T   MC

For Reference

Not to be taken from this room

MC

Children's
Literature
Review

Guide to Gale Literary Criticism Series

For criticism on	Consult these Gale series
Authors now living or who died after December 31, 1999	*CONTEMPORARY LITERARY CRITICISM (CLC)*
Authors who died between 1900 and 1999	*TWENTIETH-CENTURY LITERARY CRITICISM (TCLC)*
Authors who died between 1800 and 1899	*NINETEENTH-CENTURY LITERATURE CRITICISM (NCLC)*
Authors who died between 1400 and 1799	*LITERATURE CRITICISM FROM 1400 TO 1800 (LC)* *SHAKESPEAREAN CRITICISM (SC)*
Authors who died before 1400	*CLASSICAL AND MEDIEVAL LITERATURE CRITICISM (CMLC)*
Authors of books for children and young adults	*CHILDREN'S LITERATURE REVIEW (CLR)*
Dramatists	*DRAMA CRITICISM (DC)*
Poets	*POETRY CRITICISM (PC)*
Short story writers	*SHORT STORY CRITICISM (SSC)*
Literary topics and movements	*HARLEM RENAISSANCE: A GALE CRITICAL COMPANION (HR)* *THE BEAT GENERATION: A GALE CRITICAL COMPANION (BG)*
Asian American writers of the last two hundred years	*ASIAN AMERICAN LITERATURE (AAL)*
Black writers of the past two hundred years	*BLACK LITERATURE CRITICISM (BLC)* *BLACK LITERATURE CRITICISM SUPPLEMENT (BLCS)*
Hispanic writers of the late nineteenth and twentieth centuries	*HISPANIC LITERATURE CRITICISM (HLC)* *HISPANIC LITERATURE CRITICISM SUPPLEMENT (HLCS)*
Native North American writers and orators of the eighteenth, nineteenth, and twentieth centuries	*NATIVE NORTH AMERICAN LITERATURE (NNAL)*
Major authors from the Renaissance to the present	*WORLD LITERATURE CRITICISM, 1500 TO THE PRESENT (WLC)* *WORLD LITERATURE CRITICISM SUPPLEMENT (WLCS)*

ISSN 0362-4145

volume 113

Children's Literature Review

Excerpts from Reviews,
Criticism, and Commentary
on Books for Children
and Young People

Tom Burns
Project Editor

THOMSON
GALE

Detroit • New York • San Francisco • San Diego • New Haven, Conn. • Waterville, Maine • London • Munich

Children's Literature Review, Vol. 113

Project Editor
Tom Burns

Editorial
Kathy D. Darrow, Allison Marion

Data Capture
Frances L. Monroe

Indexing Services
Laurie Andriot

Rights and Acquisitions
Edna Hedblad, Jacqueline Key, Ron Montgomery, Susan Rudolph

Imaging and Multimedia
Dean Dauphinais, Leitha Etheridge-Sims, Lezlie Light, Mike Logusz, Dan Newell, Christine O'Bryan, Kelly A. Quin, Denay Wilding, Robyn Young

Composition and Electronic Capture
Amy Darga

Manufacturing
Rhonda Williams

Product Manager
Marc Cormier

LIBRARY OF CONGRESS CATALOG CARD NUMBER 76-643301

ISBN 0-7876-8044-3
ISSN 0362-4145

Printed in the United States of America
10 9 8 7 6 5 4 3 2 1

Contents

Preface

Literature for children and young adults has evolved into both a respected branch of creative writing and a successful industry. Currently, books for young readers are considered among the most popular segments of publishing. Criticism of juvenile literature is instrumental in recording the literary or artistic development of the creators of children's books as well as the trends and controversies that result from changing values or attitudes about young people and their literature. Designed to provide a permanent, accessible record of this ongoing scholarship, *Children's Literature Review* (*CLR*) presents parents, teachers, and librarians—those responsible for bringing children and books together—with the opportunity to make informed choices when selecting reading materials for the young. In addition, *CLR* provides researchers of children's literature with easy access to a wide variety of critical information from English-language sources in the field. Users will find balanced overviews of the careers of the authors and illustrators of the books that children and young adults are reading; these entries, which contain excerpts from published criticism in books and periodicals, assist users by sparking ideas for papers and assignments and suggesting supplementary and classroom reading. Ann L. Kalkhoff, president and editor of *Children's Book Review Service Inc.,* writes that "*CLR* has filled a gap in the field of children's books, and it is one series that will never lose its validity or importance."

Scope of the Series

Each volume of *CLR* profiles the careers of a selection of authors and illustrators of books for children and young adults from preschool through high school. Author lists in each volume reflect:

- an international scope

- representation of authors of all eras

- the variety of genres covered by children's and/or YA literature: picture books, fiction, nonfiction, poetry, folklore, and drama

Although the focus of the series is on authors new to *CLR,* entries will be updated as the need arises.

Organization of the Book

A *CLR* entry consists of the following elements:

- The **Author Heading** consists of the author's name followed by birth and death dates. The portion of the name outside the parentheses denotes the form under which the author is most frequently published. If the author wrote consistently under a pseudonym, the pseudonym will be listed in the author heading and the author's actual name given in parentheses on the first line of the biographical and critical information. Also located here are any name variations under which an author wrote, including transliterated forms for authors whose native languages use non-roman alphabets. Uncertain birth or death dates are indicated by question marks.

- A **Portrait of the Author** is included when available.

- The **Author Introduction** contains information designed to introduce an author to *CLR* users by presenting an overview of the author's themes and styles, biographical facts that relate to the author's literary career or critical responses to the author's works, and information about major awards and prizes the author has received. The introduction begins by identifying the nationality of the author and by listing genres in which s/he has written for children and young adults. Introductions also list a group of representative titles for which the author or illustrator being profiled is best known; this section, which begins with the words "major works include," follows the genre line of the introduction. For seminal figures, a listing of major works about the author follows when appropriate, high-lighting important biographies about the author or illustrator that are not excerpted in the entry. The centered heading "Introduction" announces the body of the text.

■ **Criticism** is located in three sections: **Author Commentary** (when available) **General Commentary** (when available), and **Title Commentary** (commentary on specific titles).

The **Author Commentary** presents background material written by the author or by an interviewer. This commentary may cover a specific work or several works. Author commentary on more than one work appears after the author introduction, while commentary on an individual book follows the title entry heading.

The **General Commentary** consists of critical excerpts that consider more than one work by the author or illustrator being profiled. General commentary is preceded by the critic's name in boldface type or, in the case of unsigned criticism, by the title of the journal. *CLR* also features entries that emphasize general criticism on the oeuvre of an author or illustrator. When appropriate, a selection of reviews is included to supplement the general commentary.

The **Title Commentary** begins with the title entry headings, which precede the criticism on a title and cite publication information on the work being reviewed. Title headings list the title of the work as it appeared in its first English-language edition. The first English-language publication date of each work (unless otherwise noted) is listed in parentheses following the title. Differing U.S. and British titles follow the publication date within parentheses. When a work is written by an individual other than the one being profiled, as is the case when illustrators are featured, the parenthetical material following the title cites the author of the work before listing its publication date.

Entries in each title commentary section consist of critical excerpts on the author's individual works, arranged chronologically by publication date. The entries generally contain two to seven reviews per title, depending on the stature of the book and the amount of criticism it has generated. The editors select titles that reflect the entire scope of the author's literary contribution, covering each genre and subject. An effort is made to reprint criticism that represents the full range of each title's reception, from the year of its initial publication to current assessments. Thus, the reader is provided with a record of the author's critical history. Publication information (such as publisher names and book prices) and parenthetical numerical references (such as footnotes or page and line references to specific editions of works) have been deleted at the discretion of the editors to provide smoother reading of the text.

■ A complete **Bibliographical Citation** of the original essay or book precedes each piece of criticism.

■ Selected excerpts are preceded by brief **Annotations,** which provide information on the critic or work of criticism to enhance the reader's understanding of the excerpt.

■ Numerous **Illustrations** are featured in *CLR*. For entries on illustrators, an effort has been made to include illustrations that reflect the characteristics discussed in the criticism. Entries on authors who do not illustrate their own works my include photographs and other illustrative material pertinent to their careers.

Special Features: Entries on Illustrators

Entries on authors who are also illustrators will occasionally feature commentary on selected works illustrated but not written by the author being profiled. These works are strongly associated with the illustrator and have received critical acclaim for their art. By including critical comment on works of this type, the editors wish to provide a more complete representation of the artist's career. Criticism on these works has been chosen to stress artistic, rather than literary, contributions. Title entry headings for works illustrated by the author being profiled are arranged chronologically within the entry by date of publication and include notes identifying the author of the illustrated work. In order to provide easier access for users, all titles illustrated by the subject of the entry are boldfaced.

CLR also includes entries on prominent illustrators who have contributed to the field of children's literature. These entries are designed to represent the development of the illustrator as an artist rather than as a literary stylist. The illustrator's section is organized like that of an author, with two exceptions: the introduction presents an overview of the illustrator's styles and techniques rather than outlining his or her literary background, and the commentary written by the illustrator on his or her works is called "Illustrator's Commentary" rather than "Author's Commentary." All titles of books containing illustrations by the artist being profiled are highlighted in boldface type.

Indexes

A **Cumulative Author Index** lists all of the authors who have appeared in *CLR* with cross-references to the biographical, autobiographical, and literary criticism series published by Thomson Gale. A complete list of these sources is found facing the first page of the Author Index. The index also includes birth and death dates and cross-references between pseudonyms and actual names.

A **Cumulative Topic Index** lists the literary themes and topics treated in the series as well as in *Literature Criticism from 1400 to 1800, Nineteenth-Century Literature Criticism, Twentieth-Century Literary Criticism, Contemporary Literary Criticism,* and the *Contemporary Literary Criticism* Yearbook, which was discontinued in 1998.

A **Cumulative Nationality Index** lists all authors featured in *CLR* by nationality, followed by the number of the *CLR* volume in which their entry appears.

A **Cumulative Title Index** lists all author titles covered in *CLR*. Each title is followed by the author's name and corresponding volume and page numbers where commentary on the work is located.

Citing *Children's Literature Review*

When citing criticism reprinted in the Literary Criticism Series, students should provide complete bibliographic information so that the cited essay can be located in the original print or electronic source. Students who quote directly from reprinted criticism may use any accepted bibliographic format, such as University of Chicago Press style or Modern Language Association style.

The examples below follow recommendations for preparing a bibliography set forth in *The Chicago Manual of Style,* 14th ed. (Chicago: The University of Chicago Press, 1993); the first example pertains to material drawn from periodicals, the second to material reprinted from books.

Frederick, Heather Vogel. "Cynthia Rylant: A Quiet and Reflective Craft." *Publishers Weekly* 244, no. 29 (21 July 1997): 178-79. Reprinted in *Children's Literature Review.* Vol. 86, edited by Scot Peacock, 124-26. Detroit: Gale, 2003.

Strong, Pauline T. "Playing Indian in the Nineties: *Pocahontas* and *The Indian in the Cupboard.*" In *Hollywood's Indian: The Portrayal of the Native American in Film,* edited by Peter C. Rollins and John E. O'Connor, 73-81. Lexington: The University Press of Kentucky, 1998. Reprinted in *Children's Literature Review.* Vol. 86, edited by Scot Peacock, 124-26. Detroit: Gale, 2003.

The examples below follow recommendations for preparing a works cited list set forth in the *MLA Handbook for Writers of Research Papers,* 5th ed. (New York: The Modern Language Association of America, 1999); the first example pertains to material drawn from periodicals, the second to material reprinted from books.

Frederick, Heather Vogel. "Cynthia Rylant: A Quiet and Reflective Craft." *Publishers Weekly* 244. 29 (21 July 1997): 178-79. Reprinted in *Children's Literature Review.* Ed. Scot Peacock. Vol. 86. Detroit: Gale, 2003. 124-26.

Strong, Pauline T. "Playing Indian in the Nineties: *Pocahontas* and *The Indian in the Cupboard.*" *Hollywood's Indian: The Portrayal of the Native American in Film.* Eds. Peter C. Rollins and John E. O'Connor. Lexington: The University Press of Kentucky, 1998. 73-81. Reprinted in *Children's Literature Review.* Ed. Scot Peacock. Vol. 86. Detroit: Gale, 2003. 124-26.

Suggestions are Welcome

In response to various suggestions, several features have been added to *CLR* since the beginning of the series, including author entries on retellers of traditional literature as well as those who have been the first to record oral tales and other folklore; entries on prominent illustrators featuring commentary on their styles and techniques; entries on authors whose works are considered controversial; occasional entries devoted to criticism on a single work or a series of works; sections in author introductions that list major works by and about the author or illustrator being profiled; explanatory notes that provide information on the critic or work of criticism to enhance the usefulness of the excerpt; more extensive illustrative material, such as holographs of manuscript pages and photographs of people and places pertinent to the careers of the authors and artists; a cumulative nationality index for easy access to authors by nationality; and occasional guest essays written specifically for *CLR* by prominent critics on subjects of their choice.

Readers who wish to suggest new features, topics, or authors to appear in future volumes, or who have other suggestions or comments are cordially invited to call, write, or fax the Managing Editor:

Managing Editor, Literary Criticism Series
Thomson Gale
27500 Drake Road
Farmington Hills, MI 48331-3535
1-800-347-4253 (GALE)
Fax: 248-699-8054

Acknowledgments

The editors wish to thank the copyright holders of the excerpted criticism included in this volume and the permissions managers of many book and magazine publishing companies for assisting us in securing reproduction rights. We are also grateful to the staffs of the Detroit Public Library, the Library of Congress, the University of Detroit Mercy Library, Wayne State University Purdy/Kresge Library Complex, and the University of Michigan Libraries for making their resources available to us. Following is a list of the copyright holders who have granted us permission to reproduce material in this volume of *CLR*. Every effort has been made to trace copyright, but if omissions have been made, please let us know.

COPYRIGHTED EXCERPTS IN *CLR*, VOLUME 113, WERE REPRODUCED FROM THE FOLLOWING PERIODICALS:

Book Links, v. 10, June-July, 2001; v. 12, April-May, 2003; v. 13, May, 2004. Copyright © 2001, 2003, 2004 by the American Library Association. All reproduced by permission.—*Booklist,* v. 77, May 15, 1981; v. 94, November 15, 1997; v. 99, November 15, 2002. Copyright © 1981, 1997, 2002 by the American Library Association. All reproduced by permission.—*Bookpage,* May, 2003. © 2003 ProMotion, Inc. Reproduced by permission.—*Bulletin of the Center for Children's Books,* v. 55, December, 2001; v. 56, November, 2002; v. 56, May, 2003; v. 58, March, 2005. Copyright © 2001, 2002, 2003, 2005 by The Board of Trustees of the University of Illinois. All reproduced by permission—*Childhood Education,* v. 64, February, 1988; v. 69, spring, 1993; v. 74, 1998. Copyright © 1988, 1993, 1998 by the Association. All reproduced by permission of the Association for Childhood Education International, 17904 Georgia Avenue, Suite 215, Olney, MD.—*Children's Literature,* v. 6, 1977; v. 19, 1991; v. 24, 1996. All reproduced by permission.—*Children's Literature Association Quarterly,* v. 15, 1989. © 1989 Children's Literature Association. All reproduced by permission.—*Horn Book Magazine,* v. 56, February, 1980; v. 62, July-August, 1986; v. 68, January, 1992; v. 77, March-April, 2001; v. 78, November-December, 2002; v. 81, March-April, 2005; v. 81, November-December, 2005. Copyright 1980, 1986, 1992, 2001, 2002, 2005 by The Horn Book, Inc., Boston, MA, www.hbook.com. All rights reserved. All reproduced by permission.—*Houston Chronicle,* December 19, 2001; May 11, 2003. All reproduced by permission.—*Journal of Adolescent and Adult Literacy,* v. 46, September, 2002; v. 47, December-January, 2003-2004. Copyright © 2002, 2003, 2004 International Reading Association. All reproduced by permission of the International Reading Association.—*Kirkus Reviews,* v. 49, June 15, 1981; v. 69, August 1, 2001; v. 72, December 15, 2004. Copyright © 1981, 2001, 2004 by The Kirkus Service, Inc. All rights reserved. All reproduced by permission of the publisher, *Kirkus Reviews* and Kirkus Associates, L.P—*KLIATT,* v. 37, March, 2003; v. 39, January, 2005. Copyright © 2003, 2005 by KLIATT. All reproduced by permission.—*Los Angeles Times Book Review,* December 8, 1985. Reproduced by permission.—*Mythlore,* v. 8, summer, 1981 for "Andersen: Joy, Sorrow, and the Joke Proper" by Gracia Fay Ellwood. © The Mythopoeic Society, 1981. Reproduced by permission of the author.—*The Nation,* v. 254, May 11, 1992. Copyright © 1992 by The Nation Magazine/The Nation Company, Inc. Reproduced by permission.—*New Literary History,* v. 34, autumn 2004. Copyright © 2004 The Johns Hopkins University Press. Reproduced by permission.—*Nineteenth-Century Literature,* v. 50, September, 1995. © 1995 by The Regents of the University of California. Republished with permission of University of California Press, conveyed through Copyright Clearance Center, Inc.—*Powells.com*, "Ann Brashares Embarks into Fiction: An Interview with Ann Brashares," by Dave Weich. September 7, 2001. Reproduced by permission.—*Print,* v. 58, November-December, 2004. Reproduced by permission.—*Publishers Weekly,* v. 219, April 10, 1981; v. 243, September 9, 1996; v. 244, September 29, 1997; v. 248, December 24, 2001; v. 249, June 24, 2002; v. 249, October 14, 2002; v. 251, December 20, 2004. Copyright © 1981, 1996, 1997, 2001, 2002, 2004 by Reed Publishing USA. All reproduced from *Publishers Weekly,* published by the Bowker Magazine Group of Cahners Publishing Co., a division of Reed Publishing USA., by permission.—*Reading Today,* v. 20, December-January, 2002-2003. Copyright © 2002-2003 International Reading Association. Reproduced by permission of the International Reading Association.—*Scandinavian Review,* v. 87, autumn, 1999. © The American-Scandinavian Foundation 1999. Reproduced by permission.—*Scandinavian Studies,* v. 50, autumn, 1978; v. 63, summer, 1991; v. 74, summer, 2002. All reproduced by permission of the publisher and author.—*School Library Journal,* v. 27, May, 1981; v. 47, August, 2001; v. 48, November, 2002; v. 49, February, 2003; v. 49, May, 2003; v. 51, January, 2005; v. 51, April, 2005. Copyright © 1981, 2001, 2002, 2003, 2005. All reproduced from *School Library Journal,* a Cahners/R. R. Bowker Publication, by permission—*Spectator,* v. 298, June 25, 2005. Copyright © 2005 by *The Spectator.* Reproduced by permission of *The Spectator.*—*Teenreads.com,* "Author Talk: An Interview with Ann Brashares," May, 2003. © Copyright 2002, Teenreads.com. All rights reserved. Reprinted by permission of Random House Children's Books, a division of Random House, Inc.

Thomson Gale Literature Product Advisory Board

The members of the Thomson Gale Literature Product Advisory Board—reference librarians from public and academic library systems—represent a cross-section of our customer base and offer a variety of informed perspectives on both the presentation and content of our literature products. Advisory board members assess and define such quality issues as the relevance, currency, and usefulness of the author coverage, critical content, and literary topics included in our series; evaluate the layout, presentation, and general quality of our printed volumes; provide feedback on the criteria used for selecting authors and topics covered in our series; provide suggestions for potential enhancements to our series; identify any gaps in our coverage of authors or literary topics, recommending authors or topics for inclusion; analyze the appropriateness of our content and presentation for various user audiences, such as high school students, undergraduates, graduate students, librarians, and educators; and offer feedback on any proposed changes/enhancements to our series. We wish to thank the following advisors for their advice throughout the year.

Hans Christian Andersen
1805-1875

(Also wrote under the pseudonym Villiam Christian Walter) Danish novelist, travel writer, autobiographer, playwright, poet, folklorist, editor, and author of fairy tales.

The following entry presents an overview of Andersen's career through 2005. For further information on his life and works, see *CLR*, Volume 6.

INTRODUCTION

Although he wrote in many literary genres, including novels, poems, plays, and travelogues, Andersen will forever be remembered as one of the foremost writers of fairy tales in the history of world literature. Known for such stories as "The Little Mermaid," "The Steadfast Tin Soldier," "The Emperor's New Clothes," and "The Ugly Duckling," he expanded the scope of the fairy tale genre by creating original stories drawn from a wealth of classic folklore, imagination, and his own personal experiences. In all, Andersen composed more than 150 fairy tales, primarily between 1835 and 1874, publishing his stories in various collected volumes, such as *Eventyr, fortalte for Børn* (1835) and *Danish Fairy Legends and Tales* (1846). His works revitalized and expanded the fairy tale genre—which had previously been dependent on the oral tradition—by merging the traditional folk tale with the more sophisticated literary tale. To this end, Andersen utilized the simple premise and structure of the fairy tale to transform his own theories regarding human nature into allegories, written in a conversational language that young audiences can both understand and enjoy.

BIOGRAPHICAL INFORMATION

Andersen was born on April 2, 1805, in the small town of Odense, Denmark. His father, a shoemaker, was an avid reader who encouraged his son's intellectual and creative aspirations by exposing him to works of Danish folklore, the comedies of Ludvig Holberg, *The Arabian Nights,* and the fairy tales of Jean de la Fontaine. The elder Andersen also built a marionette theatre for his son, allowing Andersen to

write and perform his own original plays. In 1819, three years after his father's death, he moved to Copenhagen to pursue an acting career. While Andersen did not succeed as an actor, Jonas Collin, a director of the Royal Theater, was impressed by Andersen's promise as a writer. He arranged for Andersen to obtain some basic schooling, including instruction at elite private schools, and by the late 1820s, Andersen had passed the entrance exams for the University of Copenhagen. In the meantime, Collin had become a sort of surrogate father to Andersen, opening his home to the young man. Eventually, Andersen secured work at the Royal Theater, appearing as an actor in minor roles and translating French plays. In 1829 Andersen's first original play was performed at the Royal Theater—the farcical *Kjærlighed paa Nicolai Taarn, elle Hvad siger Parterret.* That same year witnessed the publication of Andersen's mock travel book, *Fodreise fra Holmens Canal til Østpynten af Amager i Aarene 1828 og 1829,* which describes an imaginary walk through Copenhagen. However, Andersen's first true literary success came after his extended trip to Italy in 1833, which inspired his well received novel *Improvisatoren: Original Roman i to Dele* (1835; *The Improvisatore; or, Life in Italy*). Many scholars have contended that the trip marked a rebirth for Andersen, who subsequently turned from composing poetry to writing prose and fairy tales. Andersen began compiling his first volume of fairy tales, *Eventyr, fortalte for Børn,* during his stay in Italy. Although he had originally intended the fairy tales for both adult and juvenile audiences, he amended the title to "tales for children" after critics faulted the simplistic dialogue and style of the stories. Several of his early works were adaptations of traditional folk tales, but Andersen eventually concentrated on producing original fairy tales—all but a dozen of his 156 fairy tales are original creations. By 1837, due to the international popularity of his novels and fairy tales, Andersen was granted an annual stipend from the Danish government which funded the author's living expenses for the rest of his life. Andersen died in 1875 near Copenhagen, though his legacy as a landmark figure in world literature continues to thrive. In 2005 Denmark held a year-long festival to celebrate the bicentenary of Andersen's birth, acknowledging Andersen as the country's national author.

MAJOR WORKS

The fairy tales most familiar to English-speaking readers are Andersen's early tales, written between 1835 and 1850. These include such stories as "The Princess and the Pea" (1835), "Thumbelina" (1835), "The Emperor's New Clothes" (1837), "The Little Mermaid" (1837), "The Snow Queen" (1844), "The Bell" (1845), "The Little Match Girl" (1845), and "The Shadow" (1847), among others. Although some of his tales end on a positive note, Andersen often deviated from the traditional "happily ever after" conclusion of most fairy tales; death, for example, is the primary motif in more than three-quarters of his tales. Andersen's fairy tales fall into two general categories: adaptations of traditional Danish folktales and original creations. In his adaptations, Andersen frequently integrated plots from more than one source. "The Tinder Box," for example, is based on a combination of an old Danish tale, "The Spirit of the Candle," and an episode from the *Arabian Nights.* Andersen himself divided his original tales into two distinct classes: *eventyr* and *historier.* The *eventyr* are fairy tales in which a supernatural element contributes to the outcome of the narrative. "The Little Mer-

maid," for example, is set in a kingdom beneath the sea and tells the story of a mermaid who drinks a magical potion brewed by a sea-witch in hopes that she will be metamorphosed into a human. Andersen's *historier* are stories that do not employ a supernatural element. Frequently, the *historier* starkly portray poverty or suffering, leaving readers disturbed when good is not necessarily rewarded at the story's conclusion. The *historier* also often reveal their author's strong moralistic and religious attitudes: Andersen had a fervent faith in God and perceived death as a reward for a difficult life. This perception is perhaps most vividly portrayed in "The Little Match Girl," a grim story in which an impoverished child dies from exposure on Christmas Eve when no one will buy her matches. The child is finally freed from her suffering when her deceased grandmother arrives to lead her to Heaven. Although many of Andersen's *historier* and fairy tales end unhappily, most critics concur that the underlying attitude in his stories is ultimately positive. Andersen often offers an optimistic approach to otherwise distressing situations and invests many of his tales with a mischievous sense of humor. Of all his stories, Andersen's semi-autobiographical sketches are considered his most enduring. Stories like "The Little Mermaid," "The Nightingale," and "The Steadfast Tin Soldier" reflect, in part, Andersen's own unrequited love affairs in varying degrees of melancholy and satire. "The Ugly Duckling," the story of a homely cygnet who becomes the most beautiful of all swans, is probably Andersen's best-loved and most popular work of this type.

CRITICAL RECEPTION

During his lifetime, Andersen was celebrated for his original fairy tales not only in Denmark, but also throughout Europe and beyond. Critical assessment of Andersen's literary legacy has continued to be largely focused on his fairy tales, with some critics arguing that the popularity of his tales—along with the perception of Andersen as primarily a children's author—have overshadowed his other literary accomplishments. However, several scholars have noted that this disparity only speaks to the universality of Andersen's themes in his fairy and folk tales. According to Sven H. Rossel, Andersen's "myth-creating imagination, which broke with all literary conventions, knew how to animate the inanimate. His acute power of observation and strong sense of reality endowed the most fantastic beings with realistic traits, forcing the reader to believe in them." However, many of Andersen's contemporaries disapproved of his use of colloquialisms and originality of language, criticizing his inability to write in "proper Danish." The first published review of his *Eventyr, fortalte for Børn* declared that the tales were unfit for children. In recent years, one major trend in Andersen criticism has involved psychoanalytic studies seeking to draw connections between the suffering depicted in Andersen's stories and the troubles of Andersen's own life, including his various psychological problems and anxieties. Throughout his life, as biographers have recorded, Andersen was ashamed of his working-class background and, as such, they claim, was plagued by a sense of inferiority. Some have maintained that Andersen retold his own life story over and over again in his fairy tales—in such works as "The Ugly Duckling"—portraying himself as triumphing over evil, persecution, poverty, and scorn. There has also been interest among modern critics in Andersen's divided role as both an "insider" and "outsider" in the upper reaches of society. Believing that Andersen's tales reveal the author's desire to be accepted by the upper classes, Jack Zipes has argued that the tales also depict the humiliation, pain, and suffering that "dominated" members of society must endure in order to prove their virtuosity and nobility. Nevertheless, Andersen has been typically recognized as a consummate storyteller who distilled his vision of humanity into a simple format that appealed to audiences of all ages.

PRINCIPAL WORKS

Fairy Tales: Original Editions

Eventyr, fortalte for Børn. 2 vols. (fairy tales) 1835

Eventyr, fortalte for Børn: Tredie Hefte (fairy tales) 1837

Eventyr, fortalte for Børn: Ny Samling. Første Hefte (fairy tales) 1838

Eventyr, fortalte for Børn: Ny Samling, Tredie Hefte (fairy tales) 1841

Nye Eventyr (fairy tales) 1843

Nye Eventyr: Anden Samling (fairy tales) 1844

Nye Eventyr: Tredie Samling (fairy tales) 1845

Nye Eventyr: Andet Bind, Første Samling (fairy tales) 1847

Nye Eventyr og Historier (fairy tales) 1858

Nye Eventyr og Historier: Anden Samling (fairy tales) 1858

Nye Eventyr og Historier: Anden Række, Anden Samling (fairy tales) 1862

Nye Eventyr og Historier: Anden Række, Fjerde Samling (fairy tales) 1866

Fairy Tales: English Editions

Danish Fairy Legends and Tales [translated by Caroline Peachy] (fairy tales) 1846

Wonderful Stories for Children [translated by Mary Howitt] (fairy tales) 1846

A Christmas Greeting to My English Friends [translated by Charles Beckwith Lohmeyer] (fairy tales) 1847

The Complete Andersen: All of the 168 Stories by Hans Christian Andersen. 6 vols. [translated by Jean Hersholt; illustrations by Fritz Kredel] (fairy tales) 1949

The Complete Fairy Tales and Stories [translated by Erik Christian Haugaard] (fairy tales) 1974

Fairy Tales [translated by Tiina Nunnally] (fairy tales) 2004

Other Major Works

Fodreise fra Holmens Canal til Østpynten af Amager i Aarene 1828 og 1829 (travel writing) 1829

Improvisatoren: Original Roman i to Dele. 2 vols. [*The Improvisatore; or, Life in Italy*] (novel) 1835

Mulatten (play) 1840

Das Märchen meines Lebens ohne Dichtung [*The True Story of My Life*] (autobiography) 1847; also published as *Mit eget Eventyr uden Digtning,* 1942

Mit Livs Eventyr (autobiography) 1855

Da Spanierne var her (play) 1865

Breve til og fra H. C. Andersen. 3 vols. (correspondence) 1877-1878

Seven Poems [translated by R. P. Keigwin] (poetry) 1955

Brothers, Very Far Away and Other Poems [translated by Paula Hostrup-Jessen] (poetry) 1991

GENERAL COMMENTARY

Gracia Fay Ellwood (essay date summer 1981)

SOURCE: Ellwood, Gracia Fay. "Andersen: Joy, Sorrow, and the Joke Proper." *Mythlore* 8, no. 2 (summer 1981): 23, 42.

[*In the following essay, Ellwood offers a critical analysis of Andersen's novella-length fairy tales,* The Snow Queen *and* The Marsh King's Daughter, *comparing the title character of the* The Snow Queen *to a similar character in C. S. Lewis's* The Lion, the Witch, and the Wardrobe.]

Recently the Mydgard branch discussed Hans Christian Andersen's two novellas *The Snow Queen* and *The Marsh King's Daughter.* The sense of the meeting was that here are treasures that need to be dusted off and cherished anew. This column will therefore be a branch discussion report, so to speak. As it were.

Most of us had not read *The Snow Queen* for years, and had not heard of the other story at all before this; we were surprised by the density of the material. One luminous image after another appeared, more or less integrated in the story, exemplifying many basic motifs of Romance. Paradisal childhood innocence, capture-and-rescue, snow and ice as symbols of dehumanization, talking flowers and animals, the Wise Old Woman in her womblike hovel, the talisman, the warm, life-renewing tear, the ailing king and his languishing land, the Quest for the Grail-like marvelous object, the shapeshifting protagonist, the seizure of the maiden by the King of the Underworld, the dual-natured child of light and darkness, the life-giving sacrifice of the innocent, the return of the dead, the miraculous recovery of the king, the moment in paradise that takes up many decades on earth.

Another feature of Andersen that we had largely forgotten was his humor. Having long associated him with the sufferings of the ugly duckling, the little match girl, the little mermaid and others, we were surprised that these matters of grave import were often so cavalierly treated. *The Marsh King's Daughter* is told largely from the point of view of a pair of married storks, who discuss the ordeals and joys of the human protagonists amidst petty domestic carping and appreciative comments about mouth-watering Nile frogs.

One element in *The Snow Queen* that is bound to interest Lewis enthusiasts is of course its influence on the Narnian tales. The snow queen found her way nearly intact into *The Lion, the Witch, and the Wardrobe,* even to the sleigh, the reindeer, and the seduction and imprisonment of the foolish little boy. The submerged sexual motif is more noticeable in Andersen's story, where Kay is kissed, by the Snow Queen, and although he is described as a child, he is confused not long afterwards with the young man who courts (and presumably marries) the clever Princess.

Andersen's icy queen differs from Lewis' in that the former is identified with rationality. As Kay is carried off in her sleigh he tries to pray, but finds that all he can remember is the multiplication tables. Later, in her arctic palace, she sets him to working out a cerebral puzzle. She is almost impersonal—she destroys by virtue of what she is, in contrast to Jadis, who is gratuitously cruel and a betrayer. And correspondingly, she is not destroyed at the climax; she is simply absent when Gerda comes for Kay. Rationality cannot be slain.

Lewis uses the image of cold and snow again in *The Silver Chair,* a quest to the North, and a sinister female figure who abducts a young man. He is saved by a young heroine, though the tone is rather different in that Jill shares the honors with Eustace and Puddleglum.

In contrast to most romances, and quite un-self-consciously, the author has made the central characters in these stories female. The Quest hero is a heroine who sets out into the wide world to save someone she loves. Gerda encounters one female figure after another, vivid and highly interesting, all of whom hinder or help her in various ways until she succeeds in rescuing Kay. In *The Marsh King's Daughter,* the Egyptian princess and her daughter with whom she shares the quest do encounter male figures to be reckoned with, principally the Marsh King, who carries off the princess, and the young priest, whom the daughter rescues and who later brings about her transformation through his sacrifice. Nonetheless it is the heroines who are the focus of attention, and who give new life to the king.

Walter Wangerin, Jr. (essay date 1990)

SOURCE: Wangerin, Jr., Walter. "Hans Christian Andersen: Shaping the Child's Universe." In *Reality and the Vision,* edited by Philip Yancey, pp. 1-15. Dallas, Tex.: Word Publishing, 1990.

[*In the following essay, Wangerin presents a personal reading of some of Andersen's best known fairy tales, utilizing his own memories and reminiscence to emphasize Andersen's recurring themes of redemption, forgiveness, and hope.*]

When I was a child, I spake as a child, I understood as a child. When I became a man I put away childish things, but the man I became was shaped in childhood, and that shape remains forever.

Fairy tales shaped me. I have since "put them away." That is, the adult is a mostly rational creature, aware that fairy tales are not "real" but are a fantasy, an entertaining escape from the problems of the real world. As a man, I make such tales an object of my attention and maintain an analytical control over them: I read them. I interpret them; they don't interpret me. I master the tales, placing them within my memory and my experience exactly where I wish them to be. Fairy tales dwell within the adult.

But as a child all full of wonder I approached the fairy tale as something real indeed. Children meet the problems of the world with their imaginations, and the fairy tale honors and feeds and abets the imagination. I accepted its invitation to enter in, and dwelt within the tale. As a child I never analyzed the tale I read; I felt it; I sank inside of it; I lived its experience through to the happy conclusion, thereby enacting the solutions of imagination.

The fairy tale was like a well-built house which I inhabited safe and strong and significant. The problems outside didn't vanish when I entered that house, but its walls protected me from immediate danger. More wonderfully, when I viewed those "real world" problems through the windows of the fairy tale, they shrank to proportions equal to my child's size and I discovered marvelous ways to triumph over them. I, by the art of the tale and by the power of my magic imagination, became a citizen and a survivor in an otherwise confusing universe—and sometimes, even, a hero.

Once upon a time my mother was the problem. She, the largest figure of the real world, was beautiful beyond my deserving, and I loved her. I, the oldest child of all her brood, would truly have died for her, could it assure her happiness. But things were not so simple in those days, and I despaired of solving the problem of my mother, until a tale revised my comprehension of the world and whispered to me the secret of mothers in general.

In the dark of the evening my mother would come to tuck me into bed. When she sat on the side of the bed, her weight would sink the mattress and roll me close to her. I felt the warmth of her body. I felt the coolness of her hand upon my forehead. I smelled the holy cloud of perfume that surrounded her. I heard her low voice, thick with the thrill of loving me, and I would nearly weep with the sweetness of the occasion. How often she murmured good night to me in those days; yet always the word was new and exquisite, because this was my beloved.

We prayed together. She wore a deep red lipstick. When we finished praying, she would bend down to me and kiss my cheek, leaving the sign of her lips in red. And then she might go out for the evening, but I

could get up and run to the mirror and gaze at her love for me and carry the knowledge back to bed and fall asleep contented. Her lipstick smelled of roses.

In the morning I woke and went downstairs and sought my beloved again. How many mornings I did so, forgetting the problem which every morning I encountered!

She was in the kitchen, standing at the counter stuffing lunch bags. Her bathrobe was snagged and ratty; her hair was wild; but again and again I neglected these signs and swam in the love of the night before.

"Mom," I would say, expecting the beauty to turn and smile on me.

No answer.

"Mom? Mom?" I would repeat, prepared to say, I love you. How did you sleep? But when I touched her to get her attention, it was a different woman altogether who rounded upon me.

"Wally!" she yelled. "Where have you been? You're late!" Lashless eyes, a forehead white with anger, a mouth made stiff, an odor of soiled sheets. "Move it!" this woman would cry. "Where's your shirt? If you're not ready when I leave, you're walking to school. Go!"

If I stood in stunned wonder, this woman would grow more furious, grab my shoulder, snap me around, and push me from her.

Often I moved to my room in confusion and dressed myself slowly, injured by the injustice of it all. I could not fathom the transformation. Who was my mother now? What had happened during the night? Most important: what had I done to cause the change and to enrage her?

She meant her threat about walking. I sat with my socks in my hand, all lonely in the universe, until the car roared and beeped outside, and she and the other children drove away—and then my first feeling was panic, and the second was a bewildered guilt. I walked to school alone. I arrived there both solemn and silent, wounded by the real world, helpless to understand the problem that was my mother, let alone to solve it.

And as long as my mother was unsolvable, so was the whole world an impossibly complex and dangerous place. I didn't talk to my teacher. I withheld myself from the treacheries of friendship. I listened to everyone but spoke to no one.

One day the teacher read aloud a fairy tale whose fiction I entered, whose events I believed and experienced, whose view of the world resolved my own most troubled world—and (as a child, by the marvel of imagination) at last I understood my mother. I could love her again unhindered.

"**Snow White**" was the tale. It began with an image of simplicity and beauty, one perfectly congenial to my experience: a childless Queen sat and sewed at her castle window. It was snowing. The snow had drifted on the window sill, and the window itself was open to the evening air.

The poor Queen pricked her finger with the needle. Three drops of blood fell onto the snow. The loveliness of those drops, crimson in the white snow, moved the Queen to tears and to a prayer. "Oh, let me have a child," she prayed, "with lips as red as blood and cheeks as white as snow." It was absolutely certain that this Queen was godly and good, that she would love forever the child of her yearning and of her blood.

I recognized that Queen and gave her my immediate devotion. I knew, in fact, that if she breathed on me, her breath would be scented with roses. And when next she bore a baby, I was not surprised. I recognized that baby too.

But then the poor Queen died, and the tale struck out in strange directions. The King remarried, and a second mother appeared, as beautiful as the first, perhaps, but wicked and so self-absorbed that she talked to her face in the mirror. It was sad that the first mother died, but somehow not astonishing. What did astonish and horrify me was that the face in the mirror spoke back to the stepmother. Here was a woman divided into two parts. One part asked and the other part answered, each one independent of the other. This seemed unnatural, and it frightened me.

For a while the two parts were in harmony. "Mirror, mirror, on the wall," said the stepmother, "who is the fairest of them all?"

"You are," said her image, and she was happy.

But in time the baby developed, grew lovely, grew so beautiful, in fact, that she surpassed the beauty of the stepmother; and then the two parts of this woman were divided, for the child had come between.

"Who is the fairest of them all?"

"Well," the face in the mirror replied, "Snow White is." Snow White: the child of that other mother, the Queen, the good and godly one!

Oh, how the stepmother howled at that knowledge, torn asunder by the innocent sweetness of a child. A forehead white with anger, a mouth made stiff—I recognized that woman too. I had met her often in the mornings, in the kitchen; and now I understood (as a child understands these things) her changes and her rages.

This is the explanation which imagination could accept: that I had not one but two mothers, an original and a stepmother, a Mother of the Evening who disappeared not once but ever and again, and a Mother of the Morning who possessed a different nature indeed. What a relief this insight was for me! No longer was my mother's transformation my fault. It was a simple, sad fact of existence—but a reversible fact, since the good and godly mother could spring new every evening, just as I could reread Snow White whenever I wished.

Moreover, even when the loving mother was absent, she still continued to exist—in me! My being was the issue of her prayer, her yearning, her bright red blood, and all her purity. I was the abiding beauty of that mother, which was precisely why the stepmother couldn't stand me. Should I think evil of myself? No. As the graceful offspring of my better mother, my very existence reminded my stepmother of worth and the virtue that she lacked. Not some shame in me, but rather my very innocence enraged the stepmother. I could endure her without guilt, for her anger now became understandable to me. I, the Snow White of the story, had destroyed her self-absorption.

Thus did I peer at the "real world" through the windows of a fairy tale, and thus did I find a certain fantastic sense in all of it, and the sense preserved me. Truly, this explanation of the double mothers is more subtle than I thought it through in childhood. I merely lived it. And I knew on some functional level that Snow White was "just" a fairy tale, that I was engaged in serious pretense. But the comfort it afforded me was actual: I loved better, walked freer, was a better, healthier child on account of it.

The child psychologist Bruno Bettelheim in *The Uses of Enchantment* has affirmed my private use of the fairy tale as something common to many children. He writes that the structure of the tale (which is narrative and dramatic, not analytic and intellectual) orders and organizes the overwhelming chaos which children experience. Children are influenced by the tale not because it rationally argues certain principles (scientific, moral, or spiritual), but rather because they identify with its characters and actually experience the events of the story, which mimic in imagination the difficult events of their own lives, but which also proceed to solutions that they on their own might never find.

If, therefore, I speak of the effect Hans Christian Andersen had upon my childhood, please understand that I am not slipping into a personal and irrelevant nostalgia. I'm describing deep influences upon my adulthood, the man and the writer and the Christian under heaven. For the story that shapes a child's universe also shapes the child—and by the child, the man thereafter. The memory of a burning fairy tale can govern behavior as truly as remembered fire will caution against fire forever.

This is how the tales of Hans Christian Andersen so mightily influenced me. They were my world for a while. They named and shaped the universe in which I dwelt, and something of that shape has remained forever: not the fantasy, but the faith that created the fantasy continues even now to explain existence. By his fairy tales Hans Andersen welcomed me to his bosom, and I delivered myself for safekeeping unto him. Those things which were horrible and senseless in my external world were, in Andersen's world, horrible still; but his stories gave them a sense (often a spiritual sense) which I could grasp, by which the horror might be mastered, if not by me then by someone, by goodness, by God.

* * *

When my father bought a thick, pictureless book containing all the tales of Hans Christian Andersen and began to read them to his children, he did me a kindness more profound than mere entertainment. He began to weave a world which genuinely acknowledged all the monsters in mine, as well as all the ridiculous situations and silly asides which I as a child found significant. Andersen was my whispering, laughing, wise companion when I most needed companionship.

Night after night my father would read a story in an articulate, baritone voice. Gently the voice invited me. Slowly I accepted the invitation and delivered myself to a wonderful world, and I looked around, and lo, it was confident with solutions, and I was a citizen of some authority and reputation. I was no longer alone, no longer helpless. Even my foolish-

ness seemed canny here. I could, with the soldier and his tinderbox, marry the princess, become a king—or, with the Little Match Girl, enter heaven.

Hans Andersen's stories, though simple on the surface, contain a precise and tender perception of personal development. They are honest about the hard encounter with the "real world"—honest about evil and the tendency to evil in each of us. Andersen did not coddle me, the "me" who was revealed within his fairy tales. He didn't sweeten the bitter facts which I already knew regarding myself. But he offered me hope, for in his tales even when evil has been chosen, forgiveness may follow—therein lies extraordinary hope.

Never, never does Andersen compromise the truth of human experience for childish ears. He may tell it in outrageously fantastical terms. He may make trees to talk and darning needles to take trips, but they talk the truth, and their trips are desperately familiar to children traveling toward adulthood. In his tales, love and loneliness are equally genuine. For me his stories offered sanctuary, a sacred place to dwell in for a while, almost a temple of the observant and merciful God.

Bruno Bettelheim observes that,

> The child is subject to desperate feelings of loneliness and isolation, and he often experiences mortal anxiety. More often than not, he is unable to express those feelings in words, or he can do so only by indirection: fear of the dark or of some animal, anxiety about his body. Parents tend to overlook . . . those spoken fears. . . . The fairy tale, by contrast, takes these existential anxieties and dilemmas very seriously and addresses itself directly to them: the need to be loved and the fear that one is thought worthless; the love of life, and the fear of death. Further, the fairy tale offers solutions in ways that the child can grasp on his level of understanding.
>
> (*Enchantment* [*The Uses of Enchantment*], p. 10)

Even so did Andersen's tales express what otherwise was mute within me. If I found my feelings in his stories, then I was neither crazy nor alone. Someone shared my woe; someone invited me to chuckle at it. Andersen gave me a frame for things intangible, bewildering, elemental, and urgent. Without apology he structured his world with things of spiritual value: the eternal consequences of actions good or evil, the judging and the benevolent presence of God, the effective reality of repentance, the marvelous power of divine forgiveness. These things surrounded me when I dwelt with him.

* * *

So, then, this is the way it is: Dad sits in a chair beside my bed, one lamp low at his shoulder, his pipe clamped between his teeth. Mostly the room, an attic with slanted ceilings, is in darkness. The wind will whistle in the eaves before my father is finished reading tonight. We live in the north and the weather is winter. All that is to the good, because I will ride that black night wind.

"Ready?" Dad asks.

I nod. I curl tight beneath the covers.

"Once upon a time," Dad reads, "there lived in a village two men who had the same name; they were both called Claus. . . ."

"Little Claus and Big Claus": this is the first of all the tales my father chooses to read to us. It's an astonishing beginning. There is violence here: horse-killings, grandmother-killings, old men sent to heaven, and a great rich fool apparently drowned. But the violence accords with nightmares of my own. And fantasies that I remember, otherwise secret and frightening, are here taken for granted. The spurts of childish rage which would blot out my enemies, but which I fear I can't control, appear here in the very order of things.

And the violence is funny! I listen and laugh till the tears run down my cheeks and my father laughs too. What is happening? Violence is being reduced to something manageable; and because I am the one laughing at it, scorning it, recognizing the blustering silliness of it, then I am larger than it, capable of triumphing over it. This story does not deny the monster in me or the cruelties of the general society. Rather, it empowers me.

As Dad reads my story, I identify with Little Claus. In contrast to the big and brutal Big Claus, I am poor and weak (though cleverer by half), hobbled by kindness while he is strong in amorality. In the beginning I have one horse and he has four. All week long he plows with all five, but on Sundays the team is mine. And because I am not sinless either, vanity makes me cry out: "Giddy-up, all my horses!"

This infuriates Big Claus. "Four of those horses are mine," he yells. "If you say that again, I'll knock your horse in the head, and then you will have none."

But I am not sinless. (This is a troubling and actual fact, both in my life and in this story—which makes, of course, the story true.) In spite of his threat, the passing of churchgoers stirs my vanity again, and I cry: "Giddy-up, all my horses!"

So Big Claus comes and knocks my only horse dead.

Big Claus is an overtly violent man—as I, Wally, am too, in my secret soul. Although I may not like it, I find myself identifying with the brutal big man as much as with the clever little man. Dad is reading my own story in two ways, through two separate characters. But here is the magic of Andersen: his story divides the two tendencies within me, so that the one might be exorcised without destroying the whole of me.

Bettelheim again:

> In practically every fairy tale good and evil are given body in the form of some figures and their actions, as good and evil are omnipresent in life and the propensities for both are present in every man. It is this duality which poses the moral problem, and requires the struggle to solve it. . . .
>
> Presenting the polarities of character permits the child to comprehend easily the differences between the two, which he could not do as readily were the figures drawn more true to life. . . . Furthermore, a child's choices are based, not so much on right versus wrong, as on who arouses his sympathy and who his antipathy. The more simple and straightforward a good character, the easier it is for a child to identify with it and to reject the bad other.

(pp. 8-10)

I like Little Claus. I want to be—I am—him. I dislike Big Claus. I sever myself from—and I am not—him, even though he represents a real iniquity in me. But within the story, by laughter and luck and cleverness (but call luck "grace"), I amputate this evil which I don't want to be.

And here is how I do it. I tan the hide of my murdered horse. I take it to market to sell it. On the way I have the "luck" to witness a farmer's wife involved in an impropriety with a Deacon while her husband is absent: she's feeding the Deacon a fine dinner in her kitchen.

Just before the farmer returns, she hides the dinner in the oven and the Deacon in an empty chest. I see all this, and then the good farmer invites me inside for food.

"I'm sorry, dear, we have no food," says the farmer's wife.

But I, who am cleverer by half than Deacons and wives and Big Claus too, step on the hide of my murdered horse. I make it squeak and interpret the squeaks as a prophecy that there is dinner ready-made in the oven. There is, and the farmer is amazed by my wonderful horse-hide. Moreover, I step on it again, and it squeaks again, declaring that there's a devil-Deacon in that chest. There is! So the farmer buys my horse's hide for a whole bushel of money and sends the Deacon-in-a-chest away with me. I'm so clever that I cannot quit this cleverness: when I come to a river, I pretend out loud that I'm going to toss the chest in. The Deacon roars and pleads and bargains, until I sell him his freedom for another bushel of money. I am rich.

And what do I do to the brutal Big Claus? Why, I use his stupidity and his greed against him. I borrow his measuring pail to measure all my money, then return it to him with a few coins stuck to the bottom.

"Where did you get all that money from?" cries Big Claus, his eyes popping out.

"Oh, that was for my horse hide. I sold it last night."

Immediately Big Claus hurries home and takes an ax and knocks all four of his horses in their heads. He skins them and runs to market to humiliate himself. Who would buy horse-hides for bushels of money?

And so my story goes: I trick Big Claus into knocking his poor grandmother in the head. Ah, me, but the man is dumb! And his nature is violent altogether! Finally, I trick Big Claus into jumping into the river himself in search of a herd of cattle at the bottom, and so I am rid of dumbness, greed, and brutality all at once.

Dad closes the book. He turns out the light and leaves. But I am flying the night wind, living still in a good, good story—"good" in that evil is overcome and suffers its due, in that the Old Adam need not forever be my master. I may be forgiven—and free. But I discover the truth in experience, laughing till the tears run down my cheeks, not in remote and intellectual lessons which my poor brain can scarcely translate into "real life."

Hans Andersen has persuaded me of optimism, a tough and abiding optimism, not the pollyanna sugar which merely sweetens the facts of evil and suffering, danger, and death. I would soon reject such optimism as fraudulent—even as a child I would. It would leave no print upon my personality. But Andersen's optimism both sees and redeems the evil. We travel through it, not around it, and I am impressed forever.

Many who read my writings today are inclined to call me "melancholy." They are wrong. Andersen's fantasies schooled me, rather, in realism. I know no resurrection except that first there's been a death. And as a writer, I cannot speak genuinely or deeply of resurrection except I speak the same of death and the sin that engendered death. That I can speak accurately of death without despairing is hardly melancholic. It is liberty—and victory ("O Death, where is thy sting?"). It is the evidence of the fundamental influence which Hans Christian Andersen had upon a child who did not analyze but lived such stories as "**Little Claus and Big Claus**."

* * *

So night after night my father wreathes his head in pipe-smoke and reads to the whistle of the north wind, weaving for me experiences of genuine consolation. The number of these stories seems endless (in fact, there are 156), and that is important, for they seem to last a lifetime. As long as I need them, they are here, ever the same and ever new—exactly as are the daily encounters of my life.

I cannot run. I am short, hampered by big buttocks, hunched with a miserable miscoordination, generally inferior in the contests of children—as I say, unable to run. But in the track-meets of the fifth grade, they make me run the hundred-yard dash. It causes me a vomitus anxiety. I have nightmares of running under water. My dreams are not untrue, for when the starting gun goes off, I stumble and am the last to leave the line; slowly, slowly I suffer my way to the end of the race, and when I arrive people have departed to run in other races. I am humiliated. Ellery Yurchuck cries out, "He walks like a girl!" I do. I burn with shame. Mary Enderby slaps my cheek. Only when school is out and I am staring in the mirror of my bathroom do I realize that she had drawn lipstick lips on the palm of her hand, and that a mocking kiss has clung to my cheek the whole day through. And I cannot do what other children do so thoughtlessly. I cannot run.

But Dad, in the nighttime, reads of a duckling more ugly than others, and I curl tight under the covers and listen with unspeakable sympathy for that duck.

"I know, I know," I murmur.

Soon, I am one of the ducklings.

The ugliness alone—not wickedness, not cruelty, not any error on our part—brings shame upon us, the ugly duckling and me. Other ducklings are cute, in the image of our mother. But we were hatched from a larger, vagrant egg—an odd beginning, producing an odd shape. Therefore, we are pecked and pushed and scorned. Our wonderful mother defends us; but we only feel pity for her that she should so unjustly suffer for our own troubles, which are not hers, after all, since she is a beautiful duck. Merely that she loves us is cause for pain. Oh, it is so complicated to be ugly!

She tries to comfort us by saying, "That is the way of the world," meaning that there shall be misery on earth. It doesn't comfort us.

For our own sakes she also says, "I wish you were far away"—from pain and teasing, she means. But we take her literally. We run away to other barnyards, never to see her again.

On our own we discover "the way of the world." It includes the death of the few who befriend us: hunters kill two kindly wild ganders. It includes a sneering judgment against all the things we cannot do: can't lay eggs like chickens, can't arch our backs like cats and make sparks. Do, do, do, cries society; but we can do nothing it likes and therefore are the uglier: can't by taking thought save ourselves or add one cubit to our height.

It is utterly natural that in the end we wish to die. Sorrow drives us to such extremities, even though we are but a child and a duckling.

In the dead of a dreary winter we notice three swans moving in absolute elegance, nobility, and beauty. Surely, they too will despise our ugliness, and their spite will be as intense as their distant beauty. Surely, then, they will kill us. In fact, we desire to die by beauty rather than by any other means. It seems right. We honor the beautiful. We think to ourselves, *It is better to be killed by them than to be bitten by the other ducks.*

But here appears the outrageous grace that we never anticipated: all along, while we were ugly indeed, another mercy was working within us, uncaused by us but given to us purely as a gift. What was this mercy? What sort of gift is given now to us? Why, it is we ourselves, transfigured!

"Kill me," whispered the poor creature, and bent his head humbly while he waited for his death. So goes the story, and thus do we deny ourselves, surrender ourselves completely. "Humbly . . ." writes Andersen. "Humbly," my father reads, and I more

than hear it; I experience it: I feel fully such humility in my heart. I am the one who cannot run. But what does such humility reveal to me?

In Andersen's words: "But what was that he saw in the water? It was his own reflection; and he was no longer an awkward, clumsy, gray bird, so ungainly and so ugly. He was a swan! It does not matter that one is born in the henyard as long as one has lain in a swan's egg." And Andersen goes on to name the goodness that has existed in all our sorrow, the duckling's and mine. Andersen names the grace upon grace that we have received, and the graciousness that we shall show hereafter (which neither the chickens nor Ellery Yurchuck may ever be able to understand or to show): "He was thankful that he had known so much want, and gone through so much suffering, for it made him appreciate his present happiness and loveliness of everything about him all the more. . . . Everyone agreed that the new swan was the most beautiful of them all. The older swans bowed toward him."

But does sinful pride or vengeance then rear up in him, or in me? No, and that is much the point: for the suffering transfigures us even to the soul. Humility showed us our new selves; humility remains in our hearts to keep these selves both beautiful and virtuous: "He felt so shy that he hid his head beneath his wing. He was too happy, but not proud, for a kind heart can never be proud."

So then, there is hope—not only that there may emerge from my ugly self a beauty, but also that the suffering which my ugliness has caused is ultimately valuable, making my beautiful self also a good and sympathetic self. In the end I shall love the world the more; and even the people who once did me dishonor, I shall honor.

Can any child receive a better impress on his person, a subtler, more spiritual shape than this, that he be taught grace and to be gracious? And what is more fortified than the self-esteem that comes as a gift from God?

* * *

Night after night my father reads the stories from a thick book with pastel-colored pages, pink and blue and yellow. The book goes soft with so much reading. Night after night I live the adventures that order my turbulent days and shape my waking self, my instincts, my faith, my adulthood to come. Optimism grows in me, and hope in the midst of suffering, and this third thing, too, perhaps the most difficult thing of all: forgiveness for my own most self-centered and wretched sins. Not the doctrine of forgiveness. Not the concept. Forgiveness in fact, as a mold to my experience ever hereafter. Andersen's world is a dramatic enactment of theologies which the child simply cannot grasp in the abstract.

My father reads in a murmuring voice, so softly that the words resolve themselves into spaces and things around me. The north wind whistles at the eaves, an almost malevolent warning. This is a treacherous story. Everything is full of foreboding. The curtains stir at the attic window. Shadows twist in the corners. I would not listen if I did not trust the kinder heart of the story-teller. This story has a harmless title, but that's deceptive. The tale is frightening. It knows too well my secret faults and the evil imagination of the thoughts of my heart.

"This story," my father murmurs, the pipe gone dead beside him, "is called **'The Red Shoes.'**"

A fatherless girl named Karen appears before me. She is not aware of me, but I am of her. I join her. We are one. And we are both very vain. We think that we are more than pretty: gorgeous. Our gorgeousness so consumes us that we grow hard to those around who love and serve us. On the other hand, we want everyone to notice how splendid we are; therefore, even at inappropriate times, we slip our little feet into a pair of patent leather shoes so red, so red, O Lord, that we shine!

This is how vain we are, and this is how the story begins: at the funeral of our mother we follow the coffin in red shoes. And we are noticed. A kindly old woman notices us. We think it's because of our red shoes and our gorgeousness, but it isn't. It is her love (of which we know nothing) that sees us; she is moved by the sight of a newly orphaned child. So by grace we are granted a second mother, for the old woman takes us in and raises us as her own.

Her eyes grow dim. Ours stay sharp for red adornments. When the time of our confirmation arrives, and when we must buy shoes for the holy occasion, the old woman thinks we've bought black, but it is red we carry home, and it is red we wear to church. Everyone notices our bright red feet. Even the paintings on the wall and the bishop who blesses us stare at our feet. We are so proud! Our mind is scarcely on the words of our "covenant with God to be a good Christian." We are thinking of red shoes.

The old woman learns from others the error of our ways. She scolds us and warns us how improper are red shoes in church. But on the very next Sunday, when we will attend Holy Communion, we can't help ourselves. The red shoes cry out to us, and we put them on.

Just before we enter church an ancient figure steps into our path and stops us. We might be frightened if we would heed him, but we don't. He speaks directly to the shoes. "What pretty dancing shoes!" he says. "Remember to stay on her feet for the dance," he says. But we can think of nothing except the shoes themselves. Even when the golden cup of communion is raised to our lips, we see nothing but the shoes, as though they were reflected in the wine.

And then it happens that the old woman, our second mother, grows sick as our first mother had. Once we were ignorant of the world, of the laws of God, and of our own wicked tendencies. But now we have been taught and scolded and warned. This time we ought to know better. Nevertheless, we do again exactly what we have done before.

On the very night when the doctors say that the old woman is dying, we contemplate the red shoes, the alluring red shoes, the bright red shoes so perfect for our gorgeousness. There is a dance tonight. Looking leads to touching, and touching leads to donning; and as soon as the shoes are on our feet, we have to go. We leave the dying woman behind and steal away to dance. And we do dance. We laugh and whirl and dance the whole night through; for once we have begun, we cannot stop. It is the shoes that are dancing now. The red shoes! Dancing and dancing wherever they wish, taking us with them, down the stairs and out the door. And while they are dancing, the old woman dies. . . .

I know this only too well.

For I have divided my mother into two; and I have dealt with her as though she were only a stepmother, nothing to me. Me! I was then the center and significance of all my life. My mother the dim-eyed old woman, my mother the stepmother, who unjustly (so it seemed to me) punished me for many things, could easily be dismissed, all her wishes, all her scoldings and her disciplines, all her self! I have run out to play when (if I had thought about it) I knew she didn't want me to go. I have stayed gone too long, causing her (if I had stopped to consider it) anguish at my absence. And when she confronted me with my fault, I have whistled. I have presented her with a blank face and have whistled stupid tunes to prove I wasn't listening. I have reduced her, once or twice, to tears at my cold impertinence. Oh, I have made my mother cry, and she has gone into her bedroom and shut the door and grieved in a deep frustration—and I knew I did that by my stubbornness. Then I was burned by guilt to hear her hurt. She was ill in her bedroom, dying. She said so: Dying. "I am sick to death of your disobedience," she said. O Mama! Never again! I have vowed this in my heart: Never again! But always my demons have been too powerful for me, and I have done it again in spite of every resolution. I am Karen, surrendering to sin until my sin has taken me over completely—and even when I want to stop, I cannot. Even when my heart desires goodness, it has it not. Dancing and dancing, our shoes have taken us into the street. Oh, wretched children that we are! Is there no help for us, who cannot help ourselves?

We dance toward the church. Maybe there is help for us in church. But at the door an angel appears dressed in white, holding a shining sword.

"You shall dance," he declares, "dance in your red shoes until you become pale and thin. When you pass a house where proud and vain children live, there you shall knock on the door so that they will see you and fear your fate. Dance, you shall dance. Dance!"

"Mercy!" scream Karen and I together. But we cannot hear what the angel answers, because the red shoes carry us away and away, always dancing.

Dance we must, and dance we do. The shoes have fastened to our feet like skin.

One morning in a lonely place we dance past a solitary cottage. The man who comes out when we cry is the Executioner. "I am the one," he says, "who cuts off the heads of evil men."

"No," we plead, "for then I should not be able to repent. But cut off our feet instead."

We confess our sins (isn't this enough?), and the Executioner cuts off our feet, and the red shoes go dancing away into the forest. For us the kindly Executioner carves wooden feet. He teaches us the psalm that penitent people sing. We kiss his hand and go.

Now have we suffered enough?

We go again to the church. Is this what it takes? That we are severed of our sin? Will ritual and formality receive us now? No, no, this isn't enough. For when

we come to the door, the red shoes arrive ahead of us and dance and dance to block our way. In horror we flee. O God! The sins keep coming back! What can we do to be free?

All week long we weep on account of our sins. We are so sorry. We do repent. And by week's end we think, *I'm as good as any who sit and pray in church right now.* This gives us courage, and we go a third time. But at the gate of the churchyard the red shoes meet us, dancing, dancing, dancing, and we flee.

So now we despair. Nothing we do can save us. Not true sorrow, which we have done. Not true goodness, which we have done. Do this, do that—we've done it all, and still the shoes, they mock us.

Therefore, let us live in misery till we die. We deserve no better.

We go to the minister's house and ask for work. In pity he takes us in, gives us his roof and food. The minister's wife, also in pity, gives us work, and we work very hard though hopelessly, for we know this changes nothing. Look: our feet are still wooden. In the evening the minister reads to his children from the Bible and we listen; but we make no great account of the listening, because we are wiser now and know this changes nothing.

On Sunday the minister's whole family goes to church. We are invited, too, but our eyes fill with tears. They go without us.

We take ourselves to a tiny room and there sit down to read a psalm-book. While we sit, the wind blows hither the music of the church organ. We hear it, and we weep. We lift our face and whisper simply: "O God, help me."

All at once the sunlight seems doubly bright in the room, and the angel of God is standing before us: in the tiny room of the minister's house, in the attic bedroom where my father is reading and the north wind whistles at the eaves. This is the very same angel who held a sword at the church's door—but now he holds a rose branch thick with flowers. He raises the branch and touches the ceiling above Karen and above my bed. The ceiling suddenly sails aloft, and where he touched it a golden star appears. He brushes the walls of my attic, and they widen. Lo, here is the church organ! All around me—even though this is my bedroom and my father is reading still—the congregation is sitting and holding their psalmbooks and singing. The church has come to us, to Karen and me! When the psalm is done, someone sees us and smiles and whispers, "It is good that you came, Karen." Good to see you, Wally.

And this is what Karen replies; so these are the words in my mouth, too, brilliant with significance: "This is the mercy of God."

Mercy! It never was what we might do that could save us. It never was our work, our penitence, our goodness that would forgive us and bring us back to God again. We can do nothing! It always was the pure love and mercy of God—God's doing, given us freely as a gift. When finally we quit trying, then God could take over. When we murmured in perfect helplessness the perfect truth of our relationship, "O God, help me," then God was no longer hindered by our spiritual pride. God was God, and not ourselves—and God was our God too.

Mercy. Mercy is the healing that had waited for us all along. Love. Pure, holy love, unpurchased, underserved.

When my father reads the final sentences of this story, I am crying. I am tingling. For I am not learning, but rather I am experiencing the highest truth of our faith. Not in doctrine, but in fact it is releasing me from the sins against my mother, even as it is imprinting me for adulthood, to show in what I speak, to shine through what I write forever.

But I don't know that yet. I'm just a child, reshaped and borne outside to ride the north wind warmly to a home I shall never, never forget:

"The great organ played," my father reads, his dear head bowed above a tattered book of stories, "and the voices of the children in the choir mingled sweetly with it. The clear, warm sunshine streamed through the window. The sunshine filled Karen's heart till it so swelled with peace and happiness that it broke. Her soul flew on a sunbeam up to God; and up there no one asked her about the red shoes."

In the deeps of my bones I know and believe in forgiveness, for I have lived it. By Andersen's stories I was shaped in it—and the shape remains, forever.

Works Cited

GETTING STARTED WITH ANDERSEN:

My references to Andersen's tales come from Hans Christian Andersen, *The Complete Fairy Tales and Stories,* translated from the Danish by Erik Christian

Haugaard, Doubleday & Company, Inc., Garden City, New York, 1974. (This is not the book my father used. That has long since disappeared.)

I also recommend the foundational book on fairy tales by Bruno Bettelheim (from which my Bettelheim quotations are taken): *The Uses of Enchantment: The Meaning and Importance of Fairy Tales.* Alfred A. Knopf, New York, 1976.

Frank Hugus (essay date autumn 1999)

SOURCE: Hugus, Frank. "Hans Christian Andersen: The Storyteller as Social Critic." *Scandinavian Review* 87, no. 2 (autumn 1999): 29-35.

[*In the following essay, Hugus argues that Andersen used his fairy tales to highlight the inequities of Danish society and the struggles of the lower class, commenting that, "throughout his works, [Andersen] expresses sympathy for the poor and scorn for the pompous."*]

In the minds of most readers, the works of Hans Christian Andersen (1805-1875) are not associated with social criticism. And yet, Andersen was acutely aware of the inequities of Danish society, having experienced most of them first-hand, and throughout his works, he expresses sympathy for the poor and scorn for the pompous.

From the earliest to the very last of his 156 tales, Andersen wove criticism of social conditions into his narrative. In **"Metalsvinet"** (**"The Bronze Pig,"** 1840), for instance, he criticizes the cruelty that results from economic deprivation. **"Den lille Pige med Svovlstikkerne"** (**"The Little Match Girl,"** 1845) indicts a society that lets its children starve to death in the freezing cold of New Year's Eve. **"Alt paa sin rette Plads"** (**"Everything in its Right Place,"** 1852) demonstrates the corrupting influence of wealth and power. **"Hun duede ikke"** (**"She Was No Good,"** 1854) takes to task the upper middle class's uncharitable treatment of the working poor. Long-suffering gardener Hansen of **"Gartneren og Herskabet"** (**"The Gardener and His Master,"** 1871) is constantly put in his place by his overbearing master and mistress.

These and other tales show that if Andersen was not a firebrand revolutionary or adamant social reformer, he was from first to last the concerned observer who decried the shortcomings in Danish society and spoke out for the "little man."

THE KISS OF THE ICE MAIDEN

As paradigmatic of the mature Andersen's view on the individual's struggle with society's inequities, let us take the well known story from 1861, **"Iisjom-**

fruen" ("The Ice Maiden"). This tale, which at fifty pages is one of Andersen's longest, might at first seem to be a straightforward narrative of the young man from the ranks of the proletariat who strives for the love of a woman of the upper middle class, wins her hand against great odds, but then drowns tragically on the eve of their wedding. On another level, however, "lisjomfruen" reveals Andersen's criticism of a society in which it is virtually impossible to improve one's place.

Andersen makes clear from the outset that his protagonist Rudy is destined for failure. Not only has Rudy been born into the lower social stratum, he nearly dies in infancy when his mother and he fall into a glacial crevice in the mountains of his native Switzerland. With this "kiss" of death, the Ice Maiden, who personifies the inexorable forces of nature, has marked him as her own for the rest of his life. Rudy is thus under a double disadvantage: He is weighed down by his lower class origins and by the Ice Maiden's unwavering determination to possess him—or, put another way, Rudy carries within him the seeds of his own destruction.

From early in the story, negative prefigurations abound. When very young—Rudy is given an explicit warning by Ajola, the old dog: Things aren't evenly distributed in the world, either for dogs or for people. Ajola concludes his parable with the words: "I hope you make it into somebody's lap and ride around in a carriage. But we can't do these things by ourselves; I couldn't, either by barking or by yawning." And as Rudy enters adulthood, "society" makes its opinion known: "Rudy, was a good match, as they said, as long as he didn't look beyond his class." That he has always been perilously close to his downfall is made clear by his several physical brushes with the Ice Maiden herself. On two occasions Rudy has confronted her as a sensuous young woman in the snowy expanse of the Alps but has managed to escape.

Yet, Rudy's early years are crowned by success. He becomes an expert marksman and hunter, attributes which introduce him into the society of the wealthy miller whose daughter, Babette, Rudy loves. Before he will agree to their marriage, the miller sets a seemingly impossible condition: Rudy must bring him the young eagle that nests on the side of an inaccessible mountain crag. Rudy does so and gains permission to marry Babette. On the evening before their wedding, Rudy and Babette row out to an island in Lake Geneva. Their boat breaks loose, and Rudy swims

into the deep water to retrieve it. It is at this point that the Ice Maiden kisses him for a third time and makes him hers forever.

Rudy is only one of a long list of Andersen's lower-class figures who die or are otherwise defeated in their conscious or unconscious striving to attain something higher in life. One can mention Jørgen of "En Historie fra Klitterne" ("A Story from the Dunes," 1859), the young sculptor in "Psychen" ("Psyche," 1861), Rasmus in "Hvad gamle Johanne fortalte" ("The Story Old Johanna Told," 1872), and the washer woman of "Hun duede ikke" ("She Was No Good"). Few, in fact, are the characters who manage to jump the social chasm and remain unscathed.

Over the course of his long life, Andersen had observed that only a few individuals—those who were exceptionally capable or exceptionally lucky, or both—could transcend the constraints of their origins, that the price paid by many who attempted this feat was severe, at times amounting to personal annihilation.

SOCIAL CRITICISM IN ANDERSEN'S NOVELS

A different approach to social criticism is evident in Andersen's six novels, which are of course much less well known than the tales and stories. (With the exception of *Lykke-Peer* [*Lucky Peer*] none of the novels has been translated into English since the appearance of Mary Howitt's rather awkward translations of the mid-nineteenth century. *Lucky Peer* can be found in Jean Hersholt's *The Complete Andersen*, (1942-1949.) Social criticism, in greater or lesser portions, occurs in every one of these novels, from his first, *Improvisatoren* (*The Improvisatore*) written when he was barely thirty years of age in 1835), to his last, *Lykke-Peer* (*Lucky Peer*,) produced when the author was sixty-five years old in 1870).

Andersen's social criticism is particularly insistent in one novel, *Kun en Spillemand* (*Only a Fiddler*, 1837). In this novel, Andersen chronicles the social conditions in Denmark during the first third of the nineteenth century with an immediacy and clarity that must have impressed readers of his time as much as they impress those of us who continue to read them more than 150 years later. The larger format of the novel allowed Andersen to pen finely detailed and vividly realistic descriptions of poverty and despair.

The protagonist of *Kun en Spillemand*, Christian, like so many of Andersen's lower-class figures, struggles to lift himself out of his impoverished background by means of his talent for playing the violin. Christian is not given the opportunity to polish his artistic talents and is relegated to living out his short life as a village fiddler. Much of the novel's social criticism revolves around Christian.

When innocent young Christian arrives in Copenhagen, for instance, he is taken by two sailors to a house of prostitution. Andersen describes this scene with every bit as much social realism as any European author of the mid 19th century:

> . . . Then they entered some side streets, . . . and beautiful, fashionable ladies, dressed up as if they were going to a ball, sat in the open windows nodding politely and nicely as if they knew people. At the street corner sitting on the cold, dirty stone doorsteps was a deathly pale young woman dressed in rags. A half-naked little boy lay crying with his head in her lap. A sickly yellow infant nursed at her milkless breast. She leaned her head back and cursed, seeming not to notice the larger or the smaller of the children.

> 'She's sick!' cried Christian, "Shouldn't we tell one of the nice ladies!"

> The sailors laughed and led him into a side street where the sound of flutes and violins was coming from a low, dark building.

Charles Dickens himself could hardly have painted a more compelling picture of misery and cruel indifference.

Christian is incapable of comprehending the sordid reality behind the glittering facade that society's various classes have erected around their exploitative activities. After he and the two sailors have left Steffen Kareth's bordello, for example, Christian inexplicably continues to remain in his oblivious dreamworld, in which the house of prostitution is like a castle and the prostitutes are like royalty:

> The fairy tale about the farm boy who became emperor occurred to him. Oh, if that fashionable lady [the prostitute, Steffen Kareth] would take me under her wing, he hoped, then I could play the violin, sit with the other players, or become something even nicer. . . .

This devastatingly ironic passage defines the character of Christian; tragically, Christian's character does not evolve, and he remains credulous and susceptible throughout the novel.

In the end, Christian is overcome by his own deficiencies and almost imperceptibly slips out of existence. By this time, however, Christian has be-

come a marginal figure, and the reader has shifted his attention to the novel's female protagonist, Naomi, whose origins are equally as lowly as Christian's and who has the additional disadvantage of being Jewish. Unlike Christian, however, Naomi has the inner strength to force her way up in the world. She does so by scorning convention and by following her physical passions. Yet, even though she attains an elevated social status that Christian could hardly have imagined by becoming the wife of a French marquis, Naomi is depicted in the novel's closing pages as tortured by the knowledge that her cynical husband could abandon her at any time, that the dark secrets of her proletarian origins and her checkered past could cause her precipitous fall from social grace.

As miserable as both Christian's demise and Naomi's psychological torments are, it is the fate of a minor character in **Kun en Spillemand** that is more starkly portrayed than the fates of either of the protagonists. I refer to the figure of the above-mentioned prostitute, Steffen Kareth, whose story is so grippingly recounted that, despite its brevity, its memory stays with the reader as emblematic of the inhumanity that permeates the underside of society. In a frantic attempt to break out of the prostitution that has trapped her for more than half her life, Steffen Kareth is reduced to begging for the respectability of marriage from one of the sailors who has exploited her; not surprisingly the sailor rejects her. Equally unsurprisingly, she commits suicide, drowning herself in the icy waters between the wharf and the small ship on which the unsuspecting Christian is a crew member. Yet it is not so much her suicide that Andersen chooses to emphasize; this desperate act is treated rather perfunctorily in fact. What concerns Andersen are the implacable social forces that entrap and destroy the Steffen Kareths of this world. This problem is of such moment that Andersen interrupts the narrative flow of the novel and addresses the reader directly:

> If, eighteen years ago, you had seen the slender fourteen-year-old girl with the pure joy for life in her bright eyes, you would have thought of Semele. Yes, Semele expected Jupiter in all his majesty, and her lover arrived—but not as a sun that warms but as a fire that burns, and she became dust in his arms, . . .

But the Steffen Kareths are not all turned to ashes immediately, many linger on like the living dead:

> These apparitions breathe the poisonous stench of the grave. Don't trust the healthy-looking rosiness on their cheeks; a death's head is painted

there; . . . They are dead, but more horribly dead than our own dead. They buried the soul, but the body walks around like a ghost; like vampires they search for human blood to nourish themselves. That is why they cling fast to the drunken peasant, to the crudest farmhand, at whose sight even a man is disgusted. They are terribly unhappy spirits; but they don't descend into their graves at daybreak; oh no, then the dreams of despair arrive and sit on their breasts like nightmares singing about people's contempt, about a better life here on earth, and the tears stream down their painted cheeks. And to chase away these dreams, they take up the bottle. The death marks of the poison stand out more clearly the next night when they resume their ghostly activity. 'Save me! I'm still not completely dead. For a few minutes I can still feel how my soul is alive inside me!' one of these unlucky women will often cry out, but those who hear the voice from the grave flee in fear, and she, the woman who is half dead, doesn't have the strength to lift the coffin lid of her circumstances with sin's heavy earth pressing it down.

Despite the narrator's revulsion for prostitution, this passage is not without sympathy—a great deal of sympathy, in fact—for the unfortunate human beings who are hopelessly enmeshed in the web of this degrading profession. The target of Andersen's censure is not the unhappy "fallen" woman herself but the double standard of a society that condemns the prostitute but not the men, from all levels of society, who use her and cast her aside.

GIVING THE READER SOMETHING TO THINK ABOUT

The ills of Danish society of the mid-nineteenth century were frequently writ large in the stories and novels of Hans Christian Andersen; the author did not shrink from criticizing what he saw as egregious social flaws, many of which he had experienced personally. Andersen's prose shows that it was not at all an easy matter to climb out of one's lower social environment. That so few of Andersen's figures survive this attempt is as much a criticism of society as it is a testament to the genius and perseverance of those individuals who (like Andersen himself) were able to do so.

Hans Christian Andersen said that he wrote his tales and stories for children but that he wanted to give the parents something to think about as well. Reading Andersen's tales and stories from the perspective of his social criticism surely gives us all something to think about.

Jack Zipes (essay date 1999)

SOURCE: Zipes, Jack. "Hans Christian Andersen and the Discourse of the Dominated." In *When Dreams Came True: Classical Fairy Tales and Their Tradition,* pp. 80-110. New York, N.Y.: Routledge, 1999.

[*In the following excerpt, Zipes offers a critical reading of Andersen's fairy tales with regard to nineteenth-century, socio-cultural constructs of power, domination, and personal identity. Zipes contends that "Andersen's life was one based on servility, and his tales were endeavors to justify a false consciousness: literary exercises in the legitimation of a social order to which he subscribed."*]

> *Andersen visited me here several years ago. He seemed to me like a tailor. This is the way he really looks. He is a haggard man with a hollow, sunken face, and his demeanor betrays an anxious, devout type of behavior which kings love. This is the reason why they give Andersen such a brilliant reception. He is the perfect representation of all poets, just the way kings want them to be.*
>
> —Heinrich Heine (1851)

If the Grimm brothers were the first writers in the nineteenth century to distinguish themselves by remolding oral folk tales explicitly for a bourgeois socialization process, then Hans Christian Andersen completed their mission so to speak and created a canon of literary fairy tales for children between 1835 and 1875 in praise of essentialist ideology. By infusing his tales with general notions of the Protestant ethic and essentialist ideas of natural biological order, Andersen was able to receive the bourgeois seal of good housekeeping. From the dominant-class point of view his tales were deemed useful and worthy enough for rearing children of all classes, and they became a literary staple in Western culture. Fortunately for Andersen he appeared on the scene when the original middle-class prejudice against imaginative fairy tales was receding. In fact, there was gradual recognition that fantasy could be employed for the utilitarian needs of the bourgeoisie, and Andersen proved to be a most humble servant in this cause.

But what was at the heart of Andersen's mode of service? In what capacity did his tales serve children and adults in Europe and America? What is the connection between Andersen's achievement as a fairy-tale writer, his servile demeanor, and our cultural appreciation of his tales? It seems to me that these questions have to be posed even more critically if we are to understand the underlying reasons behind Andersen's rise to fame and general acceptance in the nineteenth century. In fact, they are crucial if we want to grasp the continual reception, service, and use of the tales in the twentieth century, particularly in regard to socialization through literature.

Despite the fact that Andersen wrote a great deal about himself and his tales and was followed by scholars who have investigated every nook and cranny of his life and work, there have been very few attempts to study his tales ideologically and to analyze their function in the acculturation process. This is all the more surprising when one considers that they were written with a plump didactic purpose and were overloaded with references to normative behavior and ideal political standards. Indeed, the discourse of his narratives has a distinct ideological bias peculiarly "marred" by his ambivalent feelings toward his social origins and the dominant classes in Denmark that controlled his fortunes. It is this "marred ambivalence" that is subsumed in his tales and lends them their dynamic tension. Desirous of indicating the way to salvation through emulation of the upper classes and of paying reverence to the Protestant ethic, Andersen also showed that this path was filled with suffering, humiliation, and torture—it could even lead to crucifixion. It is because of his ambivalent attitude, particularly toward the dominance of essentialist ideology, that his tales have retained their basic appeal up through the present day. But before we reevaluate this appeal as constituted by the socializing elements of the tales, we must first turn to reconsider Andersen in light of the class conflict and conditions of social assimilation in his day.

I

Son of a poor cobbler and a washerwoman, Andersen was embarrassed by his proletarian background and grew to insist on notions of natural nobility. Once he became a successful writer, he rarely mingled with the lower classes. If anything, the opposite was the case: he was known to kowtow to the upper classes throughout all of Europe—quite an achievement when one considers his fame! However, his success then and now cannot be attributed to his opportunism and conformism. That is, he cannot simply be dismissed as a class renegade who catered to the aesthetic and ideological interests of the dominant classes. His case is much more complex, for in many respects his tales were innovative narratives that explored the limits of assimilation in a closed social order to which he aspired. Despite all the recognition and acceptance by the nobility and bourgeoisie in the Western world, Andersen never felt himself to be a full-fledged member of any group. He was the out-

sider, the loner, who constantly traveled in his mature years. His wanderings were symptomatic (as the wanderers and birds in his tales) of a man who hated to be dominated though he loved the dominant class.

Elias Bredsdorff, the leading contemporary biographer of Andersen, maintains in *Hans Christian Andersen: The Story of His Life Work,* that

> in modern terms Andersen was a man born in the "Lumpenproletariat" but completely devoid of class "consciousness." In his novels and tales he often expresses an unambiguous sympathy for "the underdog," especially for people who have been deprived of their chance of success because of their humble origins, and he pours scorn on haughty people who pride themselves on their noble birth or their wealth and who despise others for belonging to, or having their origin in, the lower classes. But in his private life Andersen accepted the system of absolutism and its inherent class structure, regarded royalty with awe and admiration and found a special pleasure in being accepted by and associating with kings, dukes and princes, and the nobility at home and abroad.

Though Andersen's sympathy did lay with the downtrodden and disenfranchised in his tales, it was not as unambiguous as Bredsdorff would have us believe, for Andersen's fawning servility to the upper classes also manifested itself in his fiction. In fact, as I have maintained, the ambivalent feelings about both his origins and the nobility constitute the appeal of the tales. Andersen prided himself on his "innate" gifts as poet (*Digter*), and he devoutly believed that certain biologically determined people were chosen by divine providence to rise above others. This belief was his rationalization for aspiring toward recognition and acceptance by the upper classes. And here an important distinction must be made. More than anything else Andersen sought the blessing and recognition of Jonas Collin and the other members of this respectable, wealthy, patriarchal family as well as other people from the educated bureaucratic class in Denmark like Henriette Wulff. In other words, Andersen endeavored to appeal to the Danish bourgeois elite, cultivated in the arts, adept at commerce and administration, and quick to replace the feudal caste of aristocrats as the leaders of Denmark.

* * *

With a few exceptions, most of the 156 fairy tales written by Andersen contain no "I," that is, the "I" is sublimated through the third person, and the narrative discourse becomes dominated by constant reference to the location of power. The identification of the third-person narrator with the underdog or dominated in the tales is consequently misleading. On one level, this occurs, but the narrator's voice always seeks approval and identification with a higher force. Here, too, the figures representing dominance or nobility are not always at the seat of power. Submission to power beyond the aristocracy constituted and constitutes the real appeal of Andersen's tales for middle-class audiences: Andersen placed power in divine providence, which invariably acted in the name of bourgeois essentialist ideology. No other writer of literary fairy tales in the early nineteenth century introduced so many Christian notions of God, the Protestant ethic, and bourgeois enterprise in his narratives as Andersen did. All his tales make explicit or implicit reference to a miraculous Christian power, which rules firmly but justly over His subjects. Such patriarchal power would appear to represent a feudal organization but the dominant value system represented by providential action and the plots of the tales is thoroughly bourgeois and justifies essentialist notions of aptitude and disposition. Just as aristocratic power was being transformed in Denmark, so Andersen reflected upon the meaning of such transformation in his tales.

There are also clear strains of social Darwinism in Andersen's tales mixed with the Aladdin motif. In fact, survival of the fittest is the message of the very first tale he wrote for the publication of his anthology—**"The Tinderbox."** However, the fittest is not always the strongest but the chosen protagonist who proves himself or herself worthy of serving a dominant value system. This does not mean that Andersen constantly preached one message in all his tales. As a whole, written from 1835 to 1875, they represent the creative process of a dominated ego endeavoring to establish a unified self while confronted with a dominant discourse, which dissociated this identity. The fictional efforts are variations on a theme of how to achieve approbation, assimilation, and integration in a social system that does not allow for real acceptance or recognition if one comes from the lower classes. In many respects Andersen is like a Humpty-Dumpty figure who had a great fall when he realized as he grew up that entrance into the educated elite of Denmark did not mean acceptance and totality. Nor could all the king's men and horses put him back together when he was humiliated and perceived the inequalities. So his fairy tales are variegated and sublimated efforts to achieve wholeness, to gain ven-

geance, and to depict the reality of class struggle. The dominated voice, however, remains constant in its reference to real power.

Obviously there are other themes than power and domination in the tales and other valid approaches to them, but I believe that the widespread, continuous reception of Andersen's fairy tales in Western culture can best be explained by understanding how the discourse of the dominated functions in the narratives. Ideologically speaking Andersen furthered bourgeois notions of the self-made man or the Horatio Alger myth, which was becoming so popular in America and elsewhere, while reinforcing a belief in the existing power structure that meant domination and exploitation of the lower classes. This is why we must look more closely at the tales to analyze how they embody the dreams of social rise and individual happiness, which further a powerful, all-encompassing bourgeois selection process.

II

Bredsdorff notes that among the 156 tales written by Andersen there are thirty that have proven to be the most popular throughout the world. My analysis will concentrate first on these tales in an effort to comprehend the factors that might constitute their popularity in reception. Since they form the kernel of Andersen's achievement, they can be considered the ultimate examples of how the dominated discourse can rationalize power in fairy tales written for children and adults as well. Aside from examining this aspect of these tales, I shall also analyze those features in other significant tales that reveal the tensions of a life that was far from the fairy tale Andersen wanted his readers to believe it was. Ironically, the fairy tales he wrote are more "realistic" than his own autobiographies, when understood as discourses defined by dominance relationships in which the narrator defines what he would like to be according to definitions of a socially imposed identity.

Since there is no better starting point than the beginning, let us consider Andersen's very first tale, **"The Tinderbox,"** as an example of how his dominated discourse functions. As I have already mentioned, the basic philosophy of **"The Tinderbox"** corresponds to the principles of social Darwinism, but this is not sufficient enough to understand the elaboration of power relations and the underlying message of the tale. We must explore further.

As the tale unfolds, it is quite clear that the third-person narrative voice and providence are on the young soldier's side, for without any ostensible reason he is chosen by the witch to fetch a fortune. Using his talents, he not only gains a treasure but immense power, even if he must kill the witch to do so. Here the murder of the witch is not viewed as immoral since witches are evil per se. The major concern of Andersen is to present a young soldier who knows how to pull himself up by the bootstraps when fortune shines upon him to become a "refined gentleman." The word refined has nothing to do with culture but more with money and power. The soldier learns this when he runs out of coins, is forgotten by fair-weather friends, and sinks in social status. Then he discovers the magic of the tinderbox and the power of the three dogs, which means endless provision. Here Andersen subconsciously concocted a sociopolitical formula that was the keystone of bourgeois progress and success in the nineteenth century: use of talents for the acquisition of money, establish a system of continual recapitalization (tinderbox and three dogs) to guarantee income and power, employ money and power to achieve social and political hegemony. The soldier is justified in his use of power and money because he is *essentially* better than anyone else—chosen to rule. The king and queen are dethroned, and the soldier rises through the application of his innate talents and fortune to assume control of society.

Though it appears that the soldier is the hero of the story, there is a hidden referent of power in this dominated narrative discourse. Power does not reside in the soldier but in the "magical" organization of social relations that allows him to pursue and realize his dreams. Of course, these social relations were not as magical as they appear since they were formed through actual class struggle to allow for the emergence of a middle class, which set its own rules of the game and established those qualities necessary for leadership: cleverness, perseverance, cold calculation, respect for money and private property. Psychologically Andersen's hatred for his own class (his mother) and the Danish nobility (king and queen) are played out bluntly when the soldier kills the witch and has the king and queen eliminated by the dogs. The wedding celebration at the end is basically a celebration of the solidification of power by the bourgeois class in the nineteenth century: the unification of a middle-class soldier with a royal princess. In the end the humorous narrative voice appears to gain deep pleasure and satisfaction in having related this tale, as though it has been ordained from above.

In all the other tales published in 1835 there is a process of selection and proving one's worth according to the hidden referent of bourgeois power. In **"Little Claus and Big Claus"** the small farmer must first learn the lesson of humility before providence takes his side and guides him against the vengeful big farmer. Again, using his wits without remorse, an ordinary person virtually obliterates a rich arrogant landowner and amasses a small fortune. **"The Princess and the Pea"** is a simple story about the essence of true nobility. A *real* prince can only marry a genuine princess with the right sensitivity. This sensitivity is spelled out in different ways in the other tales of 1835: **"Little Ida's Flowers," "Thumbelina,"** and **"The Traveling Companion"** portray "small" or oppressed people who cultivate their special talents and struggle to realize their goals despite the forces of adversity. Ida retains and fulfills her dreams of flowers despite the crass professor's vicious attacks. Thumbelina survives many adventures to marry the king of the angels and become a queen. Johannes, the poor orphan, promises to be good so that God will protect him, and indeed his charitable deeds amount to a marriage with a princess. The *Taugenichts* who trusts in God will always be rewarded. All the gifted but disadvantaged characters, who are God-fearing, come into their own in Andersen's tales, but they never take possession of power, which resides in the shifting social relations leading to bourgeois hegemony.

In all of these early tales Andersen focuses on lower-class or disenfranchised protagonists, who work their way up in society. Their rise is predicated on their proper behavior, which must correspond to a higher power that elects and tests the hero. Though respect is shown for feudal patriarchy, the correct normative behavior reflects the values of the bourgeoisie. If the hero comes from the lower classes, he or she must be humbled if not humiliated at one point to test obedience. Thereafter, the natural aptitude of a successful individual will be unveiled through diligence, perseverance, and adherence to an ethical system that legitimizes bourgeois domination. Let me be more specific by focusing on what I consider the major popular tales written after 1835: **"The Little Mermaid"** (1837), **"The Steadfast Tin Soldier"** (1838), **"The Swineherd"** (1841), **"The Nightingale"** (1843), **"The Ugly Duckling"** (1843), **"The Red Shoes"** (1845), and **"The Shadow"** (1847).

There are two important factors to bear in mind when considering the reception of these tales in the nineteenth century and the present in regard to the narrative discourse of the dominated. First, as a member of the dominated class, Andersen could only experience dissociation despite entrance into upper-class circles. Obviously this was because he measured his success as a person and artist by standards that were not of his own social group's making. That ultimate power, which judged his efforts and the destiny of his heroes, depended on the organization of hierarchical relations at a time of sociopolitical transformation, which was to leave Denmark and most of Europe under the control of the bourgeoisie. This shift in power led Andersen to identify with the emerging middle-class elite, but he did not depict the poor and disenfranchised in a negative way. On the contrary, Andersen assumed a humble, philanthropic stance—the fortunate and gifted are obliged morally and ethically to help the less fortunate. The dominated voice of all his narratives does not condemn his former social class, rather Andersen loses contact with it by denying the rebellious urges of his class within himself and making compromises that affirmed the rightful domination of the middle-class ethic.

A second factor to consider is the fundamental ambiguity of the dominated discourse in Andersen's tales: this discourse cannot represent the interests of the dominated class, it can only rationalize the power of the dominant class so that this power becomes legitimate and acceptable to those who are powerless. As I have noted before, Andersen depersonalizes his tales by using the third-person stance, which appears to universalize his voice. However, this self-denial is a recourse of the dominated, who always carry references and appeal to those forces that control their lives. In Andersen's case he mystifies power and makes it appear divine. It is striking, as I have already stressed, when one compares Andersen to other fairy-tale writers of his time, how he constantly appeals to God and the Protestant ethic to justify and sanction the actions and results of his tales. Ironically, to have a soul in Andersen's tales one must sell one's soul either to the aristocracy or to the bourgeoisie. In either case it was the middle-class moral and social code that guaranteed the success of his protagonists, guaranteed his own social success, and ultimately has guaranteed the successful reception of the tales to the present.

Speaking about lost souls, then, let us turn to **"The Little Mermaid"** to grasp how the dominated seemingly gains "happiness and fulfillment" while losing its voice and real power. This tale harks back to the folk stories of the water urchin who desires a soul so she can marry a human being whom she loves. Andersen was certainly familiar with Goethe's "Melusine" and Fouqué's "Undine," stories that ennobled the aspirations of pagan sprites, but his tale about the self-sacrificing mermaid is distinctly different from the narratives of Goethe and Fouqué, who were always part of the dominant class and punished upper-class men for forgetting their Christian manners. Andersen's perspective focuses more on the torture and suffering that a member of the dominated class must undergo to establish her true nobility and virtues. Characteristically, Andersen only allows the mermaid to rise out of the water and move in the air of royal circles after her tongue is removed and her tail is transformed into legs described as "sword-like" when she walks or dances. Voiceless and tortured, deprived physically and psychologically, the mermaid serves a prince who never fully appreciates her worth. Twice she saves his life. The second time is most significant: instead of killing him to regain her identity and rejoin her sisters and grandmother, the mermaid forfeits her own life and becomes an ethereal figure, blessed by God. If she does good deeds for the next three hundred years, she will be endowed with an immortal soul. As she is told, her divine mission will consist of flying through homes of human beings as an invisible spirit. If she finds a good child who makes his parents happy and deserves their love, her sentence will be shortened. A naughty and mean child can lengthen the three hundred years she must serve in God's name.

However, the question is whether the mermaid is really acting in God's name. Her falling in love with royalty and all her future actions involve self-denial and a process of rationalizing self-denial. The mermaid's ego becomes dissociated because she is attracted to a class of people who will never accept her on her own terms. To join her "superiors" she must practically cut her own throat, and, though she realizes that she can never express truthfully who she is and what her needs are, she is unwilling to return to her own species or dominated class. Thus she must somehow justify her existence to herself through abstinence and self-abnegation—values preached by the bourgeoisie and certainly not practiced by the nobility and upper classes. Paradoxically, Andersen seems to be preaching that true virtue and self-realization can be obtained through self-denial. This message, however, is not so paradoxical since it comes from the voice of the dominated. In fact, it is based on Andersen's astute perception and his own experience as a lower-class clumsy youth who sought to cultivate himself: by becoming voiceless, walking with legs like knives, and denying one's needs, one (as a nonentity) gains divine recognition.

Andersen never tired of preaching self-abandonment and self-deprivation in the name of bourgeois laws.

Illustration by Arthur Rackham from Fairy Tales *(2004), by Hans Christian Andersen, translated by Tiina Nunnally.*

The reward was never power over one's life but security in adherence to power. For instance, in **"The Steadfast Tin Soldier,"** the soldier falls in love with a ballerina and remarks: "She would be a perfect wife for me . . . but I am afraid she is above me. She has a castle, and I have only a box that I must share with twenty-four soldiers; that wouldn't do for her. Still, I would like to make her acquaintance." He must endure all sorts of hardships in pursuit of his love and is finally rewarded with fulfillment—but only after he and the ballerina are burned and melted in a stove. Again, happiness is predicated on a form of self-effacement.

This does not mean that Andersen was always self-denigrating in his tales. He often attacked greed and false pride. But what is interesting here is that vice is generally associated with the pretentious aristocracy and hardly ever with bourgeois characters. Generally speaking, Andersen punished overreachers, that is, the urge within himself to be rebellious. Decorum and balance became articles of faith in his philosophical scheme of things. In **"The Swineherd"** he delights in depicting the poor manners of a princess who has lost her sense of propriety. Andersen had already parodied the artificiality and pretentiousness of the nobility in **"The Tinderbox"** and **"The Emperor's New Clothes."** Similar to the "taming of the shrew" motif in the folk tale "King Thrushbeard," Andersen now has the dominant figure of the fickle, proud princess humiliated by the dominated figure of the prince disguised as swineherd. However, there is no happy end here, for the humor assumes a deadly seriousness when the prince rejects the princess after accomplishing his aim: "'I have come to despise you,' said the prince. 'You did not want an honest prince. You did not appreciate the rose of the nightingale, but you could kiss a swineherd for the sake of a toy. Farewell!'"

The oppositions are clear: honesty versus falseness, genuine beauty (rose/nightingale) versus manufactured beauty (toys), nobility of the soul versus soulless nobility. Indirectly, Andersen argues that the nobility must adapt to the value system of the emerging bourgeoisie or be locked out of the kingdom of happiness. Without appreciating the beauty and power of genuine leaders—the prince is essentially middle class—the monarchy will collapse.

This theme is at the heart of **"The Nightingale,"** which can also be considered a remarkable treatise about art, genius, and the role of the artist. The plot involves a series of transformations in power relations and service. First the Chinese Emperor, a benevolent patriarch, has the nightingale brought to his castle from the forest. When the chief courtier finds the nightingale, he exclaims: "I had not imagined it would look like that. It looks so common! I think it has lost its color from shyness and out of embarrassment at seeing so many noble people at one time." Because the common-looking bird (an obvious reference to Andersen) possesses an inimitable artistic genius, he is engaged to serve the Emperor. The first phase of the dominant-dominated relationship based on bonded servitude is changed into neglect when the Emperor is given a jeweled mechanical bird that never tires of singing. So the nightingale escapes and returns to the forest, and eventually the mechanical bird breaks down. Five years later the Emperor falls sick and appears to be dying. Out of his own choice the nightingale returns to him and chases death from his window. Here the relationship of servitude is resumed with the exception that the nightingale has assumed a different market value: he agrees to be the emperor's songbird forever as long as he can come and go as he pleases. Feudalism has been replaced by a free-market system; yet, the bird/artist is willing to serve loyally and keep the autocrat in power. "And my song shall make you happy and make you thoughtful. I shall sing not only of the good and of the evil that happen around you, and yet are hidden from you. For a little songbird flies far. I visit the poor fisherman's cottage and the peasant's hut, far away from your palace and your court. I love your heart more than your crown, and I feel that the crown has a fragrance of something holy about it. I will come! I will sing for you!"

As we know, Andersen depended on the patronage of the King of Denmark and other upper-class donors, but he never felt esteemed enough, and he disliked the strings that were attached to the money given to him. Instead of breaking with such patronage, however, the dominated voice of this discourse seeks to set new limits, which continue servitude in marketable conditions more tolerable for the servant. Andersen reaffirms the essentialist ideology of this period and reveals how gifted "common" individuals are the pillars of power—naturally in service to the state. Unfortunately, he never bothered to ask why "genius" cannot stand on its own and perhaps unite with like-minded people.

In **"The Ugly Duckling"** genius also assumes a most awe-inspiring shape, but it cannot fly on its own. This tale has generally been interpreted as a parable of Andersen's own success story because the naturally gifted underdog survives a period of "ugliness" to reveal its innate beauty. Yet, more attention should be placed on the servility of genius. Though Andersen continually located real power in social conditions, which allowed for the emergence of bourgeois hegemony, he often argued—true to conditions in Denmark—that power was to be dispensed in servitude to appreciate rulers, and naturally these benevolent rulers were supposed to recognize the interests of the bourgeoisie. As we have seen in **"The Nightingale,"** the artist returns to serve royalty after he is neglected by the emperor. In **"The Ugly Duckling,"** the baby swan is literally chased by coarse lower-class animals from the henyard. His innate beauty cannot be recognized by such crude specimens, and only after he survives numerous ordeals, does he realize his essential greatness. But his self-realization is ambivalent, for right before he perceives his true nature, he wants to kill himself: "I shall fly over to them, those royal birds! And they can hack me to death because I, who am so ugly, dare to approach them! What difference does it make! It is better to be killed by them than to be bitten by the other ducks, and pecked by the hens, and kicked by the girl who tends the henyard; or to suffer through the winter."

Andersen expresses a clear disdain for the common people's lot and explicitly states that to be humiliated by the upper class is worth more than the trials and tribulations one must suffer among the lower classes. And, again, Andersen espouses bourgeois essentialist philosophy when he saves the swan and declares as narrator: "It does not matter that one has been born in the henyard as long as one has lain in a swan's egg." The fine line between eugenics and racism fades in this story where the once-upon-a-time dominated swan reveals himself to be a tame but noble member of a superior race. The swan does not return "home" but lands in a beautiful garden where he is admired by children, adults, and nature. It appears as though the swan has finally come into his own, but, as usual, there is a hidden reference of power. The swan measures himself by the values and aesthetics set by the "royal" swans and by the proper well-behaved children and people in the beautiful garden. The swans and the beautiful garden are placed in opposition to the ducks and the henyard. In appealing to the "noble" sentiments of a refined audience and his readers, Andersen reflected a distinct class bias if not classical racist tendencies.

What happens, however, when one opposes the structures of the dominant class? Here Andersen can be merciless, just as merciless as the people who repri-

manded and scolded him for overreaching himself. In **"The Red Shoes,"** Karen, a poor little orphan, mistakenly believes that she is adopted by a generous old woman because she wears red shoes, a symbol of vanity and sin. This red stigma is made clear as she is about to be baptized in church: "When the bishop laid his hands on her head and spoke of the solemn promise she was about to make—of her covenant with God to be a good Christian—her mind was not on his words. The ritual music was played on the organ; the old cantor sang, and the sweet voices of the children could be heard, but Karen was thinking of her red shoes." Although she tries to abandon the red shoes, she cannot resist their red lure. So she must be taken to task and is visited by a stern angel who pronounces a sentence upon her: "'You shall dance,' he said, 'dance in your red shoes until you become red and thin. Dance till the skin on your face turns yellow and clings to your bones as if you were a skeleton. Dance you shall from door to door, and when you pass a house where proud and vain children live, there you shall knock on the door so they will see you and fear your fate.'"

The only way Karen can overcome the angel's curse is by requesting the municipal executioner to cut off her feet. Thereafter, she works diligently for the minister of the church. Upon her death, Karen's devout soul "flew on a sunbeam up to God." This ghastly tale—reminiscent of the gory German pedagogical best-seller of this time, Heinrich Hoffmann's *Struwwelpeter* (1845)—is a realistic description of the punishment that awaited anyone who dared oppose the powers that be.

Though Andersen acknowledged the right of the Danish ruling class to exercise its power, he knew how painful it was to be at their mercy. The most telling tale about the excruciating psychological effects of servility, the extreme frustration he felt from his own obsequious behavior, was **"The Shadow."** As many critics have noted, this haunting narrative is highly autobiographical; it stems from the humiliation that Andersen suffered when Edvard Collin adamantly rejected his proposal to use the "familiar you" (*du*) in their discourse—and there was more than one rejection. By retaining the "formal you" (*De*), Collin was undoubtedly asserting his class superiority, and this distance was meant to remind Andersen of his humble origins. Though they had come to regard each other as brothers during their youth, Collin lorded his position over Andersen throughout their lives and appeared to administrate Andersen's life—something that the writer actually desired but feared. In **"The**

Shadow" Andersen clearly sought to avenge himself through his tale about a philosopher's shadow who separates himself from his owner and becomes immensely rich and successful. When the shadow returns to visit the scholar, his former owner wants to know how he achieved such success. To which the shadow replies that he will reveal "everything! And I'll tell you about it, but . . . it has nothing whatsoever to do with pride, but out of respect to my accomplishments, not to speak of my social position, I wish you wouldn't address me familiarly."

"'Forgive me!' exclaimed the philosopher. 'It is an old habit, and they are the hardest to get rid of. But you are quite right, and I'll try to remember.'"

Not only does the shadow/Andersen put the philosopher/Collin in his place, but he explains that it was *Poetry* that made a human being out of him and that he quickly came to understand his "innermost nature, that part of me which can claim kinship to poetry." Humanlike and powerful, the shadow can control other people because he can see their evil sides. His own sinister talents allow him to improve his fortunes, while the philosopher, who can only write about the beautiful and the good, becomes poor and neglected. Eventually, the philosopher is obliged to travel with his former shadow—the shadow now as master and the master as shadow. When the shadow deceives a princess to win her hand in marriage, the philosopher threatens to reveal the truth about him. The crafty shadow, however, convinces the princess that the old man himself is a deranged shadow, and she decides to have him killed to end his misery.

The reversal of fortunes and of power relations is not a process of liberation but one of revenge. Nor can one argue that the shadow possesses power, for power cannot be possessed in and of itself but is constituted by the organization of social classes and property. One can gain access to power and draw upon it, and this is what the shadow does. Aside from being Andersen's wish-fulfillment, the fantastic projection in this story is connected to the Hegelian notion of master/slave (*Herr/Knecht*). The shadow/slave, who is closer to material conditions, is able to take advantage of what he sees and experiences the underpinnings of social life—to overthrow his master, whereas the master, who has only been able to experience reality through the mediation of his shadow, is too idealistic and cannot defend himself. In Andersen's tale it should be noted that the shadow does not act in the interests of the dominated class but rather within the

framework of institutionalized power relationships. Therefore, he still remains servile and caters to the dominant class despite the reversal of his circumstances. In this regard Andersen's heroes, who rise in class, do not undergo a qualitative change in social existence but point more to manifold ways one can accede to power.

As we have seen, the major theme and its variations in Andersen's most popular tales pertain to the rise of a protagonist under conditions of servitude. Only if the chosen hero complies with a code based on the Protestant ethic and reveres divine providence does he advance in society or reach salvation. Though this is not explicitly spelled out, the references to real power reveal that it resides in the social organization of relations affirming bourgeois hegemony of a patriarchal nature. Even the benevolent feudal kings cannot maintain power without obeying sacrosanct bourgeois moral laws. Obviously this applies to the members of the lower classes and circumscribes their rise in fortunes. Limits are placed on their position in acceptable society. In most of the other 126 tales, which are not as widely circulated as the best-known Andersen narratives, the dominated voice remains basically the same: it humbly recognizes the bourgeois rules of the game, submits itself to them as loyal subject, and has the fictional protagonists do the same.

III

What saves Andersen's tales from being simply sentimental homilies (which many of them are) was his extraordinary understanding of how class struggle affected the lives of people in his times, and some tales even contain a forthright criticism of abusive domination—though his critique was always balanced by admiration for the upper classes and a fear of poverty. For instance, there are some exceptional tales of the remaining 126, which suggest a more rebellious position. Such rebelliousness, perhaps, accounts for the fact that they are not among the thirty most popular. Indeed, the dominated discourse is not homogenous or univocal, though it constantly refers to bourgeois power and never seeks to defy it. In 1853, shortly after the revolutionary period of 1848-50 in Europe, Andersen reflected upon the thwarted rebellions in a number of tales, and they are worth discussing because they show more clearly how Andersen wavered when he subjected himself to bourgeois and aristocratic domination.

In **"Everything in its Right Place"** (1853) the arrogant aristocratic owner of a manor takes pleasure in pushing a goose girl off a bridge. The peddler, who watches this and saves the girl, curses the master by exclaiming "everything in its right place." Sure enough, the aristocrat drinks and gambles away the manor in the next six years. The new owner is none other than the peddler, and, of course, he takes the goose girl for his bride and the Bible as his guide. The family prospers for the next hundred years with its motto "everything in its right place." At this point the narrator introduces us to a parson's son tutoring the humble daughter of the now wealthy ennobled house. This idealistic tutor discusses the differences between the nobility and bourgeoisie and surprises the modest baroness by stating:

> know it is the fashion of the day—and many a poet dances to that tune to say that everything aristocratic is stupid and bad. They claim that only among the poor—and the lower you descend the better—does pure gold glitter. But that is not my opinion; I think it is wrong, absolutely false reasoning. Among the highest classes one can often observe the most elevated traits. . . . But where nobility has gone to a man's head and he behaves like an Arabian horse that rears and kicks, just because his blood is pure and he has a degree, there nobility has degenerated. When noblemen sniff the air in a room because a plain citizen has been there and say, "It smells of the street," why then Thespis should exhibit them to the just ridicule of satire.

This degradation is, indeed, what occurs. A cavalier tries to mock the tutor at a music soiree, and the tutor plays a melody on a simple willow flute, which suddenly creates a storm with the wind howling, "everything in its right place!" In the house and throughout the countryside the wind tosses people about, and social class positions are reversed until the flute cracks and everyone returns to their former place. After this scare, Andersen still warns that "eventually everything is put in its right place. Eternity is long, a lot longer than this story." Such a "revolutionary" tone was uncharacteristic of Andersen, but given the mood of the times, he was prompted time and again in the early 1850s to voice his critique of the upper classes and question not only aristocratic but also bourgeois hegemony.

In **"The Pixy and the Grocer"** (1853) a little imp lives in a grocer's store and receives a free bowl of porridge and butter each Christmas. The grocer also rents out the garret to a poor student who would rather buy a book of poetry and eat bread instead of cheese for supper. The pixy visits the student in the garret to punish him for calling the grocer a boor with no feeling for poetry. Once in the garret, how-

ever, the pixy discovers the beauty and magic of poetry and almost decides to move in with the student. Almost, for he remembers that the student does not have much food, nor can he give him porridge with butter. So he continues to visit the garret from time to time. Then one night a fire on the street threatens to spread to the grocer's house. The grocer and his wife grab their gold and bonds and run out of the house. The student remains calm while the pixy tries to save the most valuable thing in the house—the book of poetry. "Now he finally understood his heart's desire, where his loyalty belonged! But when the fire in the house across the street had been put out, then he thought about it again. 'I will share myself between them,' he said, 'for I cannot leave the grocer altogether. I must stay there for the sake of the porridge.'" "That was quite human" the dominated narrator concludes, "after all, we, too, go to the grocer for the porridge's sake."

This tale is much more ambivalent in its attitude toward domination than **"Everything in its Right Place,"** which is open-ended and allows for the possibility of future revolutions. Here, Andersen writes more about himself and his own contradictions at the time of an impending upheaval (i.e., fire = revolution). Faced with a choice, the pixy/Andersen leans toward poetry or the lower classes and idealism. But, when the fire subsides, he makes his usual compromise, for he knows where his bread is buttered and power resides. The narrative discourse is ironic, somewhat self-critical but ultimately rationalizing. Since everyone falls in line with the forces that dominate and provide food, why not the pixy? Who is he to be courageous or different? Nothing more is said about the student, nor is there any mention of those who do not make compromises. Andersen makes it appear that servility is most human and understandable. Rarely does he suggest that it is just as human to rebel against inequality and injustice out of need as it is to bow to arbitrary domination.

The tales of 1853 demonstrate how Andersen was not unaware of possibilities for radical change and questioned the conditions of bourgeois and aristocratic hegemony. In one of his most remarkable tales **"The Gardener and His Master,"** written toward the very end of his life in 1871, he sums up his views on servitude, domination, and aptitude in his brilliantly succinct, ambivalent manner. The plot is simple and familiar. A haughty aristocrat has an excellent plain gardener who tends his estate outside of Copenhagen. The master, however, never trusts the advice of the gardener nor appreciates what he produces. He and his wife believe that the fruits and flowers grown by other gardeners are better. Yet, when they constantly discover, to their chagrin, that their very own gardener's work is considered the best by the royal families, they hope he won't think too much of himself. Then, the storyteller Andersen comments, "he didn't; but the fame was a spur, he wanted to be one of the best gardeners in the country. Every year he tried to improve some of the vegetables and fruits, and often he was successful. It was not always appreciated. He would be told that the pears and apples were good but not as good as the ones last year. The melons were excellent but not quite up to the standard of the first ones he had grown."

The gardener must constantly prove himself, and one of his great achievements is his use of an area to plant "all the typical common plants of Denmark, gathered from forests and fields" that flourish because of his nursing care and devotion. So, in the end, the owners of the castle must be proud of the gardener because the whole world beat the drums for his success. But they weren't really proud of it. They felt that they were the owners and that they could dismiss Larsen if they wanted to. They didn't, for they were decent people, and there are lots of their kind, which is fortunate for the Larsens.

In other words, Andersen himself had been fortunate, or, at least, this was the way he ironically viewed his career at the end of his life. Yet, there is something pathetically sad about this story. The gardener Larsen is obviously the storyteller Andersen, and the garden with all its produce is the collection of fairy tales, which he kept cultivating and improving throughout his life. The owners of the garden are Andersen's patrons and may be associated with the Collin family and other upper-class readers in Denmark. We must remember that it was generally known that the Collin family could never come to recognize Andersen as a *Digter* but thought of him as a fine popular writer. Andersen, whose vanity was immense and unquenchable, was extremely sensitive to criticism, and he petulantly and consistently complained that he felt unappreciated in Denmark while other European countries recognized his genius. Such treatment at home despite the fact that he considered himself a most loyal servant, whether real or projected, became symbolized in this tale. The reference to the *common plants,* which the gardener cultivates, pertains to the folk motifs he employed and enriched so they would bloom aesthetically on their own soil. Andersen boasts that he, the gardener, has made Denmark famous, for pictures are taken of this garden and circu-

lated throughout the world. Yet, it is within the confines of servitude and patronage that the gardener works, and the dominated voice of the narrator, even though ironic, rationalizes the humiliating ways in which his masters treat Larsen: they are "decent" people. But, one must wonder—and the tension of the discourse compels us to do so—that, if the gardener is superb and brilliant, why doesn't he rebel and quit his job? Why does the gardener suffer such humiliation and domination?

Andersen pondered these questions often and presented them in many of his tales, but he rarely suggested alternatives or rebellion. Rather he placed safety before idealism and chose moral compromise over moral outrage, individual comfort and achievement over collective struggle and united goals. He aimed for identification with the power establishment that humiliates subjects rather than opposition to autocracy to put an end to exploitation through power. The defects in Andersen's ideological perspective are not enumerated here to insist that he should have learned to accept squalor and the disadvantages of poverty and struggle. They are important because they are the telling marks in the historical reception of his tales. Both the happy and sad endings of his narratives infer that there is an absolute or a divine, harmonious power, and that unity of the ego is possible under such power. Such a projection, however, was actually that of a frustrated and torn artist who was obliged to compensate for an existence that lacked harmonious proportions and a center of autonomy. Andersen's life was one based on servility, and his tales were endeavors to justify a false consciousness: literary exercises in the legitimation of a social order to which he subscribed.

Whether the discourse of such a dominated writer be a monologue with himself or dialogue with an audience who partakes of his ideology, he still can never feel at peace with himself. It is thus the restlessness and the dissatisfaction of the dominated artist that imbues his work ultimately with the qualitative substance of what he seeks to relate. Ironically, the power of Andersen's fairy tales for him and for his readers has very little to do with the power he respected. It emanates from the missing gaps, the lapses, which are felt when compromises are made under compulsion, for Andersen always painted happiness as adjusting to domination no matter how chosen one was. Clearly, then, Andersen's genius, despite his servility, rested in his inability to prevent himself from loathing all that he admired.

Bibliography

Bredsdorff, Elias. 1979. *Hans Christian Andersen.* London: Phaidon.

Sven H. Rossel (essay date 2001)

SOURCE: Rossel, Sven H. "Hans Christian Andersen." In *Fairy Tales,* edited by Jann Einfeld, pp. 92-7. San Diego, Calif.: Greenhaven Press, Inc., 2001.

[*In the following essay, Rossel discusses the various origins and major thematic motifs of Andersen's fairy tales, noting that Andersen's "acute power of observation and strong sense of reality endowed the most fantastic beings with realistic traits, forcing the reader to believe in them."*]

When, at the age of fourteen, Hans Christian Andersen left home to seek his fortune in the big city, his worried mother exclaimed, "Whatever will become of you?" He confidently replied, "I shall become famous." Years later, in his autobiography, *The Fairy Tale of My Life* (1855), experience led him to say it this way: "First you go through an awful lot, and then you become famous." Single-minded in pursuit of art and recognition, Andersen as a child of the working class, with only a rudimentary education and no social connections, had even more to go through than most struggling young artists. His conviction that he had been gifted at birth with extraordinary talent, however, saw him through much. As he says in **"The Ugly Duckling"**: "It doesn't matter if one is born in a duck yard, when one has lain in a swan's egg!"

Andersen was the first prominent Danish writer of proletarian origin. Although he moved in bourgeois and aristocratic circles—in his day this was the only way for a writer to gain recognition and support—he never disguised his background but always considered himself an outsider and kept a sharp eye for the shortcomings of the bourgeoisie and aristocracy. In tales such as **"The Nightingale"** and **"The Gardener and the Lord and Lady"** Andersen's biting satire is aimed at the arrogance and selfishness of the aristocracy and court circles. Royalty itself, however, he places above criticism: when the nightingale says of the emperor of China, "I love your heart better than your crown," it continues, "and yet your crown has a scent of sanctity about it." Thus, Andersen did not become a great social writer like Charles Dickens, whose background was similar to that of his Danish friend and contemporary.

EARLY INFLUENCES AND EARLY TALES

As a child Andersen had heard retellings of old stories and tales; his father had read the *Arabian Nights* to him, and later he had become acquainted not only with the German Romantic literary tale as written by Ludwig Tieck, E. T. A. Hoffmann, and Adelbert von Chamisso, but also with the folktales collected by the Grimm brothers and with Mathias Winther's *Danish Folktales* (1823). All these sources are reflected in the first collection of tales in 1835, of which the first three are retold folktales. The fourth and weakest tale, **"Little Ida's Flowers,"** is Andersen's own invention, but still dependent on a tale by Hoffmann, *Nutcracker and Mouseking* (1819). The discovery of the folktale became the chief element in Andersen's search for artistic independence. Here he found what he had previously lacked, the short form and firm structure. Here he found the technique of retelling the same episode three times—often with increasing effect—as in **"The Tinderbox"** (1835), **"The Traveling Companion"** (1835), and **"Clod-Hans"** (1855). As in the folktale, so in Andersen's tales there is usually only one main character, and all antagonists of this hero or heroine play subordinate roles. The main character suffers hardship, but usually Andersen's tales, especially those based directly on folktales, have a happy ending.

The first six collections of tales were subtitled "Told for Children." Andersen's statement that he had written them exactly as he had heard them as a child reveals his ingenious discovery that the tales and stories have to be *told.* Andersen's tales seem so simple, but the manuscripts tell of all his patient labor to find the exact expression that would fit his intention. He read recently finished tales and stories to friends to find out if the words would fall as they should and to register the reactions of his listeners. By 1844 Andersen had dropped the subtitle. He began to write tales of greater length, and the three collections of 1852-55 bear the title "Stories." They contained such different texts as the science fiction fantasy **"In a Thousand Years' Time"** and the social commentary **"She Was No Good."** But Andersen did not give up the tale, and the last eleven volumes—from 1858 on—bear the title "Tales and Stories."

Andersen's early tales vary greatly in quality. In fact, only a third of the 156 tales and stories represent him at his best, and most of these date from the 1840s. **"The Nightingale," "The Sweethearts,"** and **"The Ugly Duckling"** appeared in 1844; three of the finest tales, **"The Snow Queen," "The Fir Tree,"** and **"The Bell"** in 1845; **"The Little Match Girl"** in 1846; **"The Shadow," "The Drop of Water,"** and **"The Story of a Mother"** in 1847. As a whole, the production after 1850 does not reach the quality of the masterpieces from the preceding decade. However, we still find some excellent though less known texts, such as **"In a Thousand Years' Time"** (1852), **"She Was No Good"** (1853), **"The Old Oak Tree's Last Dream"** (1858), **"The Butterfly"** (1861), **"The Snail and the Rosebush"** (1862), **"What People Do Think Up"** (1869), **"The Gardener and the Lord and Lady,"** **"The Cripple,"** and **"Auntie Toothache"** (1872).

AUTOBIOGRAPHICAL CONTENT OF FAIRY TALES

In his fragmentary but valuable comments on the tales printed in the collected editions of 1862-63 and 1870-74, Andersen continually emphasizes the reality behind his imaginative treatment. He once stated: "Most of what I have written is a reflection of myself. Every character is taken from life. I know and have known them all." In **"The Ugly Duckling"** we find the glorification of the author's own genius, whereas **"The Fir Tree"** is a rather harsh judgment of himself as the ambitious, always discontented artist afraid of having passed his prime. Idealized reminiscences of Andersen's childhood can be found in the opening of **"The Snow Queen."** We see self-portraits in the fortune-hunting soldier of **"The Tinderbox"** and the hypersensitive title character of **"The Princess on the Pea."** Andersen's affairs of the heart can be followed in several tales: **"The Sweethearts"** describes a meeting with Riborg Voigt thirteen years after his unsuccessful courtship; Louise Collin [daughter of patron, Jonas Collin] is probably the model for the proud princess in **"The Swineherd,"** in which the swineherd, who turns out to be a prince, is Andersen himself; **"The Nightingale"** in its contrasting of the real and the artificial is a tribute to Jenny Lind [Swedish soprano who refused his proposal of marriage]; finally, he deals with his resignation to lonely bachelorhood in the witty parable **"The Butterfly."** Portraits of friends and acquaintances can also be found. It has been suggested that the prince in **"The Bell"** is Hans Christian Ørsted, the loyal friend who praised Andersen's first tales and who was also the discoverer of electromagnetism: in **"The Bell"** the prince represents the scientific mode of approaching the Divine, while the poor boy, another self-portrait of Andersen, represents the poetic mode. It has also been posited that the poet in **"The Shadow"** represents Andersen, and the title character has the features of Edvard Collin, just as in **"The Ugly Duckling"** the cat, the hen, and the old woman portray the Collin family. Andersen also carried on literary combat in his tales. It has been suggested that **"The Snail and the Rosebush"** is another reply to [Danish philosopher Soren] Kierkegaard's harsh criticism of *Only a Fiddler* (the snail, of course, is the philosopher,

while the blooming rosebush is the poet himself), and **"The Gardener and the Lord and Lady"** is regarded as Andersen's final and wittiest settlement with his Danish critics.

PHILOSOPHICAL CONTENT

But the tales are more than disguised autobiographies and more than simple entertainment. "I seize an idea for older people—and then tell it to the young ones, while remembering that father and mother are listening and must have something to think about," Andersen says. "I write about what is true and good and beautiful," says the learned man in **"The Shadow,"** stating Andersen's own ideal of art, which reflects the Romantic philosophy of his time. But the bitter irony of **"The Shadow"** is that everyone disregards the learned man and his values, choosing to follow the title figure, undoubtedly the most demonic character in Andersen's writings. By the end of the story there is nothing left of the Romantic belief that the goodhearted person, such as John in **"The Traveling Companion"** or Gerda in **"The Snow Queen,"** has nothing to fear from evil: all human efforts are absurd. This is also the main theme of the tale **"The Story of a Mother,"** a tribute to maternal love but also a demonstration of the mercilessness of life. Here we are far from the light gaiety of **"The Tinderbox"** or the optimism of **"The Ugly Duckling."**

OPTIMISM AND PESSIMISM

It is characteristic of Andersen's tales and stories that one idea evokes its counterpart, and this duality in his mental and spiritual make-up is recognizable in all his works. The tales deal with optimism *and* pessimism. In opposition to those which posit a belief in good fortune (**"The Tinderbox," "The Traveling Companion," "The Flax," "Clod-Hans"**), in the power of goodness of heart over cold reason (**"The Snow Queen"**), and in the possibility of human experience of the Divine (**"The Bell"**), we can cite many tales that are hopeless in their pessimism: **"The Fir Tree," "The Shadow," "The Little Match Girl," "The Story of a Mother,"** and **"Auntie Toothache."** Thus Andersen's intense love of life alternates with a preoccupation with death: unable to accept the course of nature, he continually emphasizes immortality and fights death, as the mother does in **"The Story of a Mother"** and art does in **"The Nightingale."** The complete absorption in life as represented by the tiny mayfly in **"The Old Oak Tree's Last Dream"** remained Andersen's ideal.

But when Andersen aimed his satire at various inequalities in society, he never vacillated. Thus **"The Nightingale"** and **"The Swineherd"** should not only be interpreted as allegories, setting true poetry against rigid academic convention, but also as highly ironic depictions of human behavior, a critical tendency which is carried further in the social accusations in **"The Drop of Water"** and **"She Was No Good."**

REVIVING THE LITERARY FAIRY TALE

Andersen was no romantic dreamer with contempt for his own times. On the contrary, he welcomed many new events in art and science. He fantasizes about aircraft in **"In a Thousand Years' Time"** and about a magnifying glass in **"The Drop of Water."** What he welcomed was the victory of spirit over matter, and he was interested in every new discovery that seemed to represent that victory. His own contribution along these lines was the renewing of the genre of the literary tale: "The tale is the most extensive realm of poetry, ranging from the blood-drenched graves of the past to the pious legends of a child's picture book, absorbing folk literature and art literature; to me it is the representation of all poetry, and the one who masters it must be able to put into it the tragic, the comic, the naïve, irony and humor, having here the lyrical note as well as the childish narrative and the language of describing nature at his service."

If Andersen himself was able to fulfill these, his own, demands, it was primarily because he, in contrast to the German Romanticists, was able to preserve that primitive immediacy that establishes direct contact with the world around him. His myth-creating imagination, which broke with all literary conventions, knew how to animate the inanimate. His acute power of observation and strong sense of reality endowed the most fantastic beings with realistic traits, forcing the reader to believe in them. Andersen's point of departure is local, Danish—yet his tales and stories live on, even though their creator has long since died.

"Will all beauty in the world die when you die?" the little fly asks the tree. "It will last longer, infinitely longer, than I can imagine!" says the great oak tree.

Alison Lurie (essay date 2003)

SOURCE: Lurie, Alison. "The Underduckling: Hans Christian Andersen." In *Boys and Girls Forever: Children's Classics from Cinderella to Harry Potter*, pp. 1-11. New York, N.Y.: Penguin Books, 2003.

[In the following essay, Lurie explores the interplay between the narrative and thematic details of Andersen's fairy tales and various elements from his own personal history.]

In **"The Ugly Duckling"**—which generations of readers have recognized as an allegory of Hans Christian Andersen's own life—the unattractive, awkward, lowborn hero becomes a swan without any effort on his part. That ending, more than anything else in the story, makes it a fantasy. Andersen began life as one of the most gawky and disadvantaged ducks that ever waddled out of a mud pond. But he transformed himself into a swan only partially, and by long and exhausting effort.

From his earliest years as the son of a dreamy, improvident cobbler and a half-illiterate washerwoman in a small Danish town, he was what would now be called a freak. He was tall and thin and clumsy; he seldom played with other children, and his greatest delight, he wrote later, "was in making clothes for my dolls."[1]

Andersen's odd appearance was not just a childhood affliction. When he was in his sixties, a traveling companion described him as

> . . . strange and bizarre in his movements and carriage. His arms and legs were long and thin and out of all proportion, his hands were broad and flat, and his feet of . . . gigantic dimensions. . . . His nose [was] so disproportionately large that it seemed to dominate his whole face.[2]

Andersen was aware that he looked peculiar; as his most recent biographer, Jackie Wullschlager, tells us, he described himself in a letter to Charles Dickens as "one who seemed to have fallen from the skies."[3] He was suggesting that he was a kind of otherworldly phenomenon, part child, part fool, and part natural philosopher—what at the time was called a "mooncalf."

Andersen was never a fool, and only occasionally a philosopher, but in a sense he remained a child all his life, with a child's egotism and a child's intense and volatile emotions. In the language of today's psychology, he was acutely bipolar. He was often either wild with joy or in deep despair, wishing that he were dead. As he wrote at twenty-nine, "My pain is crushing when I suffer, but my joy when I'm happy is also inexpressible."[4] He also had a child's naive but penetrating view of adult pretension and self-deception, like the little boy at the end of **"The Emperor's New Clothes,"** who exclaims that the ruler has nothing on.

Also, like a child, Andersen saw everything in the world as alive and conscious. In his stories not only animals and birds, but also bugs and toys and flowers and even household objects have complex human personalities. In one of his tales a saucepan and a bunch of matches relate their life stories, and an earthenware pitcher proposes that they "have an intellectual entertainment."[5] In another tale a "decent, respectable Old Street Lamp" who is about to be retired reflects on her life. She "felt very much as a superannuated ballet-dancer feels when she is dancing for the last time, and knows that tomorrow and ever after she will sit alone in her attic chamber, morning, noon, and night, unthought of and uncared for by the generous public."[6]

For Andersen, like his Street Lamp, public attention was essential. When he was thirteen, a troupe of traveling actors came to town, and Andersen somehow convinced the manager of the theater to give him a walk-on part. To his mind, he was the center of the production. "I was always the first there, put on the red silk costume, spoke my line and believed that the whole audience thought only of me," he wrote later.[7]

From an early age Andersen sought out those who could help him toward the fame he craved. He wrote letters to well-known people and called on them, begging them to listen to him sing and recite poems and stories. Anyone who has ever been in a play or published a book will recognize the type—the awkward, odd-looking, self-conscious, very young man or woman who hangs about after the show or the reading, demanding attention, insisting on reciting a speech for you, singing a song, or showing you their half-baked, over-iced poems and stories. It is often clear from the manner of these people that they are convinced they are geniuses, and are in fact doing you a favor.

The surprising thing is that once in a while someone like this is in fact a genius. This was the case with Hans Christian Andersen; but for a long time no one agreed with him. From childhood on he was convinced of his own remarkable gifts, but by the age of thirty he had failed as a singer, a dancer, and an actor. He had managed to make a thin sort of living by writing poetry and accounts of his travels in Denmark, Germany, and Italy; his sentimental novel, *Only a Fiddler,* about a poor Italian boy who achieves fame as a singer was praised by some critics. If his life had ended then, no one would have remembered him. But instead, almost by accident, he discovered his true calling as a teller of fairy stories for children.

Today, this is a legitimate occupation: successful children's writers are world famous and often very rich. But in Denmark in Andersen's day, children's litera-

ture was moralistic and drab, and fairy tales were published only by scholars.[8] When Andersen wrote his first tales in 1835, he would probably have known the collections of Jacob and Wilhelm Grimm in Germany, and their Danish follower, Matthias Winther, whose *Danish Folk Tales* had appeared in 1823.

Unlike the Grimms and Winther, however, Andersen did not just write down the stories he had heard as a child from his mother and grandmother; he went on to compose new tales of his own. And even when he retold an existing story, he made dramatic changes. In **"The Tinderbox,"** for instance, the Princess marries the soldier at the end not because she loves him, but for practical reasons: her parents are dead, and "she liked [being queen] much better than living a prisoner in the copper palace."[9]

The heroes and heroines in the Grimms' tales and other traditional collections usually meet their reward on earth: they kill the giant, rescue the prince or princess, win a kingdom, and live happily ever after. By contrast, many of Andersen's stories end unhappily. In my collection of forty-eight of his best-known stories, twenty finish with a death, though sometimes the character who dies is rewarded by eternal life. After Andersen's Little Match Girl perishes of the cold, for instance, the spirit of her grandmother carries her off to Paradise.

In a few of his best stories, however, Andersen provides a happy ending. Little Gerda, in **"The Snow Queen,"** rescues Kai from the icy palace of the enchantress, where his heart has been frozen solid and he spends all day trying to fit sharp flat pieces of ice together in what Andersen calls "the ice-puzzle of reason." When Gerda, weeping, embraces him, the ice in his heart dissolves, and they fall into each other's arms.

Yet mutual romantic love is very rare in Andersen's tales. Again and again, his protagonists are rejected by those they court—and in this they share the unhappy experience of their author. All his life, Andersen continually fell in love with upperclass or titled persons, both male and female. Though he made many acquaintances, he had almost no romantic success: these people liked having him come to their houses, tell stories to their children, and sign books, but their attitude always remained one of friendly, slightly distant patronage. For years he tried, often in the most embarrassing manner, to get Edvard Collin, the handsome son of his first important patron in Copenhagen, to call him by the familiar pronoun

"Du"; Edvard continued to refuse, remarking that though it was a trivial thing, he had "an innate dislike" of it, similar to the dislike a woman he knew felt for wrapping paper "so much that she was sick whenever she saw it. . . . When someone whom I respect and like and have known a long time, asks me to say 'Du,' then this nasty and inexplicable feeling surfaces within me."[10]

Andersen never really recovered from this chilly rebuff, nor from the rejection he received from many other young, beautiful, and aristocratic people. Yet he continued setting his sights unreasonably high; sometimes it seems as if what he really wanted was a hopeless romantic love. Occasionally he altered facts to put a better spin on these events, declaring that he had never loved the person involved, or that circumstances, rather than their own feelings, had separated them. When he was twenty-five, he fell in love simultaneously with two siblings, Christian Voight and his sister Riborg, the children of a wealthy merchant. Riborg was already secretly engaged to a man her parents disapproved of, which may have been part of the attraction. After Riborg turned him down, he told friends that she didn't mean anything to him, but he later wrote to Edvard with a more romantic version of the story:

> . . . last summer I met a rich, lovely, spirited girl who feels the same for me as I do for her . . . certain circumstances made her marry a man who took her fortune.[11]

The emphasis on wealth in this statement leaves rather a bad taste in the mouth, and suggests that Andersen may not have felt any more real passion for Riborg than she felt for him; "certain circumstances" was a euphemism for the fact that she was in love with the other man. When, toward the end of his life, Andersen did manage to establish a happy but short-lived sexual relationship, it was with a young man.

The heroes of Andersen's tales are no more successful romantically than he was, and often for the same reasons: they aspire to union with persons or objects of a higher social class. The cardboard dancer in **"The Steadfast Tin Soldier"** pays no attention to the protagonist, and in **"The Top and the Ball,"** the Top's proposal of marriage is scorned by the Ball, "who was made of morocco leather, and fancied herself a very fashionable young lady."[12]

A recurrent theme in Andersen's tales is social snobbery and social ambition. Even inanimate objects feel it: the Darning-needle tries to pass herself off as a Sewing-needle, and the Buckwheat considers himself superior to all the other plants in the field. Andersen too was obsessed with the idea of rising in society. All his life he would seek out rich and titled people, the richer and more titled the better, and he spent some of his happiest moments as the guest of royalty. He spent months traveling among small German kingdoms, staying with one royal family after another, and entertaining them and their children by telling stories. His friends back in Copenhagen did not always approve of this. When he wrote to Jonas Collin, boasting "that while he was ignored at home, Berlin high society gathered round him," Jonas was unimpressed. According to Andersen's current biographer, he wrote back saying "what an empty life, he didn't care to crawl about on the floor with the children of dukes, wasn't Andersen going to write anything?"[13]

One thing that makes Andersen's weaknesses and faults forgivable is that from his earliest years he was aware of them. "My nasty vanity sneaks in," he wrote to a friend from the awful boarding school to which he was sent at nineteen by well-meaning patrons who wanted him to receive a proper conventional education. "[T]here is a kind of unpleasant dreaminess in me, something restless and impulsive in my soul. . . ."[14]

Andersen was also able to take a humorous attitude toward his own character. As he became more successful he developed a passion for travel, most often to warmer countries where he was already famous; and he indulged this passion constantly in spite of his continuing hypochondria and anxiety. When he was on the road, he was often seasick and consumed by fears of dogs and brigands; he had the obsessive idea that one of his fellow travelers might be crazy and planning to murder him. He recognized the irrationality of all this, though he could not overcome it. "Oh, how good I am at finding things to worry about," he once wrote in his diary.[15]

* * *

Jackie Wullschlager's extensive examination of this strange, deeply self-conscious writer and his work is a remarkable achievement: thoughtful, comprehensively researched, and wonderfully readable. Ms. Wullschlager spent many months in Denmark; she was able to read Andersen's tales and letters and journals in the original, and correct earlier translations. Her comments on the meaning of the stories, and their relation to his life, are often fascinating—and so is the impression her book gives of her own feelings about Andersen.

Biographers, who necessarily spend many years in the imaginary company of their subjects, usually end up even more devoted to them then they were at first. Yet Wullschlager's book sometimes gives the impression that as time went on she became more and more exasperated with Andersen. She portrays him as deeply annoying, vain, and egotistic, suffering from "wild imagination, inner rage, tormenting anxieties and hypochondria, insatiable ambition."[16] But she also gives him credit for his charm, brilliance, originality, and—perhaps most striking of all to the reader who knows Andersen only through his works—his sophisticated self-knowledge.

As a writer, Wullschlager has some of Andersen's own down-to-earth originality and humor. When she describes Copenhagen as Andersen would have seen it for the first time at fourteen, when he left home to make his fortune, she remarks that the city "still had the layout of a fortress. . . . Within, the buildings were forced upwards like asparagus and arranged like flowerpots on a ledge."[17]

Wullschlager attributes much of Andersen's insatiable ambition to the loneliness and persecution he suffered as an ugly, clumsy, effeminate child who was teased and bullied by other children and ashamed of his family. All his life he was painfully aware not only of his mother's drinking, but of the fact that his aunt kept a whorehouse and his uncle was in the local insane asylum. And though he gloried in the role of the poor boy who becomes rich and famous, he had a lifelong dread that these shameful connections would resurface. In Denmark, where some of his history was known, and not all his books were praised by the critics, he seldom felt properly appreciated and safe. As he grew older he began to turn against his native land. From Paris, he wrote to a friend in Copenhagen, with characteristic exaggeration:

> Here, in this big strange city, Europe's most famous and noble personalities fondly surround me, . . . and at home boys sit spitting at my heart's dearest creation! . . . The Danes are evil, cold, satanic—a people well suited to the wet, mouldy-green island . . . my home has sent me a fever from its cold, wet forests, which the Danes gaze upon and believe they love; but I don't believe in love in the North, but in evil treachery.[18]

Though he became world famous in his lifetime, Andersen's ambition was never quite satisfied. In a sense it never could be. As his biographer says, "Even after he was famous and secure, his need for constant recognition and praise was pathological, and he craved admiration like a shot of an addictive drug."[19] Andersen, of course, knew this about himself. "My name is gradually starting to shine, and that is the only thing I live for. . . . I covet honour in the same way as a miser covets gold,"[20] he admitted in a letter.

Jackie Wullschlager praises Andersen because, she believes, "he gave voice . . . to groups which had traditionally been mute and oppressed—children, the poor, those who did not fit social or sexual stereotypes."[21] It is true that in some of Andersen's tales disadvantaged persons, animals, and objects receive attention and sympathy. But very often their one-down position is also their downfall. If they aspire to higher status, and especially to union with higher-status people, animals, or objects, they are usually disappointed. The Fir Tree dreams of glory as a Christmas tree, but when he achieves this it does not satisfy him. "It must be that something still greater, still more splendid, must happen—but what?"[22] the Fir Tree muses; and he ends up dead on a rubbish heap.

It is true that Andersen's Ugly Duckling becomes a swan, and is welcomed by the other swans, but in his case heredity takes precedence over environment. As Andersen put it in his story, "It matters not to have been born in a duck-yard, if one has been hatched from a swan's egg."[23]

* * *

Although Andersen wrote more than 150 tales, only a handful of them are usually reprinted in collections for children. There is a good reason for this: though some of his stories are brilliant and moving, most are sad, distressing, or even terrifying. As a child I was frightened and upset by many of them, especially those in which a little girl misbehaves and is horribly punished. The crime that seemed to cause the most awful result was vanity, and it was always little girls who met this fate, never little boys. In **"The Red Shoes,"** for instance, Karen thinks of her new morocco-leather shoes even when she is in church, and as a result she is condemned to dance in them to exhaustion; she is only saved from death when she asks the local executioner to chop off her feet with his axe. Even worse in some ways was **"The Girl Who Trod on a Loaf."** In this tale a "proud and arrogant" child called Inger also comes to grief because of love of her new shoes. In order to keep them clean, she throws a loaf of bread into the mud for a stepping-stone. As a result of this wasteful but trivial act, Inger and her shoes sink down into the dark, muddy marsh, where she finds herself in a foul-smelling cave filled with noisome toads and slimy snakes. Little Inger fell among all this horrid living filth; it was so icy cold that she shuddered from head to foot, and her limbs grew quite stiff. The loaf stuck fast to her feet and it drew her down. . . .

Long years pass, and Inger only escapes from the toads and snakes after a good old woman, on her deathbed, remembers hearing Inger's story as a child and pities her.

I was also deeply disturbed by one of Andersen's most famous tales, **"The Little Mermaid,"** in which the heroine gives up her voice and agrees that every step she takes will feel like walking on knives, so as to have the chance of attracting the love of a prince whom she first saw at his birthday party on board a ship. When he finds the Little Mermaid on the seashore, dressed only in her long green hair, he adopts her as a kind of pet. But, like the wellborn young men and women whom Andersen loved, he does not think of her as a romantic partner, and marries a princess. The mermaid dies of grief; but after death she is transfigured, and joins the spirits of the air who "fly invisibly through the dwellings of men, wherever there are children."

Though the Little Mermaid was presented as romantically admirable, I took her story as a warning against self-sacrificial and hopeless love. I did not realize that in this tale Andersen had foretold his own future. He would be rejected again and again by those he loved most, but unlike the Little Mermaid he never gave up his voice, and the best of the stories he told would survive for hundreds of years, "wherever there are children."

Notes

1. Hans Christian Andersen, *The Fairy Tale of My Life,* quoted in Wullschlager, *Hans Christian Andersen,* p. 20.
2. William Bloch, quoted in Wullschlager, *Hans Christian Andersen,* p. 7.
3. Wullschlager, *Hans Christian Andersen,* p. 4.
4. Ibid., p. 135.
5. Andersen, *Fairy Tales and Legends,* p. 355.
6. Ibid., p. 205.
7. *H. C. Andersen's Levnedsbog,* edited by H. Topsoe-Jensen, quoted in Wullschlager, *Hans Christian Andersen,* p. 29.
8. In eighteenth-century France, however, there had been a vogue among aristocratic women for elaborate fairy tales of the sort associated with Charles Perrault and Madame d'Aulnoy, the author of "Beauty and the Beast."

9. Andersen, *Fairy Tales and Legends,* p. 107.
10. Edvard Collin, quoted in Wullschlager, *Hans Christian Andersen,* p. 109.
11. Letter to Edvard Collin, quoted in Wullschlager, *Hans Christian Andersen,* p. 110.
12. Andersen, *Fairy Tales and Legends,* p. 69.
13. Ibid., pp. 273-74.
14. Wullschlager, *Hans Christian Andersen,* pp. 70-71.
15. Journal for May 4, 1841, quoted in Wullschlager, *Hans Christian Andersen,* p. 200.
16. Wullschlager, *Hans Christian Andersen,* p. 6.
17. Ibid., p. 34.
18. Ibid., p. 215.
19. Ibid., pp. 49-50.
20. Ibid., p. 179.
21. Ibid., p. 5.
22. Andersen, *Fairy Tales and Legends,* p. 116.
23. Ibid., p. 226.

Bibliography

Andersen, Hans Christian. *The Fairy Tale of My Life.* New York: Paddington Press, 1975.

———. *Fairy Tales and Legends.* London: The Bodley Head, 1978.

Wullschlager, Jackie. *Hans Christian Andersen: The Life of a Storyteller.* New York: Simon and Schuster, 2001.

Viggo Hjørnager Pedersen (essay date 2003)

SOURCE: Pedersen, Viggo Hjørnager. "From the Flying Trunk to the Celestial Omnibus: Hans Andersen's Influence on the English *Kunstmärchen*." In *Proceedings from the 8th Nordic Conference on English Studies,* edited by Karind Aijmer and Britta Olinder, pp. 217-32. Göteborg, Sweden: Göteborg University Department of English, 2003.

[*In the following essay, Pedersen assesses Andersen's adaptations of classic fairy tales and their strong influence on such later fairy tale authors as Horace Scudder, Oscar Wilde, and E. M. Forster.*]

Fairy- and folk-tales are not quite so important in the Anglo-American tradition as in Germany and Scandinavia. In the 19th century, fairy-tales were often regarded with scepticism, and the idea that the form might be used to produce literature for adults only caught on to a very limited extent. Still, Andersen's tales did inspire a number of British and American writers, and in the following we shall compare some Andersen tales which combine realism and fantasy with similar stories by Horace Scudder, Oscar Wilde and E. M. Forster, who all belong to the Andersen tradition.

When Andersen began writing his *Eventyr* [*Eventyr og Historier*]—as early as with **"Dødningen" ("The Dead Man")** in 1830—the form was already established both in Denmark and Germany. Quite apart from the more or less authentic "folk-tales" of the brothers Grimm and other collectors, the form had for decades been used as a sophisticated medium for entertainment and criticism of manners and society. This can be traced as far back as Perrault and subsequent French 18th-century tellers of tales; but a less courtly form had been established in Germany with Musäus, whom Oehlenschläger was so surprisingly fond of, and with Hoffmann and Chamisso.[1] In Denmark, Oehlenschläger, Ingemann and Molbech, among others, used what was essentially the form developed by Musäus, and the folk-tale proper was cross-fertilised with elements from the *sagn* (local legends) which Andersen's friend Just Matthias Thiele was one of the first to collect.[2]

Musäus and his followers had an 18th-century, ironical attitude to the folktale. They did not share the superstitions of the rustics who originally had told the tales, and they did nothing to hide their amused scepticism.

This attitude also pervades Andersen's **"Dødningen,"** whose fictionality is explicit: it takes place in "Phantasiens Verden", the world of fancy, and the old king is referred to as "Hjerterkonge", the King of Hearts, a cousin of a king in a work by Gozzi. However, when that story was metamorphosed into **"Reisekammeraten" ("The Travelling Companion")**, the tone was changed. Remnants of the old flippancy are still discernible, as when the old crones drinking *schnapps* have it coloured black out of sorrow for the princess's wickedness. But otherwise we alternate between the everyday and the supernatural without batting an eyelid (although this does not always appear from H. W. Dulcken's translation):

Ude paa Marken, hvor *Johannes* gik, stode alle Blomsterne saa friske og deilige i det varme Solskin, og de nikkede i Vinden ligesom om de vilde sige: "Velkommen i det Grønne! Er her ikke ny-

deligt?" Men *Johannes* dreiede sig endnu engang om, for at see den gamle Kirke, hvor han, som lille Barn, var døbt, hvor han hver Søndag med sin gamle Fader havde været i Kirke og sjunget sin Psalme; da saae han høit oppe i et af Hullerne i Taarnet, Kirke-Nissen staae med sin lille røde, spidse Hue, han skyggede for sit Ansigt med den bøiede Arm, da ellers Solen skar ham i Øinene. *Johannes* nikkede Farvel til ham, og den lille Nisse svingede sin røde Hue, lagde Haanden paa Hjertet og kyssede mange Gange paa Fingrene, for at vise, hvor godt han ønskede ham det, og at han ret maatte gjøre en lykkelig Reise.

(I: 68-69)

Out in the field where he was walking all the flowers stood fresh and beautiful in the warm sunshine; and they nodded in the wind, just as if they would have said, "Welcome to the green wood! Is it not fine here?" But John turned back once more to look at the old church, in which he had been christened when he was a little child, and where he had been every Sunday with his father at the service, and had sung his psalm; then, high up in one of the openings of the tower, he saw the ringer [mistake for: the Nisse] standing in his little pointed red cap, shading his face with his bent arm, to keep the sun from shining in his eyes. John nodded a farewell to him, and the little ringer waved his red cap, laid his hand on his heart, and kissed his hand to John a great many times, to show that he wished the traveller well and hoped he would have a prosperous journey.

(1993:47)

"The Travelling Companion," of course, is based on a folktale. But the easy slipping in and out of the supernatural is just as characteristic of **"The Goloshes of Fortune."** This story is indeed still full of irony, but it is not directed at the supernatural element in an otherwise very realistic tale from *Biedermeier* Copenhagen. Instead, we have an imperceptible transition from the everyday to the supernatural: the story opens with a factually circumstantial account of a bourgeois household, where a party is being held, and then suddenly we meet two fairies:

Det var i *Kjøbenhavn,* paa Østergade i eet af Husene, ikke langt fra Kongens Nytorv, at der var stort Selskab, for det maa man have imellem, saa er det gjort og saa kan man blive inviteret igjen. Den ene Halvdeel af Selskabet sad allerede ved Spillebordene, og den anden Halvdeel ventede paa hvad der vilde komme ud af Fruens: "ja, nu skulde vi see til at finde paa noget!" Saavidt var man og Samtalen gik, som den kunde. [. . .]

Under al den Snak [. . .] ville vi gaae ud i det forreste Værelse, hvor Overtøi, Stokke, Paraplyer og Kalosker havde Plads. Her sad to Piger, en ung og en gammel; man skulde troe, at de vare komne for at følge deres Herskab, en eller anden gammel Frøken eller Enkefrue, men saae man lidt nøiere paa dem, saa begreb man snart, at de ikke vare almindelige Tjenestepiger, dertil vare deres Hænder for fine, deres Holdning og hele Bevægelse for kongelig, for det var den, og Klæderne havde ogsaa et ganske eget dristigt Snit. Det var to Feer, den yngste var vel ikke Lykken selv, men een af hendes Kammerjomfruers Kammerpiger, der bringe de mindre Lykkens Gaver omkring, den ældre saae saa inderlig alvorlig ud, det var *Sorgen,* hun gaaer altid selv i egen høie Person sine Ærinder, saa veed hun, at de blive vel udførte.

(II: 178-79)

In a house in Copenhagen, not far from the King's New Market, a company—a very large company—had assembled, having received invitations to an evening party there. One-half of the company already sat at the card tables, the other half awaited the result of the hostess's question, "What shall we do now?" They had progressed so far, and the entertainment began to take some degree of animation. [. . .]

While the conversation takes this turn, [. . .] we will betake ourselves to the antechamber, where the cloaks, sticks, and goloshes had found a place. Here sat two maids—an old one and a young one. One would have thought they had come to escort their mistresses home; but, on looking at them more closely, the observer could see that they were not ordinary servants: their shapes were too graceful for that, their complexions too delicate, and the cut of their dresses too uncommon. They were two fairies. The younger was not Fortune, but lady's-maid to one of her ladies of the bedchamber, who carry about the more trifling gifts of Fortune. The elder one looked somewhat more gloomy—she was Care, who always goes herself in her own exalted person to perform her business, for thus she knows that it is well done.

(1993:64)

We are invited to examine the two women in the anteroom, who are described as ordinary mortals, until we are informed that they are fairies: the transition from reality to fairyland is absolutely seamless.

The above is the 1850 version of the tale. But indeed Andersen had used this technique right from the beginning. In **"Little Ida's Flowers"** from his first collection (1835), the student introduces the supernatural as the most ordinary thing in the world in his conversation with the little girl:

> "Mine stakkels Blomster ere ganske døde!" sagde den lille *Ida.* "De vare saa smukke iaftes, og nu hænge alle Bladene visne! Hvorfor gjøre de det?"

spurgte hun Studenten, der sad i Sophaen; for ham holdt hun saa meget af, han kunde de allerdeiligste Historier og klippede saadanne morsomme Billeder: Hjerter med smaa Madammer i, der dandsede; Blomster og store Slotte, hvor Dørene kunde lukkes op; det var en lystig Student! "Hvorfor see Blomsterne saa daarlige ud i Dag?" spurgte hun igjen, og viste ham en heel Bouquet, der var ganske vissen.

"Ja veed Du, hvad de feile!" sagde Studenten. "Blomsterne have været paa Bal i Nat, og derfor hænge de med Hovedet!"

"Men Blomsterne kunne jo ikke dandse!" sagde den lille *Ida.*

"Jo," sagde Studenten, "naar det bliver mørkt og vi andre sove, saa springe de lystigt omkring; næsten hver evige Nat har de Bal!"

"Kan der ingen Børn komme med paa det Bal?"

"Jo," sagde Studenten, "smaabitte Gaaseurter og Lillieconvaller!"

(I: 43)

"My poor flowers are quite dead!" said little Ida. "They were so pretty yesterday, and now all the leaves hang withered. Why do they do that?" she asked the student, who sat on the sofa; for she liked him very much. He knew the prettiest stories, and could cut out the most amusing pictures—hearts, with little ladies in them who danced, flowers, and great castles in which one could open the doors: he was a merry student. "Why do the flowers look so faded to-day?" she asked again, and showed him a nosegay, which was quite withered.

"Do you know what's the matter with them?" said the student. "The flowers have been at a ball last night, and that's why they hang their heads."

"But flowers cannot dance!" cried little Ida.

"Oh, yes," said the student, "when it grows dark, and we are asleep. They jump about merrily. Almost every night they have a ball."

"Can children go to this ball?"

"Yes," said the student, "quite little daisies, and lilies of the valley."

(1993:12)

The little girl's opening speech is anthropomorphic: in the Danish text (though not in the English) the flowers are referred to as "dead", and she goes on to ask why they look "sick"; however, so far all the metaphor is dormant: Little Ida is hardly thinking of the flowers in human terms. This change is effected by the student, who seizes on the implicit meanings just mentioned to suggest that the flowers do indeed behave like humans.

The remarkable thing about this and similar stories is the effortlessness of the movement from fantasy to realism and back:

"Kan Professoren da forstaae Pantomime?" spurgte *Ida.*

"Ja, det kan Du troe! Han kom en Morgen ned i sin Have og saae en stor Brændenelde staae at gjøre Pantomine med Bladene til en deilig rød Nellike; den sagde, du er saa nydelig og jeg holder saa meget af dig! men saadan noget kan Professoren nu slet ikke lide, og slog strax Brændenelden over Bladene, for de ere dens Fingre, men saa brændte han sig, og fra den Tid tør han aldrig røre ved en Brændenelde."

"Det var morsomt!" sagde den lille *Ida* og loe.

(I: 45)

"Can the professor understand these signs?" asked Ida.

"Yes, certainly. He came one morning into his garden, and saw a great stinging-nettle standing there, and making signs to a beautiful red carnation with its leaves. It was saying, 'You are so pretty, and I love you with all my heart.' But the professor does not like that kind of thing, and he directly slapped the stinging-nettle upon its leaves, for those are its fingers; but he stung himself; and since that time he has not dared to touch a stinging-nettle."

"That is funny," cried little Ida; and she laughed.

(1993:14)

In this story, all supernatural events and elements are either part of the story that the student tells to the little girl, or they come to her in dreams; but this is really an exception; in most stories of this kind, from **"The Goloshes of Fortune,"** where Justitsraad Knap steps right out of his dull 19th-century existence to literally land in the mud of the Middle Ages, to **"The Storm Moves the Signs,"** where a storm moves the heavy symbols of dull everyday existence around, the central idea is the coexistence of the everyday and the supernatural, as in **"The Nisse at the Grocer's"**:

Der var en rigtig Student, han boede paa Qvisten og eiede Ingenting; der var en rigtig Spekhøker, han boede i Stuen og eiede hele Huset, og ham holdt Nissen sig til, for her fik han hver Juleaften et Fad Grød med en stor Klump Smør i! det kunde Spekhøkeren give; og Nissen blev i Boutiken og det var meget lærerigt.

(II: 255)

There was once a regular student: he lived in a garret, and nothing at all belonged to him; but there was also once a regular huckster: he lived on the ground floor, and the whole house was his; and the Goblin kept with him, for on the huckster's table on Christmas-eve there was, always a dish of plum porridge, with a great piece of butter floating in the middle. The huckster could accomplish that, and consequently the Goblin stuck to the huckster's shop, and that was very interesting.

(1993:457)

This universe, inhabited both by real people living in the real world and by supernatural beings, is perhaps not fundamentally different from that of the folktales proper. But the story does not take place "once upon a time" in fairyland, but in a closely described contemporary society; therefore we get a slight shock when the *Nisse* joins the student and the *Spekhøker,* though we might have taken the meeting of a young prince and an ogre or a speaking animal quite calmly in a real folktale.

A similar mixture of the everyday and the supernatural is found in several tales—**"The Will-O'-the-Wisps are in Town"** and **"Hvad man kan hitte paa"** (**"A Question of Imagination"** in Haugaard's translation) spring to mind.

It is this type of text, combining realism of an often very pedestrian nature with glimpses of the supernatural, or, conversely, fairy-tales that offer satirical perspectives on our everyday world, that became fashionable in Britain and America in the last decades of the 19th and the first of the 20th century. In the following we shall look at three prominent examples, Horace Scudder, Oscar Wilde, and E. M. Forster.

HORACE SCUDDER'S TALES

While still in his twenties, and before he made contact with Andersen, the American writer and publisher Horace Scudder (1838-1902) issued two collections of Andersen-inspired tales, *Seven Little People and Their Friends* (1862) and *Dream Children* (1864).

Scudder's stories have the characteristic Andersen blend of realism and animated or personified nature; animals, plants and even inanimate objects like houses may on occasion reflect or speak. Sometimes this is taken rather to excess, for unlike in Andersen, animation does not always serve a purpose. In Andersen, it always gives a specific perspective, or is used for ironical purposes, if the personified objects or creatures are used to caricature a similar human type. But with Scudder, one must sometimes ask if the information or opinion given might not just as well have taken the form of a speech from a character or an authorial comment.

Not surprisingly, then, there is little irony in Scudder, and if one gets more than enough of sentiment à la Andersen, one misses the humour of Andersen's tales. A pleasant exception is "The Rich Man's Place", which satirizes over people who go to Europe and come back to remodel everything. The story upholds the natural over the artificial, and stands up for American tradition as Scudder knew it—that of the civilized East Coast—as against far-fetched notions from abroad:

The Rich Man's Place

The rich man had a splendid place,—a house and barns, and a great pleasure-park,—but it was long since he had seen his place, for he had been travelling abroad. When people travel abroad, they expect to learn much, and the rich man when he came home had no doubt learned a great many things. He had brought away as much of other countries as he could carry,—a little in his head, but a good deal in boxes. When these were unpacked, there came forth pictures and statuary and malachite tables, and at least three cart-loads of curious things, which he arranged about the house, so that when his friends came to see him, they all said it was nearly as well as visiting foreign lands themselves; for when they entered the house, the rich man would remind them where he had been. "This hat-tree," he would say, as they took off their hats, "is made of wood from the Black Forest," and then they would shut their eyes, and fancy themselves there. "This table on which I keep my clothes-brush," he would continue, "is a malachite table from Russia." And then they would ask him if he saw the Czar. When they entered the parlor, he would take them on a tour about the room, and feed their imagination with a stone from the field of Waterloo, a splinter from John Knox's house, a piece of pottery from Herculaneum, and a scymitar from Greece; and, if left to themselves, they were given a book of views, or a stereoscope, or allowed to stand before the *étagère,* and handle the Swiss toys and Scotch pebbles. O it was precisely the same as going abroad, and so the guests all said.

But it was best when some one came who had also travelled, and perhaps with the rich man himself; then the guests would listen as one said to the other, "Do you remember that night on the Campagna?"

And the other would say, "Ah, indeed!" and look knowing. "But the Carnival, ah!" he would rejoin, and turn round to the guests, humming the "Carnival of Venice."

"What a tame country ours is!" the guests would sigh to themselves.

(151-53)

Andersen was himself a keen traveller; but as we see from his story **"Lovely,"** he also took delight in observing the ridiculous aspects of tourist life, and Scudder certainly follows him here.

Arguably the best story in *Dream Children* is "The Old House in the Wheat Forest", in which there are echoes both of **"The Story of the Year"** and **"The Old House."** The theme of the story is the relativity of time as experienced from different points of view: of a family of birds, two children, a couple who have been married for nearly 50 years, and an old house. To the birds, a year is close to a lifetime. Time is not on the children's minds as they play at building a house and starting a farm and a family, while the old couple see their past selves in the children. The house has existed for longer than any of them, being a hundred years old, but it realizes how brief even this is, pointing a moral of which Andersen would have approved:

. . . Nothing can remain young but our hearts. There love is, and love is everlasting. Yes! the couple that were married here in the parlor, just fifty years ago, are old now, but their love has left their hearts young. And the children who were with them, and who went away hand in hand, for out of my garret-window I saw them, they are young and will grow old, but love will never grow old; love will never die. The wheat will be cut down, as the forest before it. New seed will be sown. The birds that were here last spring have gone away, but there will be new ones next spring. And I shall one day fall down, and no doubt a new house will be built here, and there will be weddings in that. Ah! it is eternally beautiful, for love is eternal.

(86-87)

Of the three writers discussed here, Scudder is the closest to Andersen—often perhaps a little too close for comfort. There are many echoes of Andersen in his stories, but it is especially the sentimental stories of Andersen's later years that appeal to him, not the humour or the social criticism which are also an important part of Andersen's work. It was probably all for the best that when he came to write his *Bodley* books for children,[3] he left the fairy-tale style and instead turned to everyday situations based on history, geography, and travel.

The Rockets and Nightingales of Oscar Wilde

Oscar Wilde wrote about 20 tales and stories, many of which contain a fantastic or supernatural element, and in which the fairy-tale form is often used as a background for a criticism of life or of human character. It is especially the two collections *The Happy Prince and Other Tales* (1888) and *A House of Pomegranates* (1891) that show influence from Hans Andersen.

This influence has been variously interpreted. Briggs says that "Hans Andersen was immensely admired and very much imitated in England. Oscar Wilde reproduced almost exactly his mixture of satire and sentiment, something at once sweet and bitter" (179). Murray, on the other hand, in her introduction to *The Complete Shorter Fiction of Oscar Wilde* rather surprisingly concludes:

> Wilde probably learned from Andersen the witty, deflating touches which grace the stories, but never, even in "The Selfish Giant", is he betrayed into such depths of sentimentality as Andersen. He takes over witty talking animals and objects and uses them as frames for stories, as in "The Devoted Friend", but he avoids Andersen's cloying moments, and generally transcends him. Andersen wrote far, far more fairy-tales than Wilde; he did not write more that survive.
>
> (10)

Even if Murray probably read Andersen in rather poor translations as a child, there is really no excuse for such preposterous nonsense. But it is true that unlike Scudder's, some, at least, of Wilde's stories are fine works of art in their own right; and a more balanced comparison of the two writers is given by Bidstrup, who does not so much discuss the quality of the two writers as compare and contrast their respective messages, finding Wilde on the whole less optimistic than Andersen, who normally manages to see something good in the end, even in a tragedy like **"The Little Mermaid."**[4]

In the following I shall discuss two stories: "The Nightingale and the Rose" in order to show how Wilde's approach differs from Andersen's, and "The Remarkable Rocket" in order to investigate why Andersen's method does not always seem to work for Wilde.

"The Nightingale and the Rose" contains subtle echoes from many Andersen tales, and, in spite of the exquisite lyrical style much of it is written in, is as bitter and cynical as **"The Swineherd."** The prince of that story, we remember, offered a rose and a nightingale to a princess who was not interested. In Wilde's story, too, a student is to offer his professor's daughter a red rose to make her consent to dance with him.

Thanks to the nightingale, who gives his life in order that the rosebush may bloom for the student, he is able to offer a rose to the lady; but in the event the lady refuses the rose in favour of some jewels sent by the Chamberlain's nephew, and it is thrown into the gutter to be run over by cartwheels.

Unlike the situation in Andersen's **"Nightingale,"** the contrast here is not so much between the natural and the artificial as between beauty and money, the latter being what the young lady settles for in the end. But there is another important difference between Andersen and Wilde: unlike the prince of **"The Swineherd"** and many other Andersen heroes, the student of this story is not really a true lover; he lies down and weeps from sorrow (or vexation) when he thinks that he cannot get a rose, but soon falls asleep. He does not appreciate the nightingale's song, "for he only knew the things that are written down in books" (107), and in the end is only too willing to give up love for abstract learning:

> "What a silly thing love is," said the Student as he walked away. "It is not half as useful as Logic, for it does not prove anything, and it is always telling one of things that are not going to happen, and making one believe things that are not true. In fact, it is quite unpractical, and, as in this age to be practical is everything, I shall go back to philosophy and study Metaphysics."
>
> (109)

The idealistic nightingale, then, has died in vain.

Unlike this story, "The Remarkable Rocket" is strangely pointless and not very entertaining. It displays a whole catalogue of Andersen echoes and devices, but they do not really achieve cohesion. The frame is a fairy-tale wedding, with a prince and princess perhaps more from the French tradition than from Andersen, even though there are echoes of **"The Snow Queen."** However, we only learn that the young people are married, and then leave them in order to listen to the rocket, which was to be part of a firework-display in honour of the wedding, but which gets damp and never achieves its great moment, only exploding the next day when nobody is watching.

For all that, it is full of self-conceit, rather like Andersen's **"Darning Needle,"** and talks endlessly of itself to other pyrotechnical objects and to a number of animals.

The problem is that it is all pointless: if they were intended merely as background, the prince and princess are too prominent, and, conversely, the objects and animals are absolutely flat. An Andersen Duck talks Duck, and a needle, Needle language. But the characters of this story lack characteristic voices, and could easily exchange parts. Most surprising of all, the humour does not work,[5] and in many of the other stories there is no humour at all, only the lyrical voice.

Space does not allow consideration of other stories like "The Selfish Giant", which has little of Andersen but rather draws on Catholic legend, with the infant Christ bringing relief from all sorrows. But if one is to generalise about Wilde's stories, they tend to be lyrical and/or cynical, and many of them deal with the contrast between selfishness and altruism, but, surprisingly for any offspring of the divine Oscar, unlike Andersen's stories, they are not very funny!

E. M. FORSTER'S *CELESTIAL OMNIBUS*

In Foster's *The Longest Journey* the budding novelist, Rickie, confides to his beloved but uncomprehending Agnes the misgivings he has developed about his own work:

> They continued the conversation outside. "But I've got to hate my own writing. I believe that most people come to that stage—not so early though. What I write is too silly. It can't happen. For instance, a stupid vulgar man is engaged to a lovely young lady. He wants her to live in the towns, but she only cares for woods. She shocks him this way and that but gradually he tames her, and makes her nearly as dull as he is. One day she has a last explosion—over the snobby wedding-presents—and flies out of the drawing-room window, shouting, 'Freedom and truth!' Near the house is a little dell full of fir-trees, and she runs into it. He comes there the next moment. But she's gone."
>
> "Awfully exciting. Where?"
>
> "Oh Lord, she's a Dryad!" cried Rickie, in great disgust. "She's turned into a tree."
>
> "Rickie, it's very good indeed. That kind of thing has something in it. Of course you get it all through Greek and Latin. How upset the man must be when he sees the girl turn."

> "He doesn't see her. He never guesses. Such a man could never see a Dryad."
>
> "So you describe how she turns just before he comes up?"
>
> "No. Indeed I don't ever say that she does turn. I don't use the word 'Dryad' once."
>
> "I think you ought to put that part plainly. Otherwise, with such an original story, people might miss the point. Have you had any luck with it?"
>
> (76-77)

Then as now the general public were none too bright, and sceptical about spiritual matters. But the story referred to is not just a summary of a plot by a fictitious character—it is obviously a draft of Forster's own short story "Other Kingdom" from the collection *The Celestial Omnibus* (1911).

That story, according to Rickie, is about getting into touch with nature, and its inspiration is classical, like many of Oscar Wilde's. But quite apart from the fact that Andersen himself wrote a story about a Dryad, Forster's stories often resemble Andersen's in effortlessly mixing the supernatural with a satirical description of contemporary bourgeois society.

The stories, reissued by Penguin as *Collected Short Stories,* 1954 (from which I quote), are 12 in number. Those not taken from *The Celestial Omnibus* were first collected in *The Eternal Moment* (1928). From "The Story of a Panic" (originally 1902) to the title story of *The Eternal Moment* they are all in different ways what Forster in his introduction to the Penguin edition calls "fantasies"; but perhaps the one which is closest to the style of the Andersen who wrote **"The Goloshes of Fortune"** and **"The Nisse at the Grocer's"** is the title story of the 1911 collection, "The Celestial Omnibus".

This is a story of a boy who lives with his superficial, uncomprehending parents in an upper middle-class suburb of London. Bored, he explores the farther end of the lane where they live, and discovers a bus stop for a Sunrise and Sunset service direct to Heaven, or perhaps rather Elysium.

He goes, and encounters writers, composers, fictional characters and classical deities, but on his return nobody believes his story. Only clever and cultured Mr. Bons (try that backwards!) is at last persuaded to go with him on his next trip; but though their conductor is Dante himself, Bons is frightened, falls to the ground and is killed, whereas the boy is received into the very gay Elysium, and never returns. Spontaneous enjoyment of music, spectacle, and the people encountered in books has more value than having, as Mr. Bons, seven Shelleys in your library.

As suggested, the story has homo-erotic undertones, and the direct inspiration is Wilde rather than Andersen. But the legacy from the latter is plainly to be seen in the juxtaposition of realistic detail and the supernatural, as in the following description of "the boy" and Mr. Bons being taken heavenwards by Dante:

> [. . .] the omnibus [. . .] was large, roomy, and constructed with extreme regularity, every part exactly answering to every other part. Over the door (the handle of which was outside) was written, 'Lasciate ogni baldanza voi che entrate'—at least, that was what was written, but Mr Bons said that it was Lashy arty something, and that baldanza was a mistake for speranza.[6] His voice sounded as if he was in church. Meanwhile, the boy called to the cadaverous driver for two return tickets. They were handed in without a word. Mr Bons covered his face with his hand and again trembled. 'Do you know who that is!' he whispered, when the little window had shut upon them. 'It is the impossible.'
>
> 'Well, I don't like him as much as Sir Thomas Browne, though I shouldn't be surprised if he had even more in him.'
>
> 'More in him?' He stamped irritably. 'By accident you have made the greatest discovery of the century, and all you can say is that there is more in this man. Do you remember those vellum books in my library, stamped with red lilies? This—sit still, I bring you stupendous news!—*this is the man who wrote them.*'

> (54)

Dante, however, is not impressed. When Bons is afraid of falling to earth, and cries out for help, Dante answers that the arts must be worshipped in freedom and truth; having the classics bound in vellum is not enough.

Conclusion

Each in their own way, the three writers briefly discussed here carry on the tradition from Andersen, which he in his turn developed on the basis of German sources.

Scudder is the closest to Andersen, but his work is consequently derivative, lacking the subtlety and humour of Andersen, and only in a few of the best stories contributing an independent American perspective.

Wilde primarily uses the fairy-tale to criticise the shortcomings of most mortals, condemning their egotism, snobbery and selfishness. So, too, does Forster; but he also uses the form to satirise over the foibles of contemporary middle-class society, exactly as Andersen did himself.

One might add that what Andersen's literary descendants perhaps lack in comparison with the master is his ability suddenly to introduce a spiritual perspective, and to turn the criticism against himself: Having spent almost the entire story of **"Deilig"** (in English, **"Lovely"** or **"Charming"**) poking fun at poor stupid but beautiful Kala, whom the sculptor Alfred has come to regret that he married, Andersen suddenly turns the tables when Alfred's second wife upbraids the sculptor for suggesting that the dead Kala was all body and no spirit:

> "Det var ikke kjærligt sagt," sagde *Sophie,* "det var ikke christeligt! hist oppe, hvor der ikke skal tages tilægte, men, som Du siger, Sjælene mødes ved Sympathie, der, hvor alt Herligt udfolder og løfter sig, vil hendes Sjæl maaskee klinge i saa fuldelig Kraft, at den overklinger min, og Du—Du vil da igjen udbryde i dit første Forelskelses-Udbrud: Deilig, deilig!"

> (III: 168)

Dulcken does not quite manage to do justice to this; but here is his version:

> "That was not lovingly spoken," said Sophy, "not spoken like a true Christian. Yonder, where there is no giving in marriage, but where, as you say, souls attract each other by sympathy, there where everything beautiful develops itself and is elevated, her soul may acquire such completeness that it may sound more harmoniously than mine; and you will then once more utter the first rapturous exclamation of your love. 'Beautiful—most beautiful'".

> (517)

This is the point where criticism must bow its head and be silent; and, as Andersen puts it in **"Grief of Heart,"** those who do not understand it can take shares in the widow's tannery.

Notes

1. On the background of Hans Andersen's tales, see Rubow 1927; Rubow 1955 is a shorter English version of this study of Andersen's tales and the tradition behind them.

2. Just Mathias Thiele (1795-1874), the son of a printer, attended the famous Metropolitan School in Copenhagen, and while he was still a

schoolboy became acquainted with several of the Copenhagen *literati*. He was an admirer of Oehlenschläger and wrote several plays for the Royal Theatre. He was one of the first collectors of authentic folk material in Europe, and published *Danske Folkesagn* (Danish local legends) in four volumes (1818-23). From 1817 he worked at the Royal Library, and did valuable work in the *Kobberstiksamlingen* (the department of prints), whose director he became in 1861. He was one of the first to help the young Andersen, who was influenced by his legends, and by the *Danske Folkeeventyr* published by Matthias Winther in 1823, inspired by and in part based on Thiele's *Folkesagn*.

3. The *Bodley* series anticipates the series of children's books so widespread in the 20th century. It is good American Victoriana, describing a typical middle-class family consisting of father (very much in the centre), mother, and children, and recounting their experiences. A lot of these call for comments from all-knowing papa, but the books are quite charming and reasonably entertaining of their kind.

4. By and large I agree with this. But there is not really much consolation to be found in stories like "The Swineherd" or "Auntie Toothache", and conversely Wilde falls back on religious consolation in a story like "The Selfish Giant".

5. Only occasionally do we get glimpses of the great dramatist to come. The Selfish Giant returns to his house after a prolonged visit to his friend the Cornish Ogre: "After the seven years were over he had said what he had to say, for his conversation was limited . . ." (110).

6. Bons is wrong, of course: he might very well keep his 'speranza', hope, if he would leave his 'baldanza', (exaggerated) self-confidence.

References

Andersen, Hans Christian. 1964-91. *Eventyr og Historier.* 7 vols. Ed. E. Dal and E. Nielsen. Copenhagen: Det Danske Sprog- og Litteraturselskab.

———. (1889) 1993. *The Complete Illustrated Stories of Hans Christian Andersen.* Transl. H. W. Dulcken. (original ed. *Stories for the Household*) London: Chancellor Press.

———. (1974) 1985. *The Complete Fairy Tales and Stories.* Transl. E. C. Haugaard. Harmondsworth: Penguin.

Bidstrup, Iben K. 1999. "H. C. Andersen i Oscar Wilde—en komparativ analyse". In *Oversættelse af Litteratur II. DAO 8.* Ed. V. Appel and V. H. Pedersen Copenhagen: Center for Translation Studies, Copenhagen University, 41-61.

Briggs, Katherine M. 1968. *The Fairies in Tradition and Literature.* London: Routledge and Keagan Paul.

Forster, E. M. (1907) 1978. *The Longest Journey.* Harmondsworth: Penguin Books.

———. 1954. *Collected Short Stories.* (Earlier ed. *Collected Shorter Fiction,* 1947). Harmondsworth: Penguin.

Rubow, Paul V. 1927. *H. C. Andersens Eventyr: Forhistorien, Idé og Form, Sprog og Stil.* Copenhagen: Levin og Munksgaard.

———. 1955. "Idea and Form in Hans Christian Andersen's Fairy Tales". In *A Book on the Danish Writer Hans Christian Andersen, etc.* Copenhagen: Samvirkerådet for dansk kulturarbejde i udlandet, 97-134.

Scudder, Horace. 1862. *Seven Little People and Their Friends.* Boston: Houghton Mifflin.

———. 1864. *Dream Children.* Cambridge, Mass.: Sever and Francis.

Wilde, Oscar. 1979. *The Complete Shorter Fiction of Oscar Wilde.* Ed. by I. Murray. Oxford: Oxford University Press.

Diane Wolkstein (essay date April 2005)

SOURCE: Wolkstein, Diane. "The Finest Quality Dirt: A Look at the Life and Sensibilities of Hans Christian Andersen." *School Library Journal* 51, no. 4 (April 2005): 36-7.

[*In the following essay, Wolkstein examines Andersen's legacy as an innovative adaptor of classic fairy tales, drawing particular attention to his imaginative retelling of "Hans Clodhopper."*]

For nearly 40 years, I've been telling Andersen stories at the statue of Hans Christian Andersen in New York City's Central Park. One story that never fails to delight both the audience and me is **"Hans Clodhopper."** I had read every one of Andersen's 156 stories, but it was not until I heard Kathryn Farnsworth's wonderfully wry, whimsical telling that Clodhopper came alive for me. In celebration and commemoration of the 200th anniversary of Andersen's birth—he was born on April 2, 1805—I would like to explore this particular story, for it reveals much to us about the life of its author, his craft, as well as the storyteller's craft. Here is a brief synopsis; the full text is available with the online version of this article at www.slj.com.

The princess announces that she will marry the man who can speak for himself. Two brothers prepare by memorizing the dictionary and the local newspapers. The father gives each of them a horse. Clodhopper, the third and youngest brother, leaps onto a billy goat and takes the princess three gifts: a dead crow, a broken wooden shoe, and dirt. Dirt? Yes, but the finest quality dirt! Indeed, what could be of more importance to the well-being of a kingdom than the quality of its earth? With his outrageous yet meaningful choice of gifts, (heaven, human, earth—a bird, a shoe, dirt), Hans Clodhopper wins the princess. But winning is not keeping, and each hero must secure his own treasure. The youngest brother must now be bold and defend his treasure before the media (who were as inclined to distort facts in 1858 as they are today).

Born the child of a washerwoman and a cobbler, Andersen was an innovator, an outsider, and a daring upstart. Some even believed he was crazy, for from the time he was a child, he continually refused to accept society's norms. At six years old, when a teacher hit him, he never returned to that school. At 11, when he was working at a cloth mill and the adults shamed him by pulling off his clothes to see if he were a girl or boy, he ran away and never returned to the job. Fortunately, both his mother and father doted on their only child and protected him, refusing to allow others to abuse him.

At 14, the young Andersen had the extraordinary courage and self-confidence to leave his town of Odense to set off by himself for Copenhagen to win his heart's desire—artistic success and the possibility of being able to express himself ("speak for himself"). He first tried his luck by singing until, after a few months, his high soprano voice cracked; next he tried dancing, then acting. He persisted with his intense desire to express himself and wrote poetry, novels, plays, and travelogues until, at the age of 30, he invented a new art form that became a mixture of all the forms he had previously experimented with. Andersen's artistic success was the fairy tales he crafted.

As unexpected an innovator as Clodhopper, Andersen broke the established literary precedent with both his style and his content. Previously, Danish literature

was constructed in a formal language that had little relationship to the colloquial speech of the day. Andersen, whose background was as a performer—a singer, dancer, actor—understood the need to connect directly with his audience and was the first Danish writer to write in the language that people spoke.

In context as well, Andersen was an innovator and a revolutionary. In rewriting the folktales he had heard as a child, he gave the poor, the less fortunate, and the child the role of chief protagonist. He animated and elevated everything in the ordinary world from the beetle to the needle. And he transformed the endings. A most marvelous example of transformation (which all writers will enjoy) occurs when his story **"The Emperor's New Clothes"** was at the printer's and Andersen had a last-minute inspiration. In his original version everyone admires the Emperor's new clothes, and the story ends with the Emperor saying, "I must put on that suit of clothes." In the version that was revised at the printer's, the child murmurs, "But he hasn't anything on!" With these words, the child, like Hans Clodhopper, becomes the unexpected voice of wisdom and authenticity in the kingdom.

"Hans Clodhopper" also offers many profound insights for the craft of the storyteller. Andersen begins his tale by poking fun at memorizing as a means of connecting with oneself, with the world, as well as with achieving one's goals. The two older brothers, who fill their minds with facts and structures, prepare for the future and lose the present. When they enter the palace to speak to the princess and she does not ask them the questions they are prepared to answer, they are speechless. They are so intent on the future that they lose the joy of the moment. Most experienced storytellers learn with time that when they are too worried about the correctness of each word or transition, they lose the opportunity to enjoy and participate in a relationship with their audience, which is the soul of storytelling.

Clodhopper has no script in his mind. He has intention. He wants to win the princess and says, "If she takes me, well and good; if not, I'll take her anyhow!" He is filled with joy as well as consideration. He is the only one to think to bring her gifts. When his father doesn't have a horse for him, he improvises and jumps onto a billy goat. So, too, the storyteller or performer needs to remember that there are alternate transports to taking a journey; maybe the storyteller needs to enter the audience, maybe to stand on a crate. The means are not as important as the willingness to experiment and to communicate. Upon entering the palace, Hans, who has no answers prepared, responds to the circumstances in which he finds himself. It's summer and a stove is lit. It's hot! He does not complain about the heat, as his brothers do; rather he rejoices in the possibilities of cooking his crow.

Just as the story is about to reach a happy folktale conclusion, Andersen surprises us with his protagonist heaving the finest quality dirt at the "Quality" (those who are recording what is happening). Not only are the journalists and politician jolted, but the audience is as well. A bit of Brecht is thrown into the fairy tale, and the princess is not offended. In fact, she's delighted and says, "I would never have thought of that. But I'll learn!" If, indeed, we go to listen to stories to understand more deeply, Andersen is throwing reality in our faces.

At the moment the story reaches its happy conclusion, Andersen surprises us for the third time. He widens the context of his relationship with the story and its listeners. He walks in front of the scrim, breaks down the fourth wall, and reveals that the story we have just shared together is just that . . . a story. As the tale ends, we return to the narrator's voice. In storytelling, it is important to be aware of our voice. *Who* is telling the story? We are not the story; we are telling the story. Andersen, who experimented with all aspects of story—the writer, the director, the actor—engages us with the trickster's device of the story within the story, so that for a moment, the crack in our perceptions opens and we are all caught—storytellers and audience—in the play of imagination. The storyteller, as fool and trickster, allows us to see ourselves as mere perception.

After years of storytelling, it is clear to me that storytellers choose to tell those stories that engage the work of their soul. They continue to tell those stories until that particular work is completed. I love the character of Hans Clodhopper because he does not memorize, because he revels in the joy of life, because he appreciates what is broken, what is dead, what is ordinary. And also because he is bold.

In our times, it seems especially relevant to rescue and care for what is discarded and broken (the broken wooden shoe) and not leave it to decay but to recycle and transform its possibilities. Death awaits each of us every moment and Clodhopper does not avert his eyes before death. He honors the dead crow. He picks it up and offers it a proper, although unex-

pected, funeral by transforming it into nourishment. And as for the finest quality dirt, we are all standing on this dirt. We shall all return to this dirt. We need to acknowledge and appreciate its well being. How silly a gift—the finest quality dirt—and yet how profound; and also, revolutionary.

The fool, the simpleton wins the kingdom, for the one who can perceive and express the truth deserves to be king. Hans not only perceives reality; he is daring enough to express it, and, like a Zen monk, to deliver it directly to those who "claim" they are in search of it.

Part of the appeal of the story of **"Hans Clodhopper"** is that it touches children who relish boundary-breaking fun and silliness. Adults enjoy fun as well, and we also know that the path to such joyful liberation is through much perseverance, mindfulness, and courage. The story, for those who have come in contact with it, reaches out to every age and continues after 200 years to delight and inspire.

Is it true? The child asks.

And Andersen answers, as true as our imagination.

A Selected List of Books

Andersen, Hans Christian. *The Complete Fairy Tales and Stories.* tr. by Eric Christian Haugaard. illus. by Maurice Sendak. (Doubleday, 1983).

Andersen, Hans Christian. *Eight Fairy Tales.* tr. by R. P. Keigwin. illus, by Vilhelm Pedersen & Lorenz Frolich. (Knopf, 1982).

Frank, Jeffrey & Diana Frank. *The Stories of Hans Christian Andersen: A New Translation from the Danish.* illus, by Lorenz Frolich & Vilhelm Pedersen. (Houghton, 2003).

Yolen, Jane. *The Perfect Wizard: Hans Christian Andersen.* illus. by Dennis Nolan. (Penguin, 2005).

Stephen Pettitt (essay date 25 June 2005)

SOURCE: Pettitt, Stephen. "Is He Worth It?" *Spectator* 298, no. 9229 (25 June 2005): 55-6.

[*In the following essay, Pettitt debates Andersen's literary significance—on the occasion of the bicentenary of Andersen's birth—and argues that the general public is only familiar with an "idealised" version of Andersen's life and works.*]

I have a good Danish friend in France, as well read as anyone I know. On the door to her downstairs loo is fixed a spoof road sign. It depicts within a red circle and in instantly recognisable profiled caricature her country's greatest national hero. A red diagonal stroke through it signifies prohibition. In this house we scarcely dare mention Hans Christian Andersen. When I tried to, in connection with this article, a pair of very sage eyebrows soared to the heavens, accompanied by a cry of utter exasperation. And her reaction is shared by many Danes of taste and intellect, she assures me. Never mind that the man wrote 127 fairytales, which have been translated into the most obscure languages and dialects and published in countless editions, with illustrations by the most illustrious, and which are beloved by children and adults everywhere from Argentina to Zimbabwe, from Addis Ababa to Zurich. Setting him on a high pedestal—a pedestal that has been raised still higher this year, thanks to the fact that Andersen was born in 1805—just for that very minor achievement, my friend would contend, is absurd.

She is right, of course. In the grand scheme of matters literary, writing fairytales, however beautifully executed, cannot possibly be compared with the momentous work of creating a *Hamlet* or a *Faust*. Despite that, an essay by an academic expert called Jens Andersen—no relation, surely?—printed in the lavishly produced official programme confidently places Andersen side by side with Shakespeare and Goethe. Surely, if they were faced with the searching questioning of an Artistic Truth Commission, even Andersen's most devout apologists would find it hard to sustain such an extravagant claim faced with the hard evidence. Yes, the fairytales are very well told. Andersen's language, I'm assured by all Danish speakers, is vivid, economical, straightforward, unpretentious. The stories aren't just idyllic fantasies with princesses kissing frogs and living happily ever after, but deal unflinchingly with the darker sides of life, with poverty, ridicule, ugliness, rejection, salvation through death. Tales like **The Little Mermaid, The Snow Queen, The Ugly Duckling, The Red Shoes** and **The Emperor's New Clothes** rather touchingly reflect Andersen's own life story, his experience as an unattractive, lonely, unsettled man constantly conscious of his own background of dire poverty, constantly striving for acceptance, not least through his compulsive social climbing. Yet many of these fairytales are not Andersen's own stories, but retellings of well-known folk tales.

Moreover, they are the only works for which Andersen is now widely known. His six novels and 50 plays, modestly successful in his own time, and his collections of poems languish in one degree or another of obscurity. Most of those Danes who've read them think that they're second-rate, or worse, though one does come across the odd dissenter who thinks that they're unfairly neglected. The verdict is generally that Andersen adopts a high literary tone which doesn't suit him at all. There's an element of misguided pretentiousness in his language, a self-conscious, consistent attempt to write in an elevated manner. It's significant that it is only when he writes for children or for his own diaries that he becomes himself, that his writing gains a natural charm.

Yet, if he does not figure among the very greatest writers of all time, he's a fascinating subject for a biographer. Was his ambition absurd, and was he really just a somewhat precious mummy's boy less gifted than he himself thought? Was that bearing, that ostentatious wearing of his trademark stovepipe, a mark of arrogance or a defiant gesture in the face of a deep-rooted inferiority complex? Was he a thick-skinned man, as his infamous outstaying of his welcome at Charles Dickens's house in 1857 would suggest, or acutely sensitive? Was he a repressed or a practising homosexual? (Certainly, there was never a deep, real relationship with a woman, and fuel is only added to the gay theory by his opera queen-like adoration of the singer Jenny Lind, the 'Swedish Nightingale'.) Why was he so rootless, constantly travelling throughout Europe and beyond from the time, in the early 1830s, when he first became successful, and never owning his own property despite being well able to afford it?

Using the bicentenary to reconsider these matters, and to weigh up again the literary significance of the man, is all well and good, and the publication of a new 18-volume complete critical edition of Andersen's works is certainly not an event to be sniffed at. But the bicentenary celebrations seem to be erring heavily on the side of commercialisation. Who have the powers that be commissioned to write a full-length opera about Andersen? None other than Elvis Costello, the last person on earth I'd ask to write an opera about anything. The annual summer Green Concert, a touring rock event, this year will be saturated with hip, Andersen-related numbers, and there's to be a rock album called *Andersen's Dreams*. The year's celebrations opened with celebrity-infested open-air galas in Odense (Andersen's birthplace) and Copenhagen on 2 April, the latter starring, at notorious, budget-ruining expense, Tina Turner.

Further down the economic tree, it seems that every cultural organisation in Denmark has been more or less obliged this year to adopt an Andersen theme. In the case of classical music, that's a hard challenge to meet, since the number of existing good works inspired by Andersen is curiously small. The Danish National Symphony Orchestra has adopted a two-pronged solution. It has commissioned new works, by Bent Sorensen, Per Norgard, Poul Ruders, Bo Holten, Bright Sheng and Bobby McFerrin. And it has included pieces by composers Andersen sort of knew—Wagner, Liszt, Mendelssohn, Schumann, Grieg. The Odense Symphony Orchestra has responded even more inventively by touring some of the places Andersen visited and thereby offering itself more or less carte blanche.

Vast numbers of the great, good and mostly irrelevant in the international community have been appointed Hans Christian Andersen ambassadors for the 2005 celebrations. Britain mystifyingly boasts the quartet of David Frost, Roger Moore, Elizabeth Hurley and Derek Jacobi, as well as Sandi Toksvig (of course) and the writers Antonia S. Byatt, Michael Morpurgo and award-winning Andersen biographer Jackie Wullschlager. They are charged with helping 'to create awareness of the bicentennial events'. Thus Frost, Moore et al. will no doubt devote chunks of their time alerting Britons to Bent Sorensen's new BBC Proms commission, *The Little Mermaid,* which will be played by the Danish National Symphony Orchestra on 12 August under its conductor Thomas Dausgaard (and which forms part of the Proms's 'Fairy Tales' thematic strand this year). The libretto is by Peter Asmussen and the work interweaves passages from the diaries with the story. Sorensen is a fine composer, so this could turn out to be a worthwhile, questioning commemoration.

Otherwise, Britain escapes the bicentenary pretty lightly. The British Library last month opened an exhibition about Andersen in Victorian Britain, and the City of Birmingham Symphony Orchestra has already been involved in the international *Symphonic Fairy Tales* project, which consists of ten new Danish Andersen-related orchestral works (those poor Danish composers) given on four continents, playing Per Norgard's *The Will-o'-the-Wisps Go to Town* twice in early April. Arc Dance is repeating its 2004 Linbury Theatre staging of Kim Brandstrup's *The Anatomy of a Storyteller* in Denmark and elsewhere, and the group The Tiger Lillies will be showing its take on ***The Little Match Girl*** at the Copenhagen Theatre Festival in August.

In Odense there's a permanent museum devoted to Andersen's life and work, attached to the little house where he was born. Here you can see seemingly every last little piece of Andersen-related ephemera—that stovepipe hat, for instance, or the length of rope he insisted on carrying around with him as a kind of portable fire escape. There's also a room devoted to his artwork, including those papercuts he used to make as he told his stories. Magical, we're told. They strike me as remarkably unremarkable. But making the unremarkable remarkable is what these celebrations are about. For, just as is the case with trainers or beefburgers, it's an idealised image of Andersen, not the reality, that sells him to the world.

Brian Alderson (essay date November-December 2005)

SOURCE: Alderson, Brian. "H. C. Andersen: Edging toward the Unmapped Hinterland." *Horn Book Magazine* 81, no. 6 (November-December 2005): 671-77.

[*In the following essay, Alderson comments on the commercialization of Andersen's literary legacy—on the occasion of the bicentenary of Andersen's birth—and notes the "dubious reliability" of several translated and edited editions of Andersen's fairy tales.*]

If we allow them to, the stories of Hans Christian Andersen can pose some trenchant questions to students of narrative and its illustration. But "*which* stories?" you may ask, and I am tempted to answer "the whole damn lot"—except that few readers seem to be aware of the size and contents of that particular rattle-bag.

Self-obsessed as ever, but perhaps also trying to be helpful, Andersen was from the start given to writing notes on the origins of his *eventyr og historier,* his "wonder tales and stories." An initial brief reflection appeared in 1837 as a preface to the two stories published then only a couple of years after his first volume of *eventyr,* and the volumes of stories that appeared in 1862 and 1874 (a year before his death) contain a serial commentary on the complete collection. This confirms what is now universally accepted as the Andersen canon, and the author numbers there its constituent *eventyr og historier* at 156: "what remains of my wealth."

That quantity and that division into "wonder tales and stories" are essential factors in any attempt to assay the wealth. Andersen's collected works include novels, plays, libretti, travel books, and hundreds of poems. The 1835 arrival of the tales that would fulfill his craving for fame (and make him rich) seems inauspicious—a tiny, unillustrated book called *Eventyr, fortalte for Børn,* or *Wonder Tales Told for Children*—and indeed, at that date, the concept of anyone, anywhere, being preoccupied exclusively with a child audience would probably have seemed incomprehensible.

So it comes about that the great Andersen bicentenary brouhaha of 2005 is launched from a very flimsy bit of staging. For only about a quarter of those 156 *eventyr og historier* have currency as a "legacy to the world," while little is known about the remainder. Furthermore, that quarter, the thirty or forty tales of undisputed genius, themselves live a vulnerable existence. Publishers, promotionists, and the generality of readers are content to refer to them as "fairy tales" and to see them as belonging in the same category as the traditional tales collected or edited by such persons as Charles Perrault, or the Brothers Grimm, or Joel Chandler Harris. (Only this morning I opened the June 2005 issue of *Children's Literature in Education* to find an article on the "gender bias of the traditional fairy tales" negligently naming among the culprits "Grimm, Perrault, Lang, Andersen and Disney"!) While it is true that Andersen does acknowledge a few folktales as a source for some of his stories—**"The Tinderbox,"** say, or **"The Wild Swans"**—what arrives on his pages is not a retelling but a wholly independent creative act arising from his engagement with the original. And those few stories take their place in the canon alongside a huge preponderance of tales that have nothing of "fairy tale" about them at all. The particular-to-Andersen "wonder" in such superlative fantasies as **"The Snow Queen"** and **"The Nightingale"**; the imaginative farce and satire in **"The Collar"** or **"The Darning Needle"** or **"The Money Pig"**; the wholly Andersenian bittersweet quality of **"The Shepherdess and the Chimney Sweep"** or **"The Steadfast Tin Soldier"**—these stories come from nowhere but the author's imagination.

As if this experimentation with the potential of the short story were not enough, however, Andersen also chooses to play games with the telling. He can of course hardly be blamed for casting the stories in a language that was native to only a tiny proportion of his ultimate audience, but he exacerbates the problem by using that language not as a politely educated literary gentleman but as a companionable storyteller, catching you by the sleeve on a park bench, or ruminating over a pint in the local bar. "You should have known my old auntie . . ." begins one anecdote, or "Here's a tale I was told when I was a little lad, and

every time I've thought of it since it's seemed better and better . . ."

This insistence on the colloquial voice, which runs through tale after tale from start to finish, was reprobated by some of Andersen's countrymen at the time when he was writing and publishing the stories, and it made for particular difficulties as the news of his genius spread—to begin with via translations into German. (Seven of the first nine translations into English were made from unreliable German versions, and these formed the staple for the earliest editions published in America.) Although Edgar Taylor and his associate, David Jardine, had recognized the presence of oral tradition in their first Englishing of the *Märchen* of the Brothers Grimm in 1823, and although, at about the time when Andersen was publishing his first tales in Denmark, Charles Dickens was beginning to show the English the spirited possibilities of colloquial speech, readers and writers were not accustomed to meeting such an uninhibited storytelling vernacular and knew not how to transfer Andersen's mannerisms into another language. Observe a moderately accurate recent attempt (mine) at translating the opening of **"The Snow Queen"**—

> *Come on now—look! We're going to begin. And when we get to the end of this story we shall know more than we do now, because here's a wicked troll—really—one of the nastiest, and that's the Devil himself . . .*

—and compare it with the first-ever version (from German) by Charles Boner, as found in an early U.S. printing—

> *Now then, let us begin. When we are at the end of the story we shall know more than we know now: but to begin.*
>
> *Once upon a time there was a wicked sprite, indeed he was the most mischievous of all sprites . . .*

Quite apart from avoiding Andersen's abrupt jump into the substance of the story (and eliminating the Devil), Boner cannot help modulating the initial call to attention down to a polite request.

The reluctance of many of Andersen's translators to labor after a convincing representation in their own language of his often jokey and throwaway diction has affected for the worse countless editions of his most famous stories. (You still find Caroline Peachey's hopeless versions from 1846—the second English translation ever to appear—turning up in selections and as picture book texts.) Indeed, as one biographer remarked, he "has been so mutilated by most of his English translators it seems surprising that he should have survived at all." This bicentenary year has, however, brought forth several new, or freshly revived, translations that readily acknowledge the difficulties of the job and attain a sufficient informality.

For all this respectful behavior, though, the new translators show little interest in exploring the unmapped hinterland beyond the much-trodden pathways among the old favorites. Readers of the *Horn Book* will surely know every one of the thirteen *Tales* (Candlewick) in Naomi Lewis's selection for children, elaborately illustrated by Joel Stewart. They will know at least sixteen of the twenty-two in the *Stories* (Houghton) translated for "modern readers" by D. C. and J. Frank; and at least twenty-two out of the thirty in the *Fairy Tales* (Viking) translated by Tiina Nunnally. Only Neil Philip—an authority on our hero—in what is unquestionably the best of the new volumes, despite its vulgar get-up and illustrations, the *Fairy Tales* (Reader's Digest), offers you a more generous glimpse of lesser-known stories: seventeen in a total of forty.

Thus, thanks no doubt to the prudent conservatism of both publishers and the readers they serve, our bicentenary translators have balked not only at tackling a hundred or so of the *eventyr og historier* but also at admitting their existence. Certainly Jackie Wullschlager in her introduction to the Nunnally selection draws attention to "the pioneering new style, a high-voltage short story for adults" that characterized the later tales, but she mentions only two or three of these, while the Franks confine themselves to the damning faint praise that Andersen "wrote many more stories, most of which had moments of brilliance" but that "some were quite bad—filled with gooey sentimentality—and some were fascinating curiosities."

Such slapdash summaries really will not do. These dismissive remarks by today's Andersen celebrants consign to oblivion over a hundred stories. Can that cargo of work really be cast overboard with barely a comment—especially if there's some "high-voltage" stuff in there—and could not the new presenters of old goods at least offer readers some more literate guidance as to where access to the missing treasures might be found? It is disturbing that Nunnally confesses to never having met **"The Ice Maiden"** before she began her translating; what else hasn't she read?

In justice to the editors and translators, it must be said that complete English translations of the stories are few and far between and of dubious reliability. Even the most recent collection, ***The Complete Fairy Tales and Stories*** (Doubleday), translated by Erik Haugaard, takes many liberties with the source texts. Nevertheless, complete texts in Danish are readily accessible, and it so happens that now—in England anyway—a majestic, but overweight, reprint has arrived of ***The Complete Stories*** as translated by Jean Hersholt for the Limited Editions Club in New York in 1949—an edition that ran to six volumes, illustrated with stencil-colored drawings by Fritz Kredel.

Mr. Hersholt was more than generous in his interpretation of "complete," since he offered 155 of the 156 stories of the canon together with thirteen additional pieces. Furthermore, being both Danish and an actor with a feeling for the spoken word, he was well qualified to deal with the verbal peculiarities of his originals, even though he does seem to have had at his elbow a rather awful English translation by H. W. Dulcken from the nineteenth century.

Peculiarities certainly abound, for there's no denying that the later tales are a queer bunch—although that in itself demands that they deserve a much closer analysis than they usually get. "Gooey sentimentality" is indeed to be found in such pieces on death and retribution as **"A Story"** and **"On the Last Day,"** which have all the makings of religious tracts. But the preponderance of stories reveal a writer who has moved away from or, perhaps more tellingly, turned upside-down the fantastic or comic stories for children to probe the murkier depths of the human condition, whether in individuals, including himself, or in society. That may sound an inflated or pretentious ambition, but it gives rise to an extraordinary variety of narratives as he ventures toward the doleful, if not tragic, heart of his vision, and it is tempered always by the powers of his diction, which can give savor to many of the triter passages ("humor is the salt of the tales," he said in a late entry in his diary).

Perhaps the best way of indicating the oddity of these often-experimental exercises is briefly to describe two contrasting stories that show something of his varied inspiration. The first is **"Pebersvendens Nathue"** of 1858 (whose title Haugaard nicely translates as **"The Pepperman's Nightcap"**). This is something of an adult parallel to **"The Little Match Girl"** and seems to have been prompted by Andersen's knowledge of a street of small houses in Copenhagen where, at one time, dwelt the indigent agents of German spice-dealers. The lowly existence and death there of Anton the pepperman frames an account of his long-past disappointed love, while his nostalgic tears, falling into his nightcap—"pearls of his memories"—infect it with a melancholy for all who might subsequently wear it.

A weird conceit, no doubt partly explicable by Andersen's own woebegone experiences as a failed lover, but outdone in weirdness by the violently satirical take on **"The Ugly Duckling,"** the 1861 story **"I Andegaarden"** (**"In the Duck Yard"**)—which, had it been written today, would be seen as a parable about the fate of immigrants and asylum-seekers. A little songbird with a broken wing is chased by a cat into the duck yard. There he is adopted by a Portuguese duck (subject of much mirth throughout the tale). Pride, greed, hypocrisy, and stupidity are evinced among the fowls who inhabit the place—a very human society—and the Portuguese duck, in a tantrum, bites off the songbird's head. "Ooh!" she says, "what's up with him then? Couldn't he even take that? Well—he wasn't for this world. Why! me, with all my loving-kindness, I've been like a mother to him." And the life of the yard goes on.

Andersen's involuntary designation as a writer-for-children may well have hindered a dispassionate assessment of his later stories, with their burden of pessimism. And since they appeared in the latter half of his storytelling career, they are bunched together without the leavening of the lighter wonder tales of earlier days. When they were first published in Denmark, however, they arrived more manageably in small volumes usually containing about six tales at a time and always accompanied by the line drawings of Lorenz Frølich. As "house-illustrator" to the author, he is a vital presence in the final seventy-eight stories of Andersen's oeuvre, just as Vilhelm Pedersen, who died in 1859, had been in the first seventy-eight. Frølich's contribution to the comic, the satiric, the touching events of the late works is marvelously responsive and would in itself offer a stimulus to readers on the brink of exploring the outermost seas of Andersen's imagination.

That said, it should nonetheless be remarked that Andersen himself does not seem to have been too much preoccupied by illustration. When the first booklets of tales were published, they carried no pictures; Pedersen's work was brought into being through the urging of his German publisher in 1849. Germany had already pioneered illustrative elaboration through the drawings and lithographs of Count Pocci and Otto Speckter (which were later re-worked in English and American editions), and once Ander-

sen was well and truly launched in Great Britain, his best-known stories became fair game for artists to have a go at in every conceivable graphic form. (Among the most—inappropriately—lavish was the folio album illustrated by Eleanor Vere Boyle, dated 1872. After seeing a proof-sheet, Andersen remarked in a letter to a friend that a royalty would be even more interesting, and later commented in another letter that he could ascribe no artistic importance to the sumptuous display of color and gilding.)

In all the plethora of visualizations, though, the salient quality of those first unillustrated booklets was—like the songbird in the duck yard—ignored. Andersen's own indifference to illustrative accompaniments (except insofar as they might enhance the cash return) stemmed from his conviction that, as storyteller, he was also picture-maker and that his job was so to inspire his listeners/readers that they might discover their own big-eyed dogs, their own unclothed emperors, and (this cannot be said forcefully enough) their own Snow Queens. (While there is nothing sacrosanct about such unconvincing ladies as Little Ida or Thumbelina, the Snow Queen is a force of nature, a manifestation of Robert Graves's White Goddess, and dressing her up like a furrier's advertisement should lay the culprits open to demolition by "the next bright bolt.") The penchant that illustrators have for booking themselves ego-trips on the back of any passing classic tale is of long standing, and a proper judgment of their work hinges not on the aesthetics of the thing but on the adequacy of their response to the text that prompted it. From the days of Eleanor Vere Boyle onward, Andersen has been vulnerable to overkill by gift-book merchants and picture book publishers, and the examples set by Pedersen and Frølich still stand as a salutary corrective. The wonder in the wonder tales is in the telling.

Elena Abós (essay date November-December 2005)

SOURCE: Abós, Elena. "The Ugly Duckling Goes to the Castle: Hans Christian Andersen at the International Youth Library." *Horn Book Magazine* 81, no. 6 (November-December 2005): 681-88.

[*In the following essay, Abós examines the various celebrations surrounding the bicentenary of Andersen's birth, the history of the International Board on Books for Young People's Hans Christian Andersen Medal, and how Andersen's fairy tales have become indelibly "part of the world's cultural heritage."*]

Once upon a time, two hundred years ago in fact, Hans Christian Andersen was born in Odense, Denmark. Son of a shoemaker and a washerwoman, the poor ugly ducking managed to climb an exceedingly steep social ladder to become the most famous Danish writer of all time. He was a prolific writer, gifted storyteller, singer, actor, traveler, poet. But it was his fairy tales that earned him literary immortality. Tales such as **"The Ugly Duckling,"** **"The Snow Queen," "The Princess and the Pea,"** and many others have become part of the world's cultural heritage.

It is on his birthday, April 2nd, that we celebrate International Children's Books Day. The highest international prize for children's literature, awarded every other year by IBBY (International Board on Books for Young People), bears his name: The Hans Christian Andersen Medal. Just to have an idea of how Andersen fares as a global author in 2005, at least in quantifiable terms, I checked the Index Translationum, the UNESCO project that documents translated books published all over the world. Andersen is listed as number ten of its Top 50 Authors (after Disney, Agatha Christie, the Bible, Jules Verne, Lenin, Enid Blyton, Barbara Cartland, Shakespeare, and Danielle Steel. The brothers Grimm are twelfth and thirteenth).

Andersen's 200th birthday is being celebrated not only in his home country but all over the world. Through the year there will have been festivals, congresses, plays, and exhibitions (go to www.hca2005.com or www.andersen.sdu.dk for more information). He was remembered at the International Children's Book Fair in Bologna with exhibitions and an illustrators' meeting. And of course, there are books: many newly illustrated editions of his popular fairy tales are being published all over the world. In the U.S. and Canada, a new book on Andersen by Jack Zipes (*Hans Christian Andersen: The Misunderstood Storyteller* [Routledge]) and several illustrated biographies for young people (*The Perfect Wizard: Hans Christian Andersen* [Dutton] by Jane Yolen, illustrated by Dennis Nolan; *The Young Hans Christian Andersen* [Scholastic] by Karen Hesse, illustrated by Erik Blegvad; and *Hans Christian Andersen: His Fairy Tale Life* [Groundwood] by Hjørdis Varmer, illustrated by Lilian Brøgger), to name a few, mark the anniversary.

As part of Andersen's year, last June the International Youth Library in Munich devoted its second Illustrators' Forum to his work. Seven renowned illustrators came together to talk about their versions of his fairy tales: Dušan Kállay and Kamila Štanclová from Slovakia, Lisbeth Zwerger from Austria, Rotraut Sus-anne Berner and Nikolaus Heidelbach from Germany, and Joel Stewart and John A. Rowe from Great Britain.

The forum's location itself has earned a place of honor in the world of children's books. The International Youth Library was founded in 1949 by Jella Lepman, born out of the idea that children's books could become a bridge between people, that books could help to promote understanding and encourage new hope and values after the horrors of World War II. Blutenburg Castle, home of the IYL since 1983, is a fifteenth-century castle surrounded by a moat, with a charming inner yard and its own chapel. Its cellars house a collection of some five hundred thousand children's books in more than 130 languages (and to learn more about the International Youth Library, visit www.ijb.de).

As I approached the castle to attend the Andersen forum, I saw hanging on the sign of the IYL a brocade coat that looked as if the Emperor had just taken it off in order to try on the amazing new clothes the two swindlers had presented to him. The seminar took place in a wonderful exhibition hall with wooden rafters that could have been the Emperor's throne hall. I wish I could work a little Andersen magic to convey something of the marvelous pictures that were shown and discussed at the seminar.

Peter Nickl, from the IYL foundation, introduced the seminar, addressing the blurry line between reality and fantasy in Andersen's fairy tales and how Andersen shows the tension between them in very simple and understandable language, fancy free. Then Barbara Scharioth, director of the IYL, spoke, underlining Andersen's gift as a storyteller. Indeed, one finds many clues to the oral quality of his stories: he addresses the audience directly, uses onomatopoeia, and writes in a conversational tone. Considering childhood the most important stage in life, Andersen said that he had written his tales "as a child would have told them." Eschewing lessons or morals, he broke the rules of his time about how one was supposed to talk to children and about children. In doing so, he created a new form of telling and a new form of tale that subverted the expectations of traditional fairy tales. In his own time, it won him many critics but ultimately proved to be his passport to immortality.

Just as Andersen found new ways of storytelling, the illustrators who spoke and showed slides at the Illustrators' Forum are finding new ways to portray his tales. Dušan Kállay (winner of the Andersen Medal in 1988) and his wife Kamila Štanclová have joined forces for the first time to illustrate all 156 of Andersen's fairy tales. Kállay, professor at the Academy of Fine Arts and Design in Bratislava, is a versatile artist: book illustrator, engraver, painter, and designer. He has illustrated books, posters, stamps, and postcards, has exhibited his paintings worldwide, and received many prizes and honors. Kamila Štanclová is also a fine illustrator with many books and prizes of her own. This is the first time that the whole of Andersen's oeuvre has been translated and illustrated in Slovakia. The first of three volumes of *Märchen* (cbi, an imprint of Random House, is the publisher of the German edition; Brio, the Slovakian) is just out, and it is an impressive work of art. Some of the original pictures hang in the IYL in an Andersen exhibit, and, viewing them together, one can appreciate the sensibility and depth of the two artists' vision.

The large-format volume boasts lush paper, large print, and generous margins and is profusely illustrated with vignettes, whole page illustrations, and double-page spreads in pencil and watercolors. The rich palette, with lots of reds and blues, gives the paintings a unique lighting that I think suits Andersen especially well: it manages to depict reality with a fantastic twist, or fantasy with a realistic touch. The pictures do not try to re-create Andersen's Denmark or ancient China (as in **"The Nightingale"**), but they have their own brand of magical realism. If Andersen looked at the world with a painter's eyes, as Vincent van Gogh suggested in 1888 to his friend Rappard (and as publisher Hans-Joachim Gelberg cited in this seminar), he would have been pleased with the Slovakian artists' portrait of his world in their *Märchen.*

Štanclová and Kállay have been immersed in Andersen for three years. They divided the workload by each choosing what felt more natural to illustrate according to their tastes and styles, but it is not easy to distinguish the hands since the paintings are not signed. They recounted that Andersen (who in real life could be an exasperating guest) shared their home in Bratislava without outrageous demands, enriching their work. They were often surprised by him, by his life, by the many fairy tales they did not know, and by the quality, range, and voice of those stories.

From their talk, it struck me how humbly they came to the text. They met Andersen as if for the first time, without prejudices. They did not seem to have the need to justify their choices, to talk about overcoming dislikes or suspicions. They approached Andersen

the way Andersen approached children: taking them seriously, without talking down to them, with a brand-new language. Maybe that's why the artists have been so successful. They have managed to create a compelling, stunning Andersen that may well become a new classic and a reference for illustrators to come.

Lisbeth Zwerger is an Andersen Medal winner who needs no introduction. She first illustrated Andersen in 1980, with **Thumbelina,** and has since illustrated **The Nightingale** (both North-South), a collection of stories, and now a new edition of **The Little Mermaid** (Minedition). It would seem that Andersen fits perfectly with the melancholic mood, dreamy landscapes, and elegant line of Zwerger's watercolors, but she admitted that this assignment did not bring her much joy. Through a slide show of some of her illustrations for different tales, she expressed her dislike of Andersen, if not as literature then as illustration material. She thinks his themes are too big for picture books. In fact she finds her latest, **The Little Mermaid,** unbearably sad and tragic. It was commissioned by a Japanese publisher for a series of individual picture books of Andersen tales. In her opinion, most of the stories lack enough illustratable moments to carry a picture book by themselves. She quoted Robert Ingpen, who illustrated **The Ugly Duckling** for the same project, as saying that only somebody who has suffered would be able to illustrate Andersen. But despite Zwerger's feelings on the matter, she does a beautiful job with the tales, and her books belong to the most widely known and loved of all Andersen editions.

Rotraut Susanne Berner of Germany is a famed illustrator in Europe but not very well known in the United States. She has illustrated, among many other books, *The Number Devil* by Hans Magnus Enzensberger. Her style is bold and quirky; she always manages to surprise. She shows a preference for strong lines and colors and infuses her drawings with humor and irony. She has illustrated a collection of Andersen stories for Insel, a German publishing house. This slim, small-format volume is not aimed specifically at children, but she explains that she has them always in her mind as her audience, with the caveat that one cannot know who "the children" are; they are a group as heterogeneous as "the adults."

She finds that Andersen tales offer a mixture between innocence and sophistication in their structure, with different reading levels, and she plays with those levels in her illustrations. She describes her way of working as very tactile: she approaches the text to feel if it is "soft" or "hard," and it gives her the clues about how to illustrate it best. If, for example, the text poses questions and turns things around, she does the same with the illustrations.

British illustrator John A. Rowe, author of *Peter Piglet, Baby Crow,* and *Monkey Trouble,* among many other books, has illustrated a new edition of ***The Emperor's New Clothes*** (Minedition). Rowe brings his personal touch to this baroque emperor, a jolly fashion victim with a red clown nose. On bright white backgrounds, the courtiers and subjects are painted with eccentric detail and expressive animal faces. He found the story a little strange, too serious, and wanted to make it funnier. He sees the Emperor as quite human and even innocent, and that's why he wanted an ending without morals and with hope that could offer a change for the future. So he decided to have the portly monarch laughing with the rest of them. Rowe's is a very personal, lively take on one of Andersen's best known tales.

Nikolaus Heidelbach is an award-winning German illustrator whose books have not yet been translated into English (with the exception of his alphabet book *Where the Girls Are*). Among his most celebrated works are a collection of Grimm tales, a retelling of *Pinocchio* by Christine Nöstlinger, and several original picture books. For Andersen's *Märchen* (published by Beltz in Germany) he has painted 120 pictures for a collection of forty-three tales, freshly translated by Albrecht Leonhardt. With a mixed technique of watercolor and gouache, Heidelbach uses the thinnest of lines to create a naturalistic effect that infuses realism into his sometimes grotesque characters. His complex compositions show a precise attention to the tiniest details.

Heidelbach mentioned two hurdles that he faced, as does surely every artist attempting the task of illustrating a beloved tale. The first challenge is the images that readers already have in their minds. As a little girl once told the artist during a radio show about his Andersen, "Yes, your book is very nice. But it is wrong." She had read a different version, and of course the one she knew was the real one, the right one. The second challenge is how to reillustrate the most famous tales so that they can excite the reader as well as the artist. To overcome the sense of repetition or boredom, Heidelbach tries to surprise himself, choosing his colors as he goes or including visual jokes. For example, when the little mermaid looks toward the city at night, the jutting rocks have the nosy profile of Andersen.

Joel Stewart, illustrator of Viviane Schwarz's *The Adventures of a Nose,* Carroll's *Jabberwocky,* and his own *Me and My Mammoth,* among others, is the youngest of the group and brings his unconventional style to ***Tales of Hans Christian Andersen*** (Candlewick). This brilliantly designed volume offers new translations from Andersen specialist Naomi Lewis, including an introduction, notes on each story, and a brief Andersen biography. This book seems to me especially well suited to children and young adults. The translation reads beautifully, and the biography and introduction are accessible and interesting.

Each of the thirteen stories is preceded by a short introduction. On the opposite page Stewart introduces the tale as well, with a theater stage—props, curtain, lighting, and all—on which some character from the story appears. As an example, in the illustration for **"The Princess and the Pea,"** the king carries a ladder haughtily across the stage. As Stewart mentioned in his talk, the idea of the theater, which occurred to him before he knew how important theater was to Andersen, permitted him to put himself at a remove. The theater structure reveals the artifice of storytelling and gives the pictures a distance that the text does not have, adding extra perspective.

After the introductions, one enters the story itself and lets the pictures converse with or even contradict the text. The main illustrations whisper with muted tones and soft lines; in some instances they are tinged with somber undertones that might remind the viewer of Edward Gorey. Stewart's human figures are highly stylized, drawn with an easy, flowing line. He approaches the border between fantasy and reality with a mix of humor and matter-of-factness. For example, the beetle that carries Thumbelina away looks as if it belongs in an entomology book (in fact, that is where Stewart got every detail of his beetle, red legs and all), and so the little girl struggling to hold on to her hat also has to be real.

The most personal parts of the book, according to the illustrator, are the small characters in frequent vignettes that accompany the story and "comment" on it. The little figurines are whimsical and clever, both modern and quaint. They provide yet another perspective on the tale, often in a wholly different mood. In **"The Princess and the Pea"** one of the little figures throws a pea at the other ("look out for those rogue peas")—hardly royal behavior.

Stewart was refreshing in his openness. He talked about his work in a very self-critical, candid way, was ready to give away secrets of his art, and (gasp!)

even admitted that he uses computers as a fundamental tool in his drawing. He also admitted that before starting this project he was not familiar with Andersen and was a little reluctant to take it on because of the sentimentality he associated with the tales. But he changed his mind when he read the stories. The blending of humor and melancholy appealed to him.

After listening to these illustrators and looking at their dramatically different takes on Andersen's fairy tales, I came away with many different Andersens. The Andersen that I remembered from childhood, pure saccharine and melodrama, was a product of the puerile versions of the time, very far in spirit, picture, and word from the real thing. Most of these illustrators seem to have gone through very similar experiences. They received an offer to illustrate Andersen and had some misgivings about it. But then they found things that surprised them, even in stories that they thought they knew. They had to get rid of the image of Andersen à la Danny Kaye: sentimental and naive. The real voice of Andersen comes across in the new translations: sometimes mocking, sometimes ironic, and, yes, a bit melodramatic.

In the case of illustrated tales, the pictures are so dominant that they have the power to alter the mood of the story, and in fact what mainly remains, the aftertaste, are not the words of Andersen or his translators but the interpretation of the illustrators. With editions like these, each unique and praiseworthy, Andersen will certainly celebrate many more birthdays on the international Top 10 Authors list.

TITLE COMMENTARY

"THE EMPEROR'S NEW CLOTHES" (1837)

Hollis Robbins (essay date autumn 2004)

SOURCE: Robbins, Hollis. "The Emperor's New Critique." *New Literary History* 34, no. 4 (autumn 2004): 659-75.

[*In the following essay, Robbins addresses the frequently overlooked characters and themes in Andersen's "The Emperor's New Clothes" in order to study the story's "sociopolitical-literary-critical complexities."*]

"Custom," continues the Professor, "doth make dotards of us all."

—Carlyle, *Sartor Resartus*

Hans Christian Andersen's **"The Emperor's New Clothes"** (1837)[1] is a tale so transparent that there has been little need for critical scrutiny. Most grown-ups vaguely recall that it is the story of a king who is tricked into donning imaginary clothes (encouraged by courtiers who praise his suit) and showing them off publicly until a child cries out "but he has nothing on!" Scholars well-acquainted with the tale confirm its transparency, asserting that it is a simple story of a seeing through the trappings of power to reveal "the truth" of the Emperor's vanity and the courtiers' pusillanimity. Jacques Derrida proposes that the tale's transparency is its truth; or rather that the truth of Andersen's tale is that it flagrantly stages truth as a scene of public unveiling.[2] That is, the story not only describes a scene of reading (the little boy who "reads" the absence of the Emperor's clothes) but also assigns the position of the reader in search of (and finding) truth and closes with the reader publicly pronouncing truth to general acclaim. With its notion of "truth" as a thing that can be unveiled, Andersen's tale, for Derrida, is a fantasy for analysts. With its final image of the heroic romantic child-critic, the tale seems to suggest that anyone with a little pluck and independence can see and say "the truth."

But Andersen's tale is also a critique of criticism, Derrida's criticism suggests. As tale, teller, interpreter, and critical case study all in one, it knows what it is about in offering such a transparent fantasy. Yet if it is true that the tale's very transparency is a critique of the desire to critique—or rather, the exhibitionistic desire to unveil publicly—Derrida's privileging of the themes of analysis, truth, and unveiling in his (albeit brief) reading of **"The Emperor's New Clothes"** provides evidence that the awareness of this desire does not reduce its influence. The desire to read **"The Emperor's New Clothes"** as either a fantasy of critique or a critique of the fantasy of critique is symptomatic of our assumptions about what it means to be a reader-analyst. That is, to be a reader-analyst is to occupy the position of Andersen's child and to assert that things are not as they seem—or, rather, that things are exactly as they seem, but that few can recognize this. But this critical stance requires the privileging of (and the reinvestment in) the critical stance. The critical fantasy that Andersen's tale critiques is that when there is something wrong in the world, all that is needed is a brave, insightful individual to set things right. The tale's mythic popularity suggests that something about Andersen's account of seeing and saying the truth is attractive. The tale's truth is the fantasy-desire for the kind of truth that can be revealed.

Yet to say that **"The Emperor's New Clothes"** is actually critiquing the thing that millions of readers and admirers believe the story is "about" is to risk putting myself in the position of the little boy. To critique the story at all is to step out of the mainstream; since its publication it has been read as a simple tale of aristocratic vanity that promises little beyond the obvious.[3] For Marshall McLuhan, **"The Emperor's New Clothes"** is simply a perfect illustration of how perceptive but antisocial individuals—children, poets, artists, sleuths—can see what is really going on more clearly than "well-adjusted" individuals.[4] For Sigmund Freud, who alludes to the story briefly in *The Interpretation of Dreams,* the story simply offers proof of a "typical" desire for the natural nakedness of childhood.[5] For Derrida, as noted above, the tale offers simply another example of the truth that a text is its own best critic. (For him this is true of all texts, of course; but in Andersen's tale, the ironies are richer.) **"The Emperor's New Clothes"** is a "scene of writing" that exhibits/dissimulates "the baring of the motif of nakedness" well before the analyst arrives on the scene ("PT" ["The Purveyor of Truth"] 39). (Not surprisingly, the figure of the little boy has been used in a popular critical theory textbook to describe Derrida's early acts of speaking truth to power.[6]) But none of these observations are critiques of the story *qua* story. They are accounts of the story's illustrative power.

The story would be easy enough to critique—by this I mean to read and analyze the text following one or more of the accepted critical methodologies—and I am tempted to do so. But if I take seriously Derrida's admonition that the text also already critiqued itself before I have even begun, and if I take seriously my own observation that to read the text as a plucky, independent, "unhailed" individual is to reinvest in this critical position, then my analytical project becomes complex. I do not want to play the role of the little boy and exhibitionistically unveil the tale and all those who have refused to see its truths. But what are my alternatives? Most of the traditional metaphors for reading, especially those that are medical-surgical, vegetable, or archeological, involve some sort of opening up, stripping off, peeling, probing, and focusing light on. Is there another position the critic can take in reading a text?

I suggest that we test the effect of enlisting some new verbs in analytical criticism. I propose that **"The**

Emperor's New Clothes" offers several other critical positions besides that of the courageous romantic child. These positions are figured in the story by five very familiar "characters": the Emperor, the "rogue weavers," the ministers, the canopy, and the public. Each of these positions offers us critical verbs: to rule, to weave, to minister, to parade, and to applaud. In the critique that follows I will present and parade **"The Emperor's New Clothes"** by weaving the threads of the tale's often ignored characters and words, and in doing so, address and applaud its sociopolitical-literary-critical complexities.

THE EMPEROR

> Many years ago, there was an Emperor, who was so excessively fond of new clothes, that he spent all his money in dress. He did not trouble himself in the least about his soldiers; nor did he care to go either to the theatre or the chase, except for the opportunities then afforded him for displaying his new clothes. He had a different suit for each hour of the day; and as of any other king or emperor, one is accustomed to say, "he is sitting in council," it was always said of him, "The Emperor is sitting in his wardrobe."

To review Andersen's story and its immediate historical context, recall that the central ruse of **"The Emperor's New Clothes"** is predicated on the notion of "fitness for office." The specific setting of the tale is a bustling mercantile town whose ruler cares more about clothes than the business of state. "As it was said of other kings 'he is in council,' they said 'he is in his wardrobe.'" Two rogue weavers arrive on the scene to exploit both the king's vanity and administrative insecurity. Those who are unfit for office or are "simpletons," the rogues claim, cannot see the fine cloth they will weave.[7] By wearing a suit made from this cloth, the Emperor thinks (rather uncharacteristically), "I might at once find out what men in my realms are unfit for their office, and also be able to distinguish the wise from the foolish!"

The Emperor gives the weavers gold to set up looms and begin immediately. After some time, a faithful minister is sent in to view the cloth and is shocked that he can see nothing. "What can be the meaning of this?" he asks himself. "Can it be that I am unfit for my office?" He listens carefully while the weavers describe the colors and patterns and repeats the words back to the king. Another court official is sent in, only to ask himself "am I not fit for my good, profitable office?" He too reports back that the cloth is extraordinarily magnificent. The weavers ask for more silk and gold thread, which they put in their knapsacks.[8] Finally, the Emperor himself is shown the cloth, and he, like his ministers, is puzzled by his first deduction. "Am I unfit to be an Emperor? That would be the worst thing that could happen—Oh! The cloth is charming," he says aloud, and allows himself to be dressed in the new suit.

It is easy to make fun of this poor Emperor. Everyone does, though he is clearly the most important character, and his stature gives weight to the little boy's famous observation (*ID* [*The Interpretation of Dreams*] 242-48).[9] Yet the Emperor seems to be practicing a kind of focused undertaking that should be just as familiar to us as the little boy's critical outburst. If one character in a story is allegorical, aren't the others equally allegorical? We often expect our leaders (and ourselves) to take risks based on instinct, desire, or philosophy and to try on for size positions that they (and we) do not, or do not yet, fully understand. If so, then we, as critics who believe all perspicacious children who publicly proclaim truths that nobody seems to see, must recognize that we are also Emperors, cloistered in our closets, often ignoring much of the world around us, sifting through and trying on new ideas—partly for display and partly for vanity, but also partly because it is what we like to do.

THE WEAVERS

> One day, two rogues, calling themselves weavers, made their appearance. They gave out that they knew how to weave stuffs of the most beautiful colors and elaborate patterns, the clothes manufactured from which should have the wonderful property of remaining invisible to everyone who was unfit for the office he held, or who was extraordinarily simple in character.

These weavers resemble nothing so much as a new English Ph.D. on a job talk or a member of the MLA writing a proposal for a panel discussion. They are promising to create a text(ile) that will distinguish between the worthy and the unworthy; only the highly qualified will "get it." Theirs is a speculative endeavor but also a wholly critical one. Rather than pointing out truth, they are weaving a discourse that reveals truth.

The obvious (and all too familiar) critique is that these weavers are not really producing anything. They are rogues and frauds profiting from the insecurity and gullibility of others. Economic thought before Marx proposed that productive labor was only that which resulted in a material product, thus the labor of teachers and critics could not be considered productive. But for Marx all products of labor are "social things whose qualities are at the same time perceptible and imperceptible by the senses."[10] Andersen's weavers are merely insisting that the value of their labor be recognized apart from its material embodiment. Their presence in the text (and the fact that they are also coat-makers) signals an engagement with the highly charged political debate about the materiality of an artist's, craftsman's, or scholar's labor.[11] *Capital* opens with a sustained exploration of the handloom weavers' plight, investigating the social character of their labor and the mystical character of the coats they make.[12] Initially, the tale seems committed to a more optimistic future (or at least one less bleak) than Marx prophesies. In this bustling town, the handloom weavers'/tailors' work will lose neither its individual character nor its charm, artisans will be paid more than merely the objective cost of production, and they will convince the Emperor's ministers that it is in the town's best interest to appreciate the subjective value of their labor. The "truthful" child, who cannot see invisible labor, puts an end to this fantastic vision.

Moreover, the problem with the truth-telling child as a figure for the critic-analyst is that he does not labor prior to his outburst. The weavers, by contrast, succeed in selling the Emperor on their idea, and getting paid up front (like any good fellowship-recipient). They set up looms and request "the most delicate silk and the purest gold thread" (read: office and library privileges), which they promptly put in their knapsacks. Then they begin, "affecting to work very busily." The labor that the weavers/tailors will expend in turning the cloth into a coat may be invisible to some, they explain, but its beauty will appear to those who appreciate it. A "fit" minister or Emperor will fully perceive the artisans' labor in the coat. "Does not the stuff appear beautiful to you?" they ask. "Is not the work absolutely magnificent?"

THE MINISTERS

> So the faithful old minister went into the hall, where the knaves were working with all their might, at their empty looms. "What can be the meaning of this?" thought the old man, opening his eyes very wide. "I cannot discover the least bit of thread on the looms." However, he did not express his thoughts aloud. . . .

> The Emperor now sent another officer of his court to see how the men were getting on, and to ascertain whether the cloth would soon be ready. It was just the same with this gentleman as with the minister; he surveyed the looms on all sides, but could see nothing at all but the empty frames.

"Does not the stuff appear as beautiful to you, as it did to my lord the minister?" asked the impostors of the Emperor's second ambassador; at the same time making the same gestures as before, and talking of the design and colors that were not there.

"I certainly am not stupid!" thought the messenger. "It must be, that I am not fit for my good, profitable office! That is very odd; however, no one shall know anything about it."

Any scholar-critic who does not recognize herself (from time to time) in these subalterns is as blind as . . . well, one of the Emperor's subalterns. What is the basis for "Subaltern Studies" but the recognition that those with restricted voices speak in complicated, indirect ways? The critic or analyst who works for an institution (or within an academic field) is also a subaltern whose very dissimulation is an alternative form of critique. Literary critics are the last people who should privilege the direct speech of the little boy.

New Historicist literary critics should be especially attuned to the historical significance of the ministers' behavior. Evidently, the Emperor's court is caught up in a particularly nineteenth-century European controversy over objective qualifications for civil service. In the 1820s and '30s, the conservative Danish bureaucracy, which enjoyed power and prestige under the king's absolute rule, was under increasing pressure to respond to the needs of a growing merchant and middle class. Bourgeois liberals pressed the centralized governing structures for press freedoms, free trade, and an end to aristocratic privileges. Older bureaucrats reluctantly joined their younger, university-trained colleagues in the reform movements that would lead to a new constitutional monarchy by 1849.[13] This pattern replicated itself across Europe.[14]

Following the logic of Danish and British (as well as French and German) civil service reform, Andersen's high-level ministers and lower-level chamberlains find themselves asked to demonstrate their qualification for positions they are already holding. The old trusted minister is shocked and worried, but the reader should not be—the story suggests he and his fellow (civil) servants have proven themselves to be qualified for their jobs. The Emperor's vanity has been economically beneficial to the town: while he has been closeted with his wardrobe and ignoring his soldiers, people have prospered, and "time passed merrily in the large town which was his capital." This transparent government has been working. If the chamberlains (who are traditionally political, not sartorial) have successfully served the state by suiting the sovereign, it may be wise policy to continue.[15]

Unfortunately, however, the fashion advice that they have been used to giving has suddenly been constituted as an objective test of their fitness. They are left with a difficult choice: to acknowledge publicly that their subjective flattery has been objectively good for the capital (thus embarrassing the Emperor) or just quietly continue serving him (and keeping the peace) by admiring his clothes. All of the folk-tale precursors to **"The Emperor's New Clothes"** feature a courtier who must "see" a painting or a turban or a play or else reveal that he is illegitimate.[16] Andersen's updated version not only reflects a culture in which professional competence was quickly overtaking legitimacy and heritage as a source of aristocratic anxiety, but also weaves a new layer of complexity into the narrative. That is, while the problem of "legitimacy" follows a binary logic and is (for the most part) an objective question, professional fitness is enduringly subjective. The understandable uncertainty about the idea of "fitness" provides an incentive to admire the invisible cloth.[17] While we might indulge ourselves in picturing the Emperor's state of dishabille, the chamberlains who mime carrying the invisible train are clearly guided by their critical faculties. Their investment in the materiality of the Emperor's clothes is apparently so great that they will persist despite the public turmoil at the close of the story.

The Canopy

And now the Emperor, with all the grandees of his court, came to the weavers; and the rogues raised their arms, as if in the act of holding something up, saying, "Here are your Majesty's trousers! Here is the scarf! Here is the mantle! The whole suit is as light as a cobweb; one might fancy one has nothing at all on, when dressed in it; that, however, is the great virtue of this delicate cloth. . . ."

"How splendid his Majesty looks in his new clothes, and how well they fit!" everyone cried out. "What a design! What colors! These are indeed royal robes!"

"The canopy which is to be borne over your Majesty, in the procession, is waiting," announced the chief master of the ceremonies. . . .

The invisible "cobweb-light" fabric shares the stage with another very material piece of cloth with objectively discernible effects: the ceremonial canopy under which the Emperor will proceed. The short narrative mentions it twice. It precedes the procession and plays a crucial role in it. Its obvious critical analogue is the diploma.

The relation of the canopy to the invisible cloth (or the diploma to the journal publication) is perhaps the same relation as the physical to the metaphysical— what Adam Smith famously called a "cobweb science."[18] But it is not a binary relation; both are fabrications whose value can only be perceived by one "in the know." Not surprisingly, nobody who reads the story "sees" the Emperor's canopy. It is part of the ceremonial text of kingship.

Oscar Wilde remarks that "the true mystery of the world is the visible, not the invisible." Likewise, the riddle of the invisible cloth's—and the story's—significance is solved by the customary visible covering of the king. Seen or unseen, it is not the cloth *qua* cloth but the position and function of the cloth within the story that determines each character and produces certain of the story's effects (to paraphrase Barbara Johnson's evaluation of a certain missing letter).[19] Until the child speaks, that is, the invisible material performs the same role as the visible. The function of the canopy is to announce that the Emperor is the emperor, whatever he happens to be wearing.[20]

In Freud's reading of **"The Emperor's New Clothes,"** the "typical" invisible cloth (*not* the canopy) is evidence of repression and thus is of interest to the analyst (as might be the modern reader's active forgetting that Marx's *Capital* begins with a discussion of coats).[21] But if the invisible textile inside the text becomes for Freud the whole text, why does it, and it alone, remain so even in Derrida's whole-cloth reconsideration of Freud's reading? Why the collective critical blindness to the visible fabric of the story—kingship and the cloth that signifies it?

The Public

> So now the Emperor walked under his high canopy in the midst of the procession, through the streets of his capital; and all the people standing by, and those at the windows, cried out, "Oh! How beautiful are our Emperor's new clothes! What a magnificent train there is to the mantle; and how gracefully the scarf hangs!" In short, no one would allow that he could not see these much-admired clothes; because, in doing so, he would have declared himself either a simpleton or unfit for his office. Certainly, none of the Emperor's various suits, had ever made so great an impression, as these invisible ones.

In initially making manifest the social utility of the Emperor's invisible formal garments, the story exposes the invisible social conventions that bind the townspeople together and to the Emperor. The text suggests that the importance of these invisible customs is greatest in periods of social upheaval. But if

the problem of invisibility engages the axes of veiled/unveiled and blindness/sight simultaneously, it is unclear whether a customary act of not seeing is an act of self-protection or self-exposure.

"The Emperor's New Clothes" dramatizes the dangers of habitual blindness in the name of social discretion. "What is perfectly correct and in order if practiced within the autonomous life of sociability," cautions Simmel, "becomes a deceptive lie when it is guided by non-sociable purposes or is designed to disguise such purposes" (*SGS* [*The Sociology of Georg Simmel*] 49). The pretense of "seeing" the Emperor's invisible clothes is traditionally read as artifice at best and a lie at worst. But by foregrounding questions of sociability against a backdrop of political and economic turmoil, Andersen's tale clearly suggests that social discretion can engender democratic social solidarity. The townspeople's initial admiration for the cloth is a function of an altogether different reason. While the modern civil servant is trained to disregard (or be indifferent to) what is not in his particular purview, the townspeople remain, by contrast, fascinated with each other. "All the people throughout the city had heard of the wonderful property the cloth was to possess; and all were anxious to learn how wise, or how ignorant, their neighbors might prove to be," the narrator continues. But even while they are curious, their sense of social discretion subtly evokes bureaucratic detachment: they do not want to reveal their curiosity. Simmel observes that in all human intercourse, everyone knows more about everyone else than what is voluntarily revealed, but endeavors to be discreet about it. In general, however, "man arrogates to himself the right to know all he can find out through mere observation and reflection, without applying externally illegitimate means" (*SGS* 323). Both the townspeople and the ministers have a personal stake in admiring the invisible cloth. Their long-term economic stake, however, may be even greater.

The Little Boy

The Emperor is ecstatic, until a little boy remarks, "But the Emperor has nothing at all on!" His father exclaims, "Listen to the voice of innocence!" and the child's words are whispered from one to another. "But he has nothing at all on!" they all cry out at last. The story concludes:

> The Emperor felt most uncomfortable, for it seemed to him that the people were right. But somehow he thought to himself: "I must go through with it now, procession and all." And he

drew himself up still more proudly, while the lords of the bedchamber walked after him carrying the train that wasn't there.

Ceremonies and formal performances have played a positive role in the community. The procession through the town was apparently already planned in advance of the weavers' arrival. "All [the Emperor's] retinue . . . advised his majesty to have some new clothes made from this splendid material, for the approaching procession." As Simmel notes, the sociable world—"the only world in which a democracy of the equally privileged is possible without frictions—is an *artificial* world" (*SGS* 48). These stewards of the artifice are steadfastly maintaining the "certain reserve and stylization" that Simmel suggests constitutes the social (*SGS* 48). In their steadfastness, the chamberlains are also perhaps exhibiting a rather Hegelian act of courage: "absolute obedience, renunciation of personal opinions and reasonings, in fact complete *absence* of mind, coupled with the most intense and comprehensive *presence* of mind" in order to realize and actualize a more open government.[22] They will persist in observing the proper, albeit artificial, forms despite the little boy who "sees through" it all.

Curiously, Andersen's original version had no child. The story ended this way:

> Certainly, none of the Emperor's various suits had ever made so great an impression, as these invisible ones.
>
> "I must put on the suit whenever I walk in a procession or appear before a gathering of people," said the emperor, and the whole town talked about his wonderful new clothes.
>
> (*HCA* [*Hans Christian Andersen: The Story of His Life and Work, 1805-1875*] 312)

This original version clearly registers the growing democratic political climate of the time and closes with an image of fellowship. It is a story of a successful enchantment. The townspeople simultaneously like seeing the Emperor naked (which makes them feel powerful) and like having to pretend publicly that nobody can see him naked (which keeps the crowd in check). The magical cloth enables the people's twin desires for power and security to be satisfied.

But just before publication Andersen had second thoughts about this conclusion and told the proofreader to delete the final paragraph and replace it with the final three paragraphs we are all too familiar with, hoping, he said, to give it a more satirical ap-

pearance (*HCA* 313). He succeeds. The fairy tale that we know does not end happily. The townspeople had been quite happy to ignore the Emperor's metaphoric nakedness for years, but the child's declaration abruptly ends this charade. The ceremonial fictions of sovereignty have become a problem that needs fixing. The child's words are disruptive—not for having leveled the difference between ruler and ruled, but for endangering the formal process by which it is accomplished without being openly acknowledged. While the public outside the text applauds the boy's act of disenchantment, the community inside is fractured and diminished.[23] The rogue weavers disappear from the story, the townspeople are deflated, and the chamberlains are left holding invisible robes. Read along the grain of history, the little boy whose antisocial remark is embraced as romantic insight emerges as scandalously reactionary: he calls the people fools and tells the king to get dressed. His particular version of "transparent" social interaction is intended to expose social difference rather than foster equality, and he succeeds in utterly rending the social fabric of the town by seeing through the Emperor's clothes.

That is, the Emperor is still the emperor. The townspeople's enthusiasm for his naked vanity is exposed, but (as the canopy manifests) his sovereignty is not in doubt. To paraphrase Barbara Johnson again, if the invisible cloth poses the question of its own rhetorical status, it is answered (at least initially) by a resounding "yes": "It is [visible] 'in' a *symbolic* structure, a structure which can *only* be perceived in its effects" ("FR" ["The Frame of Reference: Poe, Lacan, Derrida"] 498). The people are traumatized not by the realization that the cloth is invisible but by the public acknowledgement that they have subscribed to its visibility. They have consented to what the Emperor's accoutrements (robes, canopy), however invisible, signify. The relationship between the robes and the townspeople is only underscored by their initial blindness to their (the robes') invisibility.

The complex social desire that **"The Emperor's New Clothes"** imagines—a vision of a certain kind of economically beneficial performance that is not publicly acknowledged as simply a performance—may have been exposed, but the number of people who labored to carry it off demonstrates its materiality. I will not say that readers of **"The Emperor's New Clothes"** have been fooled when they read the text as a story of an Emperor (and a town) that has been fooled, because Andersen's text so very much wants this to be the case. The romantic idiom (a child who seems to speak the truth) is deployed precisely to create this effect. And yet this effect is wholly a function of the belief that art is objective (that there is an essential truth), that labor is invisible, and that Emperors ought to be clothed—all of which the child is somehow already socialized to believe. The pessimism of Andersen's text is located precisely in the conservatism of this child. To read him any other way is to be blind to the fact that nakedness has its "truth" in clothing—the Emperor is not naked until the child insists that he must "truly" be clothed.

The Text

What is at the heart of this story's remarkable cultural/political relevance? Why is it that the allegorical "emperor's new clothes" circulates so widely even as we resist becoming on intimate terms with it? Lurking beneath our appreciation of the story's fairy-tale moral, I suggest, is an apprehension of the serious ontological and epistemological *social* problems it dramatizes. Recalling its much longer cognate text, *Sartor Resartus* (and sharing its engagement with metaphysics and fabrication), [**"The Emperor's New Clothes"**] vision of invisible fabric furnishes an idiom that will to some degree underwrite the investigations of the next generation of social theorists.[24] As Ruskin will ask (putting aside "tiresome and absurd" questions of objectivity, subjectivity, and truth), what is the difference between true and false appearances when under a contemplative fancy? As Marx will ask, can something invisible have value? As Weber will ask, are individual subjectivity and bureaucratic function contradictory? As Simmel will ask, why is it that secrecy—the hiding of realities—is one of man's greatest achievements? As Wittgenstein will ask, can I ever know what someone else sees or that he sees at all, when all I have is signs of various sorts that he gives me?

The brief critical attention that Jacques Derrida pays to **"The Emperor's New Clothes"** (which is largely a critique of Freud's reading of the story) functions as a kind of dumb show for his longer and more famous critique of Jacques Lacan's reading of Edgar Allan Poe's "The Purloined Letter."[25] But although the presence of Andersen's story in a critique of critique hints that the story may have something new to say about the project of critique, Derrida never proceeds beyond descrying (or decrying) the typical project of critique and truth-telling by unveiling. In Derrida's view, both Poe's story and Andersen's feature a king whose manhood is imperiled, who is surrounded by habit-driven and blindly ineffectual civil servants, and who is saved by an individual who sees what is obvious. Both Dupin and the little boy respond to the crisis of kingly exposure with flashes of insight; both save the crown further embarrassment. Both Dupin and the boy are wholly conservative and patriotic. In their view, there is never a question that a king could or should fall from grace.

It is understandable that politics in a reading of "The Purloined Letter" should take a back burner: after all, there is a woman involved, as well as a little gold knob hanging between the cheeks of a fireplace. But **"The Emperor's New Clothes"** offers no such distractions. The tale's Zelig-like appearance at the periphery of a famous twentieth-century quarrel over the nature of truth, speech, nakedness, and disclosure is all the more remarkable for the fact that the story remains essentially unexamined. Indeed, there has been surprisingly little interest in the historical, textual, and sociopolitical agenda of Andersen's story. Unlike several of his other works (notably, **"The Shadow," "The Little Mermaid,"** and *Only a Fiddler*), **"The Emperor's New Clothes"** has provoked little academic interest.[26] Perhaps, as a noted authority of the story's many folkloric antecedents suggests, the tale resists critical scrutiny because its moral is too obvious and "too bitter a pill" (AT 17).[27]

Even this briefest of readings of **"The Emperor's New Clothes"** makes manifest that it has cultural and political relevance well beyond the popular figure of the little boy. The story quite clearly rehearses four contemporary controversies: the institution of a meritocratic civil service, the valuation of labor, the expansion of democratic power, and the appraisal of art. The story's potency, I argue, is not a function of the tale's engagement with these crises but its seductive resolution of them. We are seduced by the figure of an innocent analyst who pipes up and appears to clarify.

"Andersen's text has the text as a theme," Derrida observes (PT 37). He introduces his reading of Andersen by calling it an "apologue or parabolic pretext" for his "Purloined Letter" reading that he arrives at by opening up *The Interpretation of Dreams* "somewhere near the middle." The first two texts Derrida mentions after opening the Freud are *Oedipus Rex* and *Hamlet*. Thus we find grouped together, on one page, four stories about blindness, kingship, and threatening speech. Two of these stories, remarkably, are about Danish kings. It is a point too provocative to ignore.

The weavers' text, like the ghostly voice whispering at midnight, like the existence of a lover's letter, like the words of the prophecy, threatens to bring down a king. To their auditors, the words are "true." They sell a particular idea that the king has something to be embarrassed about, whether it is fitness for office, the right to the office, or the loyalty of his wife. The material effects of these words are the basis for these four stories, all of which are "resolved" in a manner that cleans up the office of the king.

In 1835, the Danish government, like most of its European counterparts, prohibited political meetings. But that year the Society for the Proper Employment of the Freedom of the Press was formed to resist Royal encroachment on the limited right of free speech in the country. In Germany, the Carlsbad Decrees of 1835 had killed press freedoms for the most part and sent authors such as Andersen's friend Heine into exile. Andersen, as Alison Prince suggests, could not have been unaware of the dangers of his profession.[28] In this context, Andersen's tale of an Emperor who believes in the materiality of words (who clothes himself in textual description) might also be read as an exploration of a constitutional monarchy in which the public conspires to preserve the myth of monarchial fitness. But this reform could be fraught with practical problems: the Emperor risks revealing that he has nothing on because children— the most skeptical and conservative of readers—are apt to see right through the fabrication.

Notes

1. Hans Christian Andersen, "The Emperor's New Clothes," *Andersen's Fairy Tales* (E-text #1597), *Project Gutenberg,* Jan 1999, ftp:// ibiblio.org/pub/docs/books/gutenberg/etext99/ hcaft10.txt. All quotations of the story in this essay are from this e-text version, which is the most literal translation available.

2. Jacques Derrida, "The Purveyor of Truth," tr. Willis Domingo, James Hulbert, Moshe Ron, and M. -R. L., *Yale French Studies,* 52 (1975), 38-39; hereafter cited in text as "PT".

3. First published in 1837 and translated into English in 1846, there are probably thousands of versions of "The Emperor's New Clothes" extant. It has been translated into hundreds of languages and is by now a cultural icon. See Elias Bredsdorff, *Hans Christian Andersen: The Story of His Life and Work, 1805-1875* (New York, 1975), part 2, chapter 2 for specific details of this translation history; hereafter cited in text as *HCA*. See also Jon Cech, "Hans Christian Andersen's Fairy Tales and Stories: Secrets, Swans and Shadows," *Touchstones: Reflections*

on the Best in Children's Literature, ed. Perry Nodelman, vol. 2 (Summit, Pa., 1987), pp. 14-23. Cech quotes Andersen scholar Bo Gronbech: "Andersen's tales have been translated into over a hundred languages; only the Bible and Shakespeare have been translated into more" (16). The tale of the naked king and the little boy has been modernized, embellished, reimagined, and recontextualized in print, on stage, and on film. Steven Spielberg recently published a new illustrated version with himself as star. Last year Disney offered a film entitled *The Emperor's New Groove.* In a *New York Times Book Review* essay on the latest biography of Hans Christian Andersen, Brook Allen writes that "The Emperor's New Clothes" is "a masterpiece whose very title has become a byword for human vanity" (Brook Allen, "The Uses of Enchantment," *The New York Times,* 20 May 2001, late ed., section 7, 12). A quick database search reveals that the phrase "emperor's new clothes" is used hundreds of times every year in newspaper articles, congressional testimony, and academic journals as a tool for oppugning established policies and colleagues. Every field's iconoclasts, whistle-blowers, and revolutionaries want to see themselves as the little boy—the analyst who sees the *real* truth and proclaims it to the world.

4. Marshall McLuhan and Quentin Fiore, *The Medium Is the Massage* (New York, 1967), pp. 88-89. Bredsdorff sums up: "Andersen's universally applicable tale ridicul[es] the snobbery of people who pretend to understand or appreciate things they do not really understand or appreciate, in order not to be considered ignorant or stupid" (*Hans Christian Andersen,* p. 252).

5. Sigmund Freud, *The Interpretation of Dreams* (London, 1990), pp. 242-48; hereafter cited in text as *ID*.

6. Hazard Adams and Leroy Searle, eds., *Critical Theory since 1965* (Tallahassee, 1986), p. 79.

7. Freud and Derrida mischaracterize the prerequisites for seeing the cloth as "virtue and loyalty."

8. In some versions, there is a suggestion that the Emperor has paid for the cloth out of his own pocket.

9. Freud recognized the Emperor's central role but stopped short of recognizing his potential as a model for the analyst. For Freud, the Emperor is a typical dreamer dreaming the typical dream of nakedness. Freud suggested that the Emper-

or's social predicament of being naked and yet unashamed is made sense of by the weavers' deception, which he calls "the secondary revision." That is, the dream concocts the weavers in order to "clothe" the dreamer's desire for nakedness. But although Freud acknowledges his own dreams of nakedness, he does not perform his analysis from the position of the Emperor. Typically, he casts himself in the role of the little boy, stripping away the secondary revisions and revealing the desire for nakedness that shames the patient.

10. Karl Marx, *Capital: A Critique of Political Economy,* ed. Frederick Engels and Ernest Untermann (New York, 1906), p. 83.

11. For contemporary readers, fictional rogue weavers would resonate with their real-life counterparts who were actively petitioning their governments and demanding piecework rates, or being arrested and jailed for burning machines. In the first decades of the nineteenth century large-scale manufacture of power looms and expanding assembly-line production had devastated the rural economies of Europe and put thousands of handloom weavers and spinners out of work.

12. That is, Marx conceives of the relationship between the labor of a weaver/tailor and his final product as "imagined" but "invisible" material, beginning with the admonition that a product's utility is not a thing of air. Employing the idiom of invisible cloth, Marx "sees" the labor of these weavers and tailors. The coat produced by a weaver and tailor has value "only because human labor in the abstract has been embodied or materialized in it," and this labor is both visible and invisible (*Capital,* p. 45). The tailoring of the coat "shows" this labor, he continues, "but though worn to a thread, it does not let this fact show through" (60). The price of a commodity, he continues, is "a purely ideal or mental form," as is its value, which is made perceptible by its equality with gold, but which really exists only in one's head (107).

13. See Kenneth E. Miller, *Government and Politics in Denmark* (Boston, 1968).

14. The British transformation from aristocratic patronage to professionalism in the civil service began in earnest in 1802, when Parliament rather than the king became responsible for civil-service salaries. It continued through 1833 with the founding of Statistical Societies and with the merit-based reorganization of the India Office on John Stuart Mill's philosophy that "efficiency should be substituted for influence." It reached fruition in the famous 1854 Northcote-Trevelyan report, which recommended restructuring and centralizing the entire British civil service and instituting competitive exams for both recruitment and promotion. The discourse of fitness continued in fictional form in Charles Dickens's *Little Dorrit,* Honore de Balzac's *The Bureaucrats,* and Anthony Trollope's *The Three Clerks.*

15. A chamberlain is a king's (or queen's) private chamber attendant or administrator. The role of England's Lord Great Chamberlain is hereditary and requires attending upon and attiring the sovereign at his/her coronation, caring for various palaces and halls on formal state occasions, and attending upon peers and bishops at their creation. The Lord Chamberlain of the Household and the Mistress of the Robes share the oversight of all officers of the Royal Household. Shortly after "The Emperor's New Clothes" was published, the infamous 1839 "Bedchamber Crisis" in England provoked public debate about the political power of intimate advisors. In one of his first official acts, Tory Prime Minister Robert Peel demanded that several of Queen Victoria's Ladies of the Bedchamber and Mistress of the Robes be removed, because their husbands were Whig politicians. His fear, of course, was that each of these ladies would be looking after her own—that is, her political party's—best interest by discrediting Peel's government in the privacy of the Royal apartments. After the resignation of Melbourne's government in 1839, the new Prime Minister Robert Peel demanded this of Queen Victoria during his first meeting with her. His belief was that because their husbands were Whigs opposed to his government, these ladies-in-waiting would fill the Queen's ears with criticisms of Tory policy and compromise her confidence in Peel's government.

16. Archer Taylor, "The Emperor's New Clothes," *Modern Philology,* 25 (1927/28), 17-27; hereafter cited in text as AT. Taylor identifies a thirteenth-century, German jestbook tale about an artist whose paintings can be seen only by those who are legitimate. There is a fifteenth-century Turkish tale that turns on a silk turban. There is a seventeenth-century play by Cervantes in which not only does an individual

have to be legitimate to see a theatrical spectacle, but he cannot have a single drop of Jewish blood. In the source text that Andersen acknowledged, a fourteenth-century cautionary tale by Infante don Juan Manuel, translated into German as "*So ist der Lauf der Welt*," magic cloth woven by fraudulent weavers is similarly visible only to those who are legitimate. Taylor bases his genealogy on the shared characteristics of the "fraud," the "chain of falsehood," the disclosure of "the self-imposed deception," and the moral that "truth will out" (24). "All exemplify the idea [that] knaves will lie for their own supposed advantage, even if the act involves boldfaced deception" (17).

17. If the function of art is to make the invisible visible, both the weavers and the chamberlains prove themselves aesthetically (as well as ethically) proficient in their specific references to what the cloth actually looks like. Their repetitive description of the cloth's immateriality paradoxically reinforces a sense of its ontological stability. "The whole suit is as light as a cobweb," the weavers say, while fitting the Emperor; "one might fancy one has nothing at all on, when dressed in it; that, however, is the great virtue of this delicate cloth." Yet despite its existence as mere fabrication, the cloth has objectively discernible effects on the individuals it touches: the two subordinate chamberlains bend down and pick up the invisible train as the Emperor prepares to parade through the town. Their dogged determination to keep holding this train even after the little boy speaks is usually considered proof positive of the ministers' lack of common sense.

18. Adam Smith, *An Inquiry into the Nature and Causes of the Wealth of Nations* (London, 1896), book 5 "Of the Revenue of the Sovereign or Commonwealth," chap. 1 "Of the Expenses of the Sovereign or Commonwealth," article 2 "Of the Expense of the Institutions for the Education of Youth," p. 292: "When metaphysics and physics are set in opposition to one another, they naturally give birth to a third, Ontology, which treats of qualities and attributes common to both." The "subtleties and sophisms" could "compose the whole of this cobweb science of Ontology." For Carlyle, metaphysical clothes are (pun intended) a physical *habit*: "Consider well, thou wilt find that Custom is the greatest of Weavers; and weaves air-raiment for all the Spirits of the Universe;

whereby indeed these dwell with us visibly, as ministering servants, in our houses and workshops; but their spiritual nature becomes, to the most, forever hidden" (Thomas Carlyle, *Sartor Resartus* (London, 1896), book 3, chapter 8, p. 206). That is, we are blind to what is customary.

19. Barbara Johnson, "The Frame of Reference: Poe, Lacan, Derrida," *Yale French Studies,* 55/56 (1977), 457-505; hereafter cited in text as "FR."

20. Kurt H. Wolff, ed. and tr., *The Sociology of Georg Simmel* (New York, 1964); hereafter cited in text as *SGS*. As Simmel notes, "in earlier times, functionaries of the public interests were customarily clothed with mystical authority, while, under larger and more mature conditions, they attain . . . through their distance from every individual, a certainty and dignity by means of which they can permit their activities to be public" (336). Without the "mystical authority" of visible robes, the canopy gives the Emperor, his chamberlains, and the townspeople "cover," and reminds the crowd who and what the Emperor is. As an allegory of nineteenth-century political dismantling, this preoccupation with ceremony makes sense. In the emerging democratic political movements of the 1830s, a naked king—a king divested of power—was just what people were clamoring for. (Only a decade would pass before Denmark's absolute monarchy was in fact abolished and replaced by a constitution establishing a popularly elected Parliament and guaranteeing new freedoms.)

21. Recall that for Freud, Andersen's tale enacts and *is* a disguise: the dreamer, vaguely ashamed by his public nakedness, has to clothe his dream in a secondary revision—in this case the onlookers' approbation—which the analyst/boy will pull off (*The Interpretation of Dreams,* pp. 242-48). Thus Derrida: "the baring of the motif of nakedness as secondarily revised or disguised by Andersen's fairy tale, will be exhibited/dissimulated in advance by the fairy tale in a piece of writing that therefore no longer belongs in the realm of decidable truth" ("Purveyor of Truth," p. 39).

22. *Hegel's Philosophy of Right,* tr. T. M. Knox (Oxford, 1945), part 3, chap. 2, sec. 328, pp. 211-12.

23. "In comparison with the childish stage in which every conception is expressed at once, and ev-

ery undertaking is accessible to the eyes of all," Simmel argues, "the secret produces an immense enlargement of life" (*Sociology of Georg Simmel,* p. 330). The image of the naked king evokes and complicates traditionally positive metaphors of "transparent" and "open" government operating under a policy of "full disclosure." By contrast, the idea of a "cover-up" is wholly negative.

24. Carlyle's text, like Andersen's, was influenced by Goethe's writings. The similarities between the two texts are remarkable, though they are not the focus here. From *Sartor Resartus:* "Often in my atrabiliar moods, when I read of pompous ceremonials, Frankfort Coronations, Royal Drawing-rooms . . . and I strive, in my remote privacy, to form a clear picture of that solemnity, on a sudden, as by some enchanter's wand, the—shall I speak it?—the Clothes fly off the whole dramatic corps; and Dukes, Grandees, Bishops, Generals, Anointed Presence itself, every mother's son of them, stand straddling there, not a shirt on them; and I know not whether to laugh or weep. . . . What would Majesty do, could such an accident befall in reality; should the buttons all simultaneously start, and the solid wool evaporate, in very Deed, as here in Dream? *Ach Gott*! How each skulks into the nearest hiding-place; their high State Tragedy . . . becomes a Pickleherring-Farce to weep at, which is the worst kind of Farce; *the tables* (according to Horace), and with them, the whole fabric of Government, Legislation, Property, Police, and Civilized Society, *are dissolved* in wails and howls" (*Sartor Resartus,* book 1, chap. 9, p. 48).

25. To summarize Barbara Johnson, "The Emperor's New Clothes" raises the problem of the ability of subjective "seeing" to interfere with the polarity "hidden/exposed." She alludes to Andersen's tale to critique the ways that Derrida "sees" only what is within his own sight lines—that is, in focusing on a literary text solely as a signifier of literary text, Derrida is blind to what the social circulation of text signifies ("The Frame of Reference," p. 482).

26. Otto Rank treats "The Shadow" in some depth in *The Double* [1914], tr. and ed. Harry Tucker (New York, 1979). Søren Kierkegaard's first published work is a critique of Andersen's third novel, *Only a Fiddler* (1837), written the same year as "The Emperor's New Clothes" (see Bredsdorff, *Hans Christian Andersen,* pp. 128-

30, for a discussion of Kierkegaard's "From the Papers of One still Living. Published against His Will by S. Kierkegaard. About H. C. Andersen as a Novelist, with Special Reference to His Latest Work, *Only a Fiddler*").

27. See also Jack Zipes, *Fairy Tales and the Art of Subversion: The Classical Genre for Children and the Process of Civilization* (New York, 1983), pp. 71-97. Zipes claims that "the widespread, continuous reception of Andersen's fairy tales in western culture" is due to the stories' ideological embrace of "bourgeois notions of the self-made man or the Horatio Alger myth . . . [and] a belief in the existing power structure" (80-81).

28. Alison Prince, *Hans Christian Andersen: The Fan Dancer* (London, 1998).

📖 "THE LITTLE MERMAID" (1837)

Gwyneth Cravens (review date 11 May 1992)

SOURCE: Cravens, Gwyneth. Review of "The Little Mermaid" from *The Complete Hans Christian Andersen Fairy Tales,* by Hans Christian Andersen. *Nation* 254, no. 18 (11 May 1992): 638-40.

[*In the following review, Cravens alleges that Andersen's "The Little Mermaid" is an example of a thematically rich fairy tale which celebrates qualities of curiosity, love, and independence.*]

Since **"The Little Mermaid,"** by Hans Christian Andersen, was first read aloud to me by my mother when I was 4 or 5, I've read it over and over—to myself, to my own daughter and to other children. I always forget that it's a tale. It seems instead an immediate, intimate part of my life, yet suspended outside of time. When I was small, elements of the story troubled me. Growing up in the high desert of the Southwest and never having seen the ocean, I'd have given anything to be a mermaid rather than a girl, and yet the heroine yearned to become a human and live on the land. And what suffering! How could she abide the sensation, once she had legs, that she was walking on knives? But even though her trials seemed intolerable, I felt as though the deepest part of my nature were being addressed by a sincere friend, and I was satisfied and uplifted by the ending without understanding the reason.

Recently I revisited the story in **The Complete Hans Christian Andersen Fairy Tales** (edited by Lily Owens, translated from the Danish for the most part by Mrs. H. B. Paull and H. Oskar Sommer in the 1880s and published by Avenel/Crown in 1981). I was struck anew by its richness and power, and by how radical, how subversive, how steely it is in disclosing a definition of love enormously contrary to the one most commonly celebrated. What of its subtleties I could have articulated to myself back then I don't know, but some part of me readily absorbed them. Consciously I only knew that the tale somehow wanted to awaken me to the truth that there was more to my being than I thought, more possibilities than the ones that lay close at hand.

The little mermaid is a quiet, pensive child who dwells in a kingdom so accurately described, with its glowing colors and constant undulations and gliding shadows and billowy magnifications, and the sun like a purple flower with light streaming from its calyx, that you might wonder how a Dane living in the early nineteenth century before the invention of scuba diving was able to conjure up such a scene. She has a sweet singing voice, a curiosity about things human and a sense of not being at home in the element in which her elder sisters are so content. They enjoy collecting the bounty from wrecked vessels; she's pleased to have only a little statue of a handsome boy, a garden she has planted in the shape and color of the sun, and whatever impressions she can gather of the ships, towns and animals above as reported by her sisters and her grandmother. On the day she turns 15 she's allowed to visit the surface, and there she glimpses, on a boat, a prince. So begins her new life. When a storm arises and the ship founders, she rescues him from drowning, kisses his unconscious brow and leaves him on a beach. There a girl finds him, and he believes her to be his savior. The little mermaid continues to watch him longingly from a distance, remembering "that his head had rested on her bosom, and how heartily she had kissed him; but he knew nothing of all this, and could not even dream of her."

She inquires of her grandmother about the ways of mankind and learns that when mermaids die they become seafoam but that humans, after the body has been turned to dust, have a soul that lives forever. "It rises up through the clear, pure air beyond the glittering stars," says her grandmother. "As we rise out of the water, and behold all the land of the earth, so do they rise to unknown and glorious regions which we shall never see." The little mermaid, recognizing that her death means she will never again perceive the beauty of the world, asks how she can win an immortal soul. She's told that if a man were to love her

with such fidelity and wholeheartedness that his soul would flow into her body, a soul of her own would spring into being—but even attraction is impossible, because humans consider fish tails ugly.

To find a way to be with her adored prince and to achieve a soul, the little mermaid visits the sea witch in her whirlpool, braving snakelike half-plant, half-animal monsters who grasp in their clinging arms the skeletons of those who have perished at sea, and even a little mermaid, whom they've caught and strangled. As Andersen is unafraid to show—and as I must also have been aware, because children do sense such things and are always wondering about them—the darkness never stops reaching out its tentacles. "I know what you want," says the sea witch. "It is very stupid of you . . . and it will bring you to sorrow." She prepares a draught—adding a drop of her own black blood—that will turn the mermaid's tail into legs. "All who see you will say that you are the prettiest little human being they ever saw. You will still have the same floating gracefulness of movement, and no dancer will ever tread so lightly; but at every step you take it will feel as if you were treading upon sharp knives, and that the blood must flow." She adds that the mermaid can never again return to her former life, and that if the prince marries another, her heart will break and her life will end. In payment, the sea witch asks for the mermaid's voice and cuts out her tongue—the promise of love is not to be won without sacrifice. At the boundary between water and land, the mermaid drinks the potion and, feeling as if a two-edged sword were passing through her body, swoons. When she awakens, she has become human, and there stands the prince.

Just as Andersen accurately discerns the depths of the sea, he also comprehends something profound about the metamorphosis in consciousness at the boundary between girlhood and womanhood and about the hardships of that initiation: the dramatic transformation of the body, accompanied by blood and the two-edged blade of desire and pain; the irrevocable exchange of ease and freedom for the gravity and responsibilities of maturity; the solitary nature of the quest for a new sensibility and the will necessary to accomplish it; and the silence that surrounds these mysteries.

The heroine can ask for nothing; she can only hope, communing with her beloved through her expressive eyes and her enchanting—though secretly excruciating—dance. The prince, seeing a resemblance to the girl who apparently saved his life, lets his "dumb foundling" sleep on a cushion outside his room and shows her the delights of his kingdom. His parents want him to marry, but he's reluctant; if he were forced, he tells her, he'd choose her as his bride, and he "laid his head on her heart, while she dreamed of human happiness and an immortal soul." Nevertheless, it happens that he becomes betrothed to the young woman he thinks rescued him. Our assumptions and conventions can blind us to the miraculous at our door. "She is the only one in the world I could love": he tells the little mermaid. "My fondest hopes are all fulfilled. You will rejoice at my happiness; for your devotion to me is great and sincere." The mute creature can do nothing but kiss his hand.

At his wedding, aboard a ship, she carries the bridal train, thinking of all she has lost, and joins in the dancing. "She knew this was the last evening she should ever see the prince, for whom she had forsaken her kindred and her home," Andersen writes. "She had given up her beautiful voice, and suffered unheard of pain daily for him, while he knew nothing of it." And we begin to sense that it's best that the prince remain ignorant; the goal of love is not to invoke guilt and obligation.

After the couple retire for the night, the sisters of the little mermaid rise up from the swells with a knife. The sea witch, they say, has agreed to return to the little mermaid her tail and her undersea life if she will only kill the prince, and they plead with her to do it. Such is the sort of grim advice that we often receive when our fate becomes unbearable. And what disappointed lover has not cherished the impulse to turn on the person who has been everything to him or to her? With a stroke, say the inner and outer voices, you can destroy the presence of the beloved and regain your freedom, and all will be as it was before you met. The little mermaid accepts the knife. Toward morning, she goes to the dreaming prince, but upon hearing him whisper the name of his bride, she flings the knife into the water and throws herself overboard, dissolving into foam on the crest of a wave.

But this is a story suffused with light. The little mermaid has passed the crucial test: She has turned away from the temptations of darkness. Now, in the bright dawn, she finds herself rising upward surrounded by beautiful, transparent beings. Because of the purity of her endeavor, she has been turned into one of the daughters of the air, who travel about the world making helpful breezes blow. "A mermaid has not an immortal soul, nor can she obtain one unless she wins

the love of a human being" they tell her. "On the power of another hangs her eternal destiny. But the daughters of the air, although they do not possess an immortal soul, can by their good deeds procure one for themselves." The mermaid, lifting her eyes to the sun, feels them filling with her first tears. Invisible, she kisses the forehead of the bride, fans the prince and then mounts up into the sky with her companions.

The Disney movie by the same name, no doubt seen, if not memorized, by virtually every little girl in the United States since it came out a few years ago—it's one of the most successful Disney movies ever made, and it's been one of the top ten best-selling videos for over seventy weeks—has a different finale and a different agenda. If you don't know the original, or if you can expunge it from your brain, then the movie might be entertaining in the way that Las Vegas shows are. All of the sorcery of animation has been put into the service of the banal. Steel has been replaced by cotton candy. Force and magical gratification triumph. The virtues of patience and endurance are given scarcely a nod—the cute, determined heroine has three mostly fun-filled days to catch her prince. Her trials are superficial and over quickly, and she's helped along by friendly marine life. She's not interested in acquiring a soul but rather in collecting things—she has a vast cave crammed with loot from sunken ships. The "soul" comes up only in a tune about how other mermaids have sold theirs in a Faustian pact with the sea witch, who resembles the female impersonator Divine and who masquerades as the little mermaid, nearly tricking the prince into marriage as a part of her plot to rule the ocean. In a violent denouement, the witch is killed, leaving the prince free to wed the little mermaid. Now painlessly human and dressed in a snazzy outfit, she's handed over to him by her father. The screen fills with the nuptial kiss. This is how adults who know how to make money believe children should be nourished. Children, apparently happy on a diet of sugar, agree; according to my local bookseller, they now want only the Disney version, which, with its copyrighted artwork, toys and other spinoffs, threatens to crowd the original off the shelves, as has already happened, for instance, to "Pinocchio."

But I believe that Andersen's story, so full of sadness and loveliness and redemption, so subdued in its splendor, like the glimmer of the sun in the ocean depths, will survive, at least for those children—and adults—who want an experience of substance. (There's a great deal more to the story than I've mentioned here. Unlike the ending to the movie and the conclusions we learn to expect in fairy tales and in life, the little mermaid never gains the love of the prince, who remains content with counterfeit and ever oblivious to his silent friend's remarkable origins and her role as his rescuer (just as we can be to the extraordinary side of our being and its quiet help). And her fulfillment doesn't come through marriage. Rather than simply passing from the domain of her father to that of a husband, she attains an independent destiny, and her reward is her continuing capacity to give love whether or not she receives it. And that love grows beyond the particular. She even bestows affection on the bride: Real love has no rivals. Dissatisfied on the bottom of the sea and drawn toward the illumination of the upper realm by the strength of her sentiment for a man, she has, through her own efforts, now gone beyond mundane life and reached the sky, and may even arrive at something much greater that lies beyond the stars.

"THE BELL" (1845)

John L. Greenway (essay date summer 1991)

SOURCE: Greenway, John L. "Reason in Imagination Is Beauty: Oersted's Acoustics and H. C. Andersen's 'The Bell.'" *Scandinavian Studies* 63, no. 3 (summer 1991): 318-25.

[*In the following essay, Greenway explores the influence of Hans Christian Oersted's theories of physics, acoustics, and the nature of God on the narrative of Andersen's fairy tale "The Bell."*]

It may come as a surprise to those who do not consort with scientists save under duress to find that Hans Christian Oersted (1777-1851), the preeminent scientist of the early nineteenth century, discoverer of the relationship between electricity and magnetism in 1820, was the genial hub of cultural debate in Denmark for a generation. Friend and confidant of poets and critics, Oersted convinced a dubious Hans Christian Andersen to publish his *Eventyr, fortalte for Børn* (*Tales Told for Children*) in 1835. Andersen wrote to Henriette Wulff on March 16, 1835, that he had "Dernæst skrevet nogle Eventyr for Børn, om hvilke Ørsted siger, at naar *Improvisatoren* gjør mig berømt, gjør Eventyrene mig udødelig, de ere det meest fuldendte jeg har skrevet, men det synes jeg ikke, han kjender ikke Italien" [Topsøe-Jensen 1: 211] ("Then I wrote some tales for children, about which Oersted says that if *The Improviser* makes me famous, the tales will make me immortal, that they are the most accomplished things I have done, but I don't think so: he doesn't know Italy").

Discussing Andersen's use of the supernatural, Paul V. Rubow pointed out that Andersen was able to modernize the world of the *eventyr* by incorporating Oersted's theories of physics and aesthetics (Rubow 85-94). Andersen not only found the aesthetic bases of Oersted's acoustical theories congenial, but he used them to regulate the representation of reality in at least one of his *eventyr*: **"Klokken"** (1845; **"The Bell"**).

"Klokken" is not as familiar to English-speaking readers as are others of Andersen's tales, so a brief summary will help later show the importance of romantic acoustical theory to the story. Along about evening, people hear a sound like a church-bell coming from the woods. The adults search for the source of this sound, and, coming to the edge of the woods, promptly set up a store. The Emperor offers a title to the discoverer of the melodious tones' source, the award going to the theorist who concluded that the sound came from a wise owl knocking its head on a hollow tree. True, he did not go very far into the forest, but he annually published an article about the owl.

On a glorious, sunny Confirmation Day, the children hear the mysterious sweetness of this bell and decide to find it. Some stop at the store, another stops at the "kluk!" of a brook, and the others go on until they find a hut with a little bell. Yes, they all say, this must be it. All, that is, but the king's son, who says that the bell is too small to produce tones "som saaledes rørte et Menneske-Hjerte" [206] ("that so could move a human heart").

The king's son goes on alone, for as the others say, "saadan En vilde nu altid være klogere" [206] ("someone like him always wanted to be smarter"), meeting a poor boy who had left the group early. They do not go on together: the king's son goes to the left, (the side of the heart): "det var snart ligesom et Orgel spillede dertil" [207] ("it was as though an organ played along"). The boy goes to the right, for that side looked more beautiful.

At sunset, when nature was "en stor, hellig Kirke" [208] ("a great, holy church") and the colors of the day blended with the starry gleams of night, at the shining altar of the sun, in total joy the king's son "bredte sine Arme ud mod Himlen, mod Havet og Skoven" [208] ("spread out his arms toward the heavens, the sun and the forest"). The poor boy joins him then, and holding hands "i Naturens og Poesiens store Kirke" [208] ("in the great church of nature and poetry"), there sounded around them "den usynlige hellige Klokke" [208] ("the invisible holy bell").

Clearly, the story demands interpretation. Grønbech points out that, while Andersen's literary works resist being regulated by a systematic philosophy, **"Klokken"** belongs to that class of Andersen's stories where an idea regulates the narrative (177-78). True; the transcendent experience is not for all: many are misled by bourgeois motives (the shop) or deceived by empirical evidence (the bell in the hut). Still, the church of nature stands accessible to some, be they rich or poor. It exists; it can be found. So far, so obvious.

While **"Klokken"** should be a charming allegory of romantic innocence, knowledge of the acoustical theories of Andersen's scientist friend and mentor will allow us to read the story on a deeper level and help explain why, at the end, we do not find the transcendent bell. Now obsolete, Oersted's theories lent what would at the time have been a realistic dimension to Andersen's tale.

Oersted's lifelong interest in acoustics complimented the studies in electromagnetism which made him famous. In order for us to see the aesthetic role physics plays in **"Klokken,"** we must enter his imaginative world for a moment and understand the reciprocal relationships Oersted saw among sound, light, nature, and God.

Although Oersted became famous for his discovery of electromagnetism, his first serious experiments were conducted on acoustical figures (*Klangfigurer*). In 1808, he found that if one draws a bow along the edge of a pumice-covered glass plate, symmetrical patterns emerge. In the conclusion of his "Forsøg over Klangfigurer" (1808; "Experiments upon Acoustical Figures") he suggests that electricity could be generated through sound vibrations, and that light acts on the eye much as sound does on the ear. Anticipating later directions in his research, he then speaks of nature's "dybe, uendelige, ufattelige Fornuft, som igiennem Tonestrømmen taler til os" [*Naturvidenskablige skrifter* 2:34] ("profound incomprehensible reason which speaks to us through the flow of music").

He continues this line of thought in his "Om Grunden til den Fornøjelse Tonerne frembringe" ("On the Cause of the Pleasure Produced by Music") in 1808. The symmetry of acoustical figures becomes beautiful, he argues, because the oscillations express the underlying "reason in nature." Although Oersted modified his theories as he matured, he always insisted that nature's hidden reason expresses itself in tones. In his collection of philosophical essays *Aanden i Naturen* (1850; *The Soul in Nature,* 1852, 1966), appearing a year before his death, he makes the point explicit by titling an essay "The Same Principles of Beauty Exist in the Objects Submitted to the Eye and to the Ear" (325-51).

Oersted's experiments with acoustical figures seem to have been immensely interesting to non-scientists as well as to scientists, for to Oersted they demonstrated the scientific basis of beauty's physical reality. Søren Kierkegaard noted that Oersted's inner harmony reminded him of an acoustical figure; the artist Ekeberg painted him with a glass plate in his hand, and Oersted in a verse used acoustical figures as a metaphor for scientific inquiry (V. Andersen 111). Authors as diverse as Frederika Bremer and Carsten Hauch employed the image, and H. C. Andersen refers to acoustical figures in **Kun en Spillemand** (Kuehle; Rubow 86).

We may better understand the importance of acoustics in Oersted's imagination, as well as its role in Andersen's tale, by returning to Oersted's repeated emphasis upon the "unity of nature" (Knight, "The Scientist" 82-87). A second reading of **"Klokken"** leads one to notice that Andersen emphasizes the day's bright sunshine, and at the end of the story the king's son and the poor boy are inundated by color as well as sound. Oersted would read this ending as subtle and realistic: to Oersted, electricity, light, heat and sound were all forms of oscillation in the physical world and, hence, express Nature's fundamental unity, symmetry, and essential reason, much as did his early work with acoustical figures.

While Oersted's theories, with their aesthetic bent, differ markedly from our own, his contemporaries held similar views. Humphry Davy (who read the galley proofs for the second edition of the *Lyrical Ballads*) held similar theories and expressed them in poetry (Fullmer 118-26; Knight, "The Scientist" 72) while distrusting Oersted's Germanic background. If we look briefly at Oersted's view of light, we see that the transcendental epiphany at the end of **"Klokken"** becomes an aspect of romantic physics, as well as a literary phenomenon, indeed a realistic event if we remember that sound, electricity, and light are but differing expressions of the unity, of the "spirit in nature." Oersted saw the significance of his 1820 discovery of electromagnetism as proving just this unity of *Kraft* (later called "energy").

In 1815-1816, Oersted argues in his "Theorie over Lyset" ("Theory of Light") that light comes from a unification of electrical and chemical forces, heat being a slower form of light. In his "Betragtninger over Forholdet mellem Lyden, Lyset, Varmen og Electriciteten" (1829; "Observations upon the Relationship among Sound, Light, Heat, and Electricity"), he relies again upon oscillations to show that their interdependence expresses the fundamental unity of nature. In the later "Undersøgelse over Lyset med Hensyn paa det Skjønnes Naturlære" (1842; "Investigations of Light with a View to the Natural Doctrine of the Beautiful"), Oersted develops the metaphorical implications of this theory: light connects the universe and lets us feel like participants in all creation (*Naturvidenskablige skrifter* 2:509).

In "Theory of Light," Oersted describes the psychological effect of light as the bringing forth of joy, an assertion to which he repeatedly returned. The assumption of a unity in nature, an assertion which regulated his research (and that of other nineteenth-century scientists in diverse fields as well) led him in his "Observations on the History of Chemistry" (1806) to conjecture that human neural sensibility might be a form of his earlier "Law of Oscillation," operating upon the organism as a consequence of sound, light and electricity (*Soul in Nature* 320-23). With "Experiments on Acoustical Figures," Oersted argues that this operation cannot be reduced to mere mechanics, for aural effects symbolize nature's transcendent unity and reason: "det som i Tonekunsten henriver og tryller os, og lader os glemme alt, medens vor Siæl svæver hen paa Tonestrømmen, det er ikke spåndte Nervers mechaniske Pirring," he says, "men det er Naturens dybe, uendelige, ufattelige Fornuft, som igiennem Tonestrømmen taler til os" [*Naturvidenskablige skrifter* 2:34] (in acoustics, that which exalts and enchants us, letting us forget all while ascending on the stream of sound, is not the mechanical excitement of tensed nerves, but it is nature's deep, infinite incomprehensible reason which speaks to us through the stream of sound).

The mind, Oersted asserts, evolved under the same dynamics as did nature. In "On the Physical Effects of Tones," Oersted believes that the "meeting of numerous oscillations, which you assume in the nervous system, is not an exception from the usual mode of operation in nature, but belongs to her universal laws" (*Soul in Nature* 363). In the "Investigations of Light" (1842) he again draws the metaphorical implications of his theory by concluding that light is in essence an image of life, dark of death (*Naturvidenskablige skrifter* 2:507).

Oersted repeatedly admonished his many friends who wrote imaginative literature that narratives set in the present should not violate this underlying reason in nature (and hence, for him, its beauty and divine origin). In *Mitlivs eventyr* (1855; *The Story of My Life*) Andersen credits Oersted's belief that "Jeg vil at den af Digteren fremstillede Verden, med al dens Frihed og Dristighed, dog skal beherskedes af de same Love, som det aandelige Øie opdager, den virklege Verden, og uden hvilke det er ikke værd at leve deri" [2:167] ("I want the poetically represented world, with all its freedom and daring, to be circumscribed nonetheless by the same laws the spiritual eye discovers: that real world, without which it is not worth living in").

Andersen was not immune to criticism of this sort, and he took Oersted's comments seriously. He relates that when he translated Byron's "Darkness" into Danish in 1833, Oersted objected that Byron's bleak vision of entropic anarchy at the end of things was wrong: Oersted is said to have commented that "'Digteren tør tænke sig,' sagde han, 'at Solen forsvinder fra Himlen, men han maa vide, at der kommer da ganske andet Resultater, end dette Mørke, end dette Kulde, disse Begivenheder, dette er en Vanvittigs Phantasie!'" [2:10-11] ("'The artist might well imagine,' he said, 'that the sun disappears from the heavens, but he ought to know that something very different from the darkness, from this chill would occur; these occurrences are the imagination of a madman!'"). Andersen writes that, having thought about it, he agreed. After Oersted's death, Andersen recalled that "Ørsted forlangte med Rette stræng Sandhed selv i Phantasiens Raaderum" [2:245] ("Oersted correctly insisted upon strict verisimilitude, even in the chamber of the imagination").

As we return to Andersen's story after this excursion into one aspect of his friend's physics and the aesthetic judgments stemming from them, we see how Andersen could well have used Oersted's theories of sound and light to underscore his theme with what, at the time, would be realistic detail: realistic in the sense of conforming to contemporary scientific theory. The narrator of **"Klokken"** says that the sound "affected human hearts so strangely"; Oersted suggests in "The Physical Effects of Tones" that the harmony regulating the acoustical figures on glass could be extended to human sympathy. We need only recall his emphasis on the unity of nature to see how Oersted would connect chemical affinity, acoustical effects, and an affinity between nature and mind. "This accordance between nature and mind can hardly be ascribed to chance," he says in "Observations on the History of Chemistry" (*Soul in Nature* 323).

Andersen says he wrote to Oersted that *The Soul in Nature* prompted his essays on **"Faith and Science"** and **"Poetry's California"** in his collection *I Sverrige* (*In Sweden*) where he asserts that "Videnskabens Sollys skal gjennemtrænge Digteren" [121] ("the sunlight of science must penetrate the poet"). Oersted replied, according to Andersen in *Mit livs eventyr,* that "maaske bliver De Den af Digterne, der vil udrette meest for Videnskaben" [2:117] ("perhaps you are going to be that very poet, who will accomplish the most for science"). Andersen, when he received the second part of *The Soul in Nature,* replied that "hvad især gjør mig glad, er, at jeg her synes kun at se min egen Tanke, den, jeg tidligere ikke saaledes har gjort mig klar selv" [2:118] ("what above all gladdens me is that here I seem to see only my own thoughts, which I had not previously clarified for myself").

Oersted seems to have had a similar vision of the relationship between literature and science. Years before, in 1807, he wrote to his friend Adam Oehlenschläger that the scientist and the poet begin at different points: the scientist begins with the real world and ends in a sort of artistic experience; the poet, though, begins with intuition, which he strives to clarify for others: "Naar han har naaet Grendsen af sin Bane, sammensmælter han Kunsten med Videnskaben. Saaledes skiller Digteren og Tænkeren sig ad, ved Begyndelsen af deres Vej, for ved Enden at omfavne hinanden" [Oehlenschläger 3:21] ("When he has reached the end of his course, he fuses art with science. The poet and the scientist differ at the beginning of their path, only to embrace each other at the end").

Some critics have speculated that Georg Brandes's interpretation of **"Klokken"** was wrong: the king's son is not poetry; Andersen saw himself as the poor boy in the story and Oersted as the king's son (Holm 43; Rubow 94). If we accept this conjecture, interesting interpretations unfold: Andersen does not tell of the travails of the poor boy, who takes the path on the right because it is beautiful, but of those of the king's son, who takes the path on the left because that is where the heart is. The king's son knows enough empirical acoustics to realize that the small bell the children found was much too small and delicate to be heard so far away, but he is not limited by the empirical. He lets his heart guide his reason to the ultimate, transcendent experience.

If indeed Oersted was the model for the king's son, Andersen understood his older friend deeply, particularly at the end of the story. After having made a fool of himself early in his career by venturing into the speculative physics of the *Naturphilosophen* (Gower), Oersted eventually broke with Schelling and, later, Steffens over their lack of experimental rigor and their belief that one could attain ultimate knowledge through philosophy alone (*Naturvidenskablige skrifter* 1:25; Michelsen 35; Stauffer 39).[1] Oersted had a bitter feud with Grundtvig and the latter's *Verdens Krønike,* in part because of Grundtvig's assumption he could speak with God's voice. Oersted insisted that human reason could never be complete unto itself, "for our Reason, although originally related to the infinite, is limited by the finite, and can only imperfectly disengage itself from it. No mortal has been permitted to penetrate and comprehend the whole" (*The Soul in Nature* 451). Importantly, while the bell the children find in the forest is beautiful, the source of the sound is invisible to the king's son and the poor boy alike. They do not discover the bell but experience transcendence through light. Oersted maintains that light allows us to penetrate into nature and not only knits us into the universe, but catalyzes the feeling of joy as it does to the king's son (*The Soul in Nature* 113).

Michelsen points out Oersted's preference for organic metaphors over the abstract: he did not call his final collection of philosophic essays "The *Idea* in Nature," as would a Platonist or a *Naturphilosoph,* but *The* Soul [*Aanden*] *in Nature* (Michelsen 36). We have no evidence that Oersted communicated his 1807 views to Andersen, but given the continuity of Oersted's views, in particular his belief in the unity of nature, the conjecture is plausible. Indeed, I suspect Andersen pays quite a compliment to his friend and envies the moment of scientific insight: at the moment of transcendence for the king's son, oscillations fuse, and nature becomes one with mind. The waves of the ocean meet the light of the setting sun, "Alt smeltede sammen i glødende Farver," acoustically mingling: "Skoven sang og Havet sang og hans Hjerte sang med" [208] ("everything melted together in glowing colors: the forest sang and the ocean sang and his heart sang along"). When the poor boy (whose imagination we do not share) arrives, the final synthesis becomes that symmetry Oersted saw expressing creation's inner reason: in the great church of nature and poetry the last sounds we hear from the holy bell are hallelujahs of "salige Aander" ("blessed Spirits").

After Oersted's death in 1851, Andersen's view of nature seems to have changed to one extolling the drama of conquest and power, as we see, for instance, in **"Den ny Aarhundredes Musa"** [1861; **"The New Century's Muse"**] (Busk-Jensen 6:65-66). In **"Klokken,"** however, Andersen's view is the same as that of Oersted. Oersted almost paraphrases Andersen's poetic conclusion with his own elevated prose: "The holy engagement of art does not spring from conscious reflection, but from an unconscious and mystic sanctuary. . . . Every melting harmony, every resolved dissonance, is again a higher combination, which in itself bears the same stamp of reason, and which all its parts cooperate towards an inward unity" (*The Soul in Nature* 351).

As we have seen, we cannot separate Oersted's physics from his aesthetics, and Andersen, I believe, incorporated Oersted's physics of sound and light to give his tale a realistic context we no longer recognize. Thanks to Oersted, **"Klokken"** displays a physics of spiritual beauty: in a verse to Andersen, Oersted wrote: "Fornuften i Fornuften er det Sande, / Fornuften i Villien er det Gode, / Fornuften i Phantasien er det Skjønne" [*Mit livs eventyr* 2:245] ("Reason in Reason is Truth; Reason in Will is Goodness; Reason in Imagination is Beauty").

Note

1. He did, however, retain their faith in the unity of nature, which not only guided his experiments in electromagnetism but later led to the articulation of the Conservation of Energy (Stauffer, Knight, "Steps").

Works Cited

Andersen, Hans Christian. *I Sverrige. Romaner og Rejseskildringer.* Eds. Morten Borup and H. A. Paludan. Vol. 7. Copenhagen: Gyldendal, 1944.

———. *Mit livs eventyr.* Ed. H. Topsøe-Jensen. 2 vols. Copenhagen: Gyldendal, 1951.

———. "Klokken." *Eventyr.* Vol. 2. *Nye eventyr 1844-48, Eventyr 1850, samt Historier 1852-55.* Ed. Erik Dal. Copenhagen: Hans Reitzels Forlag, 1964. 204-08.

Andersen, Vilhelm. *Tider og typer af Dansk aands historie.* I, 2 (Goethe), 2 (2nd half of 19C). Copenhagen: Gyldendal, 1916.

Busk-Jensen, Lise, *et al.,* eds. *Dansk litteratur historie.* Vol. 6. Copenhagen: Gyldendal, 1985.

Fullmer, J. Z. "The Poetry of Sir Humphry Davy." *Chymia* 6 (1960): 102-26.

Grønbech, Bo. *Hans Christian Andersens Eventyrverden.* Copenhagen: Munksgaard, 1967.

Holm, Søren. "'Klokken' og de to store H. C. er." *Om Filosofi og religion.* Copenhagen: Gyldendal, 1942. 43-46.

Knight, David M. "The Scientist as Sage." *Studies in Romanticism* 6 (1967): 65-88.

———. "Steps towards a Dynamical Chemistry." *Ambix* 14 (1967): 179-97.

Kuehle, Sejer. "H. C. Ørsted og Samtidens unge Digtere." *Gads danske Magasin* 45 (1951): 167-81.

Michelsen, William. *Om H. C. Ørsted og tankebilledet bag Oehlenschlägers Aladdin.* Oehlenschlägers Selskabets skriftserie nr. 3. Copenhagen: Bianco Luno, 1963.

Oehlenschläger, Adam. *Breve fra og til Adam Oehlenschläger: Januar 1798-November 1809.* Ed. H. A. Paludan, *et al.* Vol. 3. Copenhagen: Gyldendal, 1945.

Oersted, Hans Christian. *Naturvidenskablige skrifter.* Ed. Kirstine Meyer. 3 vols. Copenhagen: Andr. Fredr. Høst, 1920.

———. *The Soul in Nature.* Trans. Leonora and Joanna B. Horner. London: N.p., 1852. London: Dawsons of Pall Mall, 1966.

Rubow, Paul V. *H. C. Andersens Eventyr. Forhistorien, Idé og Form, Sprog og Stil.* 2nd ed. Copenhagen: Gyldendal, 1943.

Stauffer, Robert C. "Speculation and Experiment in the Background of Oersted's Discovery of Electromagnetism." *Isis* 48 (1957): 33-50.

Topsøe-Jensen, H., ed. *H. C. Andersen og Henriette Wulff: En Brevveksling.* 3 vols. Odense: Flensted, 1959.

"THE SHADOW" (1847)

Christopher S. Nassaar (essay date September 1995)

SOURCE: Nassaar, Christopher S. "Andersen's 'The Shadow' and Wilde's 'The Fisherman and His Soul': A Case of Influence." *Nineteenth-Century Literature* 50, no. 2 (September 1995): 217-24.

[*In the following essay, Nassaar asserts that Oscar Wilde's "The Fisherman and His Soul" functions as a literary response to Andersen's "The Shadow" and evaluates parallels between the two works.*]

The influence of Hans Christian Andersen's fairy tales on those of Oscar Wilde has long been recognized. Peter Raby, for instance, notes that *The*

Happy Prince and Other Tales is technically and thematically based on Andersen's works.[1] Those who live in Wilde's fairy tales are stock characters from Andersen—a prince, a talking rose and nightingale, a giant, a selfish inanimate object, a rocket that boasts of its own prowess but is blinded by its vanity. Like Andersen's, the axes upon which the tales rest are sacrifice, love, and the abnegation of the self. In Wilde's tales there is a "price paid in human suffering for beauty, art, power and wealth, and . . . the corresponding salvation offered by sacrificial love" (Raby, p. 57). But this is not all. In "The Fisherman and His Soul," one of his tales in *A House of Pomegranates,* Wilde deliberately responds to and counterpoints a specific tale of Andersen's, **"The Shadow."** Wilde's reworking of this earlier tale merits detailed analysis.

"The Shadow" and "The Fisherman and His Soul" have not been linked before, probably because of the obvious influence on Wilde's tale of Andersen's famous fairy tale **"The Little Mermaid."** In this tale a beautiful mermaid abandons the sea for the dry land and acquires legs and an immortal soul for the sake of marrying a human. Wilde, in his usual paradoxical way, inverts this basic situation in "The Fisherman and His Soul." But the influence of **"The Little Mermaid"** remains technical and sharply limited; **"The Shadow"** is by far the deeper influence.

"The Shadow" is a noticeable anomaly in the body of Andersen's fairy tales, for it offers no hope of salvation, redemption, or change. Whereas the typical Andersen tale is redemptive, in the long and dark **"The Shadow,"** evil triumphs and innocence is put to death. The tale has multiple levels of interpretation, and the slow disintegration of the learned man's character is a precursor of Kafka's "The Metamorphosis," where, bit by bit, piece by piece, a man disappears.

In **"The Shadow"** a learned man visiting a foreign country sees the fleeting figure of "a graceful slender girl" and hears magical music from the apartment facing his.[2] He jokingly bids his shadow to see who lives there. The Shadow obeys, and does not return. Years pass, until the Shadow, dressed in expensive clothes and obviously having risen in the world, knocks on the learned man's door, introducing himself. The learned man, who makes his living writing of "the true and the good and the beautiful" (p. 198), graciously invites his former Shadow in and treats it courteously. Embarrassed by its past, the Shadow seeks to pay its former master for any inconvenience it may have caused in not returning or to compensate the man's new shadow. Then, more ominously, the Shadow wishes the learned man to serve as its own shadow. The man refuses, treating his former Shadow with familiarity—which the Shadow disdains.

The Shadow explains what happened to it many years before. The graceful slender girl that the learned man had seen in the facing apartment was Poetry, and the three weeks the Shadow stayed with her were equivalent to three thousand years in acquired knowledge. It learned all that man knew and wrote in verse, enough to make a shadow into a man. The Shadow, naked when in the presence of Poetry, then made its way in the world, first hiding under the skirt of a woman selling cakes, running in the moonlight, ducking against walls. It eavesdropped and spied on men, women, and children and soon learned that "it's a low-down world we live in" (p. 198). It blackmailed those whose secrets it learned, and it began to rise in the world.

The Shadow again leaves its former master, only to return some time later when the learned man, now ill and "dogged by care and sorrow," is unable to make a living because the world is as attracted to truth, beauty, and goodness as "roses to a cow" (p. 199). He agrees to go with the Shadow to a spa—he to recover his health, the Shadow to grow a beard that was not forming as it should. The Shadow insists that they go as equals, and that it will pay all expenses. The learned man agrees, but soon his familiarity with his old companion changes: the Shadow agrees to be familiar with its old master, but the former master must treat the Shadow with deference. The Shadow calls the learned man what it wants; the man must call the Shadow "sir."

At the spa the Shadow meets a princess suffering from over-acute vision who can see that it lacks a shadow. The Shadow claims that the learned man is its Shadow and that it not only has its shadow dress up as a human being, but that it also bought its shadow—at great expense—a shadow. Impressed, the princess thinks to marry the Shadow but first wants to test its intelligence. Rather than answer her questions, it sends her to the learned man, who impresses the princess. She believes that the Shadow must be that much more profound than its own shadow.

On the day of the marriage the Shadow tells the learned man that he must be its shadow and is only required to lie at its feet once a year when the Shadow and its wife show themselves to the people.

The man balks, accuses his former shadow of trying to swindle the country, threatens to reveal the truth to the princess, and is arrested on orders of the Shadow. The Shadow tells the princess that the learned man went mad, believing that he was a man and that the Shadow was his shadow. The princess commiserates, and as the cannons go off to celebrate their wedding the learned man does not hear them, for he has already been put to death.

"The Fisherman and His Soul" is Wilde's response to **"The Shadow."** The first counterpoint is when the fisherman casts off his soul. The learned man had sent his Shadow on a lighthearted mission, expecting it to return shortly, but the fisherman, in his innocence, associates with witches and with Satan himself in order to cast off his soul, which is also his shadow:

> [The witch] was silent for a few moments, and a look of terror came over her face. Then she brushed her hair back from her forehead, and smiling strangely she said to him, "What men call the shadow of the body is not the shadow of the body, but is the body of the Soul. Stand on the sea-shore with thy back to the moon, and cut away from around thy feet thy shadow, which is thy Soul's body, and bid thy Soul leave thee, and it will do so."[3]

In the fisherman's case the action is much more serious—even the witch is terrified—but his motive is love, or rather love of a specific object, the mermaid, rather than a passing fascination with "a slender pretty girl." The fisherman cannot live in the mermaid's world with a soul, for the sea-folk have no souls.

The mermaid and the slender girl who turns out to be Poetry are also counterpointed. For one thing it is the fisherman, not his soul, who goes to live with the beautiful mermaid, while it is the learned man's Shadow who spends three weeks with Poetry. The mermaid lives in a magnificent undersea world and is innocent of evil, but Poetry lives in a very different world and knows all about the dark side of life. In Poetry's antechamber the Shadow is exposed to all that she has to offer: "I saw everything," it says several times (p. 197). But seeing everything there was to see and knowing everything there was to know does not produce a wise, knowing, exalted figure, as the learned man—and the reader—would expect. Rather, it produces a self-centered, materialistic, power-hungry, manipulative human creature with the instincts of a killer. When stripped of the veneer of civilization and a manufactured religious and moral

code, the core of man's repressed self is a homicidal beast. The Shadow, during its three-week evolution to humanhood, learned of its "innermost nature." Only after its incubation with Poetry did it realize its essence: "In those days I didn't understand my own nature; in the antechamber it dawned upon me—I was a man" (p. 198). But the Shadow learns not only that it is a man: it learns also that its essence is evil. The mermaid and Poetry are both beautiful and both sing a magnificent song, but Poetry teaches a nihilistic lesson and introduces a dark world that is quite different from the mermaid's childlike, innocent one.

There are many parallels and counterpoints between the fisherman's soul and the Shadow. Both are able to exist independently of the bodies to which they were formerly attached. Both are sent without guidelines into a world that is thoroughly evil, cruel, and sinful, and both rise in this world. And both then return to the bodies from which they were separated. Survival—indeed, success—at any cost becomes for them the prime reason to exist. The ethical code upon which both the fisherman and the learned man anchor their lives is cut away for the soul and the Shadow. Both entities, by being freed, become flawed and corrupt. The soul seeks at whatever cost to reunite with the fisherman—tempting it with wisdom, riches, and finally (successfully), carnality. The Shadow, having stayed at Poetry's apartment for three weeks when it first left the learned man, does not consort, as the man imagined, with "the gods of antiquity" there, or "the heroes of old doing battle," or "darling children at play," whether in "green forest" or "holy church" (p. 197)—the stock, conventional figures and places of poetry. The Shadow's first action after learning enough to become a man is to hide in shame at its nakedness—for the Shadow there is no period of Edenic innocence in becoming human. It immediately hides under the skirt of a woman, becoming both the immaculate infant of Poetry and of the flesh of a common woman selling cakes. Left on its own, the Shadow makes its way in the world by writing letters of blackmail, while the learned man writes of the true, good, and beautiful. Finally, the Shadow tries to reunite with the learned man, but only in order to subordinate and control its former master—to turn him, indeed, into its shadow.

A clear difference between the fisherman's soul and the Shadow is that Andersen—unlike Wilde—does not catalog the evil world that the Shadow encounters in the fairy tale. He allows the reader's imagination free play, banally stating that the Shadow peeped into rooms ranging from the highest floor to the ground floor—the entire society—and saw the corruption: "I saw the most inconceivable things happening among women, men, parents and their own dear darling children" (p. 198). Being able to see exactly how humans act behind closed doors, behind their masks—this is what the Shadow will copy. The idyllic world of his former master, who saw heroes doing battle and ancient gods striding through great halls, does not motivate him. In "The Fisherman and His Soul," on the other hand, there is a litany of evil that the soul experiences. The soul worships false prophets, it lies, it steals, it inflicts pain, it kills, and it compels the fisherman to do the same when they are reunited. On dry land, in the world of experience it was forced into, treachery and debauchery become part of its existence—and Wilde describes all this in detail.

A more basic difference is that the soul becomes amoral while the Shadow becomes immoral. Both return to their respective masters with the intention of dominating them, but when the Shadow fails to control its former master it kills him, while the soul finally yields to the fisherman and is saved within the Christian framework of the tale:

> And after the second year was over, the Soul said to the young Fisherman at nighttime, and as he sat in the wattled house alone, "Lo! now I have tempted thee with evil, and I have tempted thee with good, and thy love is stronger than I am. Wherefore will I tempt thee no longer, but I pray thee to suffer me to enter thy heart, that I may be one with thee even as before."
>
> "Surely thou mayest enter," said the young Fisherman, "for in the days when with no heart thou didst go through the world thou must have much suffered."
>
> "Alas!" cried his Soul, "I can find no place of entrance, so compassed about with love is this heart of thine."
>
> (p. 270)

After the mermaid dies and her body is washed ashore, however, the fisherman's heart breaks and the soul manages to get in: "he kissed with mad lips the cold lips of the Mermaid, and the heart that was within him brake. And as through the fullness of his love his heart did break, the Soul found an entrance and entered in, and was one with him even as before" (p. 271). Having lost his heart at the beginning of the tale, the soul regains it at the end and is saved—quite unlike the Shadow, whose triumph is completely temporal and nonspiritual.

The learned man and the fisherman are also paralleled and counterpointed. The basic parallel is obvi-

ous, for they are both able to separate a part of themselves and send it out into the world independently. A difference between them is that Andersen's protagonist is very learned while Wilde's is a common man, still very young and with no education to speak of. But Wilde treats this difference in a very ironic and paradoxical way. For it is the fisherman who has real knowledge: he knows the value of love, while the learned man writes of "the true and the good and the beautiful" without focusing on love or experiencing it directly. At the beginning of Wilde's tale the fisherman's love is incomplete, for it is limited to the beautiful mermaid, but at the end it becomes all-encompassing, like that of Coleridge's ancient mariner. His education becomes complete, he is purged of all imperfection, and he enters heaven.

This brings us to the final and most basic counterpoint between **"The Shadow"** and "The Fisherman and His Soul": the ending. Both the learned man and the fisherman are innocents at the beginning of their respective tales. The learned man lives in a private world of books and writes about truth and goodness and beauty, while the soulless fisherman lives in a sparkling underwater paradise with the mermaid. Neither has any real knowledge of evil: both learn about it as their respective tales develop, the former from his Shadow and the latter from his soul.

This remarkable thematic and structural correspondence between the tales veers at the end. Wilde fixes his fairy tale in a universal moral grid that Andersen ignores. There is salvation for the fisherman within a Christian framework; indeed, the diction is steeped in the Bible. The priest, who first drove the fisherman away and cursed the sea-folk, repents—though he knows not why—and blesses all creatures in God's world. Though the fisherman cannot return to the innocence of the sea and his life with the mermaid on earth, he does return to innocence in a higher manner, with his soul in his heart, in life after death. In **"The Shadow"** there is no room for two, and the problem is resolved in a very different manner: the Shadow, who had long sought to subordinate the learned man to the status of shadow, eventually has his former master killed. The innocent—even naive—world of the man was more make-believe than real. He wrote of man's supposed higher nature—truth, goodness, beauty—but those terms meant nothing to the society of the fairy tale and were as useful as "roses to a cow." The genetic code of man in the Shadow's world is power, money, and corruption, and the Shadow can only become a full man when it kills its rival. At the spa where it meets the princess, the evil essence of man still has not fully gelled within the Shadow: its difficulty in growing a beard signifies its lack of absolute manhood. The complete dominance over the innocent can only be achieved if the learned man agrees to become its shadow, something he will never do. Therefore he is killed, with the help of the Shadow's bride, the princess. She, who is at the spa to cure her acute vision, sees only too well that the man she should marry is not the philosophical learned man who would guide her country justly, but the duplicitous Shadow whose distinguishing characteristic is that it has a shadow that has a shadow. The learned man could never merit the princess in the world of experience, but his opposite—and rival—could. When she is told that the learned man, who she believes is the Shadow's shadow, has gone mad, it is she who proposes that he be put to death: "How unfortunate for him! It would be a real kindness to relieve him of the scrap of life that is left him" (pp. 201-2). The learned man dies without having loved his Shadow or tried to save it. He deals with evil by confronting and threatening it, and it crushes him.

Wilde's tale is a Christian response to Andersen's nihilistic vision in **"The Shadow."** In Andersen's tale evil triumphs while innocence gradually disintegrates and is finally destroyed, for it can survive only if it fully submits to evil and serves it, which it cannot and will not do. There is no attempt to reconcile opposites. In Wilde's tale all-encompassing love—Christian love—is the one true road. If this road is followed, then it does not really matter how one's adventure on earth ends. The mermaid, the fisherman, and the soul all die, and they are buried in unhallowed ground on orders of the priest. But the grave blooms, signifying that they are in heaven, and the flowers cause a strange transformation in the priest that leads him to bless all the creatures in God's world, including the sea-creatures, whom he had earlier cursed. Andersen's tale was about the triumph of evil, but Wilde's is about the victory of all-embracing Christian love.

The Christian faith displayed in Wilde's tale is typical of his fairy tales. Between 1886 and 1889 Wilde wrote eleven fairy tales, most of which were published in two volumes, *The Happy Prince and Other Tales* and *A House of Pomegranates.*[4] In the earlier volume the statue of the happy prince strips itself of all its expensive gold and jewelry and gives them to the poor, and its heart, full of love and pity, finally breaks. The statue clearly develops into a Christ-figure and is elevated by God to heaven at the end of the story. In "The Selfish Giant" the giant also develops in the same direction: he acquires a heart full of love, and the tiny child he rushes to save at the end turns out to be Christ, who has come to save the giant. In the latter volume, "The Young King," which is the most obviously Christian of all Wilde's tales, relates the story of a young boy who lives in a beautiful palace and is destined to be king. On his coronation day, however, he abandons his objects of art and his wealth and becomes a Christ-figure. The people reject him, but he is crowned by God. Even those tales that are not explicitly Christian are built on the principle that Christian love is the highest value. "The Nightingale and the Rose" and "The Star-Child" are good examples.[5]

"The Fisherman and His Soul" definitely fits into the Christian pattern of Wilde's fairy tales. It is a deliberate, extended response to **"The Shadow,"** rooted in the former tale and reacting to it, but at the same time achieving an independent existence and asserting Christian values as opposed to Andersen's nihilistic ones.

Notes

1. See *Oscar Wilde* (Cambridge: Cambridge Univ. Press, 1988), pp. 56-57.

2. Hans Christian Andersen, "The Shadow," in *Eighty Fairy Tales,* ed. Elias Bredsdorff, trans. R. P. Keigwin (New York: Pantheon Books, 1976), p. 194. Further references appear in the text.

3. Oscar Wilde, "The Fisherman and His Soul," in *The Complete Works of Oscar Wilde,* ed. J. B. Foreman (London: Collins, 1966), p. 255. Further references appear in the text.

4. The earliest two tales, "Lord Arthur Savile's Crime" and "The Canterville Ghost," were published separately and are not included in either of the two volumes.

5. Although one does not usually think of Wilde as a believing Christian, he did go through a Christian phase between 1886 and 1889, as clearly evinced by his fairy tales. By 1890 Wilde's Christian convictions had collapsed and he had begun exploring human evil in *The Picture of Dorian Gray.* Toward the end of his brief life he returned to Christianity, as shown in part by his deathbed conversion to Catholicism. For a full study of the theme of innocence and evil in Wilde's works, and of his shifting attitude to Christ, see Christopher S. Nassaar, *Into the Demon Universe: A Literary Exploration of Oscar Wilde* (New Haven: Yale Univ. Press, 1974).

FURTHER READING

Bibliography

Bredsdorff, Elias. *Danish Literature in English Translation—With a Special Hans Christian Andersen Supplement: A Bibliography.* Copenhagen, Denmark: Ejnar Munksgaard, 1950, 198 p.

Presents bibliographic information on Andersen's fairy tales, novels, autobiographies, and other literary works.

Biographies

Bredsdorff, Elias. *Hans Christian Andersen: The Story of His Life and Work, 1805-1875.* London, England: Phaidon, 1975, 376 p.

Offers a comprehensive biography of Andersen with selected commentary on his fairy tales.

Enquist, Per Olov. "The Hans Christian Andersen Saga." *Scandinavian Review* 74, no. 3 (autumn 1986): 64-9.

Posits that Andersen's personal history—particularly his childhood—greatly affected his professional career.

Prince, Alison. *Hans Christian Andersen: The Fan Dancer.* London, England: Allison & Busby, 1998, 401 p.

Analyzes Andersen's life and career from the perspective that Andersen allegedly suffered from "a fiercely suppressed homosexuality."

Rossel, Sven Hakon. "Hans Christian Andersen: Writer for All Ages and Nations." *Scandinavian Review* 74, no. 2 (summer 1986): 88-97.

Examines Andersen's personal history and the international appeal of his work.

Criticism

Anderson, Christopher L. "Andersen's 'The Snow Queen' and Matute's *Primera Memoria*: To the Victor Go the Spoils." *Crítica Hispánica* 14, nos. 1-2 (1992): 13-27.

Evaluates the impact of Andersen's fairy tale "The Snow Queen" on Ana María Matute's novel *Primera Memoria.*

Burns, Mary M. "Andersen's Nightingale." *Horn Book Magazine* 62, no. 1 (January-February 1986): 78-9.

Reviews four different editions of Andersen's fairy tale "The Nightingale" and briefly discusses the story's narrative structure.

Knowles, Murray Kirsten Malmkjær. "Key Terms in H. C. Andersen's Fairytales and Their Translations into English." *Babel* 37, no. 4 (1991): 203-11.

Argues that Andersen's "The Princess on the Pea" and "The Swine Boy" revolve around a contrast of the genuine versus the artificial.

Lederer, Wolfgang. *The Kiss of the Snow Queen: Hans Christian Andersen and Man's Redemption by Woman.* Berkeley, Calif.: University of California Press, 1986, 262 p.

Studies the relationships, themes, and symbolism present in Andersen's fairy tale "The Snow Queen."

Additional coverage of Andersen's life and career is contained in the following sources published by Thomson Gale: *Authors and Artists for Young Adults,* **Vol. 57;** *Children's Literature Review,* **Vol. 6;** *DIS-Covering Authors*; *DISCovering Authors: British Edition*; *DISCovering Authors: Canadian Edition*; *DISCovering Authors Modules: Most-studied Authors, Popular Fiction and Genres Authors*; *DISCovering Authors 3.0*; *European Writers,* **Vol. 6;** *Literature Resource Center*; *Major Authors and Illustrators for Children and Young Adults,* **Eds. 1, 2;** *Nineteenth-Century Literature Criticism,* **Vols. 7, 79;** *Reference Guide to Short Fiction,* **Ed. 2;** *Reference Guide to World Literature,* **Eds. 2, 3;** *Short Story Criticism,* **Vols. 6, 56;** *Something about the Author,* **Vol. 100;** *Twayne's World Authors*; *World Literature Criticism,* **Vol. 1;** *Writers for Children*; **and** *Yesterday's Authors of Books for Children,* **Vol. 1.**

Ann Brashares
1967-

American author of young adult novels and juvenile biographies.

The following entry presents an overview of Brashares's career through 2005.

INTRODUCTION

Using the premise of a "magical" pair of pants passed between friends, Brashares created a best-selling series for young adults with *The Sisterhood of the Traveling Pants* (2001) and its subsequent sequels, *The Second Summer of the Sisterhood* (2003) and *Girls in Pants: The Third Summer of the Sisterhood* (2005). Centering on the lives of four teenage girls, the novels demonstrate the bond between the friends and illustrate the experiences associated with the adolescence and burgeoning maturity of young women. The protagonists—life-long friends—pledge to send a pair of secondhand jeans from friend to friend the first summer they are to be separated. These traveling pants thus take on a metaphoric quality, uniting the best friends across the thousands of miles separating them. The pants have ten rules concerning the possessor; the tenth rule sums up their symbolic connection to the girls' friendship: "10. Remember: Pants = love. Love your pals. Love yourself."

BIOGRAPHICAL INFORMATION

Brashares was born in 1967, in Alexandria, Virginia. She grew up in Chevy Chase, Maryland, and attended Sidwell Friends, a small Quaker school on the outskirts of Washington D.C., with her three brothers. After finishing secondary school, she enrolled at Barnard College in New York City and earned her B.A. in philosophy. Her goal was to continue her education and earn a Masters degree in philosophy, but Brashares decided to take a year off from school to earn money towards her education expenses. She took an editing job, and her experiences in this position made her reconsider continuing her education; she instead chose to pursue a career in publishing. Her first experience as a published author came in 2001

with *Linus Torvalds: Software Rebel* and *Steve Jobs: Think Different,* two nonfiction children's biographies about noted computer designers, which initially began as editing projects. Brashares eventually took over both projects and was credited as the final author. The concept for *The Sisterhood of the Traveling Pants* came from Brashares's co-worker at 17th Street Productions, whom recounted a pair of jeans that she had shared with a group of friends when she was a teen. Brashares was intrigued by the idea, eventually turning it into the manuscript for her first novel. The book quickly became a best-seller, and in 2005, Warner Brothers released a film adaptation of *The Sisterhood of the Traveling Pants,* directed by Ken Kwapis. Brashares currently resides in Brooklyn, New York, with her husband, Jacob Collins, and their three children.

MAJOR WORKS

Brashares's first two works, *Linus Torvalds: Software Rebel* and *Steve Jobs: Think Different,* were installments in the "Techies" series by Twenty-First Century Books, and each contained a brief biography of the two technological innovators. With *The Sisterhood of the Traveling Pants,* Brashares published her first work of fiction, focusing on four female teenage friends who face their first-ever separation during a summer vacation. Carmen will travel to South Carolina to stay with her father, Lena travels to Greece to visit her grandparents, Bridget journeys to Mexico for soccer camp, and Tibby remains in Washington D.C., pursuing a part-time summer job. The girls are linked by their years of friendship, correspondence, and a "magical" pair of pants—a pair of pants that looks good on each of the girls, even though they all have different physical builds. They decide that each girl will wear the pants for one week and then send it to the next friend, ensuring that the pants will travel twice around the group during the summer. As it turns out, each girl can definitely use the comfort of the pants as they experience a myriad of family and emotional struggles over the summer: Carmen has a difficult time adjusting to her divorced father's new family; Lena falls in love while in Greece; Bridget tries to seduce one of her camp counsellors; and Tibby becomes acquainted with mortality when she befriends a prickly local youth who is diagnosed with cancer. In *The Second Summer of the Sisterhood,* the four friends are now sixteen years old and again journey in different directions for the summer. This year, Carmen stays home and must deal with her jealousy over her mother's new romantic interest, while Tibby attends a film camp and contends with the anxieties associated with peer pressure. Meanwhile, Lena is reacquainted with the boy she left behind in Greece, deciding how far to let the relationship progress, and Bridget travels to Alabama and begins an incognito relationship with her estranged grandmother to find out information about her deceased mother. Brashares continues to examine the joys of friendship and the difficulties of growing up in *Girls in Pants: The Third Summer of the Sisterhood,* in which the four friends have one last summer before they head to college. The girls are—once again—faced with romantic possibilities and family issues, as Carmen adjusts to her mother's pregnancy, Lena must discover a way to finance her college tuition, Bridget becomes a counsellor at a soccer camp where she reencounters her love interest from the first *Sisterhood,* and Tibby must reconcile her feelings when a longtime friend expresses interest in starting a romantic relationship. As the series progresses, the girls trade advice, letters, and "The Pants" to each other, providing emotional support and creating a support network of strong female contemporaries.

CRITICAL RECEPTION

The critical commentary surrounding Brashares's "Traveling Pants" series has been largely favorable. Reviewers have complimented Brashares's use of "The Pants" to tie together her four divergent plotlines, though some have noted that, thanks to the author's skill with character development, the use of "The Pants" as a literary device quickly became unnecessary. Marvin Hoffman has contended that, in *The Second Summer of the Sisterhood,* "[The Pants] seem much less central to the forward movement of the story and to the underscoring of the deep bonds among the friends. The lives of the girls and their mothers are so hugely absorbing in themselves that we hardly need to rely on this device to keep us engaged." Critics have also applauded the authenticity of Brashares's narrative voice, praising her ability to thoughtfully render her teenaged protagonists. In her review of *The Sisterhood of the Traveling Pants,* Linda Bindner has purported that, "All four girls are completely realistic, and even the secondary and adult characters are fully drawn. The result is a complex book about a solid group of friends, with each one a strong and courageous individual in her own right."

AWARDS

The Sisterhood of the Traveling Pants earned a Best Book for Young Adults citation from the American Library Association. It also received an American Booksellers Book Senses Book of the Year designation and the ABC Children's Booksellers Choices Award in 2002. *The Second Summer of the Sisterhood* was a Book Sense Book of the Year Award finalist in 2004. Brashares also won the first-ever Quills Award for a Young Adult/Teen Book in 2005 for *Girls in Pants: The Third Summer of the Sisterhood.*

PRINCIPAL WORKS

Linus Torvalds: Software Rebel (juvenile biography) 2001

The Sisterhood of the Traveling Pants (young adult novel) 2001

Steve Jobs: Think Different (juvenile biography) 2001

The Second Summer of the Sisterhood (young adult novel) 2003

Girls in Pants: The Third Summer of the Sisterhood (young adult novel) 2005

Keep in Touch: Letters, Notes, and More from The Sisterhood of the Traveling Pants (juvenile fiction) 2005

AUTHOR COMMENTARY

Ann Brashares and Dave Weich (interview date 7 September 2001)

SOURCE: Brashares, Ann, and Dave Weich. "Ann Brashares Embarks into Fiction." *Powells.com* (online magazine) http://www.powells.com/authors/brashares.html (7 September 2001).

[*In the following interview, Brashares discusses the evolution of her first young adult novel,* The Sisterhood of the Traveling Pants, *her personal reading preferences, and her experiences in the publishing industry.*]

The day before splitting up for their first summer apart, four best friends discover a pair of pants that just might be magical—how else to explain a pair of jeans that fits each of them so perfectly? That night, they gather in the gym where their mothers first met (okay, technically, they break into the gym) to take the vow of the Traveling Pants.

In the morning, Carmen will reunite with her father in South Carolina. Bridget will set out for soccer camp in Mexico. Lena will board a plane to spend two months with her grandparents in Greece. Tibby, alone among the four, will stay home and work at Wallman's drugstore. The pants will circulate among them, making two rounds by summer's end if their calculations are correct.

The rules, however, took a while to sort out:

1. You must never wash the pants.

2. You must never double cuff the pants. It's tacky.

3. You must never say the word "phat" while wearing the pants. You must also never think to yourself "I am fat" while wearing the pants.

4. You must never let a boy take off the pants (although you may take them off yourself in his presence).

5. You must not pick your nose while wearing the pants. You may, however, scratch casually at your nostril while really kind of picking.

6. You must follow the procedures for documenting your time in the pants.

7. You must write your sisters throughout the summer, no matter how much fun you are having without them.

8. You may only possess the pants for the specified length of time before passing them on to one of your sisters. Failure to comply will result in a severe spanking upon our reunion.

9. You must not wear the pants with a tucked-in shirt and belt. See rule #2.

10. Remember: Pants = love. Love your pals. Love yourself.

"The pants are just pants, and life is just life, full of joys, sorrows, living, and dying," Frances Bradburn of *Booklist* raved. "This is the charm of *The Sisterhood of the Traveling Pants.* Carmen, Lena, Bridget, and Tibby are growing to adulthood, and Brashares accurately portrays one glorious, painful summer in their evolution."

The author, a seasoned editor of children's books, stole away from her own kids for a few minutes to talk about her first novel, one of the hottest young adult titles of the season.

* * *

[*Weich*]: *After working in the publishing industry for a while, writing some nonfiction and organizing various projects, what made you try a novel now?*

[Brashares]: I've done a lot of things, but not one totally full-on. For instance, the children's biography of Steve Jobs [*Steve Jobs: Think Different*] came out of an editing project. I hadn't at any point considered myself an author of nonfiction. It was more a question of who was going to write those books, and I decided to try it. I was wearing a certain hat to do that project, and it was really fun, but I was functioning more as an editor, trying to come up with ideas for children's projects.

With *The Sisterhood of the Traveling Pants,* I've made a career shift. I really want to write fiction now. I love doing it. Fiction was my first love as a child and it's where my heart is. All along, I thought if I could do anything it would be to write fiction. Finally, I'm trying to get a toehold.

So how did you start with **The Sisterhood***?*

It started with a conversation. A woman I used to work with, a dear friend, Jodi Anderson, talked about a summer where she and her friends had shared a pair of pants that wound up being lost. It was sad, but I loved the idea—a concrete thing in the middle of a great big, amorphous, rich world of fiction.

We talked about it a little more, and with some of her ideas and her blessing I went off and developed it into an outline, got characters, and got Random House on board. I just went from there.

The girls are spending their first summer apart, so each time the pants arrive with one of them in some distant part of the world they really do serve as a connection to home.

That's how I was hoping it would work, as a repository of friendship—love, hope, challenges, all of those things.

In the beginning of the story, there's a lot of talk about them being "magic" pants, but they certainly don't turn out to be lucky.

There's not so much luck along the way, no.

Why are the prologue and the epilogue from Carmen's point of view?

She has a bigger consciousness of their friendship, I think. She's less in the moment than the others.

Carmen, Bridget, and Lena are away from home for the first time. It's ironic that Tibby, who stays home, is the one who learns the most.

She's the one who's shaken up the most. The idea that that can happen at home was something I wanted to present.

That's something I found very true to life. There's so much going on in your hometown, but a child's life is circumscribed by his or her immediate contacts. Tibby, by staying home without her friends, is the first person in her group to see that. The others . . . Lena, for example, goes halfway across the globe and learns about herself, but not a whole lot about the world.

No, she doesn't. That's quite true.

When you think about this book's readership, who do you imagine it will be?

I'm assuming that it will find its way into the hands of girls. I'd love it if boys read it, too, but being realistic I think I was certainly imagining female readers.

I love the idea that it will appeal somewhat broadly. An eleven year old will enjoy it and it doesn't feel too sophisticated, but it's made me happy that people who are my age, in my thirties, and others in their twenties, are saying they like it. Of course most of them know me so maybe they're just being nice, but there's been a genuine response from people of different ages. I like to think it will have some broader appeal.

Something that jumps out, as far as appealing to adults, are the quotes that begin each chapter—everything from James Joyce to Henry Rollins to Seinfeld. They bring an older generation into the story.

I wanted the quotes to be completely random, a total mix. New stuff, old stuff, from here, from there. A lot of it is more about my age group than anybody else's. You can't try to pretend to be another age than the one you are. I wrote this book firmly as a person who's in her thirties, with powerful memories of being in my teens.

Is the quote from the Sears catalog actually true? "If you don't find it in the Index, look very carefully throughout the entire catalog." Did you really lift that directly?

I've seen it in a couple of places. I haven't verified it beyond a shadow of a doubt, but I think it's true.

How big is Carmen's butt?

I don't know! She thinks it's bigger than it is, but it's still a good-sized butt. Not quite Jennifer Lopez.

Speaking of children's books, and being a boy who really didn't read much when I was younger . . .

That's such a boy thing. Girls, particularly as middle-graders, read a lot more than boys do at their age. That's a generalization, of course.

I'd like to think I'm not a complete anomaly, but I spend my days around bookstore employees who all seem to have been reading since they were prenatal so I'm never quite sure.

Were there books for you that served the role that this one might for a girl growing up now? Are there books you'd associate it with?

I don't know if it falls into a particular category. As far as books that I loved when I was this age, I loved Judy Blume. She felt like the first author who would tell it to me like it is, expose the sensitive, painful, awkward side of things. I remember really loving that, reading those books again and again. I hope this book will have the same feeling of honesty.

I haven't read as widely in current young adult fiction as I would like, but I feel as though there are a lot of books trying very hard to deal with social issues—illness or social ills, all kinds of shocking things—and in some part of my mind I knew that I didn't want to do that. I wanted to write a book that wasn't insubstantial but wasn't really issue-driven, either. I hope I did that.

It ended up being more serious than I'd imagined. Bridget's story was meant to be fun, and it turned quite dark, though I don't know how it happened. Carmen's story was sadder than I thought it would be. That may just be my way. But I wanted it to feel accessible.

Near the end, Carmen says, "What happened in front of my friends felt real. What happened to me by myself felt partly dreamed, partly imagined, definitely shifted and warped by my own fears and wants."

That's it for me. I remember feeling that so dramatically when I left for college. Out of context, I just didn't know who or what I was. It scared me. I could only see myself reflected in other people. It's a feeling that I related to then and I relate to now.

Do you see yourself writing more children's books?

I have a desire to do a lot of things. There's a part of me that likes writing fast paced, adventure stuff that I can imagine boys enjoying more, and younger kids. I think it's fun to plot and invent that kind of stuff. But I guess I'd like to do some more young adult fiction, and I'd like to try my hand at some adult fiction at some point. I'm hoping I'll grow into that.

Maybe by your fifties.

Right, when I'm truly an adult. I think if you have a not-totally satisfied childhood, as a writer, you go back over it again and again until you get it right. Then you can move on to other stuff.

What do you read?

Since I was twelve or so, I've loved nineteenth-century novels. I'm a complete sucker for those. I still read them. Every few years when I've forgotten enough Jane Austen I read them all again. I love Dickens, Thackeray. I love the Russian novelists; I went through a phase of devouring those books. I got into a Trollope phase.

I haven't read a lot of contemporary fiction, to tell you the truth. I'd like to read more. With young children, I've read so much less than I'd like to in the last few years. I have a young baby, too.

There are some children's and young adult writers that I admire particularly. I love Karen Cushman's *Catherine, Called Birdy.* It's so wonderful. I love Katherine Paterson. Rob Thomas, who's gone on to a lucrative career in television, has written some YA books that I admire enormously. And Katherine Applegate, whom I worked with a bit as an editor, has gone on to great success; having worked with her and seen her progress as a writer, I think she's immensely talented.

With kids' books, people seem to take for granted that they're targeted toward one gender or the other. So why aren't adult books taken seriously when they're aimed at a gender?

I don't have a good answer for that. It's taken for granted that you provide different reading material for those ages, you're right. But there's a lot of great crossover now. *Harry Potter* is an absolutely cross-gender phenomenon. There are certain categories, like Fantasy, generally. Even Scary Books—take the huge popularity of the Goosebumps series.

I think that's sort of the Holy Grail if you're in children's books, that you will be the person who'll come up with something both boys and girls will like. But for the most part, it's split; people assume that's how it is and there's not much comment.

As big as unbound by demographics as Harry Potter *has become, I'm curious to see what happens when the movie comes out. It's hard to imagine it selling more books, but I know it will.*

Who doesn't already have it, right?

Right. Harry Potter and the Sorcerer's Stone *has been among our best-selling books every week for years.*

Adults are the ones who've made that happen, don't you think?

They've certainly played a large role. The other day on the bus I saw two people, both adults, reading Potter books. Since Book 4 was published, the media attention has done a lot to bring non-parents to them.

Also there's always a steady supply of kids entering that age group—I'm going to read Harry Potter *as soon as I'm old enough, that kind of thing—whereas with adult fiction, there's inevitably some new release stealing the spotlight.*

It's more stagnant. With kids' books, there's a sense of fluidity. You're always getting new potential readers.

Judy Blume is a good example. Generations of kids have read those books.

In **The Sisterhood of the Traveling Pants,** *there are references to various contemporary items—stores like Express and Bed, Bath, and Beyond, for example—but not too many, nothing that would deter a child ten years from now from reading or enjoying it.*

I hope not.

Whereas Harry Potter *is completely made up. A total fantasy.*

Although it does have the great attribute of being internally consistent. But no, this book is pretty grounded in reality. What magic there is isn't even very lucky, so what's with that? I don't know.

Considering J. K. Rowling's massive success, we haven't seen as many imitators as you'd expect.

Typically, when a children's book really succeeds you soon have a million imitators, to the point where it gets a bit shameful. But I think it's partly because *Harry Potter* is such an author-driven, unique project, so much about how she's done it and her character. Although I think it's brought a lot of energy to the Fantasy genre.

It's brought energy to the whole industry.

Do you think there's a backlash now?

Not when you consider how big it is and how long this has been going on, not since The New York Times *removed children's books from its Best-seller list about a year ago so* Harry Potter *would stop dominating. Along with Oprah and Internet bookselling, Rowling has helped reestablish the place of books in popular culture.*

There's been a lot of talk in the book industry lately about book reviews disappearing from mainstream news outlets; newspapers and magazines aren't reviewing as many books, and when they do it's a short,

thumbnail sketch. Yet I can't help but feel like more people are reading and talking about reading now than in a long time.

Arguably, they're reading fewer things, but in greater numbers.

Books have become part of our national dialogue. It's fascinating to be standing behind the curtain, so to speak. For example, we don't take any money from publishers for placement on the web site. . . .

That's an honorable thing. I remember I was so shocked, in a naïve way, to know that all that space is paid for, and all the placement in stores. I remember thinking, "Wait, they're not just picking the stuff they really like?"

Are you finding ways around that?

It's a challenge, particularly in the last year or so as more and more people new to Powell's visit our site. But it speaks to the idea that people are reading a fairly concentrated selection of titles: if we feature a book that a publishing house is promoting heavily elsewhere, it's going to sell well at Powells.com simply because people are familiar with it. They've seen it in other stores and they've seen ads for it in magazines. Whereas if we like a smaller-budget book and decide to stand behind it, we may sell some copies but people are less likely to buy it because they're hearing about it for the first time.

Once you get past the top five percent of books printed by the major publishing houses, very few people will ever hear of them. As promotional dollars sneak into more and more places, you have to find new and creative ways to generate interest in otherwise unsupported titles.

It does perpetuate, and it's a little bit sad. So many things don't get the attention they deserve.

When Ann Patchett was here over the summer, she said, "One of the most horrifying things about book tours is being in bookstores every day and just thinking, Oh, why bother? Look at all the fantastic, brilliant books."

Every time I go to a bookstore, it's a shattering experience. There are so many people trying so hard to do so many things. It can destroy your confidence. How can you have anything to say that would add to it? Yet we all persist.

And of course the flipside is that the centralization of that promotional power is largely responsible for the resurgence of books in mainstream culture. It's no different from millions of people watching Survivor *every Thursday, then talking about it at work or school the next day. Well, now that everyone's reading the same books—Harry Potter, Bridget Jones, and the like—they can talk about books, too. And that momentum helps booksellers move inventory.*

I see it in my own life. We're so brand-oriented. Life is big and complicated, and you want to simplify. You want to know what's good, what you can depend on. But a lot of books are lost. You see so much work and so much thought going into books that aren't being read.

I really should give you back to your kids. Is there anything else you want people to know about yourself or the book? I apologize for asking this question. Every time I do, I'm met with complete silence, but I can't help asking.

It's like the end of a job interview: "Do you have any questions?"

But you'd have one, right?

Well, I hope people find their way to this book and read it. Wouldn't that be great? Wouldn't it be fun? I wrote the book in an isolated way; I didn't know what people would think of it. The response so far has been such a happy surprise. I feel like it's being taken seriously, and that makes me so happy. I hope it finds its way to readers who'll like it and who'll take themselves seriously, too.

Note

Heartfelt thanks go out to Ann Brashares, who literally had to put her baby down to conduct this interview, by phone, from her home in Massachusetts on the afternoon of September 7, 2001.

Ann Brashares and Diane Roback (interview date 24 December 2001)

SOURCE: Brashares, Ann, and Diane Roback. "Flying Starts: Ann Brashares." *Publishers Weekly* 248, no. 52 (24 December 2001): 30.

[*In the following interview, Brashares discusses her inspiration for* The Sisterhood of the Traveling Pants, *the book's publishing history, and her plans for future "Sisterhood" novels.*]

For anyone who hasn't been perusing bestseller lists this fall, or hasn't visited a bookstore and seen an eye-catching pair of faded blue jeans on a book jacket, hearing someone mention "that pants book" might engender only confusion. But the many thousands of teenagers who have discovered the book and are passing it around to their friends would know instantly what you were referring to: ***The Sisterhood of the Traveling Pants,*** written by Ann Brashares (Delacorte, Sept.)

The idea for the book, in which four teenage friends spend their first summer apart but share a pair of secondhand jeans, stemmed from when Brashares was a partner at 17th Street Productions, a book packager specializing in middle grade and young adult books. As Brashares recalls, "I was talking with Jodi Anderson, an editor at 17th Street, and she was telling me how she and a friend had shared a pair of pants over one summer. That immediately sparked a bunch of ideas. I said to her that it should be a novel, that it was such a fun idea."

She took the idea to Random House, where she worked on it with Beverly Horowitz and Wendy Loggia. "Jodi was very instrumental in helping me developing the premise," Brashares says. "I'm incredibly grateful to her for letting me use a small part of her life. From the first manuscript, Jodi, then Beverly and Wendy had a lot of good ideas for revisions—not structural stuff, but line-by-line stuff."

In writing for teenagers, Brashares says, "you feel such a sense of responsibility. You want to tackle certain issues. But I didn't feel like it was an 'issues' book—I wanted it to be fun, and a pleasure. And I want the stories I write to elicit an emotional response, to get readers thinking and feeling about my characters."

The book was completed, advance copies were handed out at BEA and a publication date was set: September 11. "All summer I had that date in mind," she recalls. "But then everyone's priorities shifted." The morning of the 11th she was on her way to her local Barnes & Noble in Park Slope, Brooklyn, when she heard about the attacks on the World Trade Center, just a few miles away. "I ran home, and it wasn't until much later that night that I realized, 'Oh God, this was supposed to be my publication day. I remember thinking, 'Well, that'll be important again one day, but not right now.'"

The unfortunately timed pub date, however, didn't seem to hurt the book: it now has 160,000 copies in print after eight trips to press, and Warner Bros. has purchased the film rights. Brashares says the book's success "is giving me the confidence that I can be a writer, that it can be my job and my life." She recalls her excitement when the buzz about the book began, thanks to those BEA readers' copies. "As a writer, you live in such isolation. It's hard to imagine your book has a life beyond you. Each piece of feedback was such *fun*! And there is the sheer joy of a first book, that somehow your thoughts translate into other people's worlds."

Brashares, who shares a brownstone with her husband and their three children (all under the age of six), says she writes at home, usually in the morning. "But I tend to try to run back downstairs to the computer at night, after the kids go to sleep." Currently she is at work on a sequel to *Pants.* "It will involve the same characters," she says, "but they're a little bit older." The book is due out in fall 2002 or spring 2003.

And she hopes to do other kinds of writing as well. "I'd love to try to write an adult novel, also a book for a younger age group. But for now, I'm very happy writing for young adults. Hopefully, life will be long, and I'll get to try other things."

Ann Brashares and Heidi Henneman (interview date May 2003)

SOURCE: Brashares, Ann, and Heidi Henneman. "Pass the Pants Please: Ann Brashares Returns with a Smart Sequel for Teens." *Bookpage* (online magazine) http://www.bookpage.com/0305bp/ann_brashares.html (May 2003).

[*In the following interview, Brashares discusses the progression of her young adult characters in the second "Sisterhood" novel,* The Second Summer of the Sisterhood.]

Ann Brashares has taken the teen world by storm. A former editor, last fall she broke out from behind the scenes with her first novel, the surprise bestseller *The Sisterhood of the Traveling Pants.* This year, she returns with another book for savvy young readers, a smart sequel to her first book called *The Second Summer of the Sisterhood.*

With her newest title, Brashares again takes us into the hearts and minds of four teenage girlfriends, Tibby, Carmen, Lena and Bridget, whose mothers met at a prenatal aerobics class while they were still in the womb. "When I thought about when these girls become friends, it was never early enough," says the author. "I wanted a totally unquestioned relationship to one another, like siblings."

And Brashares has indeed created a sisterhood with these girls—a set of siblings like no other: one is Greek, one Latino, one blonde and one somewhat nondescript. While the author does hint a little at the ethnicity and background of each of her characters, she leaves much to the imagination. "I wanted to indicate that there is variety and a general openness among the girls," she explains. "It's a colorful picture, but not specifically drawn."

More important than their backgrounds, though, are their friendships. Realistically enough, each girl has her own quirks, and she is loved by the others in the group for them. Brashares expertly captures the essence of true girl power through these characters, but she is also able to express the emotions and difficulties that almost every teenager goes through.

Brashares' first book centered on a "magic" pair of jeans (any pair of pants that can fit perfectly on four unique teenage bodies *has* to have special powers). The girls pass these jeans along to each other throughout the summer and find romance, friendship and strength by wearing them. As each of the "sisters" takes her turn with the pants, she finds that the summer isn't filled with all the happiness she had hoped it would be: Tibby has to learn the hard way who her real friends and family are; Carmen jealously destroys her mother's new relationship; Bridget faces the truth about her mother's death; and Lena deals with an unexpected pregnancy. Indeed, the first passing of the pants proves to be bad magic rather than the good omen that the girls had envisioned.

But as the pants—and the summer—move on, the girls come to realize that it's not the pants that help them survive their traumas and see them through their joyous moments, but the closeness and comfort of their strong, lasting friendships.

"I think of the pants as pulling them into the plots of their lives," says Brashares, "and there needed to be a challenge, something difficult in their lives."

Compared to the first book, the second is a bit more daunting. The challenges the four mates face are somewhat more adult in nature: restoring faith in friends and family, dealing with a single parent's romantic life, coming face-to-face with death. "The girls are aging with each book and will continue to do so," says Brashares. "I felt that they were more mature and capable of dealing with some weightier issues."

Brashares' books aren't just how-to guides to surviving the curve balls of the teenage years. They are a peek into the lives of everyday people who have their own personalities, styles, histories and dreams. Love, friendship, commitment and honesty are important elements here, and Brashares combines them all flawlessly.

So what's next for the Sisterhood? "I'm not sure where it's all going," admits Brashares, "but it's going somewhere." At the very least, we'll see another summer of trials, tribulations and triumphs from the girls, and we may possibly see a glimpse of their colorful faces on the big screen. But time will tell with all of that. Until then, remember: Pants = love. Love your pals. Love yourself.

Ann Brashares and *Teenreads.com* (interview date May 2003)

SOURCE: Brashares, Ann, and *Teenreads.com*. "Author Talk: Ann Brashares." *Teenreads.com* (online magazine) http://teenreads.com/authors/talk-brashares-ann.asp (May 2003).

[*In the following interview, Brashares discusses the publication of* The Second Summer of the Sisterhood, *the impact of her first "Sisterhood" novel, and her personal connection to her teenaged protagonists.*]

Ann Brashares follows the huge success of her bestselling first novel, ***The Sisterhood of the Traveling Pants,*** with ***The Second Summer of the Sisterhood,*** which continues the adventures of four best friends and the magical pair of jeans that fits each of them perfectly. In this interview, Brashares talks about the success of her debut novel, the themes addressed in the sequel, and what the future holds for her main characters.

* * *

[*TeenReads.com*]: **The Sisterhood of the Traveling Pants,** *your debut novel, received much critical praise, awards, and adoration from readers of all ages. What are your thoughts on its success and why do you think it resonated so heavily with readers?*

[Brashares]: Its success has been a wonderful surprise each step of the way. From the outset I tried to keep my expectations very low. I know how hard it is to get a book published let alone have it succeed. I've read many excellent books that did not succeed commercially. Here I give credit to the publisher, Random House, and to the booksellers. They supported the book wholeheartedly.

To the extent that it has resonated with readers, I am grateful for it. I sense that they have responded, more than anything else, to the unconditional love and loyalty that the Sisterhood represents.

Has the success changed your writing process and expectations for **The Second Summer of the Sisterhood***?*

I tried not to let the success change anything, but it kept creeping into my consciousness anyway. I worried that I wouldn't live up to the hopes of my readers. I worried that I would forget how to write. I worried that I never knew how to write in the first place. I worried a lot and I wrote very little.

When I finally forced myself back to my computer, I worried I had fallen out of touch with my characters. They felt to me like friends with whom I'd been intensely close, but hadn't seen in a long time. It's painful, in a way, to have to ask clunky, anonymous questions of people you used to know in an intimate, hour-by-hour way. Luckily, though, when I started to spend real time with Carmen and Bee and Tibby and Lena, I relaxed. I grew close to them again and enjoyed being with them so much, I forgot all the things I was worrying about.

As for expectations, I still try to keep them in check. But I do allow myself to hope. I hope that readers who liked the first book will like the second one too.

Did you plan for the girls' relationship with their mothers to play a stronger role in **The Second Summer of the Sisterhood***? Does your relationship with your own mother resemble any from the book?*

It didn't start out that way exactly. As I was working out stories for each of the girls, I realized that most of them involved their mothers to some degree. So I just went with it. The mother-daughter bond is about as rich a subject as any I know. And I felt those relationships could give a center of gravity to a book that otherwise ran the risk of going in too many directions at once.

My relationship with my mother doesn't resemble any of the ones in the book precisely. There are some thematic similarities to Carmen, though, in that my parents were divorced and I had to come to terms with my mom having a romantic life of her own.

As the mother of three young children, do you find that you relate more to the girls or their mothers?

Even though I'm closer to the age of the mothers, I related more to the daughters. I think that's because I wrote the book from the girls' points of view. Although I tried really hard to imagine how the mothers would feel, I didn't actually spend my days thinking their thoughts the way I do when I'm writing in a character's point of view.

Also, my daughter is only one and a half. When she gets to be a teenager, then I'll really understand what those mothers go through.

Female friendship remains a central theme in the second book, do you have your own sisterhood? In your writing, you seem to have a real understanding of the importance of those bonds, how have you come to know that?

I have a few very good old friends from childhood and some more recent friends whom I love dearly. But truthfully, I think the sisterhood is more fantasy than reality for me. I grew up in a house full of boys (wonderful boys, I should mention), and always dreamed about sisters.

Do you have a sense of where the girls will be "next summer"? How do you see their growth continuing?

Next summer will be the girls' last before they split up to go to college. That's going to be a big deal for them. I suspect Tibby is going to fall in love for the first time. I have a feeling Bridget might encounter Eric, the soccer coach, again. I have a few other plans up my sleeve, but I think I better keep them secret.

What do you hope readers will take away from this second book?

I don't really write with the idea of trying to teach any lessons. I want to tell a story as truthfully and engagingly as I can, and then let the chips fall where they may. But I realize when I get to the end of the story, I care very much that my characters evolve and grow. In spite of their torments and their selfish impulses, I care that they are guided by a spirit of goodness. I want them to set a high standard for compassion and for friendship.

TITLE COMMENTARY

📖 *THE SISTERHOOD OF THE TRAVELING PANTS* (2001)

Linda Bindner (review date August 2001)

SOURCE: Bindner, Linda. Review of *The Sisterhood of the Traveling Pants,* by Ann Brashares. *School Library Journal* 47, no. 8 (August 2001): 175.

Gr. 9-Up—[In *The Sisterhood of the Traveling Pants,* b]est friends Lena, Tibby, Bridget, and Carmen are preparing to spend their first summer apart since they were born. Before leaving to visit her father, Carmen buys a pair of second-hand jeans on a whim, and when the others discover that the pants fit all of them, they create the sisterhood of the traveling pants. Each teen gets them for a few weeks before sending them on, and thus they travel from Washington, DC, to Greece to Baja California to South Carolina, linking the friends even as they are apart. The summer and the pants come to represent more than any of them can ever anticipate in this four-part coming-of-age story. Before the season ends, each teen must deal with some unpleasant problem, reach a real low, then confront her personal flaws and pull herself back up again. Brashares deftly moves from narrative to narrative, weaving together themes from the mundane to the profoundly important, from death to raging hormones, from stepfamilies to dead-end minimum-wage jobs. The endings aren't pat, yet each story line comes to a satisfying conclusion. All four girls are completely realistic, and even the secondary and adult characters are fully drawn. The result is a complex book about a solid group of friends, with each one a strong and courageous individual in her own right. They form a true sisterhood of acceptance and support, resulting in a believable and inviting world.

Kirkus Reviews (review date 1 August 2001)

SOURCE: Review of *The Sisterhood of the Traveling Pants,* by Ann Brashares. *Kirkus Reviews* 69, no. 15 (1 August 2001): 1117.

In [*The Sisterhood of the Traveling Pants,*] this feel-good novel with substance, four teenage girls, friends since they were all born just weeks apart, are about to embark on their first summer as separate young women. Carmen, half-Hispanic, has a knack for math; Lena, the beauty of the group and self-conscious about her appearance, demonstrates artistic talent; Bridget is the tall soccer star; and Tibby, the rebel, sports a nose ring. Visiting grandparents for the first time in Greece, attending soccer camp in Mexico, spending the summer with dad in South Carolina, or working at home, how will these girls survive their time alone? Leave it to a pair of secondhand jeans, which, despite their various body shapes, fits all four perfectly. These magical jeans, dubbed the Traveling Pants, span the world, one week at a time, lending their mystical powers wherever they go. The pants become a metaphor for the young women finding their own strength in the face of new love, unexpected friendships and death, a father's remarriage, and a reckless relationship—and without their best friends. Debut novelist Brashares renders each girl individual and lovable in her own right, emphasizing growing up without growing apart. Move over, Ya Ya Sisters. (*Fiction. YA*)

Deborah Stevenson (review date December 2001)

SOURCE: Stevenson, Deborah. Review of *The Sisterhood of the Traveling Pants,* by Ann Brashares. *Bulletin of the Center for Children's Books* 55, no. 4 (December 2001): 132-33.

[In **The Sisterhood of the Traveling Pants,**] four inseparable friends—Carmen, Lena, Tibby, and Bridget—are facing separation, if only for a summer; they're reconciled somewhat to this fate by their plan to share the magic jeans that Carmen has discovered, jeans that look fabulous on each of the girls and seem to bring confidence and maturity to their wearer. All four turn out to need all the help the Pants can provide: Carmen discovers that her long-awaited summer alone with her father is really her first meeting with Dad's fiancée and her teenage kids; Lena's visit with her Greek grandparents goes awry when they misunderstand her disconcerting chance encounter with a neighbor boy as something more serious; Tibby finds herself oddly attached to a sharp-tongued younger girl who proves to have cancer; Bridget throws her considerable talents into securing the affections of an assistant coach at soccer camp and finds she may have gotten more than she bargained for. Brashares handles the disparate threads well, with a companionable, sisterly tone that carries the reader through the quick and constant changes from viewpoint to viewpoint (usually bridged by a letter from one of the girls to another) even before the girls' identities are clearly established. That establishment doesn't take long, however, and the personalities are strong and original and true to their fifteen-year-old selves, capable of maturity but also prone to lacking it when it's needed. It's no surprise that all four move farther along the road to adulthood by the end of the summer, but the book's loving depiction of enduring and solid friendship will ring true to readers, who will appreciate this recognition of one of life's most important relationships.

Marvin Hoffman (review date 19 December 2001)

SOURCE: Hoffman, Marvin. "Summer of Growth, a Growing Mystery." *Houston Chronicle* (19 December 2001): 19.

[*In the following review, Hoffman characterizes* The Sisterhood of the Traveling Pants *as a "very impressive first novel."*]

I was in one of my favorite independent bookstores in Chicago recently when I saw a note peeking out from the pages of a book on the Recent Arrivals counter. The book was **The Sisterhood of the Traveling Pants** by Ann Brashares, which the store owner, in her neat block print, had taken the time to personally recommend as one of the best books for teenage girls she had read in a long time. So when the book arrived on my reviewer's pile, it got a quick promotion to the top.

The owner's recommendation did not fail me. This very impressive first novel by a young New York author contains a rich mix of all the major elements in the lives of teenage girls in today's America. It is not a "problem" book, but its characters struggle with issues of friendship, sexual awakening, death, divorce, competition, jealousy and much more.

Carmen, Bridget, Tibby and Lena have been part of each other's lives in a Washington, D.C., suburb since their mothers met during pregnancy. They have spent every summer together swimming, playing, riding their bikes—until the summer of the story. At age 15 they are about to spend three months apart for the first time.

Carmen is headed to South Carolina to be with her divorced dad; Lena and her younger sister are off to Greece to visit her grandparents; Bridget will spend the summer at a sports camp in Mexico's Baja California to hone her considerable soccer talents; Tibby is sentenced to staying at home and clerking in the town's discount drugstore.

Before they head off to their various adventures, they discover a pair of jeans that Carmen bought on impulse in a thrift shop and left unworn on her shelf. During a pre-departure get-together they decide to try them on. Although the girls come in all different sizes and shapes, the jeans have the miraculous quality of looking good on all of them.

They decide the jeans will serve as their summer link and immediately draft a set of guidelines governing their movement from one summer locale to the next, where each girl will report on her experiences while wearing them. I need to be clear that this is not a fantasy novel; there is nothing magical about the jeans beyond the "real" magic of the deep love among the friends who will not allow life and geography to weaken the bonds that have kept them together since birth.

It is impossible to recap the complex plot lines of these four separate yet intertwined summers. The novel is structured like so many current TV shows—multiple intercut stories, with the traveling pants serving as the device that keeps the narrative from flying apart. Although the stories are told in the third person, the book is framed by a prologue and epilogue in the voice of Carmen, who is in many ways the most reflective and introspective of the group.

Let the following suffice. Carmen arrives in South Carolina expecting to have a summer alone with her father but discovers that he is about to remarry into a family that includes two other teenagers. Lena, the cold beauty of the group, spends her summer fighting off her grandmother's attempt to fix her up with a handsome young man on the island. Guess where this one is headed.

Bridget quickly emerges as the star athlete in her camp, but her attention is directed to breaking the camp's fraternization rules to be with a counselor to whom she is dangerously attracted. Stay-at-home Tibby decides to make a film about her dismal work life. She is assisted by Bailey, an obnoxious 11-year-old who invades Tibby's life and provides some of the most tragic and heartwrenching moments in the story.

All the girls grow and discover things about themselves that are moving and dramatically credible. Although the tone is basically serious, there is humor in the premise of the traveling pants as well as in the clever aphorisms that punctuate the story in the form of chapter headings: "Luck never gives; it only lends." "Today is the tomorrow we worried about yesterday."

Although Carmen is half Puerto Rican, this book is mainly about the experience of white, middle-class suburban girls, but its themes are universal and should appeal to a broad audience. I'm going to look for more notes protruding from volumes in that bookstore. This one worked out fine.

James Blasingame (review date September 2002)

SOURCE: Blasingame, James. Review of *The Sisterhood of the Traveling Pants,* by Ann Brashares. *Journal of Adolescent and Adult Literacy* 46, no. 1 (September 2002): 87-8.

[In *The Sisterhood of the Traveling Pants,*] Carmen, Tibby, Lena, and Bridget have been best friends for as long as they can remember. Their mothers first met 16 years earlier in an aerobics class for pregnant women, and since that time the girls have never known a summer apart. This summer will be different, however, as three of the friends leave their homes in the Washington, D.C., area and head for different parts of the globe. Although they are separated, they will continue to share two important things, their lifelong friendship and a pair of pants.

The pants are only thrift-store blue jeans that Carmen picked up for US $3.49, and although they aren't truly magical, they do have some surprising properties. They fit each of the four girls perfectly despite their completely different body sizes and types, accentuating each girl's positive physical characteristics and minimizing negative ones. Whoever has the pants in her possession experiences powerful moments of romance, athletic triumph, or resolution of whatever issue is foremost in her life at the time. The girls call this the "power of the pants," and although they don't believe it to be magic, they do believe that the pants serve as a reminder of the strong friendship and advocacy they share. As the title suggests, the pants really do travel from girl to girl over the course of the summer, and while each girl has the pants she is reminded that her three best friends are with her in spirit if not in person.

The novel is really four different stories, each one told in several parts as the novel goes back and forth among the girls just like the pants. Carmen travels to South Carolina to spend the summer with her father, just the two of them, but discovers on her arrival that her father has a new family. Bridget travels to a big-time soccer camp in Mexico where the reckless abandon with which she plays soccer also shows up in her first exploration into romance. Lena spends her summer with her grandparents, lifelong residents of a beautiful village on the coast of Greece, where she thwarts her grandmother's plan to connect her with the village's most eligible bachelor. Tibby, the only member of the sisterhood to remain at home, starts a new job at Wallman's Drugstore and with a strange new friend attempts to make a documentary about quirky but interesting people. In the Epilogue all the girls meet for their annual birthday party at the site of the now long-disbanded aerobics class their mothers attended. Although each girl's story has its own ending, the author uses this final scene to add a note of resolution.

This novel addresses issues that young people quite often face, such as blended families, painful relationships, death and grieving, and dealing with adversity, but the approach is not heavy-handed, and the story is enjoyable. Ann Brashares's first fiction attempt is a successful one.

THE SECOND SUMMER OF THE SISTERHOOD (2003)

Claire Rosser (review date March 2003)

SOURCE: Rosser, Claire. Review of *The Second Summer of the Sisterhood,* by Ann Brashares. *KLIATT* 37, no. 2 (March 2003): 8.

Another summer and more adventures for the four friends—Bridget, Tibby, Carmen, and Lena—we met in the first book. Yes, the magical pants are still with them [in *The Second Summer of the Sisterhood*] and are passed one to the other as the weeks pass by. The four are again separated and yet are constantly connected by e-mail, letters, and phone calls. Bridget is in the small Southern town where her mother grew up—she is hiding her identity and trying to get to know the woman who is her grandmother. Tibby is at a film camp at a local university, admiring a rather sophisticated fellow student and ashamed of her loyal friend Brian. Carmen is at home angry with her mother for falling in love and doing her best to sabotage that relationship. Lena has broken up with her boyfriend from last summer's trip to Greece, but Kostos appears unexpectedly on her doorstep and she is thrown back into the whirlpool of love.

Like the style of the first book, the four stories of the four girls proceed at a fast clip, with their care for each other and the pants themselves connecting the four narratives. The author cuts from one narrative to the next neatly and cleanly; and the reader has no trouble feeling part of these four lives. Brashares manages this juggling act well. She also has great love for many other characters; for instance, the adults of the story are developed as full characters, especially the mothers. The girls are smart, thought-ful, introspective, resourceful, creative, and flawed. They can also be self-destructive, angry, jealous and deceitful. This is longer than most YA novels, and filled with conversations, action, and life.

Elizabeth Bush (review date May 2003)

SOURCE: Bush, Elizabeth. Review of *The Second Summer of the Sisterhood,* by Ann Brashares. *Bulletin of the Center for Children's Books* 56, no. 9 (May 2003): 351-52.

The Traveling Pants, those miraculous jeans that fit each wearer to a "T" and seem to conjure life-changing events (*The Sisterhood of the Traveling Pants, BCCB* 12/01), are off to an unpromising start this summer [in *The Second Summer of the Sisterhood*]. Lena's stuck clerking in a clothing store; Carmen's babysitting and seeing a guy she can't quite seem to focus on; Tibby's off at film school, courting the attention of a fellow student with considerable talent and an overload of attitude; and poor Bridget, who's put on so much depression-induced weight that she can't even zip The Pants up, is sweating in Alabama, getting to know the grandmother her father will have nothing to do with. So disappointing are The Pants, in fact, that the girls barely keep them for the week before shipping them off to the next destination. Ah, there's still some magic left, though, as Carmen's mother finds out when she borrows them for a date herself. It's the Motherhood of the Sisterhood, if you will, that becomes the unifying motif in this outing, as each girl learns that there's more to Mom than she thought. Tibby's mother really does care for her as much as she does for the younger siblings; Carmen's mother is still a vibrant babe with a shot at romance; Lena's mother had a past amour that threatened her marriage; Bridget's deceased mother was as deeply beloved as she was intensely troubled. This is no Ya Ya Redux, though; the girls still hold center stage, floundering in romances, wrestling with extra-Sisterly friendships, and relying on the unwavering love and support of the quartet. Last year's Sisterhood fans can start passing around this new installment, sharing like all good Sisters do.

Susan W. Hunter (review date May 2003)

SOURCE: Hunter, Susan W. Review of *The Second Summer of the Sisterhood,* by Ann Brashares. *School Library Journal* 49, no. 5 (May 2003): 144-45.

Gr. 8-Up—Carmen, Lena, Tibby, and Bee are back in this long, engaging sequel to *The Sisterhood of the Traveling Pants* (Delacorte, 2001) [*The Second*

Summer of the Sisterhood]. The four best friends are beginning their 16th summer with new expectations for personal growth, romance, and deepening friendship, all enhanced by the magic of a shared pair of thrift-store jeans. Brashares has deftly interwoven the story's strands to convey the relaxed intimacy of the girls' friendships as well as the many parallels in their individual experiences. The dialogue is natural and helps build nuances of character; the use of metaphor and insightful language renders a narrative that is highly readable and marked by emotional truth. Bee, whose mother died when she was 11, heads to Alabama under an assumed name to visit her estranged maternal grandmother. Carmen and Lena both become entangled in emotional spats with their mothers, and Tibby makes an edgy documentary film about her mother for a screenwriting course. This is a summer for coming-of-age, and for people materializing out of the blue, but making an impact—Tibby's old friend Brian appears unbidden at her dorm; Lena's Greek boyfriend, Kostos, arrives suddenly; and Carmen's stepsister comes seeking sanctuary. Meanwhile, the traveling pants are circulated among the friends. It may just be the power of wonder, but the jeans undoubtedly play a role in the happy resolution of this big-hearted, complex tale of living, learning, and caring. Brashares's novel can be enjoyed by readers who have not yet discovered the previous book. It is certain to delight those readers who have.

Marvin Hoffman (review date 11 May 2003)

SOURCE: Hoffman, Marvin. "*Sisterhood* Sequel Works, but Hang up the Pants (Device)." *Houston Chronicle* (11 May 2003): 19.

[*In the following review, Hoffman compliments Brashares' skill with characterization in* The Second Summer of the Sisterhood, *but argues that the "traveling pants" plot device is no longer an essential component of the "Sisterhood" storyline.*]

According to Ann Brashares' publishers, her first novel, *The Sisterhood of the Traveling Pants,* sold more than 350,000 copies in hardcover.

When I reviewed it in this column two years ago, I counted myself among its many enthusiasts, most of whom, I suspect, were female. In *The Sisterhood,* Brashares follows the adventures of four teenage friends—Lena, Tibby, Carmen and Bridget—as they spend their first summer apart from each other. The pants of the title are a pair of jeans that pass from torso to torso through the summer and on which the girls inscribe memories of a truly memorable season.

I had no idea that a sequel was in the works until *The Second Summer of the Sisterhood* arrived in the mail. I welcomed the opportunity to refresh my memories of the quartet's earlier adventures and to see what was in store for them in this following summer of their teenage lives. The author tells this story, like the first book, through a lens that pans continually across the friends in a skillfully interwoven narrative.

The Second Summer is a mother-daughter book. Each of the girls is engaged in a struggle to define herself in relation to her mother and to come to some understanding of her mother's own defining experiences.

Bridget, the only one of the four whose mother is no longer alive, has been forbidden contact with her maternal grandmother since she was 7. She is the athlete of the group, having spent the first summer at soccer camp where she had her first romance, with a staff member, which did not end well. She has given up athletics, put on weight and darkened her blond hair in an attempt to redefine herself.

She has also decided to spend the summer in the small Alabama town where her grandmother lives without revealing who she really is. She rents a room in a boarding house and is hired by her grandmother to clean out a memory-laden attic so it can become a guest room for a bed-and-breakfast.

As her relationship with her grandmother deepens, Bridget learns about her mother's own troubled past, and this enables her to understand the causes of her early death.

Lena spent the previous summer on the Greek island where her grandparents live. There, Kostos, an extraordinary young man, managed to break through her legendary emotional reserve to begin a torrid romance. But once back on her own turf, Lena's defenses reasserted themselves and she broke off the relationship. When Kostos appears in the States for a summer internship, the relationship is reignited.

Meanwhile, in what appears to be an unrelated subplot, Lena learns from her friends' mothers, all of whom have known each other since they were students together in a birthing class, that there was a mystery man in the life of Ariadne, Lena's mom, whom she refuses to acknowledge or discuss.

In the end, the two tracks merge as we see Lena's romance following the same tragic path as her mother's.

Tibby spent the previous summer close to home dealing with the death of Bailey, an extraordinary 12-year-old whom she befriended. This summer she is off to a college campus where she is taking a film course and, more important, figuring out which relationships really matter.

She connects with a set of shallow friends who encourage her to produce a mocking portrait of her mother as her project for the film course. When her mother appears at the showing, she is crushed by her daughter's cruelty.

Tibby is shocked into reassessing the direction in which her life is going and reconnects with the lessons she learned from Bailey as she lived out her last days.

Finally, there is Carmen, who spent a turbulent summer with her father and his new family, struggling with her anger over the breakup of her parents' marriage and with her jealousy of the life her father has created apart from her.

This summer she is home with her mother, feeling doubly angry and abandoned as her mother embarks on a romance with a colleague at work. Carmen does her best to sabotage this relationship, but watching her mother crumble as the romance falters, she comes to see her as a woman with her own right to happiness, independent of Carmen's self-indulgent needs.

As in the first volume, the semi-magical pants, which manage to fit all four very differently configured bodies, circulate from one friend to another throughout the summer and even wind up being worn by one of the mothers.

However, they seem much less central to the forward movement of the story and to the underscoring of the deep bonds among the friends. The lives of the girls and their mothers are so hugely absorbing in themselves that we hardly need to rely on this device to keep us engaged.

These are great stories about complex, not always admirable, characters. *The Second Summer* may be intended as a chick book, exploring friendship among women and the tangled world of mother-daughter relationships, but this guy, for one, can't wait till next summer.

James Blasingame (review date December-January 2003-2004)

SOURCE: Blasingame, James. Review of *The Second Summer of the Sisterhood,* by Ann Brashares. *Journal of Adolescent and Adult Literacy* 47, no. 4 (December-January 2003-2004): 348-49.

Let's quickly review background information from the predecessor to *The Second Summer of the Sisterhood* (Delacorte, 2001). Our four protagonists, Tibby, Carmen, Lena, and Bridget have some very special and unusual things in common. Their mothers all belonged to the same aerobics class for pregnant women, delivered their daughters close together in time, became good friends, and set the four girls up for a lifelong friendship. Although their mothers have now drifted apart and the girls live in different areas of the city, the four teenagers have remained close friends.

One unusual nuance of their friendship is the shared ownership of an almost-magical pair of jeans from a secondhand store. Although the girls have different physiques and sizes, the "traveling pants" fit each one perfectly. Not only are they a perfect fit, but also they have the uncanny quality of complementing each girl's figure. The girls share the pants—which they believe to be good luck, as well as good fashion—by mail so that each girl has a turn with them.

We now join the foursome one summer later. As in the first novel, each girl has her own conflict. Tibby and Bridget have totally different conflicts from those they experienced the previous year. After dealing with the death of a slightly eccentric and younger friend last summer, this year Tibby goes away to film school, where she encounters older (but still eccentric) teenage filmmaker-hopefuls and deals with the issue of genuine friendships. After spending last summer at soccer camp and experimenting with romance, Bridget attempts to covertly contact her estranged grandmother this year by traveling to the deep South and keeping her true identity a secret.

Carmen's and Lena's problems are not unlike those of the year before. Last summer Carmen had to deal with the fact that her father, who had moved away, now had a new and apparently happy family life of which she did not feel a part. Now Carmen feels a parent is being stolen from her life again, but this time it is her mother, who has just begun dating someone special. Lena's summer is very much a continuation of the previous one, when she traveled to her grandparents' home in Greece and fell in love with a handsome young man—who loved her in spite of her hard-to-get machinations. It's ironic that Lena is sentenced to spend this summer pining for Kostos, having told him they would be better off not contacting each other. Imagine her emotional roller coaster when Kostos shows up.

This book is at least as good as the previous one, and, as sequels go, it is no disappointment at all. The author has a talent for seamlessly moving from one girl's story to the next without disruption or the need for too much explanation. The girls are a year older and their problems are more complicated, as befits their age. Brashares is again thoughtful and insightful when handling the issues that confront young women as they move into adulthood, such as identity, nontraditional families, romantic relationships, finding real friends, and being true to one's conscience and values.

GIRLS IN PANTS: THE THIRD SUMMER OF THE SISTERHOOD (2005)

Kirkus Reviews (review date 15 December 2004)

SOURCE: Review of *Girls in Pants: The Third Summer of the Sisterhood,* by Ann Brashares. *Kirkus Reviews* 72, no. 24 (15 December 2004): 1199.

[In *Girls in Pants: The Third Summer of the Sisterhood,*] Tilly, Carmen, Lena and Bee are graduating from high school and heading to college—Brown, RISD, NYU, and Williams. In the summer before college, before getting on with "their real lives," the girls have the Pants to keep them connected as they go their separate ways. Brashares provides a prologue for those new to the saga, explaining the sisterhood and the magical powers of the Pants they share—one at a time, of course—during the summer. The Pants offer a kind of spiritual link between the girls, providing love, security and connectedness as they face various dramas with boys, parents, new siblings and uncertain futures. The theme of this volume is change, as the girls understand they are leaving one life behind, but in one way or another, each realizes that leaving home doesn't mean giving up home or friends. Four intersecting story lines, snappy dialogue, empathy for characters and humor make this installment as enjoyable as the others. Legions of fans will enjoy spending another summer with the girls. (*Fiction. 12+*)

Publishers Weekly (review date 20 December 2004)

SOURCE: Review of *Girls in Pants: The Third Summer of the Sisterhood,* by Ann Brashares. *Publishers Weekly* 251, no. 51 (20 December 2004): 61.

Fans of the Traveling Pants series will be delighted to welcome back the four life-long friends [in *Girls in Pants: The Third Summer of the Sisterhood,*] as they face their last summer together before separating for college. Though each girl has her own problems—and her own romance—to deal with, the quartet is there for each other, as are the magical pants that look good on them all (even if the pants themselves take a back seat in this installment). The author expertly splices together each friend's struggle with growing up: Bee's first love turns up as a fellow soccer coach at the summer camp where she is also coaching, Carmen's mother is expecting a new baby, Lena's father, as punishment for her sneaking off to an art class, will not pay for her education at Rhode Island art School of Design and Tibby is afraid when a long-time friendship turns into romance. Though readers new to the series may have trouble catching on to the back story, and a couple of plot points strain credibility (e.g., Tibby becomes Carmen's mother's last-minute labor coach), the girls are once again wonderfully drawn, with all their realistic faults. Readers will laugh as tough Carmen faces off with a police officer who stops her on her way to the hospital, and be touched when Lena draws a portrait of her recently widowed grandmother. Even in moments that edge toward melodrama (such as a parting shot of the four friends holding hands as they face the ocean surf), it's the girls' genuine love and tenderness that will win readers over and make them envious of the friends' strong bond. Ages 12-up.

Linda L. Plevak (review date January 2005)

SOURCE: Plevak, Linda L. Review of *Girls in Pants: The Third Summer of the Sisterhood,* by Ann Brashares. *School Library Journal* 51, no. 1 (January 2005): 125-26.

Gr. 7-Up—Four friends embark on their third summer of adventures [in *Girls in Pants: The Third Summer of the Sisterhood*], beginning with their high school graduation. Tibby ponders the change in her relationship with a male friend who now wants to date her. She is devastated when her little sister is seriously injured after falling out a window that Tibby accidentally left open. Lena's plans to attend art school are disrupted when her conservative father discovers her sketching a nude male model during a summer class and refuses to pay the tuition. Carmen takes a job looking after Lena's cantankerous grandmother. She decides to attend college locally when she discovers that her mother and new stepfather are expecting a baby. Bridget goes to summer camp and is surprised to learn that her ex-fling is also a counselor. As in the previous books, the pants move from girl to girl weaving their special magic, but they are mentioned only briefly and it is easy to forget who has them when. The multiple story lines abruptly switch within chapters, building suspense. However, reluctant readers may miss having more solid transitions. The novel will appeal to those wanting light fare as the girls spend most of their time fretting about boys and all of their tribulations end happily. Fans will clamor for the latest in the series. The story stands alone, but references to the previous summers will attract readers to the other books.

Claire Rosser (review date January 2005)

SOURCE: Rosser, Claire. Review of *Girls in Pants: The Third Summer of the Sisterhood,* by Ann Brashares. *KLIATT* 39, no. 1 (January 2005): 6.

Fans of this delightful series of books will eagerly grab this third part [*Girls in Pants: The Third Summer of the Sisterhood*]. (It has been announced that a movie will be made of this series and released in the summer of 2005, which will only encourage more readership.) To recap: it concerns four friends, four families, linked by a lifetime of memories and also by a magical pair of pants that brings out the best in the girl wearing them. This third summer of the sisterhood is the summer after graduation, before the friends—Tibby, Bee, Lena and Carmen—separate and go to college, so there is a bittersweet quality to the story. Each girl is a thoughtful, articulate, attractive person with her own set of talents and interests; connecting them all is the friendship they treasure. They may get their feelings hurt, they may stagger around in despair, they may be confused, they may be celebrating and happy—they are absolutely believable characters. As they pursue their activities this third summer, they frequently are in touch with one another, which is how the reader finds out what's going on in each life. It's best to start with the first book, but each book is equally enjoyable.

Elizabeth Bush (review date March 2005)

SOURCE: Bush, Elizabeth. Review of *Girls in Pants: The Third Summer of the Sisterhood,* by Ann Brashares. *Bulletin of the Center for Children's Books* 58, no. 7 (March 2005): 282-83.

Unwashed, uncuffed, and unbelted according to "the rules," the mystical jeans are back in summer circulation [in *Girls in Pants: The Third Summer of the Sisterhood*], ready to inspire and document milestones in the lives of their collective owners. Tibby, Carmen, Bridget (Bee), and Lena have blustered their way through high-school commencement and stand at the threshold of college with duffels full of second thoughts and mixed emotions. Lena's father is outraged at his little girl's figure drawing (nude figure drawing, that is) summer class and pulls the plug on her finances for Rhode Island School of Design, so now it's up to her to win scholarship money on her own. Carmen's mother and stepfather are expecting a baby, and Carmen is reluctant to leave home for school in Massachusetts, fearful of losing her place in her tenuous new family. Bee is off to soccer camp and an unsought reunion with the counselor she rashly seduced at sixteen (see *The Sisterhood of the Traveling Pants, BCCB* 12/01). Tibby, who trembles the most at impending change, learns some life lessons from her three-year-old sister and finds romance with an old-friend-turned-hunk. With the focus returned squarely to daughters rather than mothers, the signature cascade of story fragments flowing into a unified whole, and the heightened aura of raw emotion endemic to the "last summer" theme, the Pants set will bruise their fingertips on this page-turner. Whether the pants ritual has come to an end at the final sob-inducing scene at Rehoboth Beach is, of course, for the friends and their creator (and her publisher?) to decide, but fans who share the girls' separation anxiety had better keep a box of tissues close at hand.

Jennifer M. Brabander (review date March-April 2005)

SOURCE: Brabander, Jennifer M. Review of *Girls in Pants: The Third Summer of the Sisterhood,* by Ann Brashares. *Horn Book Magazine* 81, no. 2 (March-April 2005): 198.

The Traveling Pants and the girls who wear them are back for a third summer [in *Girls in Pants: The Third Summer of the Sisterhood*]. Tibby, Carmen, Bee, and Lena are graduating from high school and at summer's end will head off to four different colleges. While the Pants only play a bit part this time around, the starring role still goes to those unbreakable bonds of Sisterhood that carry the girls through all kinds of family and boyfriend dramas. The girls nicely show how they've grown and matured over the last two years, and if Brashares too obviously spells out the lessons each learns, that overtness is one of the books' strongest appeals for fans, who can just sit back, relax, and be armchair travelers.

FURTHER READING

Criticism

Brashares, Ann. "How I Write." *Writer* 118, no. 7 (July 2005): 66.

> Brashares discusses her inspirations, her method for writing fiction, and her advice for developing young adult writers.

Brashares, Ann, and James Blasingame. "Interview with Ann Brashares." *Journal of Adolescent and Adult Literacy* 47, no. 4 (December-January 2003-2004): 350.

> Brashares discusses *The Second Summer of the Sisterhood,* her connection with her readership, and future writing projects.

Eagleman, Daphne, and Lisa Armitage. Review of *Girls in Pants: The Third Summer of the Sisterhood,* by Ann Brashares. *Journal of Adolescent and Adult Literacy* 49, no. 4 (December-January 2005-2006): 356.

> Evaluates the strengths and weaknesses of *Girls in Pants: The Third Summer of the Sisterhood.*

Leahy, Christine. Review of *The Sisterhood of the Traveling Pants,* by Ann Brashares. *New York Times Book Review* (10 March 2002): 21.

> Provides a positive assessment of *The Sisterhood of the Traveling Pants.*

Additional coverage of Brashares's life and career is contained in the following sources published by Thomson Gale: *Authors and Artists for Young Adults,* **Vol. 52;** *Contemporary Authors,* **Vol. 218;** *Literature Resource Center***; and** *Something about the Author,* **Vol. 145.**

Golden Age of Children's Illustrated Books

Nineteenth- and twentieth-century publishing era that witnessed the release of some of the most significant and influential works of children's illustration of all time.

INTRODUCTION

The so-called "Golden Age" of children's illustrated books—a period dating from around 1880 to the early twentieth century—is today regarded as a literary epoch that produced some of the finest works of art ever created for children's literature. The culmination of a progressive movement that, for the first time, focused on producing texts specifically oriented to appeal to children, this era continues to be cited as a major source of inspiration for modern juvenile authors and illustrators. During this period, the sheer number of published children's texts increased exponentially, with publishing houses releasing thousands of new books annually. While most were substandard in quality, earning the label "toy books," the highest echelon featured a roster of acclaimed artists that produced painstaking illustrations which continue to be reproduced in new editions even today. Many of the top artists of this era either earned lasting fame as a result of their work in children's publishing, such as Randolph Caldecott and Kate Greenaway, or solidified already well-established reputations by crossing over to juvenile-themed illustrations, such as George Cruikshank and John Tenniel.

As a movement, the "Golden Age" can be difficult to define given the dramatically varied artistic visions, subject matter, and broadly attributed period of time over which it is said to have occurred. However, several generalizations regarding the underlying themes and motifs of the Golden Age can be made. In theory, artists ascribed to this period are remembered for their interest in providing a more intuitive connection between the text and image than had been present in children's literature prior to the Victorian Age. As a result, they introduced the first aspects of realism into popular children's illustrations with the intent of creating a gateway to the text rather than drawing attention away from the text. Additionally, while the subject matter for Golden Age artists primarily revisited previously published material—most commonly, revised editions of famous novels, educational primers and alphabet books, or classic folk stories, including the works of George MacDonald or the Brothers Grimm—Golden Age illustrators distinguished themselves through their use of modern art theories to reinterpret these more classical texts. As a result, facets of several different artistic styles were used to reinvigorate conventional children's publications, evincing the influences of the Pre-Raphaelite and Aesthetic Art movement, Art Noveau, and *Les Nabis,* among others. But perhaps most importantly, the Golden Age oversaw a new devotion by artists and publishers to children's literature that was focused solely on young audiences, fostered largely by improvements in printing methods—a result of the dawning Industrial Age—which allowed better quality illustrations to accompany these works.

As a result of the Golden Age's broad scope and time period, critics tend to divide the movement into three phases defined by three leading schools of illustrators—the early Victorians, a group of innovative masters who helped enable the ascendancy of color illustrations; the Victorians, whose work is generally ascribed as being the artistic peak of the movement; and the Brandywine School, a group of American illustrators formed under the tutelage of Howard Pyle who reinterpreted traditional Victorian motifs to create an uniquely American artistic style. There are two primary figures who are commonly associated with the Golden Age's early Victorian period: George Cruikshank and John Tenniel. Both men achieved early fame as political caricaturists for such magazines as *The Scourge* and *Punch.* While working almost exclusively in black-and-white plates drawn in ink, they laid a structural and stylistic framework that edged away from earlier children's illustrations which simply served a decorative purpose. Indeed, some critics even label Cruikshank's illustrations of Jacob and Wilheim Grimm's first English translation of *German Popular Stories* (1823) as the first manifestation of the Golden Age. Cruikshank was also renowned for his early collaborations with Charles Dickens, providing the illustrations for the first edition of *Oliver Twist; or, The Parish Boy's Progress* (1838). John Tenniel found similar acclaim with his groundbreaking plate illustrations for the first editions of Lewis Carroll's children's classics *Alice's Adventures in Wonderland* (1865) and *Through the Looking Glass, and What Alice Found There* (1871).

The second epoch of the Golden Age—the mid- to late-Victorian period—witnessed, what some consider, the zenith of children's illustration, a result of the culmination of a cultural shift in both societal thought and color image reproduction capabilities. Printer Edmund Evans published many of the most acclaimed children's texts from this era, including the works of three of the most prominent Golden Age illustrators: Walter Crane, Randolph Caldecott, and Kate Greenaway. Crane was an admirer of the Aesthetic Art movement, which sought to incorporate contemporary art into the mass-produced publications of industrial England. Crane believed that a balance could be achieved between the seemingly disparate forms of mass entertainment and great art; the success of his efforts is highlighted by some of his best known works such as *The Frog Prince* (1874) and *The Baby's Opera, A Book of Old Rhymes with New Dresses* (1877). As Crane's contemporary, Randolph Caldecott suggested an appreciation for adventure and experimentation as well as a strong belief in the use of clean bold lines that nonetheless expressed a nostalgic undercurrent for a simpler era, the details of which are readily apparent in what is perhaps his most famous work: *The Three Jovial Huntsmen* (1880). In books such as *Under the Window, with Coloured Pictures and Rhymes for Children* (1879) and *A Apple Pie: An Old-Fashioned Alphabet Book* (1886), Kate Greenaway also invoked a sentimental revisiting of the pre-Victorian era, presenting a bevy of young children playfully enjoying sunny scenes of everyday events, all facets of her characteristic images of an idealized childhood. But where Caldecott's broad strokes attempted to incorporate the stylistically impressionist forms of such artists as James Whistler, Greenaway's illustrations were slavishly detail-oriented recreations of eighteenth-century pastoral scenes. Despite their fundamentally disparate approaches to engaging their young audiences, as clients of the same publishing house, Crane, Caldecott, and Greenaway were friendly rivals, and their work remains as examples of some of the most resplendent illustrations to ever accompany a children's text.

The third phase of the Golden Age revolves around Howard Pyle's American Brandywine School. Drawing upon the legacy of Crane, Caldecott, and Greenaway, Pyle blended Victorian realism with romanticism, a style that brought a new artistic vigor to the author/illustrator's own juvenile adventure books

such as *The Merry Adventures of Robin Hood* (1883) and *The Story of King Arthur and His Knights* (1903). While the Victorian Golden Age artists would frame their illustrations with no trace of action or consequence, Pyle's artwork was fraught with the tension and drama of the text he was illustrating. In this sense, Pyle was faithful to the doctrines of the Victorian belief that illustration should be more than decorative, working to advance the plot as much as the words on the page. But as important as his artistic contributions were, Pyle's greatest personal legacy might be his instruction of a group of illustrators that is collectively called the Brandywine School. Composed of such luminaries of American illustration as N. C. Wyeth, Jessie Willcox Smith, Elizabeth Shippen Green, Maxfield Parrish, Frank Schoonover, Harvey Dunn, and Violet Oakley, the Brandywine artists were all pupils of Pyle and evince varying aspects of his tutelage in their work. Of all the Brandywine students, N. C. Wyeth's artistic style most parallels the works of his teacher. His efforts in children's literature were largely within the realm of adventure novels—including *Treasure Island* (1911) and *Robinson Crusoe* (1920)—texts that featured explosions of bright color and raging action. Like Pyle, Wyeth's work served to underscore the action, linking thought to the visual stimulation offered by the illustration. However, while Wyeth was the scion to Pyle's illustrative style, other Brandywine artists—particularly his female students—demonstrated a willingness to explore other aspects of illustration. For example, in some ways, the works of Jessie Willcox Smith seem more reminiscent of Kate Greenaway than the works of Howard Pyle. Like Greenaway, Smith dabbled with the idealized mold of drawing gently romanticized portraits of happy children sedately content in their own warm homes. But, unlike Greenaway's sentimental universe, Smith's works showed the complete family, not just the fantasy realm of the child.

By the late twenties, the era of the Golden Age began to slowly fade, with only a few illustrators such as Beatrix Potter and Arthur Rackham taking up the mantle of the Victorian and Brandywine traditions. And even though these artists can lay claim as being the equals of any of their forebears, they are sometimes considered an afterthought due to their late prestige. Indeed, Arthur Rackham's illustrations for Kenneth Grahame's *The Wind in the Willows* (1940) is generally regarded as the final great issue of the Golden Age. Still, the influence of these early masters remains widely felt in almost every picture book published today in terms of format and intent. Further, the Golden Age illustrators are credited for helping save hundreds of traditional folk tales from obscurity through their faithful retellings, even as the Industrial Age threatened their existence as society continued its dramatic shift away from the countryside and into more urban settings. But more importantly, the Golden Age illustrators saw the value that art could play in children's literature, appreciating that good art could teach and motivate. Despite the gains made to children's literature over the years, the Golden Age remains remarkable for its contrast of vivid beauty and realism while maintaining its roots in traditional illustration. In honor of their contributions to the genre, many of the most prestigious awards in children's literature bear the names of the Golden Age masters, including the Caldecott Medal for best American children's book and the Kate Greenaway Medal given annually to the best British children's illustrator.

REPRESENTATIVE WORKS

Randolph Caldecott

The Diverting History of John Gilpin [illustrator; written by William Cowper] (picture book) 1878

The House that Jack Built (picture book) 1878

Sing a Song for Sixpence (picture book) 1880

The Three Jovial Huntsmen (picture book) 1880

The Queen of Hearts (picture book) 1881

Hey Diddle Diddle, and Baby Bunting (picture book) 1882; also published as *Hey Diddle Diddle and Other Funny Poems*

A Frog He Would a-Wooing Go (picture book) 1883

Some of Aesop's Fables with Modern Instances [illustrator; edited and compiled by Alfred Caldecott] (picture book) 1883; also published as *The Caldecott Aesop: Twenty Fables*, 1978; and as *Aesop's Fables,* 1990

Jackanapes [illustrator; written by Juliana H. Gatty Ewing] (picture book) 1884

Lob Lie-by-the-Fire; or, The Luck of the Lingborough [illustrator; written by Juliana H. Gatty Ewing] (picture book) 1885

Walter Crane

Farmyard Alphabet (picture book) 1865

The House that Jack Built (picture book) 1865

Sing a Song of Sixpence (picture book) 1866

Baby's Own Alphabet (picture book) 1874

The Frog Prince (picture book) 1874

Goody Two-Shoes (picture book) 1874

Puss in Boots (picture book) 1874

The Yellow Dwarf (picture book) 1874

Jack and the Beanstalk (picture book) 1875

The Baby's Opera, A Book of Old Rhymes with New Dresses (picture book) 1877

The Baby's Bouquet, A Fresh Bunch of Old Rhymes and Tunes [illustrator; compiled by Lucy Crane] (picture book) 1878

Baby's Own Aesop, Being the Fables Condensed in Rhyme [illustrator; text by William Linton] (picture book) 1886

George Cruikshank

German Popular Stories [illustrator; by Jacob and Wilhelm Grimm] (fairy tales) 1823

Oliver Twist; or, The Parish Boy's Progress [illustrator; by Charles Dickens] (juvenile novel) 1838

George Cruikshank's Fairy Library. 3 vols. [editor and illustrator] (picture books) 1853-1854; also published as *The Cruikshank Fairy-Book,* 1911

Cinderella and the Glass Slipper [editor and illustrator] (picture book) 1854

The History of Jack and the Beanstalk [editor and illustrator] (picture book) 1854

Puss in Boots [editor and illustrator] (picture book) 1864

Kate Greenaway

Under the Window, with Coloured Pictures and Rhymes for Children (picture book) 1879

Kate Greenaway's Birthday Book for Children (picture book) 1880; reprinted as *Kate Greenaway's Birthday Book,* 1980

Mother Goose; or, The Old Nursery Rhymes [illustrator] (picture book) 1881

Little Ann and Other Poems [illustrator; by Ann and Jane Taylor] (picture book) 1882

Marigold Garden: Pictures and Rhymes (picture book) 1885

A Apple Pie: An Old-Fashioned Alphabet Book (picture book) 1886

The Pied Piper of Hamelin [illustrator; by Robert Browning] (picture book) 1888

Kate Greenaway's Book of Games (picture book) 1889

Howard Pyle

The Merry Adventures of Robin Hood (juvenile fiction) 1883

Pepper and Salt; or, Seasoning for Young Folk (juvenile fiction) 1886

Otto of the Silver Hand (juvenile fiction) 1888

Wonder Clock [with Katharine Pyle] (juvenile fiction) 1888

The Story of King Arthur and His Knights (juvenile fiction) 1903

The Story of the Champions of the Round Table (juvenile fiction) 1905

The Story of Sir Lancelot and His Companions (juvenile fiction) 1907

The Story of the Grail and the Passing of Arthur (juvenile fiction) 1910

Arthur Rackham

Fairy Tales of the Brothers Grimm [illustrator; by Jacob and Wilhelm Grimm; translated by Mrs. Edgar Lewis] (fairy tales) 1900

Gulliver's Travels into Several Remote Nations of the World [illustrator; by Jonathan Swift] (juvenile fiction) 1900

Rip Van Winkle [illustrator; by Washington Irving] (juvenile fiction) 1905

Peter Pan in Kensington Gardens [illustrator; by J. M. Barrie] (juvenile fiction) 1906

Alice's Adventures in Wonderland [illustrator; by Lewis Carroll] (juvenile fiction) 1907

A Midsummer Night's Dream [illustrator; by William Shakespeare] (play) 1908

Aesop's Fables [illustrator; translated by V. S. Vernon Jones] (fairy tales) 1912

Arthur Rackham's Book of Pictures (picture book) 1913

Mother Goose—The Old Nursery Rhymes (nursery rhymes) 1913

A Christmas Carol [illustrator; by Charles Dickens] (juvenile fiction) 1915

The Legend of Sleepy Hollow [illustrator; by Washington Irving] (juvenile fiction) 1928

The Arthur Rackham Fairy Book (fairy tales) 1933

The Wind in the Willows [illustrator; by Kenneth Grahame] (juvenile fiction) 1940

Jessie Willcox Smith

An Old Fashioned Girl [illustrator; by Louisa May Alcott] (juvenile fiction) 1902

In the Closed Room [illustrator; by Frances Hodgson Burnett] (juvenile fiction) 1904

A Child's Garden of Verses [illustrator; by Robert Louis Stevenson] (children's poetry) 1905

A Child's Book of Old Verses (children's poetry) 1910

The Jessie Willcox Smith Mother Goose (nursery rhymes) 1914

The Water-Babies [illustrator; by Charles Kingsley] (juvenile fiction) 1916

The Princess and the Goblin [illustrator; by George MacDonald] (juvenile fiction) 1921

John Tenniel

Alice's Adventures in Wonderland [illustrator; by Lewis Carroll] (juvenile fiction) 1865

Through the Looking Glass, and What Alice Found There [illustrator; by Lewis Carroll] (juvenile fiction) 1871

N. C. Wyeth

Treasure Island [illustrator; by Robert Louis Stevenson] (novel) 1911

Kidnapped: Being Memoirs of the Adventures of David Balfour in the Year 1751 [illustrator; by Robert Louis Stevenson] (novel) 1913

The Boy's King Arthur: Sir Thomas Malory's History of King Arthur and His Knights of the Round Table [illustrator; edited by Sidney Lanier] (folklore and legend) 1917

Robin Hood [illustrator; by Paul Creswick] (novel) 1917

The Last of the Mohicans: A Narrative of 1757 [illustrator; by James Fenimore Cooper] (novel) 1919

Robinson Crusoe [illustrator; by Daniel Defoe] (novel) 1920

Rip Van Winkle [illustrator; by Washington Irving] (short story) 1921

The Deerslayer; or The First War-Path [illustrator; by James Fenimore Cooper] (novel) 1925

The Yearling [illustrator; by Marjorie Kinnan Rawlings] (novel) 1939

OVERVIEWS AND GENERAL STUDIES

Anne Lundin (essay date 2001)

SOURCE: Lundin, Anne. "Victorian Horizons: 'Sensational Designs.'" In *Victorian Horizons: The Reception of the Picture Books of Walter Crane, Randolph Caldecott, and Kate Greenaway*, pp. 21-57. Lanham, Md.: Scarecrow Press, 2001.

[*In the following essay, Lundin provides a comprehensive analysis of the "cultural discourse" surrounding the works of several major illustrators from the "Golden Age of Children's Literature," including Walter Crane, Randolph Caldecott, and Kate Greenaway. Lundin presents ten traditional aspects of review that she uses as criteria to evaluate the impact of the Golden Age illustrators on their intended audiences.*]

The twentieth-century picture book bears the mark of Walter Crane, Randolph Caldecott, and Kate Greenaway. They are our historical horizon, the cultural landscape against which our modern books are foregrounded, silhouetted. Indeed, children's books, particularly from the late Victorian period, look familiar to us today. Instead of the plain fare of instruction, books for the young appealed to adult as well as child fancies. Picture books were celebrated as works of art and enjoyed a large following. From the largesse of the literati, with its tradition of authoring and editing children's books, to the speculative market of sensational fiction, children's books shared a public literary culture of young and old. The popularity of children's literature can be determined not only by the diversity of books produced but also by the nature of the productions and the manner in which they were presented. In essence, by looking at what the critics said.

The Victorian periodical press both reflected and constructed the response of the public to a literature of childhood. Literary journalists reviewed children's books in response to a heightened interest in children's reading and to a concomitant rise in the juvenile book market. Journals and magazines included essays on children's literature in its relationship to education, book arts, and the marketplace. These reviews and commentary constituted the criteria by which children's books were interpreted and given value in the late Victorian period.

How were children's books received in the formative period of the late nineteenth century? What contributions did the critics make in shaping the cultural discourse over children's books? How does this reception compare to the climate that shapes contemporary book publishing? To answer these questions, we turn to the cultural gatekeepers of the age—the periodical reviewers, the cultural mediators—to see how they perceived and promoted children's books. I embarked on what was an immersion in the cultural discourse of the late Victorian age, as revealed by their voices across a century. To understand these critical years of the Golden Age of Children's Literature, seventy-five British and American periodicals were chosen from a twenty-five-year period. The primary question was to what extent late Victorian criticism reflected and constructed a certain climate that encouraged the growth and development of what has become modern children's literature. Readings in reception theory afforded a foundation for a study of historical readership.

Reception Theory

Reception theory is a modern approach to literary history that examines the ways in which literary works are received by readers. The examination of "reception" began in the 1950s in the fields of jurisprudence, theology, and philosophy. The application of "reception" to literary studies developed in the late 1960s as a way to relate the three elements of aesthetic communication—author, work, and recipient (reader, critic, or audience). The approach is a reaction to the limitations of intrinsic literary study, of-

ten known as "New Criticism," in which a literary work is considered complete unto itself, autonomous and apart from the reader. Reception theory was launched by the theories of Hans-Georg Gadamer, Hans Robert Jauss, Wolfgang Iser, and furthered by the work of Stanley Fish, Jane Tompkins, Jonathan Culler, among others, who argue for the role that audiences play in the scheme of things. Reception theory is central to the larger field of Cultural Studies, which shares interest in the social history of how culture is produced and received.

Reception theory is related to other rhetorical studies, such as reader-response criticism. What they have in common is an interest in the relationship between the literary text and its reader, between what is being communicated and how it is received. Each reader-oriented approach acknowledges that literary works do not exist within a vacuum—a departure from formalist criticism—but have meaning from their interaction with readers. Reception study is distinguished by its greater concern with historical changes affecting the reading public than with the solitary reader. Literary meaning is determined over time, by a series of readings constituting its history of influence. The history of reception includes those literary and sociological factors that shape individual responses in a given time and place. The context of reception is defined in material and ideological terms, in aesthetic terms, or in terms of evaluative interpretive communities that mediate between the literary product and audience.

Readers of a certain social group—what Stanley Fish calls "interpretive communities"—shape readings and evaluations of a literary work. Historically situated, the community of interpreters are a work's first readers. Wolfgang Iser suggests that audiences play an important part in what he calls the "realization" of a text.[1] Jane Tompkins views historical reception as the only way to re-create the original context from which the books emerged and responded to the cultural discourse of their time.[2] The history of reception includes those literary and sociological factors that shape individual responses in a given time and place, often called "the horizons of expectation" that frames the impact and interpretation of a work. To Gadamer, the concept of a horizon is "the range of vision that includes everything that can be seen from a particular vantage point," which includes the shared meanings or "prejudices" of an age.[3] A work's first readers are privileged for their proximity to the text's cultural formation and their critical role as the audience of ideal readers—and consumers—for whom a work is conceived. In Jauss's words, the horizon "conditioned the genesis and effect of the work."[4] Examining the contemporary reception of a literary work at the moment of its emergence offers insight into why and for whom a work is conceived—an impact that may be lost to a modern reader.

Historicizing the context to a book's reception provides the opportunity to see texts in a different light. Instead of embodying universal themes of transcendent value, literature bears the cultural realities of its age, the national, social, economic, and institutional interests and concerns of an historical context from which texts arise and continue to speak. This way of looking at literature challenges canonical notions and allows for a broader consideration of "literary" and "extraliterary" texts. Children's books and picture books matter and make sense as agency, what Tompkins calls "sensational designs" that seek to move readers and make things happen as "attempts to redefine the social order."[5] A text's "cultural work" arises from its influence in the culture as a discourse of power. A literary text's particular historical audience responds to the work in a dialectical relationship by the way it answers the fundamental questions of its age. The questions and answers embedded in a literary work in a particular historical moment can only be understood by a later age through reconstructing the horizons of expectations of that time, which reveal how the readers of that day viewed and understood the work.

Allowing historical contingencies to be part of our perception of literature also offers a glimpse into the politics of reputation. Tompkins considers how works deemed classic are embedded in a network of circumstances, which are political, "since they involve preferences, interests, tastes, and beliefs that are not universal but part of a particular reader's situation."[6] Some of these circumstances are artfully crafted, and others are serendipitous interventions by figures of status and influence. Readers are always situated in relation to a work in a particular framework of beliefs and social practices. This insight does not deny a text's aesthetic value but explains, in part, why some texts reach a wide audience and rich reward, while others remain obscure. Whatever a text's intrinsic merit, a literary work succeeds or fails in terms of its cultural production, which includes publishing practices, pedagogical and critical traditions, economic structures, social networks, and national needs. Classics are made, not born.

A key to the interpretation of cultural production lies in the historical studies of reader response criticism.

The salient features that shaped literary fashions and critical reputations in the late nineteenth century were embedded in the horizons of expectations of the age—the assumptions of the readership as to childhood and its literature. The horizons of expectations with respect to children's literature in the 1880s and 1890s constituted the framework in which juvenile books were received. These standards are implicit in the Victorian periodicals of the day, in which reviewers and commentators of literary magazines and journals, as well as the popular press, articulated their expectations for literature and art. The careers of Crane, Caldecott, and Greenaway must be seen within the context of children's literature with its cultural assumptions and presuppositions, and within the context of periodical publication, in which critics embraced children's books as a valid subject and authorized their existence as text and image. Drawing on reception theory and on my own readings into the cultural discourse on children's books in late nineteenth-century England and America, I construct my sense of the spectrum of these contextual perspectives. I turn to the documentary evidence of the reviews and commentary of contemporary readers, drawing on approximately seventy-five periodicals as representative of the leading review journals of the day, as determined through *Poole's Index, Nineteenth-Century Readers' Guide,* and *Wellesley Index.*

My research reveals which periodicals, in part, reviewed children's books, something we have not known in children's book history. Of this number, forty-six periodicals, or 61%, did some reviewing of juvenile literature. On the inclusion of commentary on children's literature, fifty periodicals, or 67%, were represented. Some periodicals that did not review children's books included articles about issues related to children's reading, noted children's book authors, or classic children's books of an earlier era. The high percentage of periodicals covering children's books is significant, considering that most were literary reviews or magazines oriented to a general adult readership. As this late Victorian period was prior to the establishment of professional journals in the field, these periodicals represent the nature and extent of cultural discourse concerning children and their literature.

Based on my reading of the contemporary cultural discourse of the period (1875-1900), and in the process of determining the context for the reception of Walter Crane, Randolph Caldecott, and Kate Greenaway, I constructed the following horizons, realizing that Crane, Caldecott, and Greenaway's contemporary reception could be examined only by understanding the larger cultural context of the day: the historical situation of which both the readers and the works were a part.

VICTORIAN HORIZONS OF EXPECTATIONS

The horizons of expectations with respect to children's literature in the last quarter of the nineteenth century constituted the context in which, I believe, juvenile books were received. The literary discourse of the period can be described as including the following spectrum of positions:

(1) Treatment of children's books as a commodity

(2) Elevation of children's books as works of art

(3) Emphasis on illustration and pictorial effects in literature

(4) Lack of rigid demarcation between adult and children's literature

(5) A growing gender division

(6) Diversification of the didactic tradition

(7) Continuing debate on fantasy and realism

(8) Romantic idealization of childhood and its literature

(9) Attention to the historiography of children's literature

(10) Anxiety about the changing character of children's literature

These characteristics of the literary climate describe the complex and often conflicting critical reception of children's books in the late Victorian period. While these issues have been present to some extent since the advent of children's book publishing in the mid-eighteenth century, they converged to create a unique climate for the reception of children's books in England and America in the late nineteenth century.

TREATMENT OF CHILDREN'S BOOKS AS A COMMODITY

Victorian children's books were perceived as commodities, in the sense of prizes or rewards, gift books, and toy books. Books as prizes had a long tradition in juvenile publishing. They were originally designed to impart moral guidelines, to reinforce exemplary behavior, and to caution against the evils of intemperance or profanity. The Religious Tract Society, with evangelical leanings, and the Society for Promoting Christian Knowledge, with a broader base, were two pioneer publishers in the field whose influence continued throughout the century. By the 1870s prize books were more secular in content and more

attractive in appearance. Many of the mainstream publishers, such as Cassell, Routledge, Ward Lock, Nelson, and Nisbet, developed reward series. Reviewers rarely discussed prize books as such, but covered the leading publishers; the *Times* regularly reviewed new works of the Society for Promoting Christian Knowledge, noting that they excelled in storybooks with a wide range of tone and subject matter.[7] The visibility of prize books in the marketplace was most evident in periodical advertisements: the Religious Tract Society announced its list in the *Spectator* (1879) as "Christmas Presents and School Prizes"; Mudie's headlined an extensive list as "Christmas Presents and Prizes."[8]

However, while this "prize book" market was more institutional, geared to Sunday Schools and other educational purposes, most of the children's book trade was centered on the home. The multitude of periodicals, the promotion of books as designed for family reading, and the timeliness and publishing zeal in late autumn months for the holiday gift market all pointed to the significance of the family as a responsive market for children's book publishing. For instance, the appearance of children's books at the Christmas season promoted the association of juvenile books as illustrated holiday books or annuals. Illustrated gift books, often called "Keepsakes," "Forget-Me-Nots," or "Friendship's Offering," were produced from the beginning of the nineteenth century. They were essentially booklets of verse, by whatever famous personage could be cited as a contributor, and illustrated with steel engravings. Seasonal themes were common. The gift books were meant to be ornamental, in the style of our "coffee table books" today, something more to adorn a room rather than to be read.

The annuals began to be fashioned into illustrated Christmas stories by popular authors. It was in this tradition that the public received Dickens's *A Christmas Carol* (1843) and Thackeray's *The Rose and the Ring* (1855). This fashion died out, too, but after this the illustrated magazines revived the "Annual" tradition in their special Christmas numbers. In the late 1860s holiday gift books, illustrating a favorite poem or other literary masterpiece, began to appear on the shelves at Christmastime. Publishers vied with each other as the demand for the books grew. While only a few publishers were associated with the Christmas book trade at mid-century, by 1880, as the *Dial* noticed, the leading publishers, both English and American, were competing and employing "much of the finest literary, artistic, and inventive talent that clusters around the publishing craft."[9] Much of this attention was directed to a young audience. The *Graphic* (1882) noted a marked change in the character of Christmas literature: "Formerly the season produced a host of handsome and elaborately illustrated 'drawing-room' volumes; now such works are few and far between, and publishers' energies seem concentrated on the childish public."[10]

The concentration of children's book publishing at the Christmas season promoted the notion of the book as commodity. The *Times* (1883) began one of its Christmas book surveys by connecting the "English manner of celebrating Christmas" and "the development of popular English art." The fashion for exchanging gifts promoted the publishing of books, especially with "the growing taste for reading" and "the publishers of many classes" eager to provide competition.[11]

Juvenile books regularly appeared approximately two months before Christmas. Most publishers featured children's books only at this season, a practice that elicited commentary. The *Graphic* considered "how little juvenile literature is published at any other time."[12] The *Nation* noted in 1879, "Every holiday season brings a fresh assortment of stories for the young which, as being new, recommend themselves as gifts and do their share in the cultivation of juvenile ethics."[13] In 1880 the *Saturday Review* commented that the quantity is much more remarkable than the quality: "A flock of brilliant cloth covers, a crowd of woodcuts, is the general impression left on the weary eye and brain"[14]; in 1882 the journal observed that Christmas books come out earlier all the time, now appearing by late September[15]; and in 1886 Christmas picture books were "sufficiently numerous to engage the whole of the fabulous family of the old lady that lived in a shoe."[16] The *Illustrated London News* (1882) defined the gift book genre as consisting of handsome editions of popular classics, illustrated with pictorial designs; new flights of fancy, such as narrative poems or fairy tales, also furnished with graphic illustration; and children's books, nursery tales, rhymes, or "new ones specially composed for the beloved infant race of this present time."[17] The *Graphic* stated in 1892 that the juvenile literature of the year was crowded into a few weeks, "a custom too deeply rooted for change."[18] This custom, according to the *Bookman* (1896), impeded literary criticism, since the books appeared as a great bulk, impossible to characterize except in a cursory manner.[19]

Victorian children's books developed in part from the gift book tradition. John Newbery's pioneer works in the mid-eighteenth century were gift books, containing miscellaneous verse, pictures, and marketing ploys. *A Little Pretty Pocket-Book* (1744) included toys as rewards and gimmicks of promotion: balls for boys, pincushions for girls. Nineteenth-century children's books perpetuated these associations with the designation of "toy books." Largely a publisher's invention, the term was used to describe contemporary picture books, often issued in series, which depended for their impact on the use of color. The emphasis was indeed on color, not text, which was often slighted, until Edmund Evans transformed the genre with high quality artistic books: the works of Walter Crane, Randolph Caldecott, and Kate Greenaway.

By 1895, the *Dial,* noting the proliferation of Christmas books for children, commented that their imaginative composition could "supply a modern school of fiction," but was instead contained in fifty or so volumes of "impractical and impossible extravagances." To *Dial,* these books potentially might stimulate the heroism and genius of the future, but, more practically, their sheer volume and excess might just as readily "crush them."[20]

ELEVATION OF CHILDREN'S BOOKS AS WORKS OF ART

Children's books were transformed during this period from utilitarian fare to objects of art. The *Dial* (1881) admired the beautiful volumes, resplendent in gilt covers and exquisite illustrations, heaped on the booksellers' shelves, and recalled, in contrast, the books of the writer's own childhood, "plain and clumsy to ugliness in their exterior."[21] The *Art Journal* (1881) noted, too, the startling difference between the toy books of twenty years ago and those of the present: the earlier books were described as "primitive" and "clumsy" in conception and craftsmanship, characterized by crude lines and harsh colors, devoid of beauty. Acknowledging Randolph Caldecott's influence, the critic, William Henley, stated, "Art for the nursery has become Art indeed."[22] The *Magazine of Art* (1882) chronicled the rise of illustration in children's books, from its infancy in the mid-eighteenth century when the expectations were low; now the standards were high in the use of paper, type, and, especially, color printing, which gave the books the status to be considered as works of art.[23]

Gift books and toy books attained artistic status through technical as well as aesthetic changes. The revival of etching and invention of photomechanical methods of reproduction provided a medium for a

Illustration by Randolph Caldecott from his R. Caldecott's First Collection of Pictures and Songs.

new school of illustrators. The success of children's magazines stimulated greater attention to book arts. The competition for subscriptions and quality stories and art work raised the standards in general for children's literature.

The decade of the 1880s was attuned to art reform. Aestheticism was the name given to the heightened emphasis on art principles in domestic manufacturing, including furniture, ceramics, textiles, wallpapers, and books that began in mid-nineteenth-century England. Its most visible impact was on architecture, where it was known as the "Queen Anne style." This progressive ideal of style led to a greater interest in aesthetics for children. The Aesthetic movement in illustration was heralded by books written for children, with adults in mind, particularly the work of Crane, Caldecott, and Greenaway.

Contemporary reviewers were aware of the phenomenon. Grant Allen in the *Fortnightly Review*

(1879) related the work of Robert Louis Stevenson, Walter Crane, and Randolph Caldecott to "the many products of the Queen Anne revival," which he characterized as a reaction to "the formless solidity of the age wherein we live." He astutely observed that literary revivals tended to look back to an idealized world while incorporating touches of the modern spirit as well.[24] The *Critic* (1881) praised the number of excellent toy books on the market, which should help children learn at an early age to distinguish good art from bad.[25] The *Graphic* (1881) surmised that "children of the nineteenth century ought to grow up with well-cultured artistic tastes if they profit by the daintily illustrated books provided for their delectation."[26] The *Dial* (1881) observed that books best show the influence of "art-culture" in America. Children's books were touted as a measure of the progress of the American people in applying art to decorative purposes and to the techniques of art. A skillful use of color—"the last and most sacred element of beauty"—was considered essential. Holiday books for children revealed the extent of this "genuine feeling for the beautiful and a correct interpretation of its laws and possible interpretations."[27] This description, which could function, in itself, as a contemporary definition of Aestheticism, suggests how children's books related to the extension of the movement.

A children's book could hope for no higher praise than the word "artistic." Publishers even advertised their books as such. An advertisement by E. P. Dutton in the *Critic* (1884) was entitled "Artistic Children's Books" and included promotional blurbs that cited one book as a model for students in water-color drawing and another as "the most charming specimen of really artistic children's books that we have met for a long time."[28] By the late 1870s, children's books stood at the forefront of fashion, reflecting contemporary artistic motifs and attracting a sizable, sophisticated market.

While the Aesthetic movement peaked in the 1860s-1870s, its influence lingered in the status accorded children's books as art. In 1882 the *Graphic* noted that Aestheticism was beginning to wane, but not in children's books, where it was more influential than ever. The reviewer mentioned the familiar aesthetic themes still so prominent in juvenile books: "fancies of olden times, soft refined colouring, and humour suggested rather than strongly expressed."[29] In 1900, the *Dial* wrote about Walter Crane's picture books, "the pictures are sufficiently decorative to be used on the nursery walls by lovers of life and beauty."[30] Aesthetic principles were embodied in the Arts and Crafts movement, with its emphasis on hand craftsmanship and what the English artist William Morris called "The Book Beautiful."

Emphasis on Illustration and Pictorial Effects in Literature

In the Victorian period art became increasingly important not only in illustrating the text but also in influencing literary discourse. As a visual art, illustration was able to extend the concerns of the journalist and the novelist. In its opening issue in 1842, the *Illustrated London News* declared that art had become the bride of literature. In the serial novels of Dickens, the illustrations and pictorial narrative worked as one. A public receptive to art was instrumental in the response to illustrated children's books. The use of illustration in both children's and adult literature—picture books, periodicals, and novels—helped to educate the expectations of the public and stimulate a close relationship between books for young and old.

The popularization of visual elaboration coincided with technical progress in printing for a mass audience. The development of wood engraving was instrumental in creating a popular audience for illustration. Wood engraving was a traditional woodcut technique, dating back to the thirteenth century, in which the parts of a design that are to be white are cut away, while the black parts are left in relief. Thus, both text and illustration can be printed together. Wood engraving had been developing steadily since the mastery of the craft by Thomas Bewick (1753-1828), who perfected the process that was used extensively throughout the nineteenth century, which necessitated hard-wood blocks and tools of metal engraving. He demonstrated the effect of light and shade by lowering parts of the block to print faintly and to create delicate designs by using the close-grained end of boxwood. Bewick's techniques were adapted by news periodicals, which found the unity of the page conducive for mass production.

From the 1840s illustrations played a role in periodicals, but by the 1860s visual matter was prominent. Wood engraving was suitable to the large print runs of popular journalism. The development of a workable process of picture reproduction stimulated creativity and the emergence of artists. Professionally trained artists were engaged to illustrate appealing images of Victorian life to accompany serialized fiction, poetry, travel literature, and news stories. Illustration became a staple of popular journalism. The receptivity of the public to these images increased the use of wood engraving to produce publications in greater abundance and economy. The number of new publishers of books and periodicals grew rapidly, as did the reputation of these artists, who enjoyed an unprecedented public following and influence.

Further technical innovations changed the direction of printing by the mid-1860s. Thomas Bolton developed a technique of transferring a photographed image of a drawing to a wooden block, which enabled the engraver to work on the surface and to preserve the original drawing. George Baxter pioneered a process of using aquatinting to produce a design in color; the technique was further refined by J. M. Kronheim to produce similar effects at a lower cost. Color printing by wood engraving was perfected in the work of Edmund Evans, a printer in direct lineage to Bewick. Evans, apprenticed to Ebenezer Landells, a pupil of Bewick, developed a mastery in color printing from wood blocks and worked closely with his artists—Walter Crane, Randolph Caldecott, and Kate Greenaway—to exploit the possibilities and limitations of the medium. Evans demonstrated that it was possible to produce inexpensive illustrated books of fine color and taste.

Artistic styles and technical methods were further expanded toward the end of the century by Oriental influences and the Arts and Crafts movement, with its revival of interest in early illustration. The tradition of the decorated book had waned over the course of the century, only to be revived by the Pre-Raphaelites, in particular the edition of Tennyson's *Poems* (1857) and the title page by Rossetti to *Early Italian Poems* (1861). Book decorators and book printers worked toward an ideal of design as beautiful in its own right and its relationship to the whole of the book. As Walter Crane—who was the person most vocal on the subject—writes, "Book illustration should be something more than a collection of accidental sketches. Since one cannot ignore the constructive organic element in the formation—the idea of the book itself—it is so far inartistic to leave it out of account in designing work intended to form an essential or integral part of the book."[31] In effect, the illustrator, often collaborating with the author, became more interested in interpreting the text than in decorating the page, and the whole book—from cover to cover—was now considered text. The emphasis on the visual, on the physical attractiveness of a book, created a stimulating book environment.

Art was so prominent in literature that a writer in the *Critic* (1883) stated, "The spirit of the times takes much more kindly to the art of the painter than to that of verse-making."[32] The prevalence of illustration accompanying text in periodicals and novels affected the expectations of the public for the reading experience. The impact was on the serialization process as well as on the framework of illustrated texts. In suggesting character, advancing plot, stating dialogue, and infusing moral significance, the illustrator's creativity shared the novelist's dramatic quality. The inherent rivalry was exacerbated by a practice of matching text to preexisting pictures. The traditional role of text and illustration was reversed as well in the practice of gift books; often the illustrations were completed first, with verse then written to complement the pictures.

Reviewers frequently noted the dominance of illustration in contemporary literature. To the *Critic* (1882), "A savage dropped into a modern bookstore would undoubtedly suppose literature to be something to look at; something like Wordsworth's Nature, with 'no charm unborrowed from the eye.'"[33] The *Literary World* (1881) was struck by the proliferation of illustration, once so diffuse, which was now directed toward two distinct lines: "the pictorial poem and the children's quarto."[34] The *Dial* (1880)

Illustration by Howard Pyle from his Wonder Clock *(1888).*

noted the stock of holiday juvenile books, most of which were illustrated, and commented as an aside, "A holiday book without pictures is like a Christmas pudding without plums."[35] To Walter Crane, children's book illustration was the only imaginative outlet available for the creative artist who rebelled against "the despotism of facts."[36]

Heightened attention to art was perceived by some as a threat to the future of literature. An 1880 essay in *Lippincott's* on "Cheap Books" attributed a decline in quality literature to the ascendancy of Aestheticism. The author noted, "Literature is out of fashion, and Art is having its day." Art was defined not in the abstract but in the commercial sense—"pocket-art." The public was perceived as seeking not the distinguished literary works of the past but handbooks to art, guides to decoration and ornamentation. In such a cultural climate, books lessened in value as well as cost. All that mattered was art and adornment. The writer was concerned that women's advancement would be jeopardized by a preoccupation with aesthetic touches in artistic needlework and china painting, at the expense of higher goals of intellectual merit.[37]

Lack of Rigid Demarcation between Adult and Children's Literature

Children's books were read frequently by adults in the nineteenth century. Six of the ten best-sellers in the United States between 1875 and 1895 were children's books: *Heidi, Treasure Island, A Child's Garden of Verses, Huckleberry Finn, Little Lord Fauntleroy,* and *King Solomon's Mines.*[38] The generation after 1880 was the era of Robert Louis Stevenson, Howard Pyle, L. Frank Baum, Beatrix Potter, and Laura Richards. Richards's poetry was often featured in the *Ladies Home Journal,* suitably illustrated by Kate Greenaway. The genre of adventure fiction appealed to both children and adults, who made popular such works as *Ben Hur,* Rudyard Kipling's fables, and the scientific fantasies of Jules Verne as well as the magical creatures of Palmer Cox's *The Brownies.*

This dual readership was recognized in the reviews. The *Atlantic Monthly* in 1894 described the phenomenon as "not juvenile literature but books for the big about the little."[39] The *Times* (1889) found that "some of the stories for younger children are far more amusing reading to our minds than nineteen-twentieths of the three-volume novels."[40] The *Art Journal* (1881) distinguished between two classes of children's books: those actually written for children and those catering to "the pleasure of grown-up as well as infantile minds" and noted the continuing trend of publishing high-class works "nominally intended for the little ones, but also catering to the grown-up folks."[41] Reviewers frequently made reference to books "delighting all children between the ages of six and sixty," or "pleasing the old as well as the young."

Younger children and adults shared picture books. Older children read books whose subject matter attracted a broad popular audience. Some examples included Charles Dickens's novels, G. A. Henty's imperialistic adventures, James Fenimore Cooper's *Leatherstocking Tales,* Harriet Beecher Stowe's *Uncle Tom's Cabin,* Louisa May Alcott's *Little Women,* Mark Twain's *The Adventures of Huckleberry Finn,* and Frances Hodgson Burnett's *Little Lord Fauntleroy,* which was described in *Murray's Magazine* (1887) as "one which appeals equally to the old-young reader and the young-old reader."[42]

Other evidence exists about the breadth of child/adult reading practices. The *Pall Mall Gazette* conducted a poll in July 1898 to determine the best books for a ten-year-old. As a summary of children's leisure reading, it was instructive, suggesting the longevity of many of the books that children—and adults—read in the late nineteenth century. Most popular was *Alice's Adventures in Wonderland,* followed by two perennial favorites, the fairy tales of Grimm and Andersen. *Robinson Crusoe* and *Little Lord Fauntleroy* followed, with *The Water Babies*—sixth, *The Heroes*—seventh, *The Jungle Book*—eighth, *The Pilgrim's Progress*—ninth. Next came *The Arabian Nights,* then *Through the Looking-Glass,* the books of Alcott, *Ivanhoe,* and *Masterman Ready.* Fifteenth were the fairy tale anthologies of Andrew Lang, and the final favorites were the books of Mrs. Molesworth and G. A. Henty.[43]

Some critics tried to construct or preserve the distinction between books for and books about children. The *Art Journal* (1883), recounting the history of children's books, noted that *Alice's Adventures in Wonderland* appealed to both adults and children, and its enormous popularity and commercial success encouraged authors to write for both; the drawback to this approach, of course, was that in trying to please both, an author would please neither.[44] *Blackwood's* (1896) stated that books that were "avowedly designed both for children and for grown-up people are apt to please neither."[45] Mrs. E. M. Field's *The Child and His Book* (1891) noted that many recent books for children had not been stories *for* children, but stories *about* children, of greater interest to grown people than to the young. While her book surveyed older traditions in children's literature, her comments on the contemporary scene showed some concern for the appropriateness of the dual audience. To Field, contemporary artists were, if anything, "too good." As she said,

> The nursery picture-book has a curious tendency to find its way to the drawing-room table and to the smoking-room lounge, even perhaps to the serious study shelf. And uncles and aunts who buy these charming productions "for the children" are frequently discovered to be themselves gloating over them in a corner.

While admiring the beauty of these books, she found some of the older illustrators, such as Bewick, to be superior in their directness and simplicity.[46] Horace E. Scudder, the *Atlantic Monthly* editor, wrote *Childhood in Literature and Art* in 1894, which distinguished between books in which the child merely furnished the subject matter and those which were written to be read by the children themselves.[47] The *American Review of Reviews* noted this distinction, adding that many children's books were sources of entertainment to grown-up people, and that no rigid classification should be made.[48]

By the end of the century, there were hints of coming changes. Compared to the prime period of "the Golden Age" of children's book publishing, fewer distinguished prose writers showed an interest in writing for children. The *Dial* (1901) noticed this tendency and expressed concern for the adverse effects on children's literature. Recalling that the masters of English fiction a generation ago had not found children's books to be beneath them, the reviewer detected "a great gulf" between children's book authors, who "have little or no reputation in the broader paths of literature," and those who wrote for adult audiences.[49]

A GROWING GENDER DIVISION

The decades of the 1880s and 1890s displayed a growing consciousness of gender and a more rigid classification of children's books. Reflecting the broader discourse on gender roles, children's books during this period often dealt with themes of the "test of manhood" or "true womanhood." While books for the youngest readers tended to be more gender-inclusive, those for older children divided largely into adventure fiction for boys and domestic chronicles for girls. Robert Louis Stevenson's *Treasure Island* and Louisa May Alcott's *Little Women* stood as quintessential examples.

Historians agree that gender division in children's books became a marked trend in the 1860s, the "After-Alice" boom period of publishing. Edward Salmon, a prominent author and authority on children's books in the 1880s and 1890s, addressed the subject in various periodicals and in a collection of essays, *Juvenile Literature As It Is* (1888). In "What Girls Read," appearing in the *Nineteenth Century* (1886), Salmon was critical of the writing for girls, not in quality but in subject matter, which lacked the dynamism of boys' books. Domestic dramas, described as "goody-goody," appeared lackluster after the hairbreadth escape of boys' fiction. Girls' books existed as a transition to adult reading and to prepare young women for their social roles ahead. Well-known female authors were discussed, with Alcott the most esteemed. A poll of girls' and boys' reading, conducted by Charles Welsh, indicated a strong preference among both sexes for the works of Charles Dickens and Sir Walter Scott, and little reference to girls' fiction. While Salmon questioned the validity of the survey, he was struck by the omission and suggested that authors reconsider before producing "another story on the usual lines."[50]

Reviewers began in earnest to differentiate between boys' and girls' books in the 1890s. *Current Literature* (1899) defined the gender differences by suggesting that morals should be introduced indirectly into stories, so that little boys would intuitively recognize the requisite qualities behind the heroes of adventure fiction, and little girls would be stirred in their feminine stories with "sweetness and innocence in charming profusion."[51] While earlier columns grouped fiction for boys and girls in composite columns labeled "Juveniles," separate divisions now appeared. The *Review of Reviews,* a periodical originating in 1890 to reprint work from other periodicals, distinguished between them in their coverage of "Gift Literature." The *Academy,* which had long reviewed children's books and had recently begun a Christmas book supplement, announced in 1900 that "children's books" had become too large a designation, and that distinction would now be made between "Picture Books," "Story Books," and "Books for Boys and Girls."[52]

From the 1880s, the *Times* devoted separate review essays to boys' and girls' literature. Of all the reviewing outlets, the *Times* was the most critical of popular fiction for the young, particularly books written especially for girls. One reviewer in 1885 admitted an unsympathetic response to books written for girls and added complaints about boys' books being monotonous in plot and motive. However, even in the stalest adventure story for boys, there would be some excitement, which contrasted sharply with girls' fiction:

> However often the hero may be blown up or shot down . . . although we know he has more lives than any cat, and are assured that he will be returned to his home and parents, nevertheless there is always the exciting question as to how to scrape through each particular peril; while feminine authors writing for their sex seldom dare or care to stir the pulses, except in a quietly sentimental fashion.[53]

Commenting in 1886 on girls' fiction, the *Times,* in another prescient note, suggested that publishers would be more successful "if they occasionally gave a clever authoress her head, remembering that girls, as well as boys, delight in life and action."[54] The *Dial* (1899) noted differences in the quantity of books written for boys and for girls. The reviewer found it curious that fiction for adults was largely peopled with female characters, while fiction for youth was decidedly slanted toward boys' interests.[55]

A Diversification of the Didactic Tradition

The Victorian age as a whole was preoccupied by moral concerns. As one contemporary essayist wrote in the *Bookman* (1897), Victorian literature was "a literature of the pulpit—always self-conscious, always 'moral.'"[56] Children's literature has been dominated by the didactic tradition from its beginnings: the expectation that books for the young must in some way inform and instruct. The late Victorian period has been distinguished in the literature for its departure from the strictures of didacticism. An essay in *Saturday Review* (1886) marked this trend in the growing rise of fiction for the young. The writer noted the scarcity of books available earlier in the century, citing a brief canon of acceptable works: books by authors Maria Edgeworth, Sarah Trimmer, Anna Barbauld, Lucy Aiken, and Thomas Day; a few periodicals and an occasional annual; and, in more progressive homes, classics like *Gulliver's Travels, Arabian Nights, Don Quixote, Robinson Crusoe, Tales from Shakespeare, Tales of the Genii,* and *Rasselas.* Now all had changed, as children's books reflected "the development of a theory of fiction-making for the young at which our own worthy fathers and mothers would have stood amazed, if not absolutely 'aghast.'" The writers marveled at the abundance of juvenile stories available, in a variety of illustrations and price. Fiction was now considered appropriate family reading. The author estimated that for every one book of fiction read by the young earlier in the century, fifty fictional works were now consumed.[57]

A few years later, an 1870 *Graphic* vividly described the developments in this growing genre. Using the image of the nursery rhyme of Jack Horner and his Christmas pies, the reviewer remembered his own childhood reading, where he felt lucky to find "one plum of incident or adventure amidst the solid mass of suet of instruction and the flour of moral precepts." Contemporary children were now able to have their instruction by itself and their amusement by itself, "unspoiled by any dread of being trapped into 'lessons' in the midst of 'play.'"[58]

While it has been a commonplace to view the period of the mid-1860s through the turn of the century as "the Golden Age" of imaginative literature, there was no great departure from didactic aims in children's books. Indeed, the 1866 *Saturday Review* noted the appropriation of fiction by religious authors, whereby "the ingenuous youth of today are to be seduced into the paths of virtue."[59] Most children's books throughout the period exhibited pronounced moral or instructive themes, although there were changes in tone.

Exemplary behavior could shape destiny, given the right amount of persistence.

One evidence of the survival of didacticism in the late Victorian period was the continued publication of many of the older didactic classics. Books by Sarah Trimmer, Mary Sherwood, and Thomas Day appeared in revised editions, with more engaging illustrations and abridged texts. New editions of Mrs. Trimmer's *Fabulous Histories* (1786) were reprinted under the more whimsical original subtitle, *The History of the Robins,* and were published well into the twentieth century. Mrs. Sherwood's *The Fairchild Family* (three parts, 1817-1847) was reprinted in one-volume editions, with some textual changes. For instance, some of the more extreme religious exhortations were deleted as well as the notorious incident in the book when the children are escorted to a gibbet to see the decaying remains that ensued from quarrelsome behavior. Thomas Day's *Sandford and Merton* (three parts, 1783-1789) was reprinted many times, translated into French, and appeared in a greatly condensed chapbook edition.

The persistence of instructional works was stimulated by periodical essays and reviews which revived the childhood classics. In the *New Review,* and reprinted in the *Eclectic Magazine,* popular author F. Anstey wrote a long tribute to *The Fairchild Family,* a work of "didactic piety" and "portentous instructiveness" that has maintained its popularity and appeal for "even the most secular-minded child."[60] An *Academy* editorial of 1905 touted the older works for their clarity of vision and directness in discipline, as opposed to "the introspective literature offered to the youth of our day."[61] *Blackwood's,* surveying the contemporary landscape of children's literature in 1896, commented that "the collapse of baldly and blatantly didactic literature which took place a quarter of a century ago has not been an unmixed blessing." Tracing the evolution of a new tone in children's literature, the *Blackwood's* reviewer concluded that the children now have the good fortune of possessing excellent entertainment plus "the pick of the didactic literature, which has lost all its sting." The writer praised the quality of the old didactic tales, which children could still enjoy, especially since they would not take them seriously but would "revel in their archaic oddity."[62] Biographical essays appeared on the classic Georgian children's authors, including Hannah More, Maria Edgeworth, Anna Barbauld, and Lucy Aiken.

Most discussions of children's books in periodicals of the day included references to didactic intentions. The *Outlook* included a long essay on "Literature for

Children" (1883), which was excerpted in the *Critic,* in which the author stated that "every story should have an aim or lesson," the truth of which would be revealed, not by explicit authorial observation, but by narrative development.[63] *Current Literature* (1900) expressed a similar aim: "Let them have the joy of their childhood in the little time while they may, and make them moral by example rather than by precept—at least, such precepts as are found in books avowedly didactic."[64] But adults were counseled to be indirect in their religious exhortation, to avoid, in the words of the *Critic* (1884), "harping on the golden strings."[65]

This debate on the virtues of literature was part of the larger discourse on literacy and education. In England, the passage of the Forster Elementary Education Act in 1870, which created state-run elementary Board schools, promoted an awareness of educational needs and created a growing market for the publishers. For the first time the government made provisions to use the power of "the mighty engine of literature," in Matthew Arnold's words. By 1880 Parliament established compulsory education laws for all English children under twelve. The advent of universal education demonstrated the necessity of revising the conventional ideas of moral and social behavior, which had been long established within a settled middle-class society. Educational aims became so dominant that one writer in the *Quarterly Review* (1886) warned against excluding amusement and reminded readers that it is through the imagination that a child's interest is aroused, without which our "educational labours will be worthless."[66]

In America, where expansion of public education progressed since the late eighteenth century, expressions of faith in the social and individual benefits of education also influenced the publishing of children's books. The *Critic* commented in 1887 that educational works were beginning to overwhelm the market. The writer described the field as a table to which the choicest dishes were brought, where "didactic blackbirds vociferating the most useful information are packed, as it were, in innumerable tempting pies."[67] *Current Literature* (1888) viewed the growing list of distinguished writers creating books for children as a landmark of American civilization—"this attention to the mental needs of the young."[68] *Dial* (1894) noted the phenomenon as well, remarking that "some of the best writers, alive to the importance of this field, are sharing in the production of books of information."[69]

The didactic tradition was being redefined and reshaped into diverse formats. Earlier evangelical concerns were being replaced by a new scientism, and technical changes in Victorian printing made illustration a prominent feature of publishing for children. While most works in the earlier tradition of the moral tales were unillustrated, since illustration was perceived as incompatible with earnest content, contemporary instructive works exploited the potential of the pictorial effect. Picture books offered a new format for conveying instructive messages. The growth of literacy and the expansion of the reading and visually oriented public shaped a diversified object and medium for children's books.

CONTINUING DEBATE ON FANTASY AND REALISM IN LITERATURE FOR CHILDREN

The question of whether fact or fantasy was more appropriate reading for children has deep roots in the nineteenth century. The early reformists like Maria Edgeworth and Sarah Trimmer were concerned with educating children to live in a material world and feared that children's imaginations might be damaged by contact with mystical worlds of enchantment and mystery. Fairy tales were a subject of controversy. Fantasy in general had long been considered objectionable because it blurred truth and fiction and because it distracted children from the serious business of learning facts and moral lessons. The first objection, that fairy tales were untruthful, persisted in one form or another throughout the century, although it diminished over time. The second objection, that fairy tales were frivolous distractions from serious pursuits, was particularly pronounced during the first third of the nineteenth century, when children's books were invariably instructional in nature.

The issue continued to be debated in the periodical press into the late nineteenth century. In 1895, a column in *Punch,* "Meeting of Fairy Folk," satirized an article from the *Educational Times* by a Mr. H. Holman, school inspector, who expressed his aversion to the fairy tales for their primitive, immoral nature. *Punch* then imagined the fairy tale characters meeting to protest their expulsion from the nursery and to defend their intrinsic utilitarian worth.[70] *Good Words* also commented on Holman's views, citing his recently published book, *Education: An Introduction to Its Principles and Their Psychological Foundations,*[71] which included a critique of fairy tales as "intellectual and moral atavism."[72] While Holman questioned fairy tales for their unrealistic depiction of experience beyond a child's world, William Canton's column in *Good Words* affirmed that very quality as a virtue, the anticipation of "a world of delight beyond the region of law." To Holman's claim that facts provided satisfying subject matter, Canton argued that the cost was too great: the acquisition of "a handful of crude facts" at the expense of "that divine sense of wonder, that spiritual vision, that imaginative sympathy."

Punch could well jest, and *Good Words* rejoin, particularly since esteemed scholars like Andrew Lang shared their sentiment. As a prominent man of letters, Lang helped to popularize fairy tales and to impart an academic respectability to the field. *Current Literature* (1890) called Lang "unquestionably the foremost literary power in London at the present time."[73] His fairy book series, which began with the *Blue Fairy Book* in 1889 and ended with the *Lilac Fairy Book* in 1910, helped to shape a receptive public. To Lang, folktales were not the debased remains of higher literary myths, but the very foundation of them. Lang's name was cited in an essay on fairy tales in *All the Year Round* (1893), in which the author urged the creation of such tales for adults, described as "the children who have grown up."[74]

Fairy tales became fashionable fare in many literary magazines of the period. Even publications which normally did not cover children's literature included pieces on fairy tales as reading for adults. In *Pall Mall Magazine,* Evelyn Sharp commemorated Hans Christian Andersen's publishing centennial and acknowledged that fairy tales led the children first and the grown-ups afterwards.[75] The *Nineteenth Century* included scholarly studies of fairy tales, notably "Cinderella" and "Puss in Boots."[76] The *Gentleman's Magazine* revealed a newly discovered fairy tale in verse by Charles Lamb.[77] The *Edinburgh Review* (1898) published an extensive history of "Fairy Tales as Literature," which was one of many that expressed what the author called "the gospel of childhood's imagination." Fairy tales were viewed as opening the door to the nursery for the adult, so that the eyes of the child lingered on in the adult as "eclipsed illusions." Even when the adult learned the scientific basis of reality, there would still remain a link to "the imagination of grown years with the fairy-nurtured imaginations of the nursery."[78]

America seemed more resistant to fairy tale enchantment, and the reviewers lamented this opposition. A reviewer in the *Critic* (1887) stated pragmatically, "Fairy-tales are hardly in fashion. If you doubt it, write one for the children's magazines, and see what becomes of it."[79] An editorial in *Current Literature*

(1900), in defense of fairy tales, expressed the main objection to be an exploitation of the supernatural "to an objectionable and harmful extreme."[80] An essayist in the journal *Education* (1900) argued that "well meaning but unimaginative teachers" substituted books of facts for books of fancy, whereas fairy tales had a strong ethical element that expressed symbolically the truths of Nature.[81] What was peculiar to American children's literature was an emphasis on practicalities and self-reliance rather than imaginative play, exemplified in the popular "Peter Parley" series. These instructional works on the subjects of history, natural science, geography, biography, and mythology featured a fictionalized narrator and generous use of illustrations. As late as 1897, the *Dial* noted the prevalence of factual books of this type, which they attributed to "the worship of false gods."[82] The reviewer lamented the lack of imaginative content, citing barely half a dozen books that "give the imagination a chance to grow." He decried the absence of fairy tales, which had a truth and authenticity that spoke to the needs of generations of children. The reviewer quoted a current essay by Harry Thurston Peck, who called for a "Renaissance of the Natural, when they will no more be fed with formulas and made to learn so many improving things." *Dial* (1897) noted that children were so satiated with formulas and facts, with "only practical commonplaces to digest," that the imagination was threatened by "death from inanition."[83]

ROMANTIC IDEALIZATION OF CHILDHOOD AND ITS LITERATURE

The 1880s and 1890s were an age of romanticism and escapism. The *National Review* (1891) repeated the description of the period as "the Age of Children."[84] *Good Words* (1904) described the nineteenth century as "the Children's Century," noting the enhanced value placed on the child, as the subject of reform movements as well as scholarly studies and fictional narratives.[85] *Scribner's* (1898) explored the literary preoccupation with the child as "a second childhood in literature," in which writers looked back to a "golden age" for solace in uncertain times.[86]

Aestheticism had popularized childhood as a contrast to the excesses of modern technology, its commercial vulgarity and industrial blight. The aesthetes of the Queen Anne movement looked back to a greener time, an older time. Country life, not town life, was preferable. The old-fashioned became fashionable. The adjectives "delicate," "quaint," and "old-fashioned" were high praise, epitomizing a nostalgic romanticism of the past. The late Victorians envisioned childhood as preserving the innocent world that adults had lost. Childhood was considered a separate state of life, and the child became the focus of major imaginative and philosophical speculation—as well as commercial exploitation. Childhood for the Victorians became a symbol of mediation in a period of spiritual crisis. One poem in particular became the cultural text for this mediation—Wordsworth's "Ode: Intimations of Immortality from Recollections of Early Childhood" (1807). Throughout the nineteenth century, lines from this poem were summoned to evoke sentiment for reform as well as nostalgia. The child was viewed as one who was fresh from God and still remembered a heavenly home, while the aura surrounding childhood faded into the common light of adulthood. Writers indulged themselves in an imaginary return to the simplicity of childhood. *Scribner's* (1896) noted the outpouring of child literature, which seemed to be more about the child than for the child, more an expression of a state of mind than a dramatic literature. Adults seemed to be receiving, in their words, "unalloyed enjoyment" out of this new child literature, which was enjoying a kind of Elizabethan age.[87] The *Atlantic Monthly* observed the trend as well. In a review of Frances Hodgson Burnett's *The One I Knew Best of All,* the reviewer noted the prevalent fashion of interpreting the life of the imaginative child in terms that produced not "juvenile literature," but "books for the big about the little."[88] The *Critic* (1901) noted in an article, "The Literary Cult of the Child," that the nineteenth century had indeed discovered childhood, that it had awakened to its "dramatic" and "picturesque" possibilities, and that the effect of the child-cult was not its moral effects but its artistic value.[89] The image of the pastoral garden of childhood was pronounced for a whole framework of authors making up "the Golden Age" of children's literature: Charles Kingsley, Lewis Carroll, George MacDonald, Louisa Alcott, Richard Jeffries, Kenneth Grahame, E. Nesbit, Beatrix Potter, J. M. Barrie, and A. A. Milne. Children were viewed as having a clear, even heightened vision of the world so that by the end of the century, children and childhood became critical elements in the literary imagination.

Such romanticism became sentimentalized in the popular culture. The *Illustrated London News* (1890) described the broad nostalgic appeal of childhood:

> The pleasures of children supply the sweetest part of parents' pleasures; and to many a kindly heart, among good old maids and other childless persons, or the aged whose own sons and daughters have grown up to men and women, there is noth-

ing so delightful, in the whole spectacle of life, as the innocent joys of the little people, without whose presence the world, indeed, would be horridly dull and dreary.[90]

The periodicals reflected this iconization of the child in popular culture. In advertising, these images were used to peddle soap, insurance, silverware, or literature. Infants reading a book graced the 1880s cover of *Tinsley's Magazine,* a literary review of adult fiction. The child was extolled as "The New Hero," in an article by that title in the *English Illustrated Magazine* (1883), which was revived more than a decade later in the *Review of Reviews.*[91] Articles began to appear on the social welfare of children, on the reading responses of slum children to popular books. An essay in *Atlantic Monthly* (1901), "The Child in the Library," began, "He was an only child and a motherless one," and then chronicled the great works of literature within the library that provided solace.[92]

Romanticism was also evident in the historical themes prevalent in art and literature. There was a revival of interest in the late eighteenth century and early nineteenth century, the Regency period that represented to the late Victorians a simpler, more innocent time, just as for the Pre-Raphaelites the medieval period served as an alternative image to its modern age. Grant Allen noted in the *Fortnightly Review* (1879) "the many revivals of the Queen Anne period," in which are found "touches of the modern spirit everywhere interwoven with the older style."[93] The *Dial* (1899) related the contemporary trend of historical fiction—tales of colonial times—to romantic yearnings for a nation's childhood at a time of enormous growth into maturity. Leaving behind simpler times, the country looked back to its origins, "when the nation was still in swaddling clothes."[94]

ATTENTION TO THE HISTORIOGRAPHY OF CHILDREN'S LITERATURE

The growing attention to classic books reflected the backward glance of romanticism. As the culture focused on the golden past, it looked to its own literature of childhood. The remembered books of the turn of the century were perceived as more wholesome, less corrupted by the marketplace. The *Spectator* (1899) examined "Modern Nursery Books" and concluded that contemporary authors would be well-advised to return to the old models.[95] Mrs. E. M. Field did just that in her history, *The Child and His Book* (1891), ending her discussion with books of the 1820s.[96] Art critic and editor Gleeson White wrote a seminal essay on the history of children's book illustration that consumed the whole issue of *Studio*

(1897-98).[97] Andrew Tuer compiled *Pages and Pictures from Forgotten Children's Books* (1898), *Stories from Old-Fashioned Children's Books* (1898), and wrote the definitive work, *The History of the Horn-Book* (1899).[98] Facsimiles began to appear of classic books like *Goody Two-Shoes,* with an introduction by Charles Welsh, noted bibliophile and biographer of John Newbery.[99] The first textbook anthology of "Classics for Children" appeared in 1885 by the press of Ginn, Heath & Company, to the rave reviews of the *Dial.*[100]

Essays on the history of children's literature appeared in a wide range of periodicals, some of which did not regularly cover children's books: the *Atlantic Monthly* reviewed "The History of Children's Books" (1888) by Caroline Hewins, the children's library pioneer who was busily promoting old and new in the *Library Journal*[101]; the *Strand* surveyed "Grandfather's Picture-Books" (1892), "Favorite Books of Childhood" (1894), and "Some Old Children's Books" (1898)[102]; *Eclectic Magazine* reprinted an article that appeared in *New Review,* a tribute to "On an Old-Fashioned Children's Book: The History of the Fairchild Family," (1896) by popular author F. Anstey[103]; *Blackwood's* surveyed contemporary literature in "On Some Books for Boys and Girls" (1896), concluding with an historical appraisal[104]; the *New England Magazine* offered Charles Welsh's "The Early History of Children's Books in New England" (1899)[105]; *Critic* savored "Christmas Books of the Past" (1899), finding most contemporary holiday books "unwholesome and depressing"[106]; *Longman's* explored "Some Eighteenth-Century Children's Books" (1901)[107]; and, in that same year, *Edinburgh Review* covered "Schoolroom Classics in Fiction."[108] The interest in the origins and development of children's books indicate a maturing field, an independent branch of literature, and a romantic longing for the past—for one's own childhood reading and the childhood of the genre.

ANXIETY ABOUT THE CHANGING CHARACTER OF CHILDREN'S LITERATURE

To establish a canon of childhood literature became critical as its very foundations were considered threatened. The field was being glutted with cheap publications, products of the new rotary press, which made accessible what was popularly called "sensational fiction." The "penny dreadfuls," as they were known in England, or "the dime novels," as they were known in America, created great turmoil in the press. Many in the educational establishment felt threatened by such encroachment on the perceived purity of lit-

erature for the young. To Edward Salmon, "no element of sweetness and light" entered their dark forays into bloody revenge and base passions, improbably plotted and crudely executed.[109] Others nostalgically looked back to the simpler texts of their childhood and reminisced over the great classics so removed from what was now, in the words of the *Dial* (1888), "the large amount of trash which goes under the name of children's literature."[110] A few argued for greater tolerance of popular literature. One notable example was the essay, "Sensational Literature," in *All the Year Round* (1892), in which the author examined the conventional wisdom about the adverse effects of cheap publications on culture and morality and refuted the charges in a strong defense of popular literature.[111]

More common was the sentiment expressed by H. V. Weisse in "Reading for the Young" that cheap literature poisons the mind with its dubious moral tone and unwholesome stimulus; Weisse even suggested that a life of crime might result from such literary consumption.[112] The essayist in *Outlook*'s "Reading for Children" (1901) pointed out that the matter of reading was of great importance and presented "so many perplexities" to parents eager to train the impressionable child.[113] In 1886, the *Quarterly Review,* after surveying new editions of the great classics, called—"pleads" is its word—for a guide to children's books.[114] The following decade would provide an abundance of such guides, in the way of polls, reading lists, essay reviews and published books. One British newspaper, the *Daily News,* organized a survey of "the best one hundred books for children," the results of which appeared in the *Academy* and were reprinted in the *Eclectic.*[115] This cultural discourse over children's books articulated the formation of a canon, a prescribed list of revered texts, which the Victorians were the first to create and redefine according to a complex historical process that involved aesthetic ideals, educational theories, psychological insight, and contemporary fashion. These perceived classics function within the horizons of expectations, which to the late Victorians included a cultural consciousness of children and their growth toward "life and beauty," two hallowed words that were common to contemporary reviews and that, curiously enough, also described the themes of the great works of the "Golden Age" of children's literature.

PAST AND PRESENT

As the nineteenth century neared its end, children's literature was shaping its identity as a separate genre and fledgling field of no small import. At the same time, children's literature was being shaped by the diverse expectations of its many publics. The literary marketplace swelled with children's books, second only to novels in book production, as the yearly notices in the *Bookman* indicate. The horizons of expectations for Victorian children's books, as expressed through contemporary reviews and commentary, reinforced the notion of a literature taken seriously. The horizons suggest the deep significance for the Victorians of a literature of childhood.

My construction of the horizon of expectations yields the following assumptions about the late Victorian, Anglo-American cultural landscape.

First, the treatment of children's books as a commodity revealed the profitability of children's books in the marketplace, the appropriation of the gift book genre, and the association of children's books as holiday fare and family reading.

Second, the elevation of children's books as works of art indicated a dual audience for picture books, an aesthetic autonomy, and a perceived status as the apotheosis of art-culture.

Third, the emphasis on illustration and pictorial effects in literature lent a credibility to children's literature as a highly visual narrative form.

Fourth, the lack of rigid demarcation between adult and children's literature created broad appeal for picture books and adventure fiction and encouraged the participation of the literati.

Fifth, the growing gender division led to further classification of children's books by gender and age categories, the expansion of the juvenile market, and the disappearance of a unified audience.

Sixth, the diversification of the didactic tradition reflected the attention of the commercial trade to secular moralities and the move from narrow prescription and instruction toward the satisfaction of a wider range of interests.

Seventh, the continuing debate on fantasy and realism reflected the overt rejection of didacticism, the belated effects of romantic sensibilities, the conflicts of puritanism and scientism, and the adoption of the fairy tale as a fashionable Victorian genre.

Eighth, the romantic idealization of childhood and its literature invested the child with cult status, brought child-study to the forefront of scholarly and popular interests, and distinguished between books *for* and *about* children.

Ninth, attention to the historiography of children's literature developed out of scholarly interest in book collecting, bibliography, and the book arts, a romantic nostalgia for childhood reading, and a conservative response to a rising tide of pluralism.

Tenth, anxiety about the changing character of children's literature was expressed in research and in the criticism of children's books, the articulation of a literary canon of classic works, and the perception of the book as tool rather than art.

These horizons, in my reading of a vast landscape of discourse, informed the criticism and commentary on children's books in the late nineteenth century. Publishers created a niche for children's books, which became enlarged through expanding literacy as well as periodical coverage in reviews, commentary, and advertisements. The result was an unprecedented reviewing of children's literature in the leading literary periodicals of the day and a heightened awareness of children's social, educational, and artistic development. Specialized children's libraries and children's book publishing followed, along with the professionalism of these new networks.

The influence of these Victorian horizons persists into the twentieth century. In a continuity of cultural discourse, one horizon leads into another. While modern reading of Victorian children's books differs decidedly from the contemporary reception, we view these books with subtle lines of influence leading the reading backward and forward in time. Their horizons form part of our own. Curious variations of expectations exist in the reception of children's books in the late-twentieth century, some of these which have historical roots in the late nineteenth century. Unlike the extensive coverage of the mainstream literary press, children's books are now reviewed in a vast professional framework of publications and yet virtually ignored by literary periodicals. The public knows only the few leading names of bestselling titles or larger than life figures like Maurice Sendak. Debate continues over the book as text or tool, as instruction or amusement. Fantasy and imagination are suspect. Didacticism is diversified into social messages and technological formats that reflect and shape competing ideologies. In a hot-wired electronic culture, children learn nonlinearity and interactivity. The publishing of children's books is largely directed to adult consumers and a mass market. Multinational corporations, with children's book publishing a small subsidiary of their big business, control the literature of childhood. The book itself as historical and aesthetic artifact is threatened with extinction. Some predict the end of childhood as we knew it or would wish it to be. Experts construct lists of the best books of the century and debate such canons. Literacy is defined by those who not only can read but who continue to do so beyond the schoolroom. Children and their literature are both marginalized and mythologized. The contemporary interest comes from familiar provinces of psychological, sociological, political, and spiritual needs as the modern age, like the late Victorian, turns a new century.

Notes

1. Wolfgang Iser, *The Implied Reader* (Baltimore, MD: Johns Hopkins University Press, 1974), 274.

2. Tompkins, xiii.

3. Hans-Georg Gadamer, *Truth and Method* (London: Sheed and Ward, 1975), 269.

4. Hans Robert Jauss, *Toward an Aesthetic of Reception,* trans. Timothy Bahti (Minneapolis: University of Minnesota Press, 1981), 146.

5. Tompkins, xi.

6. Tompkins, 9.

7. "Christmas Books," *Times* (December 20, 1883), 8.

8. *Spectator* 52 (December 6, 1879), 1549, 1555.

9. "Books for the Holidays," *Dial* (December 1880), 159.

10. "Christmas Books," *Graphic* (November 4, 1882), 494.

11. "Christmas Books," *Times* (November 20, 1883), 4.

12. "Christmas Books," *Graphic* (October 20, 1888), 418.

13. "Christmas Books," *Nation* (December 11, 1879), 408.

14. "Christmas Books," *Saturday Review* (November 20, 1880), 655.

15. "Christmas Books," *Saturday Review* (November 25, 1882), 711.

16. "Christmas Books," *Saturday Review* (November 27, 1886), 733.

17. "Illustrated Gift-Books," *Illustrated London News* (October 28, 1882), 454.

18. "The Christmas Bookshelf," *Graphic* (October 29, 1892), 534.

19. "Books for Boys and Girls," *Bookman* (December 1896), 385.

20. "Books for the Young," *Dial* (December 1895), 339.

21. "Illustrated Juveniles," *Dial* (December 1881), 182.

22. W. E. Henley, "Randolph Caldecott," 212.

23. "Art in the Nursery," *Magazine of Art* (December 1882), 129.

24. Grant Allen, "Some New Books," *Fortnightly Review* (July 1, 1879), 154.

25. "Children's Books," *Critic* 1 (November 5, 1881), 307.

26. "Christmas Books," *Graphic* (November 5, 1881), 471.

27. "Illustrated Juveniles," *Dial* (December 1881), 180.

28. "E. P. Dutton's & Co.'s New Books," *Critic* (December 6, 1884), xi.

29. "Christmas Books," *Graphic* (November 18, 1882), 559.

30. "Pictures and Stories for Little Readers," *Dial* (December 1900), 507.

31. Walter Crane, *Of the Decorative Illustration of Books Old and New* (London: G. Bell & Sons, 1896), 174.

32. James Herbert Morse, "Robert Browning," *Critic* (June 9, 1883), 263.

33. "Children's Books," *Critic* (December 2, 1882), 327.

34. "Illustrated Books," *Literary World* (September 24, 1881), 327.

35. "Books for the Holidays," *Dial* (December 1880), 163.

36. Walter Crane, *Of the Decorative Illustration,* 158.

37. "Our Monthly Gossip," *Lippincott's* (May 1880), 641.

38. Hellmut Lehmann-Haupt, *The Book in America: A History of the Making and Selling of Books in the United States* (New York: Bowker, 1952), 160-61.

39. "Books for and about Children," *Atlantic Monthly* (June 1894), 853.

40. "Christmas Books," *Times* (December 5, 1889), 13.

41. "Children's Christmas Books," *Art Journal* (December 1881), 380, 408.

42. "Our Literary List," *Murray's Magazine* (March 1887), 288.

43. Gillian Avery, *Nineteenth-Century Children: Heroes and Heroines in English Children's Stories, 1780-1900* (London: Hodder and Stoughton, 1965), 137.

44. "Children's Books," *Art Journal* (January 1883), 21.

45. "On Some Books for Boys and Girls," *Blackwood's Edinburgh Magazine* (March 1896), 389.

46. Mrs. E. M. Field, *The Child and His Book* (London: Wells Gardner, Darton, 1891), 314.

47. Horace E. Scudder, *Childhood in Literature and Art, With Some Observations on Literature for Children* (Boston: Houghton Mifflin, 1894).

48. "Juvenile Literature," *American Review of Reviews* (December 1894), 698.

49. "Books for the Young," *Dial* (December 1901), 449.

50. Edward Salmon, "What Girls Read," *Nineteenth Century* (October 1886), 449-50.

51. "Juvenile Literature," *Current Literature* (March 1899), 206.

52. "Books for Children," *Academy* (December 8, 1900), 558.

53. "Christmas Books," *Times* (December 9, 1885), 13.

54. "Christmas Books," *Times* (December 21, 1886), 13.

55. "Books for the Young," *Dial* (December 1899), 432.

56. Clement K. Shorter, "The Reader: Victorian Literature," *Bookman* (January 1897), 58.

57. "Notes for Family Reading," *Saturday Review* (February 24, 1886), 238.

58. "Children's Christmas Books," *Graphic* (December 17, 1870), 590.

59. "Notes for Family Reading," *Saturday Review* (February 24, 1866), 238.

60. F. Anstey, "On an Old-Fashioned Children's Book," *Eclectic* (May 1896), 698.

61. M. E. Francis, "A Literary Causerie," *Academy* (September 9, 1905), 825.

62. "On Some Books for Boys and Girls," *Blackwood's Edinburgh Magazine* (March 1896), 387.

63. "Literature for the Young," *Critic* (May 26, 1883), 243.

64. "Fairy Literature," *Current Literature* (June 1900), 246.

65. Edward Hale, "On Writing for Children," *Critic* (December 6, 1884), 267.

66. "Books and Reading," *Quarterly Review* (1886), 512.

67. "Minor Notices of Books for the Young," *Critic* (December 3, 1887), 285.

68. "General Gossip of Authors and Writers," *Current Literature* (December 1888), 472.

69. "Books for the Young," *Dial* (December 1894), 339.

70. "Meeting of Fairy Folk," *Punch* (December 14, 1895), 287.

71. H. M. A. Holman, *Education: An Introduction to Its Principles and Their Psychological Foundations* (London: Isbister, 1896).

72. "Bits about Books," *Good Words* (1896), 214.

73. "General Gossip of Authors and Books," *Current Literature* (April 1890), 333.

74. "Fairy Tales," *All the Year Round* (August 26, 1893), 199.

75. Evelyn Sharp, "Footsteps to Fairyland," *Pall Mall Magazine* (January 1901), 132.

76. W. R. S. Ralson, "Cinderella," *Nineteenth Century* (November 1879), 832-53; "Puss in Boots," *Nineteenth Century* (January 1883), 84-104.

77. Richard Herne Shepherd, "An Unknown Fairy-Tale in Verse by Charles Lamb," *Gentleman's Magazine* (August 1885), 188-96.

78. [Una Ashworth Taylor], "Fairy Tales as Literature," *Edinburgh Review* (July 1898), 59.

79. "Minor Notices of Books for the Young," *Critic* (December 3, 1887), 285.

80. "Fairy Literature," *Current Literature* (June 1900), 246.

81. Anna Hamlin Wikel, "The Child and His Book," *Education* (May 1900), 544.

82. "Books for the Young," *Dial* (December 1897), 342.

83. "Books for the Young," *Dial* (December 1897), 342.

84. H. Sutton, "Children and Modern Literature," *National Review* (December 1891), 507.

85. Florence Maccunn, "Children's Story-Books," *Good Words* (1904), 341.

86. "The Point of View: The Golden Age—Second Childhood in Literature," *Scribner's Magazine* (January 1898), 123.

87. "The Point of View: 'The Child's Garden'—of Verses and Other Literature," *Scribner's Magazine* (April 1896), 519.

88. "Books for and about Children," *Atlantic Monthly* (June 1894), 853.

89. Louise Betts Edwards, "The Literary Cult of the Child," *Critic* (August 1901), 167.

90. "Joies D'Enfants," *Illustrated London News* (December 13, 1890), 739.

91. Theodore Watts, "The New Hero," *English Illustrated Magazine* (December 1883), 181-990; "The 'New Hero' and His Picture Books," *Review of Reviews* (1897), 604.

92. Edith Lanigan, "The Child in the Library," *Atlantic Monthy* (January 1901), 121.

93. Grant Allen, "Some New Books," *Fortnightly Review* (July 1, 1879), 154.

94. "Books for the Young," *Dial* (December 1899), 432-33.

95. "Modern Nursery Books," *Spectator* (December 2, 1899), 841-42.

96. Mrs. E. M. Field, *The Child and His Book* (London: Wells Gardner, Darton, 1891).

97. Gleeson White, "Children's Books and Their Illustrators," *Studio* (Winter 1897-98), 3-68.

98. Andrew Tuer, *Pages and Pictures from Forgotten Children's Books* (London: Leadenhill, 1898); *Stories from Old-Fashioned Children's Books* (London: Leadenhill, 1898); *History of the Horn-Book* (London: Leadenhill, 1899).

99. *Goody Two-Shoes,* facsimile reprint of 1766 ed. with introduction by Charles Welsh (London: Griffith & Farran, 1881).

100. "Briefs on New Books," *Dial* (June 1885), 51.

101. Caroline Hewins, "The History of Children's Books," *Atlantic Monthly* (January 1888), 112-26.

102. "Grandfather's Picture Books," *Strand* (1892), 199-208; Francis Low, "Favorite Books of Childhood," *Strand* (1894, 128-36; Alice Waters, "Some Old Children's Books," *Strand* (1898), 32-40.

103. F. Anstey, "On an Old-Fashioned Children's Book," *Eclectic* (May 1896), 698-705.

104. "On Some Books for Boys and Girls," *Blackwood's Edinburgh Magazine* (March 1896), 386-91.

105. Charles Welsh, "The Early History of Children's Books in New England," *New England Magazine* (March 1899), 147-60.

106. Annie Russell Marble, "Children's Books of the Past," *Critic* (December 1899), 1122-32.

107. L. Allen Harker, "Some Eighteenth-Century Children's Books," *Longman's* (October 1901), 548-57.

108. "Schoolroom Classics in Fiction—A Survey," *Edinburgh Review* (October 1901), 414-37.

109. Edward Salmon, "What Boys Read," *Edinburgh Review* (1886), quoted in "What Boys Read," *Punch* (February 20, 1886), 96.

110. "Books for the Young," *Dial* (December 1888), 211.

111. "Sensational Literature," *All the Year Round* (September 24, 1892), 294-300.

112. H. V. Weisse, "Reading for the Young," *Contemporary Review* (1901); "Reading for the Young," *Eclectic* (September 1901), 228-46.

113. "Reading for Children," *Outlook* (December 7, 1901), 866.

114. "Books and Reading," *Quarterly Review* (1886), 512.

115. "The Best Hundred Books for Children," *Eclectic* (June 1900), 802.

VICTORIAN MASTERS OF THE GOLDEN AGE

Patricia Demers (essay date 1989)

SOURCE: Demers, Patricia. "Walter Crane's *The Baby's Opera*: A Commodious Dwelling." In *Touchstones: Reflections on the Best in Children's Literature, Volume Three: Picture Books,* edited by Perry Nodelman, pp. 46-54. West Lafayette, Ind.: ChLA Publishers, 1989.

[*In the following essay, Demers provides an introduction to the life and canon of "Golden Age" illustrator and author Walter Crane, paying particular attention to his seminal work* The Baby's Opera, A Book of Old Rhymes with New Dresses *and noting the various influences that inspired his oeuvre.*]

Artist and teacher, enthusiast and critic, romantic and socialist, Walter Crane devoted his life to the ideal of beautification. He remains a byword for elegance and design in illustration. We are still attracted by the gentle drape of the gowns and balletic grace of his women, by the cheerful insouciance of his children and the muscular proportions of his men, and by his often humorous exploitation of the full page. Symbols, emblems and quirky jokes so abound in his vibrantly coloured work that few of his real fans need to search for the identifying signature rebus (a bird and W within a semi-circle): we instantly recognize the Crane "look."

In his *Papers and Addresses on Art and Craft and the Commonweal* (1911), Crane enumerated these "essential qualities of beauty": "harmony, proportion, balance, simplicity, charm of form and colour" (*William Morris to Whistler* 214). Unfortunately, some of Crane's admirers have isolated certain of these features and disregarded others, making their commentaries on his work clear examples of the Aesopic moral that "the story depends on the teller."

For instance, Edmund Evans, the water-colour artist and businessman who worked with Crane, recognized him as "a genius," and was especially impressed with the accuracy of Crane's animal drawings, which were executed "in the most intelligent way, without a fraction of hesitation in the line" (32). This "great ability in drawing," fostered no doubt by Crane's three-year apprenticeship to the engraver J. W. Linton and his frequent visits to London's Zoological Gardens in Regent's Park, distinguished his earliest collaborations with Evans—*Railroad Alphabet* and *Farmyard Alphabet* (1865)—and also sparked the success of the sixpence Toy Books of 1865-86 and the larger shilling series of Toy Books of 1874-76.

Quite differently, it is Crane's fascination with the black outlines and flat colours of the Japanese printmakers Hokusai, Hiroshige and Bari in the late eighteen sixties, and his absorption in the Renaissance masters during his extended honeymoon in Italy (1871-73), that inform William Feaver's comments on his "pure but eclectic manner." According to Feaver, Crane set a standard for "stylish quality": "one could assume that every item he showed was available from Liberty's shop in Regent Street" (16). As the first president of the Arts and Crafts Exhibition Society, an association of painters "against the Royal Academy and its narrow views of art and exclusiveness" (Crane, *William Morris* 95), Crane secured a platform for his passionate views about the needed blend of utility and beauty in all the interrelated aspects of daily living—clothes, furniture and architecture. "Modern life," Crane said in discussion "Of the Progress of Taste in Dress in Relation to Art Education," lacked "beauty and romance" because it was "ruled by the dead weight of the prosaic, the prudent, the timid, the respectable . . ." (185). In fact, because Crane declared in his *Reminiscences* (1904) that his work was the "vehicle" of his ideas, Alan Suddon has made Crane's essay about taste in dress the basis of an argument about the surprising, venturesome and uncorsetted costumes of Crane's illustrations. Suddon goes as far as to suggest that the non-restricting kimono styles modelled by Crane's nursery adults actually influenced the softer lines of turn-of-the-century and Edwardian fashion.

Evans, Feaver, and Suddon are all partially right. But Crane is more than a gifted line drawer, or a purveyor of stylized Japonaiserie, or a Pre-Raphaelite couturier. He heralds an exuberant development in the design of children's books, particularly because he demonstrates that a book can be a work of art: in his own words in "A Decorative Ideal," "the home of both thought and vision" (*Ideals* 184).

Not only does Crane's extended, poetic description of a book as a commodious dwelling provide a fine introduction to his work for children, it also establishes Crane's place as an artist in his own time. His remarks about books emerge from a discussion of one of the foremost innovations of his era: photographic reproduction, which was as transforming in his day as computer technology is in our own. While Crane was quick to realize its advantages, he was not unaware of the losses involved. Among the most significant of these, in his opinion, was the confusion and deterioration of "the faculty of inventive design, and the sense of ornament and line." Since complete control and mastery of the layout of each page was an essential tenet, it is natural that he would want a book to beckon its reader, not with a rough hewn realism but with its friendly "architectural plan." He envisions the reader welcomed by the "facade" of the frontispiece, the "inscription over the porch" of the title page and the "votive wreath" of the dedication, and being led by the author and artist "from room to room, as page after page is turned, fairly decked and adorned with picture, and ornament, and device; and, perhaps, finding it a dwelling after his desire, the guest is content to rest in the ingle nook in the firelight of the spirit of the author or the play of fancy of the artist" (184).

Crane's own fancy never disappoints a reader. From the earliest eight-page, paperbound Toy Books of 1865-66—*Sing a Song of Sixpence, Cock Robin, The House that Jack Built, Dame Trot and Her Comical Cat* and *The Waddling Frog*—to the more stylistically advanced work in this format of 1867-69—*1, 2 Buckle My Shoe, Multiplication Table in Verse* and *Grammar in Rhyme*—he ingeniously blended text and illustration on each page. With the improved colour processing of later works like *Old Mother Hubbard, Little Red Riding Hood* and *The Sleeping Beauty,* with Crane's easy self-portraiture as the master of *Puss in Boots* (1873), and with the splendid double-page centrefolds of each of the shilling Toy Books—especially *Goody Two Shoes, Beauty and the Beast, The Yellow Dwarf, Bluebeard, Princess Belle Etoile* and *Aladdin*—his reputation in the forefront of children's book illustration was assured. We can hunt for the Botticelli-inspired poses in *Beauty and the Beast,* point to the influence of Pre-Raphaelitism in *Princess Belle Etoile,* notice the confusion of Japanese and Chinese styles in *Aladdin* and ferret out the Flaxman bias in *The Yellow Dwarf*; but the essential thing is the unique stamp of design and execution that marks Crane's work.

Only with the publication of *The Baby's Opera* in 1877, however, did Crane's intense love of detail, powerful line and instinct for full-page adornment truly affect the final product. *The Baby's Opera* signals the beginning of his mature work for many reasons. Although the texts are still borrowed and traditional, in this case "old rhymes . . . by the earliest masters" chosen and arranged by Crane's beloved sister Lucy, the "dresses" he concocts for them are wonderfully new. In this charming book tailored to the small hand (16.8 × 15.7 cm.) and captivating young and old reader alike, each of the thirty-six rhymes and eleven complete illustrations is full of

Crane's personal response to the particular nursery ditty. His borders picture the song, not merely by encapsulating its events but by echoing its rhythms, exploiting its humour and emblematizing its world. They also frame these simply played tunes with an extended palate of colors, ranging from sienna to gamboge, flesh tint to bisque, azure to deep marine.

Crane's quietly unobtrusive "architectural plan" nevertheless controls the whole book. The jovially rotund figure of King Cole drawing on his hookah and beaming at his musicians, who are clad in jerkins embroidered with emblems of their art, supplies the facade. What could be friendlier, we wonder, than the inscription over the porch of Crane's title page, with one line of feline fiddlers and another of a nursery rhythm band framing the stage curtain that announces this production. Encircled in laurel and enjoying the central position is the infant, rattle in one hand and book in the other, while a knowledgeable-looking long-billed bird peeks out from the side of the screen. The book is dedicated to Mrs. George Howard (whose husband later became the ninth Earl of Carlisle); the votive wreath for this page consists of a baby gleefully sailing in a coracle-lyre that is prowed with a crane and propelled, we assume, by the Aeolian breeze of the artist Crane's fancy. The book's own medallion, on the verso of the title page, features an infant Pan or Orpheus charming the animals with his pipe and sitting beneath a tree festooned with a palate bearing Crane's rebus and a banner marked with a double E, to indicate his collaboration with Evans. There is nothing recondite about this symbolism, which provides such a hospitable welcome to the musical works ("opera" at its roots) which follow.

In the opening song, girls and boys are invited to "come with a good will, or not at all." Crane's world is indeed one of cheer and good will. Although the ice cracks under three children at play "all on a summer's day," and an aristrocratic womanizer wishes to dally with the pretty milkmaid, and King Arthur is a gourmandizing thief who steals the ingredients for a plum pudding, their situations are neither dreadful nor threatening. Crane's penchant for drollery and light-hearted burlesque dictates his treatment of these three old rhymes. As Iona and Peter Opie explain, "Three Children" could have originated in a Caroline ballad about the burning of London Bridge (282); but Crane exults in the mock-cautionary tone with its tongue-in-cheek warning to "parents all that children have, / And you that have got none." In the "carefully rewritten" ditty that had existed in a more

Illustration by Walter Crane from Favorite Poems of Childhood *(1993). Simon & Schuster, 1993*

bawdy version since the days of James I, Crane's articulate milkmaid handles the gentleman as capably as Ralegh's nymph answered Marlowe's passionate shepherd; in addition, his bonneted maid—winsome, nubile but sensible—encountering the frock-coated squire contrasts nicely with Randolph Caldecott's treatment of *The Milkmaid* (1882), a jauntily bodiced lass whose back only is seen as she walks briskly and converses with a young, horsebound cavalier. Whether the original ballad was about King Arthur or King Stephen, and whether the Queen involved was "good Quane Bess" (Opie 56) or Guinevere, Crane chooses to spotlight the use to which the frugal and talented queen puts her husband's theft; without any of the sultriness of William Morris's *Queen Guinevere* (reproduced in Harding's *The Pre-Raphaelites* [95]), Crane's queen is a capable, handsomely proportioned cuisiniere who feeds the noblemen and fries the leftovers for breakfast. This illustrator takes pleasure in physical attractiveness.

His women are less angular, histrionic and lantern-jawed than many of the models of his Pre-Raphaelite contemporaries; either in empire waists or Grecian draperies, they have fuller figures and curlier hair, and embody a gently maternal comeliness.

As in most nursery rhymes, incongruities are plentiful in *The Baby's Opera*. The black sheep never accounts for one of his bags of wool, yet there is still "none for the little boy that lives down the lane." Crane, though, attenuates any stress on pain or discomfort. Baby's cradle will fall, but the gentle tendrils bordering the song suggest a cushioned descent. The bucolic sturdiness of Jack indicates that he will probably recover quickly from the cranial fracture. Crane does not moralize or admonish; he is content to entertain. He clearly delights in such eccentrics as the "jolly miller," a happy curmudgeon whose world is coloured in yellows and pinks on an outline of soft blue. The illustration might even be a fanciful document. Although he was born in Liverpool, Crane was raised in the south of England, in Torquay and London; he may have heard childhood stories about the old Dee mill at Chester or actually have visited the site where, the Opies tell us, the legendary miller of Dee is supposed to have plied his trade (302). Since the mill burned down in 1895, we cannot check Crane's drawing against the original, but we can conjecture that there was probably considerable accuracy in his representation. He imparts a cartoon quality to the donnish activities of Dr. Faustus, whipping his scholars first in one direction and then the reverse. The ferule borders this ditty as fittingly as the crook surrounds "Little Bo Peep," "Baa! Baa! Black Sheep" and "Over the Hills & Far Away."

Crane's real genius in *The Baby's Opera* resides in the deft harmonizing of ornament and design with the mood and rhythm of each song. "Xmas Day in ye Morning" is a clear-voiced street cry that strikes a thrilling minor key when the dame and her maidens are enjoined to bake their pies. The blue and bisque enclosure of this song suggests not only the outside brick wall of a house, with windows illustrating specific quartets, but also the arched masonry and entablature of oven openings. Crane creates an entirely different kind of harmony for "My Lady's Garden," in which the calm passage up and down the F major scale is echoed in the neat borders of blue and pink silver bells and cockle shells as well as by the perfectly alternated sweet human faces of the flowers, superintended by a gardening Mercury, in the full-page illustration.

Crane's hand exercises masterful control over this whole production. He orchestrates the leap of the cow, the dance of the plate and spoon, the tune of the cat cellist and the paw-tapping chortle of the gentleman dog on the front cover as surely as, in the guise of a tuxedoed crane, he presents the "Hey diddle diddle" rhyme to a pair of youngsters in evening costume on the back cover. Such a delightful ebullience is in no way belittling to children, and does not reduce them to miniature adults. It does, however, express Crane's fervent belief in the need to expose them to art and beauty from the earliest age.

A companion volume, *The Baby's Bouquet, A Fresh Bunch of Old Rhymes and Tunes,* was issued the following Christmas, and maintains Crane's distinctive stress on an aesthetically pleasing and joyous milieu. Once again, the emphases on comfort, grace and artistic design—consistent with his theory of illustration as a vehicle for his ideas about modern life—are

announced at the outset. Nothing could be further from what Crane in *William Morris to Whistler* called the "vulgar smartness and stuffiness" of mid-Victorian furniture, "afflicted with curvature of the spine" and showing "design-debauchery" (52), than the inviting nursery scene which provides the frontispiece of *The Baby's Bouquet*. The children wear no-waist pinafores; one pushes the other in a wonderful wicker perambulator; and they receive a floral bouquet from a winged, Aphrodite-like enchantress. Toys are strewn about the room; the wainscoting is decorated with Crane's nursery friezes and the wallpaper above it is also a real paper of his own design. Here is illustration as both advertisement and tour-de-force. The votive wreath, called "Pegasus," highlights not the infant mariner but the hobbyhorse-riding child, who plays an enlarged French horn which actually surrounds the whole design. Crane seems to have been especially fascinated with the Pegasus figure, and drew "a Pegasus to all little passengers aspiring to run, and read, or write" as a cover-device for a collection of three books, *A Romance of the Three Rs,* in the first of which, *Little Queen Anne and Her Majesty's Letters,* appear more of the wicker furniture and nursery toys from *The Baby's Bouquet*. Lucy Crane again collected and arranged the tunes for the *Bouquet*; forecasting their later collaboration in Lucy's translation of *Household Stories from the Collection of the Brothers Grimm* (1882), her influence is evident in the number of German and French pieces included. His long-standing interest in folk music also resulted in Crane's partnership with Theophilus Marzials, the head of the music section at the British Museum, who supplied the arrangements for *Pan Pipes. A Book of Old Songs* (1882); its bitter sweet ballads, such as "The Three Ravens," "Early One Morning" and "Barbara Allen," are directed at an older readership than the three Baby books.

The last of the "triplets," *The Baby's Own Aesop* (1887), is definitely the most skilled and challenging. Crane felt free to adjust, to add "a touch here and there" to the rhymed version of the fables supplied by his old master W. J. Linton. The dedication—"to the possessors of *Baby's Opera & Baby's Bouquet* with Walter Crane's compliments"—indicates some of the changes that have taken place during the nine-year interval. An infant stevedore operates a mechanical crane or winch, from whose beak the new cargo descends to the vessel already carrying the *Opera* and *Bouquet*. An owl is perched on the bow, while a quill stuck in an inkpot serves as a mast. Crane often treats four fables on a double page, and never provides a full-page illustration uninterrupted by text.

He seems at pains to squeeze as much of the worldly, pragmatic, frequently cynical wisdom of the Greek fables into his design as possible. With the pithiness of the rhymes and morals, the zoological precision of his drawings and his penchant for caricature, Crane leads the young reader to an understanding of the tactics of gamesmanship ("The Fox & the Crane"), the strategy of politics ("The Fox & the Mosquitoes") and the emptiness of masks ("The Fox & the Mask"). It is a more sobering work than the two earlier Baby books; perhaps Crane felt that its unflattering assessment of human nature, by means of illustrating old saws, was the necessary counterpoint to the amiable ditties. When George Routledge issued all three under the title *Triplets* (1899), Crane probably considered that they represented a healthy combination of the beautiful and the useful.

So established was Crane's reputation that he was commissioned as the illustrator of stories by Mrs. Molesworth, Robert Louis Stevenson, Mary de Morgan, Oscar Wilde and Nathaniel Hawthorne and of such textbooks as *The Golden Primer* (1884) and *The Dale Readers* (1899-1907). Although Ruari McLean can state categorically that "the typical fault of Victorian book design was feebleness" (6), that judgement must be adjusted—if not overturned—in the case of Crane. His prolific invention, it is true, did not extend to the elaborate tracery which distinguished his friend William Morris's Kelmscott imprints. But his excellence *was* recognized and celebrated. He was the first president of the Art Workers' Guild established in 1884, and of the Arts and Crafts Exhibition Society begun in 1888. He was appointed as Director of Design at the Manchester Municipal School of Art in 1893, Art Director of Reading College in 1896 and Principal of the Royal College of Art, South Kensington, in 1898. As well as contributing cartoons regularly to the socialist periodicals *Commonweal* and *Justice,* he wrote idiosyncratic theoretical books, such as *The Bases of Design* (1898), *Line and Form* (1900) and *Ideals in Art* (1908). He continued to paint while illustrating and designing books; in fact, in the same year that *The Baby's Opera* was published he also completed an ambitious oil painting, *The Renaissance of Venus.* He knew the other members of the famous illustrating trio, having met Kate Greenaway once and having welcomed many friendly visits from Randolph Caldecott to his Shepherd's Bush studio.

Crane was an indulgent father and sought-after-artist—a duality that sounds both quaint and anomalous today. He provided illustrations for works by Spenser and Shakespeare, Cervantes and Plutarch, but also, as Margaret Crawford Maloney tells us, found time to toss off "at odd moments" private entertainments for his three children, Beatrice, Lionel and Lancelot (8). Most of these over-thirty family works remain in manuscript; the few that have been published—*Legends for Lionel* (1887), *Lancelot's Levities* (1888), *Mr. Michael Mouse* (1956) and *Beatrice Crane Her Book (The 2nd)* (1983)—offer privileged glimpses of a close, witty, fun-loving Victorian family.

Indeed, these experimental miscellanies reveal the childlike pleasures that animated Crane's life. The most recent assessment of his work and character, in Humphrey Carpenter and Mari Prichard's *Oxford Companion to Children's Literature,* cites the eulogy of his friend, C. R. Ashbee, about his naiveté as the blissful "Commendatore" living devotedly alongside "Mistress Crane." I think his way of life, that seems to have had all the popular associations of the fairy tale, was a deliberate and artistic decision. Neither regressive nor reactionary, he openly admitted a perpetual fascination with "the rich tapestry of story and picture . . . , the warp of human wonder and imagination . . . crossed with many coloured threads of mythological lore, history and allegory, symbolism and romance." (134) Recognizing in design his own succinct language for talking to his fellow men, Crane pursued his art with a dedication that made blitheness and ardour uniquely compatible.

References

Carpenter, Humphrey, and Mari Pritchard. *Oxford Companion to Children's Literature.* Oxford: Oxford Univ. Press, 1984.

Crane, Walter. *The Baby's Opera: A Book of Old Rhymes with New Dresses by Walter Crane, Engraved & Printed in Colours by Edmund Evans. The Music of the Earliest Masters.* London and New York: George Routledge & Sons, 1877.

———. "Preface." *The Romance of the Three Rs: Penned and Pictured by Walter Crane.* London: Marcus Ward & Co., Ltd., 1886.

———. "The Lion and the Statue." *The Baby's Own Aesop: Being the Fables Condensed in Rhyme with Portable Morals Pictorially Pointed by Walter Crane.* London and New York: George Routledge & Sons, 1887.

———. "Of the Progress of Taste in Dress in Relation to Art Education." *Ideals in Art: Papers Theoretical, Practical, Critical.* London: George Bell & Sons, 1905.

————. *William Morris to Whistler; Papers and Addresses on Art and Craft and the Commonweal.* With Illustrations from Drawings by the Author and Other Sources. London: G. Bell & Sons, Ltd., 1911.

Evans, Edmund. *The Reminiscences of Edmund Evans.* Ed. Ruari McLean. Oxford: Claredon Press, 1967.

Feaver, William. *When We Were Young: Two Centuries of Children's Book Illustration.* London: Thames and Hudson, 1977.

Harding, James. *The Pre-Raphaelites.* London: Academy Editions, 1977.

Maloney, Margaret Crawford. "About *Beatrice Crane Her Book* and Her Family." *Beatrice Crane Her Book (The 2nd) June 1st, 1879. A Manuscript by Walter Crane.* Toronto: Reproduced by the Friends of the Osborne and Lillian H. Smith Collections, 1983.

McLean, Ruari. *Modern Book Design from William Morris to the Present Day.* London: Faber & Faber, 1958.

Opie, Iona and Peter, ed. *The Oxford Dictionary of Nursery Rhymes.* Oxford: At the Clarendon Press, 1951.

Suddon, Alan. "Walter Crane, Dress, & Children's Illustration." *Canadian Children's Literature* 4 (1976).

Alison Lurie (essay date 1990)

SOURCE: Lurie, Alison. "The Child Who Followed the Piper: Kate Greenaway." In *Don't Tell the Grown-Ups: Subversive Children's Literature,* pp. 51-66. Boston, Mass.: Little, Brown, and Company, 1990.

[*In the following essay, Lurie charts the publishing career of "Golden Age" illustrator Kate Greenaway, suggesting that Greenaway's seemingly idealized portraits of childhood are subtly subversive protests against industrialization. Lurie also expounds on how Greenaway's relationship with John Ruskin impacted the illustrator's overall body of work.*]

One of the gifts an artist may have is the ability to create what J. R. R. Tolkien called a "secondary world"—a fully imagined alternate universe, as consistent as our own or possibly more so. Such a secondary world may make visible some aspect of the primary one, so that once we have seen, for instance, a landscape by Corot, a play by Chekhov, or a film by Chaplin, we will find echoes of it ever after.

Not all artists have this gift. Some painters of the first rank lack it, while some of the second rank are given it in abundance. It can even coexist with a level of skill that would keep its possessor out of most galleries today. Kate Greenaway, who was famous in her own time for her pictures of pretty children in pastoral landscapes, is hardly visible when measured against the best artists of her period. She began her career as, and in many ways remained, a designer of greeting cards. Her color sense was refined but timid, her range of subjects narrow. As a draftsman she was at times almost pathetic: her trees seem to be made of green sponge, her sheep look like poodles, and even John Ruskin, her greatest fan, could not teach her perspective. All she could really draw was flowers and children, especially good little girls—and even here she sometimes faltered: Ruskin irascibly described the feet of her figures as "shapeless paddles or flappers."[1] Yet she was as popular in her own time, and is probably better known today, than either Randolph Caldecott or Walter Crane, the other members of the trio that revolutionized the picture book in the late nineteenth century—though Crane was a better graphic designer and Caldecott a superior draftsman.

Outwardly Kate Greenaway seems in no way a subversive artist. Yet her little boys and girls are far freer than most middle-class children in Victorian England, when well-to-do children, especially girls, wore heavy, stiff, uncomfortable clothing and were almost never observed running barefoot on the grass. Greenaway's world was also completely rural and preindustrial; it can be seen as a silent protest against what the railways and the factories were doing to the English countryside and the towns.

Kate Greenaway's work is also subversive in another, less obvious sense—one that most of her readers might never have noticed and of which she was probably unaware herself. Underneath the innocent surfaces of her drawings and rhymes there occasionally appears a kind of sentimental sensuality about childhood that was one of the darker secrets of the Victorian age and that, as we shall see, brought her at least one dubious admirer.

The classic makers of children's literature are not usually men and women who had consistently happy childhoods—or consistently unhappy ones. Rather they are those whose early happiness ended suddenly and often disastrously. Characteristically, they lost one or both parents early. They were abruptly shunted from one home to another, like Louisa May Alcott, Kenneth Grahame, and Mark Twain—or even, like Frances Hodgson Burnett, E. Nesbit, and J. R. R. Tolkien, from one continent to another. L. Frank Baum and Lewis Carroll were sent away to harsh and bullying schools; Rudyard Kipling was taken from India to England by his affectionate but ill-advised parents and left in the care of stupid and brutal strangers. Cheated of their full share of childhood, these men and women later re-created, and transfigured, their lost worlds. Though she was primarily an artist rather than a writer, Kate Greenaway belongs in this company.

In the more than eighty years since Kate Greenaway's death there have been only two biographies of her. The first, M. H. Spielmann and G. S. Layard's *Kate Greenaway* (1905), is a rambling, lavishly illustrated, eulogistic whitewash, which does its best to make her into one of her own quaint, old-fashioned figures. Rodney Engen's serious and perceptive study, published in 1981, was long overdue. As he shows, Greenaway's childhood, in the classic pattern, was marked by turbulence and sudden deprivation.

Though Kate Greenaway was born in London, when she was eight months old her mother became ill, and Kate was put out to nurse on a farm in Nottinghamshire. Kate called the farmer's wife, Mary Chappell, "Maman" and wrote of her later as "the kindest, most generous, most charitable, the cheerfulest and most careful woman"[2] she had ever known. "In all things she was highest and best."[3] No description by Kate of her real mother has survived; she is said to have had a "stern, religious nature . . . resolved to do what was, in her view, morally right."[4]

After two years in the country, Kate was brought back to gray, grimy, working-class Victorian London, where her father, a wood engraver, was struggling with decreasing success to support his increasing family. When Kate was five the family moved again, to Islington, and her mother opened a small shop selling children's and ladies' dresses and trimmings. It prospered, but Mrs. Greenaway was now at work from eight a.m. till eight p.m., and the care of Kate and her younger sister and brother was transferred to twelve-year-old Lizzie, the eldest child. Since their house had no yard or garden, the four children spent most of their time wandering about the London streets. In the summer, when there was enough money to spare, they would be sent to Nottinghamshire, and Kate would stay with the Chappells in what she always insisted was her real home.

Unlike the little girls in her books, Kate Greenaway was an odd, awkward, plain child—intensely shy, strong-willed, and moody. When she was sent to school she had trembling fits that lasted for days, or

until she was removed; as a result, she was educated largely at home. She was subject to recurrent nightmares, including one in which her father's face would change to that of a stranger; "she would desperately tear off the false face, only to be confronted by another and yet another, but never his own."[5] The prospect of becoming an adult held no attraction for her: as she wrote later, "I hated to be grown-up, and cried when I had my first long dress."[6]

Kate Greenaway's skill at drawing persuaded her parents to send her to art school when she was twelve. She was a docile and dedicated student who made few friends and won prizes for delicate, carefully executed, academically correct work. She went on to become a moderately successful but undistinguished commercial artist, whose greeting-card designs and magazine illustrations clearly derived from the best-known figures of the time: Walter Crane, Richard Dadd, and Sir John Tenniel. The breakthrough did not come until she was thirty-two, when she began *Under the Window,* a collection of verses and drawings in what was to become her famous and characteristic manner. The book was published for Christmas, 1879, and was an instant popular success.

What Kate Greenaway had done was to imagine and portray a world that thousands of people then and since have wanted to enter in imagination. Her vision was of an idealized childhood in an idealized English country landscape: of sweet babies and delicately pretty girls and boys playing in perfectly tended gardens, gathering flowers in cow pie—free meadows, and dancing on the tidy village green. In the Greenaway world it seldom rains and is nearly always springtime or summer; everyone is graceful, charming, and prettily dressed. Though her books appeared in the 1870s and 1880s, her figures usually wear the styles of Wordsworth's time rather than her own— the simple loose frocks and smocks and slippers of the ideal Romantic child. These quaint, old-fashioned costumes are appropriate, since what Kate Greenaway presents is a greeting-card version of Wordsworthian innocence, untouched by age, dirt, poverty, illness, care, or sin. Ultimately, perhaps, her vision derives from William Blake, particularly from the illustrations to his *Songs of Innocence,* many of which show an ideal rural scene peopled by children in loose, light-colored clothes.[7]

Though the popularity of Kate Greenaway's world seems easy to understand, in fact it has certain odd aspects that are not apparent at first glance. For one thing, there is the extreme, almost obsessive attention

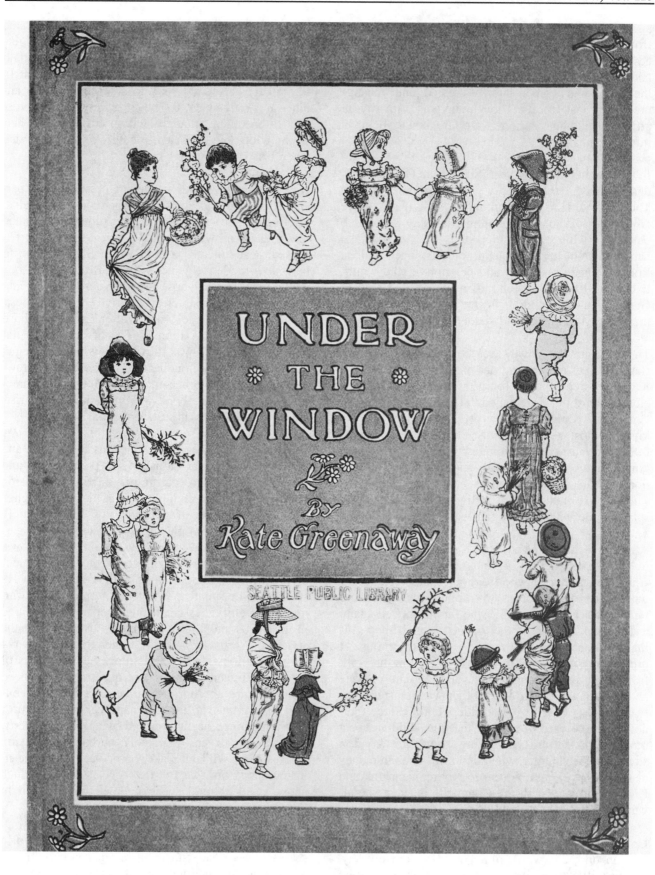

Cover illustration from an edition of Kate Greenaway's Under the Window, with Coloured Pictures and Rhymes for Children *(1879).*

to costume. The clothes her children wear were often sewn for her models by her own hands, and details of construction and trim are so carefully noted that they could be—and sometimes have been—reproduced as if from a fashion plate. Possibly we should expect this from someone who was the daughter of a ladies' milliner and outfitter—and also from someone who, disliking her own appearance, wore drab, dowdy clothes. Other factors must be responsible for the strange air of disengagement and even melancholy that often hangs over her scenes. Greenaway children are as a whole remarkably quiet and well behaved. They seldom quarrel or fight; they smile infrequently and almost never laugh or cry. Even when they are playing together they do not seem to be much aware of one another; their habitual expression is one of dreamy self-absorption. The only close relationships occur between mother and child, or between an older girl and smaller children.

Another odd thing about Kate Greenaway's world is that most of the people in it are young and female. She shows a few old ladies, but not many women between twenty and sixty. And—except in *The Pied Piper of Hamelin,* of which more later—there are almost no males over the age of ten. Moreover, the little boys are greatly outnumbered by the little girls, and those who do appear are often rather girlish-looking.

A fantasy world populated largely by sweet, pretty, charmingly dressed, dreamily innocent little girls was well suited to the Victorian cult of the child—especially the female child. The preference for childishness and innocence in adult females was widespread, and some Victorians carried it to the point of preferring actual little girls to grown women. This taste might be expressed harmlessly in friendship, as in the case of Lewis Carroll. Or it might become overtly and destructively sexual, as Steven Marcus has shown in *The Other Victorians.* Kate Greenaway's most famous fan, John Ruskin, seems to have fallen between these two extremes. The story of his disastrous, unconsummated marriage to Effie Gray and his thwarted love for the neurasthenic Rose La Touche is too well known to need retelling here; but it is worth recalling that Effie was thirteen years old when Ruskin first became interested in her, and Rose nine, and that they were both physically very much the Greenaway type. Ruskin himself had been deprived of his full share of childhood happiness, and in a more thoroughgoing way than Kate had. As a child prodigy, he was allowed no playmates and almost no toys by his puritanical but obsessively devoted mother; most of his time was spent in lessons or in solitary contemplation.

In 1879, when *Under the Window* was published, Ruskin was sixty, "a weary, broken man, famed throughout Britain for his books and lectures, but plagued by fits of madness triggered by overwork."[8] He had resigned his professorship at Oxford and retired to his country house in Lancashire, "where he received a steady stream of well-wishers and maintained a voluminous correspondence with his admirers, particularly young, unmarried women . . . his 'pets' as he called them."[9] Another favorite activity was having little girls from the local parish school to tea. The dainty nymphet charm of Greenaway's figures was almost guaranteed to appeal to Ruskin, who, as he put it, wanted only to be loved "as a child loves."[10] His enthusiasm for *Under the Window* was immediate; and shortly after it appeared he wrote Kate Greenaway a long letter in a highly playful and somewhat feverish tone:

> My dear Miss Greenaway—I lay awake half (no a quarter) of last night thinking of the hundred things I want to say to you—and never shall get said!—and I'm giddy and weary—and now can't say even half or a quarter of one out of the hundred. They're about you—and your gifts—and your graces—and your fancies—and your—yes—perhaps one or two little tiny faults:—and about other people—children, and grey-haired, and what you could do for them—if you once made up your mind for whom you would do it. For children only for instance?—or for old people, me for instance—[11]

What Kate Greenaway could do for Ruskin soon became evident. He was still haunted by the memory of Rose La Touche, who had died four years earlier, and, as Rodney Engen points out, "*Under the Window* abounded in suggestive images: drawings of pink roses, bowls of rose blossoms, a girl in a pale frock clutching a bouquet of roses ('Will you be my little wife, If I ask you? Do!')."[12] He wanted original drawings, sketches, and watercolors of pretty young "girlies" (his term), the more of them the better. For the rest of his life Kate recognized this need and kept Ruskin supplied with what an unsympathetic modern critic might describe as soft-core kiddie porn—though Ruskin's public position was that her drawings expressed an almost spiritual ideal: "The radiance and innocence of re-instated infant divinity showered again among the flowers of English meadows."[13] Apparently he never repaid Kate Greenaway for any of these gifts, some of which took days to complete—though he was a rich man and she an overworked artist struggling to support not only herself but her parents.

All pornography, even of the most rarefied and decorous kind, appears to be subject to a law of diminishing returns. After a while a new and slightly different version of the same stimulus is necessary in order to produce the desired response. If this were not so, one copy of *Hustler* would last its purchaser a lifetime, and most of the shops in Times Square would be out of business. The pictures of pretty "girlies" that Kate Greenaway sent to Ruskin aroused almost embarrassing raptures of appreciation, but more were always wanted. If he thought only of himself, he once wrote, "I could contentedly and proudly keep you drawing nicest girls in blue sashes with soft eyes and blissful lips, to the end of my poor bit of life."[14] Even the most delightful of her figures, however, seemed to Ruskin to have one fault: they were overdressed. He wrote to her persistently on this topic: "Will you—(it's all for your own good—!) make her stand up and then draw her for me without a cap—and, without her shoes,—(because of the heels) and without her mittens, and without her—frock and frills? And let me see exactly how tall she is—and—how—round. It will be so good of and for you—And to and for me."[15] But Kate Greenaway was deeply prim; she might spend days working on a gift for Ruskin, but she refused to undress her figures.

Though his need for Kate's drawings was private, Ruskin's enthusiasm for her work soon became public. In a lecture at Oxford in 1883 he spoke of her "genius" and "tried to convince his amazed audience that Kate ranked among the most important of old master and contemporary artists."[16] To understand the effect of this we must imagine someone like Sir Kenneth Clark speaking at Harvard on the genius of Norman Rockwell. Privately, Ruskin went even further: writing to thank her for a hand-painted Christmas card, he remarked, "To my mind it is a greater thing than Raphael's St. Cecilia."[17]

At other times and in other mental states Ruskin was quite aware that Kate Greenaway was not the equal of Raphael. He took on the task of correcting her "little tiny faults"[18] and directing her artistic career as he had in the past, unsuccessfully, tried to direct those of other artists, among them J. M. W. Turner, Dante Gabriel Rossetti, John Millais, and Edward Burne-Jones. In Kate Greenaway's case he was no more successful, but he was more readily obeyed. He com-

plained of the clumsiness of her drawing and demanded that she make detailed realistic copies of plants, rocks, and domestic objects ("When are you going to be good and send me a study of . . . the coalscuttle or the dust pan—or a towel or a clothes screen—"[19]). She accepted his criticisms humbly and carried out his assignments conscientiously, but without any noticeable effect on her published work. The studies she did for Ruskin are largely without interest and show that his dedicated scolding had succeeded only in temporarily turning a gifted professional illustrator into a mediocre and conventional Victorian art student. Fortunately, Kate Greenaway was wise enough not to abandon the style and the subjects that had made her famous.

Patrons of porn shops are notoriously unwilling to make eye contact with the proprietor, let alone to form a close acquaintance, and Ruskin showed a similar reluctance to meet Kate Greenaway. Though he wrote to her as "Sweetest Katie" and signed his letters "loving J. R.," it took him two years to propose a meeting. Before he came to tea in her studio Kate Greenaway was so nervous she almost wished she had not invited him; but the visit was a great success, and from then until his death he was the most important person in her life.

In 1883 Ruskin was sixty-three, and to the disinterested observer a person of no particular charm. Beatrix Potter, who met him a year or so later, described him in her diary as a "ridiculous figure," untidily dressed and "not particularly clean looking"[20]—in other words, a dirty old man. Nevertheless, he had many female admirers of all ages, and he soon also became the focus of Kate Greenaway's affections. She was deeply flattered and excited by Ruskin's praise, thrilled by the intimate, playful tone of his letters and conversations, and awed by the willingness of this famous man to consider her as a friend and a pupil. As Rodney Engen shows, she was soon thoroughly in love and regarded Ruskin with an almost religious reverence. Men like him, she wrote to another friend, were "far above and beyond ordinary people," and she hoped that "whilst I possess life I may venerate and admire with unstinted admiration, this sort of noble and great men."[21] After she had spent a month visiting Ruskin in the country, she confided to his cousin, Joan Severn, "Words can hardly say the sort of man he is—perfect—simply."[22]

Ruskin, on the other hand, was in love with Kate's work, not with Kate herself. She was no graceful Greenaway "girlie," but a plain, dumpy, dowdy spinster of thirty-six, with a working-class background, a shy, nervous manner, and a pronounced lisp. The resulting tragicomedy was of a sort familiar to all painters and writers who do not have the good fortune to be as handsome, charming, and eloquent as their work. This happens fairly often, since many—perhaps most—artists are partly motivated by a wish to create something superior to themselves. As a result, fans who meet them for the first time often feel a pang of disappointment, expressed in remarks like "He was smaller than / older than / fatter than I thought he'd be" or "She didn't say anything all that interesting."

The relationship between Ruskin and Kate Greenaway was an uneven one in both senses. He lectured and teased, praised and criticized; he asked her to stay with him in the country and then withdrew the invitation; he promised to visit her studio and then made flimsy excuses not to, or came only briefly and spent all his time there flirting with her child models. As Engen puts it, "He wanted attention, but on his own terms; while he urged her to write often, he stressed the importance of his own silence."[23]

Rodney Engen, like most biographers, is a partisan of his subject, and he indignantly accuses Ruskin of having "played a cruel game with Kate's emotions; his letters encouraged her with lavish praises; then, when she became too affectionate, he became cool and turned away from her."[24] This, on the evidence given, does not seem quite accurate. Ruskin's treatment of Kate Greenaway was cruel, but it was not a deliberate game: rather it was the result of his mental instability, his recurring attacks of depression and his constant fear of madness. Kate apparently did not understand how precarious his mental health was or why, when he would not come to see her, he remained in contact with other—usually younger, prettier, and less emotionally exhausting—admirers. In fact Ruskin, though flattered, was also embarrassed and perhaps even frightened by the intensity of Kate's feelings for him, and by the alternately demanding and pleading tone of her letters. "My dear Kate," he wrote in 1886, "There is not the remotest chance or possibility of you or anybody else in London seeing me this year and if you begin snewsing [*sic*] and probing again—I close correspondence on the instant. . . . You ought to have known my heart world is dead—long ago."[25]

A definite rejection like this certainly might have made Kate Greenaway's life easier, if it had been consistently maintained; but Ruskin, unbalanced as

Illustration of a "Little Girl Dreaming about Christmas," by Kate Greenaway. Bettmann/Corbis.

he was and eager for her drawings, blew hot and cold. Sometimes he refused even to open Kate's letters; a few weeks or months later he might write to her so warmly and intimately that all her hopes would revive. Like Kate's father in her childhood nightmare, he showed her first one false face and then another.

It was during this period that Kate Greenaway began to write a series of awkward and often unfinished but deeply felt love poems, of which only a few have ever been published. Her first biographers print several of these verses, while assuring the reader that they had nothing to do with Kate's life; rather it merely "pleased and soothed her to work out a poetic problem. . . . The case was not her own."[26] Rodney Engen, who takes the opposite view, seems to be nearer to the truth. The poems do not suggest someone who is pleased and soothed:

Nothing to do but part dear
Oh love love love, my heart
Is slowly breaking and coldness creeping
Nearer into my every part.[27]

During this same period of emotional turmoil Kate Greenaway produced her two most unusual books. The first one, *A Apple Pie,* published in the fall of 1886, was much larger in format than most of her work, and the figures were also larger and more active. Perhaps significantly, the drawings had never been submitted for Ruskin's approval, though she usually consulted him about all her major work. The Mother Goose rhyme she had chosen to illustrate describes the struggles of a group of alphabetically named individuals (in her pictures, mainly little girls) for the possession of what she shows as an outsize pie.

A apple pie
B bit it
C cut it
. . . . .
F fought for it
G got it
H had it
J jumped for it
K knelt for it[28]

In the traditional versions, K either "kept it" or "kicked it."[29] That Kate should make this change suggests that she felt herself to be in a one-down position, having to beg for what she wanted.

It may not be too farfetched to view this large pie as John Ruskin, and the children as his various "pets" and admirers competing for a share of his attention as they so often did—and in the end literally eating him up. Whether or not Ruskin got the message, his reaction to *A Apple Pie* was very hostile. According to Engen, "he considered the project a personal affront, an insult to their friendship"[30] and wrote Kate Greenaway a series of scathingly critical letters. In fact, *A Apple Pie* is one of Kate Greenaway's most attractive books; it has a boldness of design and energy of execution that are missing in much of her work.

The next uncharacteristic Greenaway project, *The Pied Piper of Hamelin* (1888), was undertaken with Ruskin's approval and under his supervision. He approved of her plan to illustrate Robert Browning's poem, adopting for the purpose a somewhat Pre-Raphaelite style and a palette dominated by rust, ocher, and olive tones instead of her usual pastels. He sent her copies of his favorite paintings as models, and also exercises in perspective which she carried out conscientiously but without noticeable result.

To illustrate any text is also to interpret it, and Kate Greenaway's *The Pied Piper* is an excellent example of this process. In Browning's poem the Piper is an eccentric trickster figure, "tall and thin, / With sharp blue eyes, each like a pin."[31] Greenaway pictures him as a kind of romantic hero: pale, dignified, melancholy, and mysterious, with a resemblance to portraits of Ruskin that can hardly be accidental. (The echo between the titles of these two books—Pie / Pied Piper—may be mere coincidence. It might be noted, however, that Kate Greenaway had already thought of illustrating Browning's poem in 1885 and had written to him for permission to do so. In this case it would be the Piper who turned into a pie, and not vice versa—which makes more sense.)

As Browning tells it, *The Pied Piper* is a moral fable. The burghers of Hamelin hire the Piper to charm away the rats that are plaguing the town, but once the rats have been drowned in the river they refuse to pay him. In revenge he plays a different tune, which draws all the children of Hamelin skipping and dancing after him. This enchanted procession (consisting, by my count, of 128 girls and only 46 boys) follows the Piper out of town and into a mountain crevice that supernaturally opens to receive them. Browning never reports what was inside the mountain. One child who was too lame to keep up with the rest says later that they were promised "a joyous land . . . Where waters gushed and fruit-trees grew, / And flowers put forth a fairer hue";[32] but of course these promises may have been as illusory as the visions of tripe and pickles with which the Piper lured the rats to their doom. The final lines of the poem provide a matter-of-fact moral:

So, Willy, let me and you be wipers
Of scores out with all men—especially pipers![33]

Kate Greenaway's illustrations, however, make good on the Piper's promises. She added a final scene, reproduced as the frontispiece and cover of her book, which shows the Pied Piper sitting and playing in a springtime orchard while beautiful Greenaway children dance round a tree and others embrace him. Ruskin, who followed this project closely, "supervised her work on this one scene with unswerving dedication," and he later wrote, "Yes, that is just what it must be, the piper sitting in the garden playing. It perfects the whole story, while it changes it into a new one."[34] He tried to get her to undress at least some of the children—"I think we might go the length of expecting the frocks to come off sometimes"[35]—but Kate, as usual, ignored this hint. She did, however, follow Ruskin's instructions in substituting flimsy white dresses and wreaths of flowers for the heavier, darker clothes in which the children had left Hamelin. So the "new story" was made to end with the Piper surrounded by beautiful girlies in what Ruskin called the "paradise scene"[36] and said represented his idea of heaven. Kate, in this story, is nowhere—though perhaps we are to imagine her as the feminine-looking lame boy left outside the mountain.

The Pied Piper, in this view, would represent a final act of self-sacrifice on Kate's part: an acceptance of the fact that there was no place for her in Ruskin's life except as the provider of images that might comfort him and lift him out of his increasing melancholy. But she was denied even this satisfaction. As Ruskin's mental condition worsened, even her drawings did not always cheer him up; sometimes they seemed only a painful reminder of how much he had lost. When she begged for news, he asked if she realized how sad he always was, "how the pain and failure of age torment me—what an agony of longing there is in me for the days of youth—of childhood—here every one of your drawings is as of heaven into which I can never enter—?"[37] Gradually, as he sank into the depression and confusion of his final years, he broke off relations with her completely.

Kate Greenaway's own poems suggest that eventually she realized that her idealized great man was an illusion:

> The You I loved was my creation—mine,
>   Without a counterpart within yourself.
> I gave you thoughts and soul and heart
>   Taken from Love's ideal.[38]

But she never abandoned Ruskin; during the nine years of silence before his death she continued to write to him and to send him drawings and watercolors.

For Kate Greenaway too the last years of the century and of her life (she died in 1901) were hard ones. She was lonely and often ill, and her drawings were going out of fashion in a world that had discovered Aubrey Beardsley and the Impressionists. Yet she had, and still has, her passionate supporters. Many of her books remain in print today, and nice little girls all over the Western world can be seen wearing versions of the styles she made famous. To the general public she is probably much better known than John Ruskin. Even the most major criticism is time-bound and speaks mainly to its own contemporaries; but the most minor work of art, if it creates a true secondary world, can seem as fresh after a century as on the day it was made.

Notes

1. Quoted in Engen, *Kate Greenaway: A Biography,* p. 141.

2. Ibid., p. 19.

3. Ibid.

4. Ibid., p. 8.

5. Ibid., p. 46.

6. Ibid., p. 26.

7. I am indebted to my friend James Merrill for this observation.

8. Engen, *Kate Greenaway,* p. 67.

9. Ibid., p. 67.

10. Ibid., p. 69.

11. Ibid., p. 64.

12. Ibid., p. 70.

13. Ibid., p. 90.

14. Ibid., p. 103.

15. Ibid., pp. 93-94.

16. Ibid., p. 90.

17. Ibid., p. 76.

18. Ibid., p. 64.

19. Ibid., p. 105.

20. Ibid., p. 108.

21. Ibid., p. 77.

22. Ibid., p. 87.

23. Ibid., p. 132.

24. Ibid., p. 109.

25. Ibid., p. 136.

26. M. H. Spielmann and G. S. Layard, *Kate Greenaway,* p. 258.

27. Engen, *Kate Greenaway,* p. 109.

28. Kate Greenaway, *A Apple Pie.*

29. See Opie, *The Oxford Dictionary of Nursery Rhymes,* p. 47.

30. Engen, *Kate Greenaway,* p. 141.

31. Robert Browning, *The Pied Piper of Hamelin,* p. 14.

32. Ibid., pp. 43-45.

33. Ibid., p. 47.

34. Engen, *Kate Greenaway*, p. 145.

35. Ibid., p. 148.

36. Ibid., p. 145.

37. Ibid., p. 151.

38. Spielmann and Layard, *Kate Greenaway*, p. 260.

Leonard S. Marcus (essay date March-April 2001)

SOURCE: Marcus, Leonard S. "Medal Man: Randolph Caldecott and the Art of the Picture Book." *Horn Book Magazine* 77, no. 2 (March-April 2001): 155-70.

[*In the following essay, Marcus theorizes that Randolph Caldecott and his fellow "Golden Age" artists, Walter Crane and Kate Greenaway, fundamentally altered the way picture books are created and influenced all subsequent generations of illustrators.*]

The picture book was born on the fly, as an art form for, by, and very often about people in a hurry. Children, of course, are always on to or into the next new thing. But during the 1860s, 1870s, and 1880s, it was industrial Britain's upwardly striving middle class who clamored for illustrated storybooks for its children. And it was in response to that great and growing demand that ambitious young artists such as Walter Crane, Kate Greenaway, and Randolph Caldecott turned to picture book making; and that Caldecott, in particular, went on in a few short years to produce a series of books that represented a new kind of book for young people.

Thanks to the Caldecott Medal, more people than ever recognize Randolph Caldecott's name. Yet nowadays, more adults than children—and of the adults probably more librarians and collectors than anyone else—know any of the sixteen picture books that Caldecott illustrated, at the rate of two a year, from 1878 to 1885. And few people know very much at all about the artist himself. The home page of the one website devoted to him leads with the headline: "Randolph Who?" Who, indeed? What follows is an attempt to renew our acquaintance with the medal man himself; to show in pictures and words something of who Randolph Caldecott was, the world he belonged to, the work he did, and in what ways that work still has value.

Caldecott was born in March 1846, in Chester, England, a small town well to the north and west of London. The son of a hatter, he was a tall, bright,

physically frail, good-natured child. The elder of two sons, he taught himself to draw at an early age, and in his last year of school he earned the Head Boy's silver badge, which he wore, by all accounts, with none of the comic self-importance of *Harry Potter*'s Percy Weasley. One of Caldecott's most engaging personal traits, his readiness to poke fun at himself, set the tone for the best of his illustration, in which all but the most ridiculous characters look to be worth knowing. It is as though Caldecott could not help putting himself in the other person's bowed or buckled shoes. This gift of empathy stood him in good stead especially when, as a much-in-demand thirty-two-year-old magazine illustrator, he turned to artmaking for children. At a time when many contemporary illustrators, including Kate Greenaway, perched the young on pedestals of unattainable moral perfection, Caldecott approached his audience at eye level, as flesh-and-blood folk no better and no worse than himself.

Caldecott's tradesman father did his best to talk him out of a career in art, and the good son obliged, first by taking a clerk's job at a nearby bank and later, at age twenty-one, at a bank in more cosmopolitan Manchester. He never gave up sketching, however, and there is always plenty of paper in a bank. Manchester's dynamic art scene soon absorbed his evenings, and in 1868, within a year of his arrival in that city, Caldecott published his first humorous illustrations in a local magazine.

Things happened fairly quickly for him after that. In 1871, he published his first drawings in the prestigious *London Society* magazine; the next year, he moved to London, set up as an illustrator, exhibited a painting, published in *Punch*, and illustrated his first book, a travelogue for adult readers called *The Harz Mountains: A Tour in the Toy Country*, by Henry Blackburn. Another travel book followed, along with work for American magazines, including *Harper's Monthly*; then a commission, in 1876, to reillustrate Washington Irving's *Old Christmas*. It was this last project that solidified his reputation, prompting the renowned printer, Edmund Evans, to approach him about the possibility of launching a picture book series alongside the series Evans had already printed by Walter Crane. Caldecott created his first two picture books—*The House That Jack Built* and *The Diverting History of John Gilpin*—in 1878, in time for the Christmas trade, and he continued the series at the same pace for the next seven years running. The Caldecott Picture Books were an instant success, both in their original, eye-catching paperbound "Yellow Back" editions, which during the artist's lifetime had initial print runs of up to 100,000 copies each, and in the more costly gift editions that followed, in which four and later eight of the picture books were bound together.

The world in which Caldecott came of age was in some ways much like our own. New technologies were transforming the way people worked, traveled, communicated, and pictured themselves. The steam locomotive telescoped distances for travelers, making it possible, for instance, for Lewis Carroll to make the sixty-mile journey from Oxford to London any time he wished for a weekend of theater-going; Carroll was riding the rails when the chapter titles for his first *Alice* book came to him. As an illustrator on assignment and later as an ailing thirty-something-year-old artist in search of warmer climes, Caldecott was another frequent traveler who worked well while in motion. In the spring of 1879, he wrote a friend that he had just dashed off the complete dummy for one of his two picture books for that year—either his *Elegy on the Death of a Mad Dog* or *Babes in the Wood*—while hurtling along by train between Florence and Bologna. Rapidly executed, preliminary drawings such as these came to be known as his "lightning sketches." Victorian rail travelers were book buyers, and Caldecott's popular picture books sold briskly at the bookstalls to be found on train platforms throughout Britain. The canny artist went so far as to take this fact into account in his cover designs, aiming for images bold enough to be "catching," as he told a friend, "from the top of an omnibus or out of the passing window of a railway carriage."

The telegraph not only shot words through a wire at unimaginable speeds but, just as the advent of e-mail has done, prompted the invention of a new up-tempo style of written communication. Emily Dickinson was the first poet of the telegraph age. Caldecott brought to the picture book a similar taste for verbal punch and compression, showing time and again that what could be pictured in a book did not also have to be stated; and that, with the right drawings to help spirit them along, a very few lines of text could be made to speak volumes.

The inventions that most directly influenced Caldecott's work were in the field of mechanical reproduction—Edmund Evans's domain. During Caldecott's childhood, high-quality color printing still lay beyond the practical reach of the publishers of books

and magazines. Whatever books the young Caldecott read would either have been hand-colored or color-printed by primitive methods yielding garish results. Edmund Evans was not only a master wood engraver and color printer but also something like a modern-day packager. Evans gambled that, given the choice, the newly educated English public would prefer children's books of superior artistic quality, and that high demand for the books would help keep them competitively priced. Evans was right, and the various series illustrated for him by Crane, Caldecott, and Greenaway set a new standard for the picture book that in some ways has yet to be surpassed.

The combined impact of these three artists can be seen in the contrast between two anonymous nineteenth-century English alphabet books on that most Victorian of subjects—trains—the first published in 1852, the second around 1889. *Cousin Honeycomb's Railway Alphabet* is a book of the old school, illustrated with hand-colored woodcuts and designed more or less the way bricks are laid, text and pictures fitted one on top of the other. But the 1889 *Railroad Alphabet* shows a different, more fluid Crane-Greenaway-Caldecott-like approach to design, in which pages no longer merely warehouse content but instead serve as platforms for the artist's inventiveness and the viewer's imagination.

Each of Evans's illustrators left a different mark on the picture book. Walter Crane was essentially a decorative artist who brought a lusty delight in design to the genre. Fey, theatrical Kate Greenaway was something like the Laura Ashley of her day, and a fervent spear-carrier for the Victorian cult of innocent childhood. Caldecott's impact, which far exceeded that of his two rivals, was more in the nature of an explosion: an unhinging of the basic conventions of the illustrated book. Caldecott books were free-wheeling experiments at a time of feverish experimentation in the visual arts.

J. M. W. Turner's *Rain, Steam, and Speed* of 1844, for example, represented one of the earliest attempts by an artist to record the propulsive rhythm and energy of the age. The French Impressionists, several of whom were living in exile in London in 1871, learned from Turner and were guided by his example. Under the spell of Turner and Monet alike, James McNeill Whistler, the American-born bad boy of English painting in Caldecott's day, stripped and streamlined his canvases to such an extent that in 1877 the great—if also mentally erratic—art critic and Kate

Illustration by Randolph Caldecott from his R. Caldecott's First Collection of Pictures and Songs.

Greenaway supporter, John Ruskin, publicly accused him of artistic fraud. (Later that year, Whistler sued Ruskin for libel; though he won, he was soon forced into bankruptcy.)

Caldecott, who had moved to London in 1872, was by then a member of Whistler's circle, sharing key artist-friends and two London galleries in common with him. And although he and the famously self-dramatizing painter were not close, the illustrator also shared some of the older artist's most basic ideas about picture making. Caldecott's most often quoted comments on drawing—"the art of leaving out [is] a science" and "the fewer the lines, the less error committed"—read like notes straight from Whistler's own play-book. And in an 1883 letter, Caldecott sounds the Whistler-note again as he explains why the work of Walter Crane always leaves him cold: "He is a clever man; but he does not enough follow his natural bent. He is in the thrall of the influence of the early and most intellectual Italian painters and draughtsmen"—artists of the type, that is, who met with fussy Ruskin's, but not Whistler's, approval.

Caldecott also shared Whistler's fascination with the Japanese woodblock prints that had only just become widely known in the West. Caldecott's inventive use of the three major design-elements in his picture books—text type, color plates, and sepia line draw-ings—often gives his page layouts a beguiling asym-metry clearly derived from Japanese prints.

Still, vast differences separate Whistler's work from Caldecott's. Whistler was an art-for-art's-sake firebrand. Caldecott, though he exhibited his paint-ings and sculptures with modest success, was quite content to be known as an illustrator-for-hire. Calde-cott was a storyteller, who set several of his picture books in the eighteenth-century English countryside. In this one important respect, Caldecott applied the brakes to the modernizing tendencies in his art, offering his contemporary readers an idealized backward glance at their grandparents' less hurried world. Whistler, in contrast, believing that art ultimately should be about itself, was suspicious of narrative and "subject matter" generally.

Whistler could nonetheless get off a fine portrait now and then. As an instinctive caricaturist, Caldecott made a point of turning down portrait commissions. As he told a friend, "I fear that I ought not to approach Mrs. Green brush in hand—my brush is not a very reverent one." Everyone knows "Whistler's Mother." But take a look at "Caldecott's Mother," as seen in the picture book *An Elegy on the Glory of Her Sex: Mrs. Mary Blaize,* based on a text by Oliver Goldsmith.

During Caldecott's lifetime, photography turned traditionally labor-intensive portraiture into instant art for nearly everybody. Critics at first were uncertain whether images produced by mechanical means should be considered art at all. Lewis Carroll, who was sure photographs could be art-worthy, countered with a tongue-in-cheek fantasy called "Photography Extraordinary" in which he imagined a machine for the mechanical production of novels. Whistler became an avid photographer in his later years; it is a good bet that had he lived a while longer, Caldecott, with his keen interest in reproduction techniques and growing impatience with printers, might have also.

The photographer whose work bears the most striking affinity with Caldecott's is Eadweard Muybridge (1830-1904), an Englishman living in California who in the years just before Caldecott published his first picture books began a series of pioneering stop-action photographic studies of animals and humans in motion. Muybridge's fascinating experiments forged the missing link between still photography and the soon-to-be-invented motion picture. Caldecott's picture books can be seen as having a comparable historical role as the bridge, or certainly one of the bridges, between traditional print illustration and animation. Consider, for instance, the helter-skelter sequence in *The Three Jovial Huntsmen,* in which Caldecott has his hard-riding comic protagonists— and us—literally going in circles. No wonder that Maurice Sendak, though he grew up not on Caldecott's *The House That Jack Built* but Disney's *Steamboat Willie,* is the American artist who has had the most to say about Caldecott's preeminence (about which more later).

Caldecott never considered himself a writer, but he had the confidence to make small changes to suit his purposes in the traditional texts he chose for

illustration. In *Sing a Song for Sixpence,* for example, one of his pair of picture books for 1880, he replaced the *of* in the title of the traditional rhyme with *for.* In making this small revision, he sharpened the focus of the cryptic old verse so that it could be fairly read as a story about singing for one's supper or, more plainly, working for a living. To sing a song *for* sixpence could mean to earn one's living as an artist for hire; Caldecott's Picture Books sold for a shilling— twice sixpence. (Walter Crane, who had advised Caldecott to demand a royalty from Evans, was nonetheless said to have been bothered when Caldecott succeeded in having his compensation pegged to "results"; Crane himself received a flat fee.) In addition to altering the title, Caldecott added a last couplet— "But there came a Jenny Wren and popped it on again"—in which the Maid gets back her nose. By 1880, Caldecott, who had just married, may have been thinking more closely about his young audience than he had before.

He had made no such concessions a year earlier, when he illustrated *The Babes in the Wood,* the plotline of which can be summed up as "Hansel and Gretel" minus the gingerbread house and the happy ending. Everyone in that strange little book just ups and dies. What emerges from the carnage, however, is the realization that the last thing Caldecott wanted a children's book to be was sentimental, and for setting that precedent we have a lot to thank him for. Here is his response to a letter from a writer-friend who had offered some advice about an illustration-in-progress:

> What you say of chins is true—I make a note of it—but the suggestion to 'give a touch more size to the eyes' makes one think that one must be careful in accepting—or rather in acting upon— criticisms of this kind. . . . I have altered the eye of the lady in question: but I have made it rather smaller. . . . It is a very cheap way of making a pretty face to draw large eyes. . . .

Another time, after a proud parent tried to foist her children off on the artist as models, Caldecott wrote a friend: "A history of the twins was kindly given by the mother, how they lived together, ate together, slept together, walked together, did everything together. Interesting. My opinion was that they were 2 fat, ugly children. . . ."

One of the artist's most devoted contemporary fans, it turns out, was Rupert Potter, father of Beatrix, who purchased from him the complete set of original drawings for *The Three Jovial Huntsmen* as well as two from *Sing a Song for Sixpence,* and hung them in his young daughter's nursery. The old story told about Beatrix Potter's early years was that she largely "lived" in her room as the cloistered prisoner of domineering Victorian parents. That may have been partly so. But her childhood was far from uniformly grim. She and her father, who was an accomplished amateur photographer, often visited London galleries and artists' studios together. And she learned to draw in part by copying her very own Caldecotts. Later in life, as the author and illustrator of some of English children's literature's most tough-minded tales, Beatrix Potter revealed a very Caldecott-like impatience with Victorian primness and sentiment. If the emotional undercurrents running through picture books could be tracked, there would be a straight line from Caldecott to Beatrix Potter, and from Potter to Margaret Wise Brown and Maurice Sendak.

Brown, as a nonillustrator, may seem the odd man out of the group. But it was Brown who once told the Russian émigré artist Esphyr Slobodkina, when the latter woman expressed doubt in her own ability to author a picture-book text, "Don't worry, Phyra, you write like a painter!" Brown did, too. And Brown, perhaps more than any writer before her, understood how to leave Caldecott-style openings in a picture-book text for the illustrator to elaborate on—as for example in the opening line: "Night is coming. Everything is going to sleep," trusting that Jean Charlot would come up with a suitably all-encompassing image for the first page of *A Child's Good Night Book.* And it was Brown who, in the Caldecott spirit again, wrote the line for which the perfect illustration was no illustration at all: "Goodnight nobody."

Nor was it just Margaret Wise Brown's lively grasp of the interplay between pictures and words that links her work to Caldecott's. *The Runaway Bunny* and *Little Fur Family* are every bit as much hunting stories as Caldecott's own *Three Jovial Huntsmen* and *The Fox Jumps over the Parson's Gate,* and in fact cut a lot closer to the bone as tales about quickness and cunning. Like Caldecott, Brown, who hunted rabbits on Sundays and wrote books about bunnies during the rest of the week, took care not to idealize her subjects, who ultimately of course were not rabbits at all, but vulnerable, resilient, flesh-and-blood boys and girls.

Margaret Wise Brown's career had just begun in 1938, the year that the American Library Association awarded the first Caldecott Medal to Dorothy P. Lath-

rop for *Animals of the Bible,* a picture book with biblical quotations selected by Helen Dean Fish. By the late 1930s—the time of Lawson, Bemelmans, Burton, Flack, and so many others—the American picture book was coming of age as an art form independent of, yet still strongly influenced by, British models. The establishment of the medal was meant both to celebrate and help solidify the achievement. It is surprising to realize that in 1938 Beatrix Potter was still alive, as was L. Leslie Brooke, the English illustrator most often mentioned at the time as Randoph Caldecott's immediate successor. There was even some talk of a Brooke Medal rather than of a Caldecott one. But Frederic G. Melcher, the publishing visionary who put up the money for the award (as he already had done for the Newbery), held out for the artist he rightly considered the founding father of the genre in question. One consequence of this was that when the British decided in the mid-1950s to follow the American lead and create an illustration prize of their own, the best name for the award was already taken; English illustrators must be content to win the Kate Greenaway Medal.

In another sign of Americans' continued reverence for English cultural models, *The Horn Book Magazine* had long since adopted Caldecott as its unofficial house artist, posting an image redrawn from *The Three Jovial Huntsmen* on every cover. In March 1946 the *Horn Book* devoted a special issue to a celebration of the hundredth anniversary of both Caldecott and Kate Greenaway's birth. The number's best piece, "Caldecott's Pictures in Motion," was by Hilda van Stockum, a prolific Dutch-born American author and illustrator, who wrote perceptively about Caldecott's special achievement:

> When leafing through his Picture Books it is [the] ebb and flow of perpetual motion which strikes one first. Other artists like to dwell on the scenes they are creating, either from contemplative joy in their beauty or from a psychological joy in their social values. Not so Caldecott. He is always aiming at the next picture; his very figures seem to be pointing to it; one cannot wait to turn the page and see what happens next. . . . As an artist, I am interested to see how Caldecott achieves this effect of continuous movement. I think he does it through a lavish use of horizons; his people are either coming at you, large as life, or vanishing over a hill. You can never be sure of them; now they're here, now they're gone. . . . It is this vigorous action which endears Caldecott to children, who don't look at pictures to admire, but to participate. As a daughter of mine put it, they want to be "in the book."

By mid-century, Caldecott's example had left its mark on the American picture book in numerous ways. His legacy could be glimpsed in the vibrant wordless sequence in Helen Sewell's *A Head for Happy* (Macmillan, 1931); in the warm, sepia line and adventurous shifts in perspective of Robert Mc-Closkey's *Make Way for Ducklings* (Viking, 1941); and in the balletic interplay of pictures and words in Ruth Krauss's *A Hole Is to Dig* (Harper & Brothers, 1952), illustrated by Maurice Sendak.

The story of how Harper's editor, Ursula Nordstrom, met Sendak at New York's F.A.O. Schwarz toy store, where the latter was then employed in the display department, has become well known. Such was her first impression of his talent that Nordstrom immediately began contemplating the possibility of a Margaret Wise Brown/Maurice Sendak collaboration, a dream-project that failed to materialize only because of Brown's unexpected death in the fall of 1952.

With her death, Sendak assumed Brown's mantle of boldness and experimentation. In 1955, he produced a dummy for a picture book that aimed at giving the Head Boy of the grand English picture-book tradition a run for his money.

The book Sendak was after was not going to be a Caldecott nostalgia-fest, decked out with hunting horns and crumpets. Nowhere in Caldecott is there anyone like the hero who (eight years later) finally emerged as Max; nowhere is there anyone or any *thing* like Sendak's Wild Things. But the energetic pacing in *Where the Wild Things Are* unmistakably bears the Caldecott mark—as does Sendak's sure grasp of the sonnet-like picture book form. In his 1964 Caldecott acceptance speech, Sendak, taking up where Hilda van Stockum had left off, pointed to the elements of Caldecott's work that he had learned from:

> No one in a Caldecott book ever stands still. . . . Characters who dance and leap across the page, loudly proclaiming their personal independence of the paper—this is perhaps the most charming feature of a Caldecott picture book. . . . [But] for me, his greatness lies in the truthfulness of his personal vision of life. There is no emasculation of truth in his world. It is a green, vigorous world rendered faithfully and honestly in shades of dark and light, a world where the tragic and the joyful coexist, the one coloring the other. It encompasses three slaphappy huntsmen, as well as the ironic death of a mad, misunderstood dog; it allows for country lads and lasses flirting and dancing round

the Maypole, as well as Baby Bunting's startled realization that her rabbit skin came from a creature that was once alive.

To which one might add that, placed beside the books being published today, one of the most striking features of Caldecott's picture books is the seldomness with which child characters become the major focus in them. Caldecott's books have less to do with the world children know than with the alluringly off-limits adult world about which they wish to know more. The promise of a stroll—or *gallop*—into that forbidden territory is central to the Caldecott appeal.

All his life, Randolph Caldecott suffered from weak lungs and a weak heart, and it was in search of better health that he and his wife Marian set sail for the United States in late October 1885. Landing in New York a day late following a stormy crossing, they immediately boarded a train and headed south for the Florida sun. Caldecott was fascinated by America, and hoped to bring home a big book of drawings based on his travels, which were to have taken him all the way to California and back, after which he planned to settle in for an extended East Coast visit. Caldecott's work was well known in the United States, and had the trip gone as planned, he doubtless would have been the toast of literary New York and Boston. Instead, after stopping briefly to sketch in Philadelphia, Washington, and Charleston, he fell ill, took a sudden turn for the worse, and died in St. Augustine in February 1886.

A rush of posthumous publications followed the famous artist's death. Among these was a picture-book *Jack and the Beanstalk,* retold by Hallam Tennyson, son of the poet laureate, and a book of Caldecott's lightning sketches for *The House That Jack Built.* Caldecott's widow is said to have tried at first to discourage the publication of the sketches. The drawings look so hurried, the argument went. Perhaps recalling the Whistler-Ruskin lawsuit, Marian Caldecott feared that the revelation of drawings executed with such apparent freedom and speed would be put down as un-art-worthy and would damage her late husband's reputation.

Quickness and freedom were of course what Caldecott's art was all about. His reputation as an illustrator's illustrator—an artist whose work held a treasure trove of innovative pictorial narrative techniques and ideas—continued to grow as English illustrators, and later also Americans, scrambled to lay claim to his legacy.

That legacy—Caldecott's ongoing influence on the world of children's books—remains great today, notwithstanding the fact that few contemporary picture book artists study his work. Artistic influence, like the party game of Telephone, can take untraceable twists and turns. Some modern illustrators "meet" Caldecott without ever knowing it, via the work of Beatrix Potter, for instance, or Sendak. Others may share with Caldecott a common source of inspiration, such as Japanese Ukiyo-e prints. Whatever their provenance, the underlying ideas about pictorial storytelling that Caldecott developed still work, and they continue to define the picture book as an art form.

And what of Caldecott himself—artist of "lightning sketches" and bold, spare, action-packed images; freelancer with a keen grasp of publishing economics and a roiling impatience with traditional printing methods? If Caldecott could be fast-forwarded in time into our media-saturated world, what place would he find in it? Would he be illustrating children's books? Designing websites? Drawing *New Yorker* covers? Storyboarding big-budget Hollywood animations? All these possibilities are implied in his still-resonant hundred-plus-year-old illustrations.

For his own amusement, Caldecott once drew a parody of a Kate Greenaway illustration in which he played up for comic effect the latter artist's tendency to idealize cute little girls in oversized bonnets. It is not hard to imagine that, were he among us today, Caldecott might take similar aim at the grandiosity of much contemporary illustration. One reason that his picture books are so supercharged with life is that Caldecott held his own ego in check as he made them. Caldecott drawings suit their occasion—robustly, modestly, and with a fine sense of proportion. Friends and critics alike who claimed more for his art than that left themselves open to his subtle scorn. As he once wrote a fawning but self-important collector:

Dear Sir:

Your note of 22 May is very complimentary to me—in it you tell me that you are going to *preserve* for future generations a copy of my volume of *Picture Books.* I am very glad. I hope others will do the same, and that future generations will feel blessed, be content, and not knock the nose off my statue.

Yours pictorially, Randolph Caldecott

THE BRANDYWINE SCHOOL OF CHILDREN'S ILLUSTRATION

Christa Kamenetsky (essay date 1977)

SOURCE: Kamenetsky, Christa. "Arthur Rackham and the Romantic Tradition: The Question of Polarity and Ambiguity." *Children's Literature* 6 (1977): 115-29.

[*In the following essay, Kamenetsky debates whether Arthur Rackham—an influential nineteenth-century children's illustrator—qualifies as either a Victorian or a Romantic artist. Kamenetsky argues that Rackham evinced qualities of both artistic disciplines in his work, noting that, "[b]y never committing himself completely either to the one world or the other, Arthur Rackham developed a certain spirit of ironic detachment in his illustrations, which we recognize as his peculiar sense of humor."*]

The question of identity has puzzled many critics of Arthur Rackham. Judging by the many contradictory essays written about his work, he still appears to be an artist of various styles that escape a definite classification in the history of the English graphic tradition. Was Rackham a Victorian artist or was he a Romantic visionary? Selma Lanes pointed out Rackham's philistine middle-class tendencies. Although she did not deny his magic in uncovering the fairyland beneath the countryside, she underscored to a greater extent his emotional detachment, his "matter-of-factness," and his affection for detail, texture, and elaborate design in "cozy English interiors replete with rugs, quilts and bric-a-brac."[1] Henry Pitz felt that Rackham's drawings had more "conviction" than those of Caldecott and Greenaway and that he was "English to the very core."[2] This was also Derek Hudson's view, who saw him as close to his British "Cockney origins."[3] Eleanor Farjeon, on the other hand, saw in him an artist capable of transporting the commonplace into a sphere of the imagination, a romantic "wizard" bringing to life a world of fairies, elves, and dwarfs.[4]

How do we reconcile such differing opinions, which emphasize the realistic as well as the imaginative perspectives of Rackham's work? Margery Darrell came to the conclusion that in his "strange mix of magic and materialism" lay the very key to the credibility of his work. "Perhaps it was his very worldliness that made his drawings so believable," she suggested.[5]

Without attempting to minimize the British influences upon his work, we will proceed to view Rackham within the broader perspective of European Romanticism, of which English Romanticism was a definite part. A brief exploration of the nature of European Romanticism, in all its complexity, may throw some light upon the complexity of Rackham's subject choice and on the puzzling ambiguities of his style.

Around 1920, Arthur Lovejoy pointed to the diversity of the term "Romanticism," suggesting that one should refer to it only in the plural form. He felt that the confusion of terminology had led not only to the present "muddle" of critical thought, but also to the unfortunate ambiguity now associated with the word.[6] Twenty years later, René Wellek contradicted Lovejoy by asserting that there were three unifying principles of Romanticism that could be detected throughout the art and literature of Europe. He identified them as: the role of the imagination as the very basis for poetry and art; the organic view of all natural objects; and the creative use of myths and symbols.[7] In more recent times, Morse Peckham tried to reach a synthesis of Lovejoy's and Wellek's views. He felt it was more important to acknowledge the inherent contradictions of Romanticism as an integral part of the movement than to quarrel about "multiplicity" versus "unity." "Since the logic of Romanticism is that contradictions must be included in a single orientation, but without pseudo-reconciliation," he wrote, "romanticism is a remarkably stable and witful orientation."[8]

Keeping in mind Peckham's observation, we will now move on to examine the seemingly contradictory forces in Rackham's work on the basis that they may correspond to those inherent in European Romanticism as a whole. In this connection, we will give particular attention to his subject choice, his use of the imagination, his organic view of nature, and the ambiguous qualities of his style.

In looking at the wide range of Rackham's illustrations, we notice that he gave considerable attention to folklore and imaginative literature. Among the folk literature of the oral tradition which he illustrated—with a natural feeling for the mood and the cultural uniqueness in the heritage of other lands—were such folk tales as Grimms' *Fairy Tales,* Stephens' *Irish Fairy Tales,* and Aesop's *Fables.* Of the illustrations of his native folklore we may mention Steele's *English Fairy Tales* and *Mother Goose.* Among the literary adaptations of traditional folklore we find his unique illustrations of Wagner's *Rhinegold,* and his *Twilight of the Gods,* Ibsen's *Peer Gynt,* Fouqué's

Undine, Shakespeare's *Midsummer Night's Dream,* Irving's *Rip Van Winkle,* and Hawthorne's *Wonder Book.*[9]

Rackham's emphasis on universal folklore reflected his romantic interest in the life, language, and literature close to the common folk tradition. As such, it corresponded to the Romantic dream of reviving the folk heritage around the world—a dream echoed also in the so-called color fairy books of Andrew Lang. It was Herder, during the *Sturm und Drang* movement in Germany, who initiated this revival trend by collecting folk songs of many lands. He was followed by von Arnim and Brentano, Tieck, and later the Brothers Grimm. The Grimms' *Household Tales* were still widely read in England at Rackham's time. In 1914, Rackham wrote to one of his friends: "In many ways, I have more affection for the Grimm drawings than for the other sets. . . . It was the first book I did that began to bring success (the little earlier edition, that is)."[10]

Rackham's illustrations of Grimms' fairy tales demonstrate his fine perception and great skill in getting close to another country's folk heritage. The universality of folktale motifs may have helped him in part. Yet it remains a remarkable fact nonetheless that his illustrations of Grimms' *Märchen* made their way back across the channel to give many generations of German children a first glimpse of their own folktales.[11] How well he did capture the spirit of German folklore may be perceived also from his *Mother Goose* illustrations, which were later adapted to an edition of German nursery rhymes. Though some verses in this edition were translated from the English, most of them were of German origin. Yet Rackham's silhouettes seem to fit the text perfectly.[12] Similarly, we may notice that his illustrations of *Rip Van Winkle* capture the very essence of the book, and it would not readily enter an observer's mind that in this case a British artist illustrated an American book. Rackham's illustrations fit Irving as they fit American folklore. We can't well imagine Rip any other way than Rackham has perceived him.

Viewed from the Romantic perspective, Rackham well demonstrated in his work what Coleridge called "the coloring of the imagination." In Wordsworth's "Preface" to the *Lyrical Ballads* we read: "The ordinary things should be presented to the mind in an unusual aspect."[13] Like the Romantic poets, Rackham often chose to illustrate the commonplace, rendering it colorful in the light of his imagination. Whether he illustrated scenes from folklore or fantasy, his drawings always reflected a certain mood or atmosphere. He achieved this partially by using soft pastel colors, in which even the most meticulously drawn details were blended to an antique tone, giving the effect of ancient parchment. In his paintings the soft browns and grey-greens dominate, here and there illuminated by a warm ivory. His colors vary from light, fluffy tones to rich, dark ones of the kind one may find in Flemish or Dutch landscape paintings. The warm hues of Rackham's colors add much to the impression that the imaginary world of fantasy and folk tale is part of the here and now. One is therefore perhaps less surprised than one ought to be at discovering fairy tale creatures amid a world drawn, otherwise, with much attention given to realistic detail.

A second device has helped Rackham in projecting the spirit of imagination into the world of realism, namely, his independent and very peculiar selection of captions for his illustrations. Instead of searching out highlights of plot and action, he would focus upon scenes or lines often overlooked by even the most attentive reader. Selma Lanes observed in this connection: "Thus he often chose to illustrate the unillustrable, or to rescue from oblivion words the reader had most likely never noticed. From Charles Dickens' *A Christmas Carol* he plucked the line: "The air was filled with phantoms, wandering hither and thither in restless haste and moaning as they went."[14] From *Wind in the Willows,* we may add, he captured the very atmosphere of a golden afternoon, when "the smell of the dust kicked up was rich and satisfying."[15] Rackham thus created a mood that did not leave the observer untouched. He himself felt that the most fascinating form of illustration for the artist was the one in which he expressed "an individual sense of delight or emotion, aroused by the accompanying passage of literature."[16] Again we are reminded of Wordsworth's theory of poetry, in which he expected the poet to arouse the reader's passions and to give him a certain sense of pleasure and delight.

In regard to Rackham's ambiguity of style, we find another striking correspondence with Romanticism, in the element which Morse Peckham called "the illusion of mutability."[17] Peckham had in mind a certain amphibian quality emerging from Romantic art and literature that belonged neither entirely to the world of reality nor entirely to the world of fantasy. By recognizing its kinship to metamorphosis, he re-evaluated imaginative ambiguity as a positive force,

suggesting that it represented the Romantic striving for unity between the internal and the external world or toward the "perfect identification of matter and form."[18] By tracing certain correspondences in the art of Constable and the poetry of Wordsworth, Peckham tried to establish their similar views of the concept of "organic nature." In Constable's cloud studies, for example, he noticed an attempt to bring together the appearances of landscape and sky through certain parallel lines, movements, and colors—an attempt which he felt corresponded to Wordsworth's view of nature as a creative soul. In "Tintern Abbey," Wordsworth had spoken of the eye and ear in terms of "what they half create, / And what perceive," whereas Constable had said, "It is the business of a painter not to be content with nature, and put such scene, a valley filled with imagery fifty miles long, on a canvas of a few inches, but to make something out of nothing, in attempting which he must almost of necessity become poetical."[19] Both of these quotes also seem to illustrate Arthur Rackham's view of nature. Miss Farjeon well described his landscapes drawings as "delicate webs of leafless branches traced against a wintry sky; . . . pale marbled clouds . . . and strange patterns upon the water."[20] In Rackham's drawings, as much as in Wordworth's poetry, we sense that "there is a spirit in the woods." His illustrations make trees, grass, flowers, and the very fieldstones come alive. In looking at the strangely twisted, gnarled, and knotty trees in his drawings, we can never be quite sure if nature, man, or a creature from the netherworld is speaking to us. What appears to be a knothole turns out to be an eye or a mouth—and yet, it may be a knothole after all.

In the landscapes of Rackham the very concepts of "manhood," "treehood," and "dwarfhood" often become strangely fused and blurred, leaving the observer with a feeling of ambiguity. We recognize in the ambiguity the Romantic world view, according to which the same spirit flowed through all things. Both macrocosm and microcosm, the animate and the inanimate object, were humanized and alive, revealing at their very source the deepest secrets of God and nature.

In some of Rackham's drawings we may witness the very process of a strange metamorphosis at work, gradually fusing natural objects and imaginative perspectives. At times, his illustrations are gloomy and frightening, suggestive of a dark and evil netherworld, and at other times, they are light and gay—or even grotesque. One can never be sure what mood to anticipate. In *Rip Van Winkle,* for example, we may feel a bit apprehensive while trying to decide whether some of the roots of an old twisted tree might belong as arms or legs to a withered and misshapen dwarf leaning against its trunk. Another illustration in the same book, no less ambiguous in style, makes us smile, as we discover among some hybrid creatures seated high on top of a branch the plumes of birds and the faces of men. Particularly amusing is a female creature among them, who is busily engaged, of all things, in knitting a sock. Her ball of yarn, hanging from her nest in a hopeless tangle, is drawn so realistically that one is tempted to pick it up.

Such opposing moods are very pronounced in Rackham's drawings. Side by side we may observe in them idyllic as well as grotesque elements—moods so contradictory that they do not seem to have been created by the same artist. And yet, it is precisely this sense of contradiction that illustrates the Romantic striving toward unity. Viewed separately, these polarities present such contrasts as those between the contemplative and peaceful mood of Wordsworth, for example, and the grotesque and nightmarish mood of Coleridge. In Germany, the polarities are represented by the "light" bourgeois Romanticism (*bürgerliche Romantik*) of Eichendorff and Brentano on the one hand and the "Dark" or "night side" of horror Romanticism (*Schauerromantik*) of Tieck, Novalis, and E. T. A. Hoffman on the other.[21] Oscar Walzel commented on these seemingly contradictory forces of European Romanticism: "I maintain that two antithetical methods of forming a work of art may be distinguished from each other. . . . The first is rather calm and simple and lays no claim on emotional intensity. The other is more roaring and pathetical and at times grotesque, and even inclined to hyperbolic expression. The current conception of baroque, or as Wörringer terms it, "Gothic," is applicable only to the latter."[22] In some of Rackham's illustrations we find an echo of the idyllic world of the *bürgerliche Romantik,* as seen in the engravings of Ludwig Richter (first German illustrator of the Grimms' *Household Tales*), the paintings of Moritz von Schwindt (well known for his enchanted forest scenes), and later in the works of Karl Spitzweg, master painter of the small town atmosphere. In both Spitzweg and Rackham we discover a similar fondness for crumbling medieval walls bathed in late afternoon sunlight, rooftop scenes, and quaint characters. In some other Rackham drawings we perceive the dark world

Illustration by Arthur Rackham from The Annotated Christmas Carol: A Christmas Carol *(1976), by Charles Dickens. Clarkson N. Potter, Inc., 1976.*

of the *Schauerromantik* and certain moods reminiscent of E. T. A. Hoffmann. In visual terms, Rackham expressed the dark sphere of Romanticism by means of bizarre line movements and tensions in forms. By using a fairly dark tint of raw umber, he would create the atmosphere of the netherworld, in which the real and the unreal lived together side by side in an ambiguous relationship.[23]

Rackham's dual vision of life comes out well in a work not meant for children. His illustrations for Walton's *The Compleat Angler* show well fascination with both the idyllic and the grotesque. And yet, there are drawings, interspersed with contemplative fishing and village scenes, that seem to have lost their way from the children's bookshelf: insects with spectacles are scribbling something into books; dwarfs are engaged in frog hunts; and fish skeletons, equipped with crutches, are contemplating their future fate in the angler's frying pan. The last drawing, ironically, is accompanied by a delicious fish recipe in the text, which reads: ". . . and pour upon it a quarter of a pound of the best fresh butter, melted and beaten with half-a-dozen spoonfuls of the broth. . . ."[24]

Although we smile at these drawings, we perceive quite a different mood in another one, which is reminiscent of a tale by Edgar Allan Poe or E. T. A. Hoffmann. An odd old couple is bent over what appears to be a huge book of knowledge. Their wrinkled, grinning faces seem out of place in the museumlike surroundings of skeletons and weird-looking stuffed fish and birds. There is a striking incongruity between the rich folds of the neatly arrayed silk and brocade clothing of the couple and the bare spiny bones hanging overhead. The open book may suggest a Romantic symbol of the hieroglyphics of life, yet the facial expressions are far remote from radiating a sense of wonder. Instead, they suggest something resembling more closely the features of the grotesque.

The Romantic grotesque may be translated as ungraceful, out-of-harmony, or incongruous. It was capable of taking on a humorous as well as a horrifying quality, depending upon the emphasis of the writer or artist. Paul Ilie characterized it as "a low keyed disquietude."[25] In analyzing the fantasies of Bécquier, Ilie called attention to the hybrid and ambiguous nature of his portrayals of transformation that showed but little resemblance to Ovid's portrayal of metamorphosis. Whereas Ovid had clearly indicated changes from one form to another, the Romantic grotesque remained ambiguous and hybrid in nature, thus transmitting the eerie feeling of metamorphosis still in process. It is just such a feeling which emerges from many of Rackham's drawings. We are never quite sure about his portrayal of nature as nature, of man as man, or of a symbol as a symbol.

It may well have been Beardsley who inspired Rackham with the element of the grotesque. Hudson noted a strong influence, especially with respect to some nightmarish scenes, one of which in fact is entitled: *A nightmare: horrible result of contemplating Aubrey Beardsley after supper.*[26] Further, Hudson noted the influences of Gothic and Italian primitives and also of "Cruikshank, Caldecott, Dickey Doyle, Arthur Boyd Houghton, [and] the artists of Germany and Japan."[27] It is also possible, however, that Rackham received inspiration along these lines from the very

writers of the German *Schauerromantik*, not to mention, of course, Edgar Allen Poe, whose works he illustrated. We know that Rackham frequently spent his holidays on the continent, usually in Germany and also that his wife, Edythe, studied art there prior to her marriage.[28] One of Rackham's admirers pointedly commented in 1905 "I have at last been able to get to your exhibition which I enjoyed immensely. Hitherto one had to go to the Continent for so much mingled grace & grotesque as you have given us. . . ."[29]

A study of all of the influences on Rackham will lead us to a complex and varied pattern that easily might distract our attention from his own original contributions to the art of illustration. And yet, a study of some affinities of mind may give us a clue as to the direction of his thoughts—particularly since Rackham himself acknowledged above all other influences his affection for the spirit of the Germanic North. When once asked by a friend how he would explain a peculiar Indian flavor in his drawings, Rackham responded: "I think I myself am more conscious of Teutonic influence."[30] Indeed, Rackham visited Wagner's Bayreuth several times while traveling in Europe, and he was as fond of Wagner's Nordic operas as he was of Norse mythology.[31] It is possibly from here that he drew his inspirations for the thievish, gray, and grotesque dwarfs who appear in his various fairytale illustrations. The Nordic *alb* (later Elberich or Oberon) had nothing whatever in common with the dainty dwarfs of Disney. Jacob Grimm in his monumental work *Teutonic Mythology* also commented on the dark or gray complexion of the "dark elves," as he called them.[32] According to the Edda they had emerged originally as maggots from the rotten flesh of the slain frost giant Ymir.[33] It may be noted that Norse or Teutonic mythology represents a common heritage for both the English nation and the German nation alike—a fact which may explain why Rackham's illustrations are so very much at home in the Nordic folk heritage of both countries.

From the perspective of European Romanticism, the double nature of the netherworld of dwarfs and elves held a special interest for writers and artists because it seemed to correspond to their own view of the world. Ricarda Huch characterized the Romantic movement as one that upheld the contrast between spirit and nature, light and darkness, force and materialism. Swaying back and forth between these opposites, the poets of the time hoped to achieve a synthesis of mind and spirit.[34] Walzel saw in this polarity a reflection of the Romantic dream of harmony. By oscillating between thesis and antithesis, he said, one hoped to recover the "golden age" of the ancient past. This oscillation, in turn, gave birth to Romantic irony, as the inherent contradictions were not resolved but kept alive.[35]

By never committing himself completely either to the one world or the other, Arthur Rackham developed a certain spirit of ironic detachment in his illustrations, which we recognize as his peculiar sense of humor. It was his special gift to create an illusion of reality by giving minute attention to realistic detail. Unnoticeably, he would then introduce, by means of color or ambiguous forms, the spirit of the imagination. It seems that he very much enjoyed the freedom of belonging to both worlds and to neither, thus asserting the very freedom of his creative mind.

There is an odd little drawing among his letters and notes that served as a wedding announcement for his daughter Barbara.[36] It shows an old, twisted, knotty, and leafless willow tree with grotesque branches sticking out like sinewy arms at the sides and like windblown hair on the top. Strangely enough, this tree bears the very features of Arthur Rackham— glasses, long nose, and all. On one of the "branches" sit two little birds ready, it seems, to build their nest. Who was Rackham, we may wonder—a man, a dwarf, or a tree; a "realist" or a "fantasist"?

If we have viewed Rackham's work within the context of European Romanticism, it should be remembered that there is nothing rigid about this attempt. Classifications remain constructs of the mind and, like metaphors, can only be carried so far in bringing out certain affinities of thought. In his work *Beyond the Tragic Vision,* Morse Peckham wrote: "Thus even a single work of art must not be regarded as culturally coherent, as reflecting one and only one aspect of a construct model."[37] Periods or movements were "constructs" or "operational fiction," he warned, and they should be used with caution. In the case of Romanticism however, as both Peckham and Walzel agreed, we have to do not with a single coherent construct but with a multiplicity of patterns characterized by polarity and imaginative ambiguity. For this reason alone, there is little danger that an application of Romantic theories to Rackham's work might lead to a rigid interpretation of his art.

The perspectives of European Romanticism open up new possibilities of viewing the seeming contradic-

Illustration by Arthur Rackham from Gulliver's Travels into Several Remote Nations of the World *(1900), by Jonathan Swift.*

tions in Rackham's illustrations as complementary forces arising from a dialectical approach to nature. To Rackham and the Romantics, nature was humanized and alive. By swaying back and forth between the worlds of fantasy and reality, he imparted to both the spirit of his creative imagination.

Like the European Romantics, Rackham felt at home in the folklore and fantasy of many nations. His interpretation of both reflects his capacity to perceive a living creature behind every bush and tree, in the ripples on the water, or in the movement of the clouds. Ambiguity and metamorphosis to him became a way of seeing which corresponded to the Romantic search for a mythopoeic vision of life. As if he were holding up a mirror to the complexity of our souls, Rackham cunningly revealed to us our dreams of beauty as well as the distorted features of our nightmares and secret fears. In that sense, polarity and

Ali Baba's son, who one day invited him to his father's house. On hearing that the new guest would eat no salt with his meat, Morgiana's suspicions were aroused, and she recognised him as the captain of the robbers. After dinner she undertook to perform a dance before the company, and at the end of it pointed a dagger at the captain, and then plunged it into his heart. Ali Baba was very much shocked, until Morgiana explained the reasons for her conduct; he then gave her to his son in marriage, and they lived in great prosperity and happiness ever after.

Illustration by Arthur Rackham from A Treasury of the Great Children's Book Illustrators, *by Susan E. Meyer. Harry N. Abrams, Inc., Publishers, 1983.*

ambiguity not only mark his poetic vision, but also the special sense of humor that places him, beyond doubt into a class of his own.

Notes

1. Selma Lanes, *Down the Rabbit Hole: Adventures and Misadventures in the Realm of Children's Literature* (New York: Atheneum, 1972), pp. 67-79.

2. Henry Pitz, *Illustrating Children's Books: History-Technique-Production* (New York: Watson-Guptill Publ., 1963), pp. 42 and 86.

3. Derek Hudson, *Arthur Rackham: His Life and Work* (New York: Scribner, 1960), p. 156.

4. Eleanor Farjeon, "Arthur Rackham: The Wizard at Home," *St. Nicholas,* XL (March, 1913), 391.

5. Margery Darrell, ed. *Once upon a Time: The Fairy World of Arthur Rackham* (New York: Viking Press, 1972), p. 12.

6. Arthur O. Lovejoy, "On the Discrimination of Romanticisms," *Publications of the Modern Language Association,* XXXIX (1924), 229-253.

7. René Wellek, "The Concept of Romanticism in Literary History," *Comparative Literature,* I (1949), 1-23, 147-172.

8. Morse Peckham, "Toward a Theory of Romanticism." *Publications of the Modern Language Association,* LXVI (1951), 5-23. See also: *Studies in Romanticism,* I (1961) 1-8.

9. For more detailed information on Rackham's various illustrations, consult Sarah Briggs Latimore and Grace Clare Haskall, *Arthur Rackham: A Bibliography* (Los Angeles: Suttonhouse, 1937). Also Hudson, Appendix.

10. Hudson, pp. 46-57. For the reception of Grimms' *Household Tales* in England, see Iona

and Peter Opie, *The Classic Fairy Tales* (New York: Oxford University Press, 1974), pp. 25-28.

11. See: Ethel M. Chadwick, "Arthur Rackham," *Dekorative Kunst,* II (Munich, Dec., 1909), 23-34.

12. George Dietrich, ed., *Mein Kinderhimmel: Gesammelte Kinderlieder und -Reime,* ill. by Arthur Rackham (Munich: Mohn Verlag, 1919).

13. William Wordsworth, "Preface to the Second Edition of Lyrical Ballads (1800)" in *Selected Poems and Prefaces of William Wordsworth,* ed. Jack Stillinger (Boston: Houghton Mifflin Co., 1965), pp. 446-447.

14. Lanes, p. 68.

15. Darrell, p. 7.

16. *Ibid.*

17. Morse Peckham, p. 11. See also: Robert F. Gleckner and Gerald E. Enscoe, eds., *Romanticism: Points of View,* 2nd ed. (Englewood Cliffs: Prentice Hall, 1970), pp. 231-258.

18. *Ibid.*

19. Morse Peckham, *The Triumph of Romanticism* (Columbia, S.C.: University of South Carolina Press, 1970), pp. 105-122.

20. Farjeon, p. 391.

21. See Marianne Thalmann, *The Romantic Fairy Tale: Seeds of Surrealism* (Ann Arbor: University of Michigan Press, 1964). Also: Ricarda Huch, *Die Romantik: Blütezeit-Ausbreitung-Verfall* (Tübingen: Rainer Wunderlich Verlag, 1951), p. 397.

22. Oscar Walzel, *German Romanticism* (New York: Ungar Publ. Co., 1965), pp. 51-78.

23. Robert Lawson, "The Genius of Arthur Rackham," *Horn Book* (May-June, 1940) p. 150.

24. Izaak Walton, *The Compleat Angler, or the Contemplative Man's Recreation,* ill. by Arthur Rackham (Philadelphia: D. McKay, 1931). The book was originally published in 1653. It includes not only instructions on angling but also proverbs, superstitions, legends, and popular rhymes. Obviously, it was the folklore that inspired Rackham to illustrate this work.

25. Paul Ilie, "Bécquier and the Romantic Grotesque," *Publications of the Modern Language Association* LXXXIII (1968) 319-322.

26. Hudson, p. 45. Hudson thought that Rackham's subject choice was healthier than Beardsley's and wider than Tenniel's. He accordingly called him "a loveable grotesque."

27. *Ibid.,* p. 44.

28. *Ibid.,* pp. 54-55.

29. *Ibid.,* p. 58.

30. *Ibid.,* p. 46.

31. *Ibid.,* p. 92.

32. Jacob Grimm, *Teutonic Mythology* II (New York: Dover Publications, 1966), pp. 439-517. See also Reidar T. Christiansen, ed., *Folktales of Norway* (Chicago: Delacorte Press, 1966), Introduction.

33. Jean Young, ed., *The Prose Edda of Snorri Sturluson* (Berkeley: University of California Press, 1960), p. 41.

34. Huch, p. 512

35. Walzel, pp. 45-67.

36. Hudson, p. 138.

37. Peckham, cited in *Triumph,* pp. 151-152.

Susan R. Gannon (essay date 1991)

SOURCE: Gannon, Susan R. "The Illustrator as Interpreter: N. C. Wyeth's Illustrations for the Adventure Novels of Robert Louis Stevenson." *Children's Literature* 19 (1991): 90-106.

[*In the following essay, Gannon studies the symbiotic relationship between Robert Louis Stevenson's adventure novels and N. C. Wyeth's illustrations in the Scribner's Illustrated Classics series.*]

Castles, sailing ships, a pirate cave; tall, big-boned figures caught in mid-gesture; and all the swords, boots, swirling cloaks, and flintlock pistols a romantic could wish—dramatically lit and freely painted. The illustrations for Stevenson's adventure novels in Scribner's Illustrated Classics series are obviously N. C. Wyeth's. But though all Wyeth's pictures share a family resemblance, each sequence of illustrations also renders a markedly personal reading of a single novel and has its own mood, tone, palette, and recurrent images. Wyeth's pictures, like all good illustrations, create for each novel a rich and rhetorically powerful narrative sequence well able to modify a reader's experience in significant ways; for, if narrativity is "the process by which a perceiver actively constructs a story from the fictional data provided by any narrative medium," it is clear that the reader's own active narrativity is susceptible to the powerful impact of an illustrator's vision as he or she works on the cues provided in the discourse "to complete the process that will achieve a story" (Scholes 60).

Stevenson himself appreciated this, commenting approvingly of a set of illustrations that its "designer also has lain down and dreamed a dream, as literal, as quaint, and almost as apposite as . . . [the author's]; and text and picture make but the two sides of the same homespun but impassioned story" ("Bagster's Pilgrim's Progress" 296). And Stevenson's discussion of those illustrations goes on to trace the interactions between text and picture as they might be experienced by a perceptive reader. Following Stevenson's lead, I would like to examine some of the choices Wyeth made in illustrating Stevenson's novels—choices which can shape a reader's experience of a novel in significant ways—and then to offer a reading of the way Wyeth's illustrations for *Treasure Island* (arguably his best) work together in sequence to interpret that text.

N. C. Wyeth illustrated four of Stevenson's adventure novels for Scribner's Illustrated Classics Series: *Treasure Island* (1911), *Kidnapped* (1913), *The Black Arrow: A Tale of the Two Roses* (1916), and *David Balfour* (1941). Wyeth's illustrations for each of these novels set up an immediate field of reference for the reader, enacting and embodying the story like a play or a film in specific visual terms. When the details of a verbal description are turned into visual images they become more precise and limited. A hat or coat must be cut a certain way; a human figure must be of a certain height and build; a house must have specific architectural features. Each choice which "places" details for the reader both limits and—paradoxically—offers a potential enrichment of the reading experience as the illustrator puts his own complex experience of the text at the reader's service.

One of the most important choices an illustrator can make is the selection of scenes to be shown. All of Wyeth's pictures accent thematic and structural development in the novels, but in the design of an illustrated book there are some illustrations which hold positions of special rhetorical force. In illustrating Stevenson's novels for the Illustrated Classics Series, Wyeth used cover, endpapers, and title page to make a strong thematic statement and set the tone for his whole interpretive reading of each novel. The cover of *Kidnapped* shows young David Balfour apparently

stranded on the "island" of Earraid, unaware that he will be able to walk to freedom when the tide goes out. The cover of *David Balfour,* Stevenson's sequel to *Kidnapped,* dramatizes an important thematic difference between the novels. Highlighting the older David's inability to make any decisive moves for himself, it shows him bound hand and foot and carefully guarded, a real prisoner on a real island.

Wyeth also used endpapers to sum up the conflict in a book. In *Treasure Island* and in *The Black Arrow,* novels filled with violent contention for power and wealth, brutal pirates and members of an outlaw band stride purposefully across these pages, whereas the endpapers in *David Balfour* depict the Bass—the rocky islet on which David is helplessly imprisoned during much of the action. The title page sketches for both of the David Balfour novels metaphorically express the central concerns of the books. In each case the figure of David is more clearly realized and substantial than the shadowy and rather fantastic background, suggesting that the picture really shows what is on his mind. On the title page of *Kidnapped* a thoughtful David contemplates a dreamlike rendition of the House of Shaws; in the title sketch for *David Balfour,* a shadowy gibbet with its swinging noose looms over the frightened boy. Wyeth draws attention to the terrible dilemmas David faces. In the first book he must risk enslavement and death in order to claim his inheritance; in the second, if he offers the testimony needed to clear an innocent man of murder, he risks the gallows himself. Wyeth's cover and endpapers for *David Balfour* pinpoint at once the conflict between freedom and bondage, between action and passive acceptance of the status quo, which will dominate the story.

The illustrations for a book, by epitomizing the plot, can often serve as a sort of trailer for it, much like the "previews of coming attractions" familiar to us from the movies. Wyeth thought "a person should be able to walk into the book store and just thumb through a book and get the idea of the story by the drama of the illustrations—very quickly" (*An American Vision* 80). His pictures represent carefully chosen moments more or less evenly spaced throughout the story and so arranged as to provide not only a sense of the story's continuity, its drama and emotional force, but to complement each other aesthetically, offering contrast and comparison in subject matter, coloring, and design.

Andrew Wyeth has described his father's way of setting about deciding which moments in a novel to foreground for the reader: "after initially reading the story, especially if it was a good yarn, Pa would re-read it carefully and underline the passages that he felt were the essence of the story" (*An American Vision* 80). When he looked for moments which would show "the essence" of a story, Wyeth sometimes chose obvious moments of crisis or decision—Jim Hawkins's confrontation of Israel Hands in *Treasure Island* is a good example. But sometimes he chose a moment which would capture his idea of a character (Ebenezer Balfour in *Kidnapped* crouched over his porridge, plotting murder) or a relationship (Silver in *Treasure Island* leading Jim Hawkins on a leash) or a situation (Dick Shelton and Joan Sedley in *The Black Arrow* at bay in the forest). In Stevenson, Wyeth was working with a writer who had a marvelous ability to paint vivid and succinct word pictures of people and places, an artist with a knack for setting up important scenes in a very dramatic way. Yet often Wyeth would avoid the very scenes Stevenson made most striking. In explaining to his son why he chose to illustrate a scene an author had not described very fully, Wyeth once said: "'Why take a dramatic episode that is described in every detail and redo it? Instead I create something that will *add* to the story'" (*An American Vision* 80).

That something is often a symbol of the whole as much as a simple image of one small part. Wyeth ignores the famous scene from *Kidnapped* in which David climbs the unfinished staircase at Shaws only to find himself poised on the brink of an abyss; instead, he settles on a less obvious scene which serves as an even better visual emblem of the entire situation in which David has been caught. The illustrator shows the boy stranded on a rock in the middle of a dangerous current, unable to move forward or backward until Alan Breck forces him to take a blind leap to safety. Wyeth focuses attention here on a moment of choice involving that combination of trust and daring which will be vital to David's ultimate salvation.

Highlighting two scenes which might easily have been passed over by the reader of *Treasure Island,* Wyeth uses them to symbolize the complex relationship between Jim Hawkins and Long John Silver. The first picture of the two together shows Silver as an amiable substitute father; the second reveals him to be a cruel bully. And the self-defeating confusion which prevents Dick Shelton in *The Black Arrow* from knowing who his real friends are is brilliantly captured in Wyeth's picture of him knee-deep in an icy sea, fighting his own potential ally Lord Foxham on so dark and snowy a night that neither of them can really see the other.

From the 1919 edition of The Last of the Mohicans, *by James Fenimore Cooper, illustrated by N. C. Wyeth.*

In most cases when Wyeth departs from Stevenson's text, it is because he is deliberately adding or omitting details for artistic and interpretive reasons of his own. Often Wyeth extends Stevenson's narrative, picking up some symbolic touch and giving it a clear visual reference which Stevenson never supplied. He captures very well Stevenson's intent to supply his hero with a series of "doubles" in *The Black Arrow,* older men who represent in various ways the kind of person Dick Shelton might grow up to be. Dick is given a vividly recognizable appearance. He is a tall, well-built boy with dark hair, an oval face, a strong profile, and straight brows that meet across his nose. As Dick Shelton and the outlaw appropriately named Lawless prowl stealthily through the snow toward Lawless's lair, they look almost like identical twins. The young Richard III who appears in the book seems older in the illustrations than he is said to be, resembling more the traditional image from historical portraits, but there is a speaking family resemblance between the infamous king and Dick—the same straight browline and profile; in his effort to create this effect, Wyeth even minimizes Richard's "crookback" so that it is hardly noticeable. Further, in the final illustration, depicting the last scene in the book, the scowling and dour Ellis Duckworth (the Robin Hood figure in the novel) who bids farewell to Dick is dressed exactly like him and could be the boy's older brother.

Wyeth uses his own recognition of an elaborately coded world to place the details of each Stevenson story firmly in a social and historical context. His use of physical types which have come to be associated in our culture with certain values is an important part of his rhetorical strategy. The brutal, battered-looking pirates who stride across the endpapers of *Treasure Island* announce their ruthlessness in their very physical presence. The wiry, lithe Alan Breck who fights best when cornered has a distinctly rodent-like grin as he battles the invaders of the roundhouse in *David Balfour.* His face tells you something of his mindset. Wyeth makes David Balfour a handsome, brawny boy, whose burly shoulders and well-developed, muscular arms and legs seem too powerful for his sensitive and almost girlish face. The artist adds a certain charm to this character, conveying David's boyish clumsiness as he sits awkwardly in a delicate Queen Anne chair in a fussy and crowded lawyer's office. The posture of the boy suggests strongly his sense of being not only a dirty and ragged stranger in this respectable place but also something of a young bull in the china shop.

If bodies have a language, then so do the shadows they cast; indeed, the human shadow has a rich and highly conventionalized set of meanings in art and literature, and Wyeth often uses it to symbolize a character's inner nature. Thus, Ebenezer Balfour's shadow looms ominously on the wall behind him as he eats his porridge and plots to murder his nephew, and Alan Breck's dances, twice his size, on the walls and ceiling of the roundhouse as he gamely fights off a pack of sailors aboard *The Covenant.* Sometimes a person's shadow is thrown before him, portending the ill effects of his actions, as in the case of the pirate Billy Bones on the cliffside, and sometimes a figure is surrounded by shadows which suggest an atmosphere of all-encompassing evil, as in the treasure cave scene in *Treasure Island.*

Wyeth gives his Stevenson characters eloquent body language, often presenting them in the act of making slightly exaggerated gestures which "mime" their intent. This slight exaggeration draws attention to the gesture and creates a certain fictionality about it— puts it in quotation marks, so to speak. Figures gesturing like this rely for some of their impact on arousing a kinesthetic response in the viewer like that evoked by Marcel Marceau "walking against the wind." Thus Dick Shelton and his henchman, Lawless, prowl through a snowy forest, bent forward intently, miming "stealth" with every muscle. Wyeth prided himself on his ability to convey this sort of effect, claiming that his early work on a farm had given him an "acute sense of the muscle strain . . . the feel . . . the protective bend of head and squint of eye that each pose involves." In fact he complained that "after painting action scenes I have ached for hours because of having put myself in the other fellow's shoes as I realized him on canvas" (quoted in Wyeth 6). That Stevenson shared Wyeth's appreciation of this particular effect is evidenced in his admiration for an illustrator's depiction of Bunyan's "Christian, posting through the plain, terror and speed in every muscle" and Mercy eager to go her journey with "every line" of her "figure yearning" ("Bagster's Pilgrim's Progress" 300).

There is, of course, a veritable lexicon of body language which can be called upon in drama, fiction, and illustration, so sometimes Wyeth need only quote from an already coded social text to make his point. A bereft mother in *Treasure Island* hides her face in her apron, and a conventionalized message is conveyed immediately about her social class, her powerlessness, her maternal feeling. When one of the Black Arrow's band climbs a tree to get the lay of the land his costume makes a silent allusion to Howard Pyle's illustrations for Robin Hood, while his brow-shading hand evokes "sailor searching the horizon" in a gesture at once conventional and mimelike.

Stevenson is famous for his use not only of gesture but of costumes and props to suggest aspects of character, and Wyeth follows him closely here. "Character," Stevenson once said, "to the boy is a sealed book; for him, a pirate is a beard, a pair of wide trousers, and a liberal complement of pistols" (*Essays* 261). He signals the outlaw status and desperate situation of Alan and Davie in *Kidnapped* by the increasingly wretched state of their clothes. Wyeth carefully shows the two declining into raggedness, picture by picture, until David suddenly springs forth in the final illustration in a fine brown suit, carrying a fashionable cane (not mentioned by Stevenson). The differing lots of the young gentleman and the man with a price on his head are brilliantly summed up by the contrast in their appearance in this last picture.

One of Wyeth's trademarks as an illustrator is his fondness for depicting actions caught in midmovement. Catriona's skirts billow out around her as

"Robin and the Tinker at the Blue Boar Inn," drawing by Howard Pyle. From The Merry Adventures of Robin Hood *(1883), by Howard Pyle. Charles Scribner's Sons Publishers, 1951.*

she leaps from one ship to another; an inn sign just nicked by a sword blow swings violently from the impact; a sturdy inn table is shown tipping over and spilling its burden of pewterware. Though he is working in a static medium, Wyeth creates the illusion that each scene represents part of a rapid, almost headlong sequence of action. In doing so, he well reflects the speed and action of Stevenson's narrative, and he captures an effect Stevenson himself admired in another illustrator whose pictures he felt captured an author's "breathing hurry and momentary inspiration" ("Bagster's Pilgrim's Progress" 304).

It is not just choice of subject that determines Wyeth's interpretation of a particular novel but also choices of color, design, light, and shade. Wyeth's artistic choices operate as an effective visual rhetoric, creating pictures the viewer can "read." Each of his sets of illustrations has its own palette. The Balfour novels are set in a world of soft blues, greens, and

silver-grays. The pictures for *The Black Arrow* suggest medieval illuminations in their clear colors and decorative detail, though a number of the scenes are dark and somber in tone: two young people drink from a forest pool under the stars; armed men struggle desperately in snowy battle scenes; a wounded spearman returns home just before dawn. Wyeth's *Treasure Island* is a place of harsh tropical sun and dark shadows, highly theatrical in the posing and lighting of the major scenes. The sunlight is dazzling as Jim leaves his seaside home for a shadowy world where good and evil will be strangely mixed. The shocking difference between two ways of life is symbolized by the arresting blocks of sharp and uncompromising light and shade in this picture. The same effect is repeated in one of the last pictures for the novel as Jim is marched from the bright cliffside into blue shadows by John Silver. In another picture, harsh yellow light from an oil lamp pours down on the cabin where the brutal Israel Hands struggles with his shipmate O'Brien, turning everything in the room flat brown and gold. And as Jim looks through a loophole in the stockade wall he sees a group of pirates crouched in a semicircle lit luridly from below by torchlight. In the final scene, a masterpiece of artistic restraint, Jim kneels in a fairy-tale cavern all in sepia tones, where the only bright spots are the glittering gold coins that seem dimly to illuminate the cave.

For Stevenson it is "the triumph of romantic storytelling" when the reader consciously plays at being the hero: "Then we forget the characters; then we push the hero aside; then we plunge into the tale in our own person and bathe in fresh experience; and then, and then only do we say we have been reading a romance" (*Essays* 231). Wyeth's use of perspective cleverly conveys the feel of Stevenson's narrative method. Over-the-shoulder views in which we see "with" the protagonist, who is placed in the foreground as an observer of action rather than a participant, are common in the pictures for those novels which are narrated in the first person. When David Balfour bids farewell to his old teacher, his back is to the viewer, and over his shoulder we see the old man and the landscape David must leave. Another device for emphasizing the first-person perspective is the presentation of a scene from an unusual angle distinctively identified with the narrator in the text. When David lies in bed, looking up at Alan and Cluny playing cards, the illustrator shows us the scene from a low angle, as David would have seen it; and when Jim Hawkins peeps through a cabin window or a chink in the stockade wall, we see what he sees.

The structural design of Wyeth's illustrations often underscores their meaning. When Catriona leaps dramatically from boat to boat in a rough sea, she falls right into David Balfour's outstretched arms. In this picture, his arms and her billowing petticoats form a small but attention-getting circle in a picture full of strong, thrusting diagonals. The completion of the circle also works well to suggest that David and Catriona, who in many ways represent different but necessary aspects of a single personality, belong together and cannot be "whole" unless each has what the other can give.

Color, lighting, and design are all used by Wyeth to convey his own reading of a scene in his portrait of Lord Prestongrange in *David Balfour.* The picture illustrating David's confrontation by the powerful Lord Advocate of Scotland shows them meeting in a dark-

ened room. The tall figure of Prestongrange, looming in the darkness, dominates the scene. The shape of his elongated figure is echoed in the two candles he has lit—which give off a dazzling light—and in the wine decanter, glass, and candle snuffer on the table before him. One fist is on the table, knuckles down; and in the other hand, the taper he used to light the candle points down and toward the viewer. There is a dark shadowy area to the right of him, and the paneling behind him forms a large cross—suggesting again the gibbet, but also, perhaps, David's willingness to sacrifice himself for his friends. The picture dramatizes forcefully the emotional effect of interrogation by a judge whose power to condemn or free his prisoner is absolute, and Wyeth cleverly puts the viewer in the position of the prisoner.

Each set of illustrations Wyeth did for a Stevenson novel constitutes a highly personal reading of the written text, often accenting the undertones of tragic conflict which appealed to the artist. His pictures for *The Black Arrow* capture Stevenson's lightly satiric treatment of knighthood but also stress a darker suggestion that, in the corrupt world of this novel at least, the possibility of heroic action is no longer available.

Those of Stevenson's stories which are told in the first person by a mature narrator who explains both how he felt at the time of his adventures and what they mean to him now offer a special challenge to the illustrator. The ironic perspective the mature David Balfour can give to the story he relates in *Kidnapped* is rarely felt in the illustrations, which show us David as victim or—at best—survivor rather than as the foolish, stubborn prig the narrator feels himself to have been. Wyeth's pictures emphasize external events, dominated by the figures of energy and menace which seem so often to threaten David. But the essence of Stevenson's story, David's awkward, moment-to-moment struggle to appreciate and assimilate the virtues of his alter ego, Alan Breck, in order to become a more complete human being, cannot effectively be dramatized in fourteen pictures, though it is emblematized in several of them. Similarly, the pictures for the sequel, *David Balfour,* project effectively David's inability to act and the consequent aura of guilt which hangs about him, but the social comedy of Stevenson's story and the pained irony of the narrative voice are again missing.

Wyeth's pictures for *Treasure Island,* on the other hand, convey wonderfully well the intriguing doubleness of that novel, which from one perspective seems like a stirring adventure story; from another, something of a tragedy. Without ever picturing Stevenson's mature narrator, Wyeth has managed to create a parallel narrative to Stevenson's which stresses the difference between the way the story was experienced by its focal character and the way the teller understands it, now that he is older and wiser. But only a more detailed examination can do justice to the way Wyeth manages, in a brilliantly structured sequence of pictures, continually to remind the reader of the shadow side of young Jim Hawkins's blindness to the future without downplaying in the least the glamor and sheer romantic appeal of his adventures.

Wyeth's choice of moments to illustrate in *Treasure Island* is as carefully calculated as Stevenson's own choice of scenes to narrate in detail. His pictures are deliberately arranged so that the meaning of each picture is related both to the pictures that surround it and to the text in which it is set. The cover illustration showing three pirates raising the Jolly Roger does not correspond to any particular scene in the novel but offers a generic reference to that grim moment in any pirate saga when the buccaneers run up their colors in preparation for an attack. Thus the pirates appear to prepare an attack on the cover, sweep down the beach on the endpapers, and pause guiltily on the title page, reflecting on the price they are likely to pay for their crimes as they bury their treasure.

Stevenson divided his story into significant parts, each of which is carefully subtitled and develops a particular phase of the action. Wyeth takes advantage of the way Stevenson sets his story up, arranging his illustrations so that those grouped together play off one another effectively. In the pictures for the opening sequence of the story, called "The Old Buccaneer," Bill Bones stands lookout in the first illustration and lunges out of a darkened doorway in the second; then Blind Pew moves menacingly toward the viewer in the third, tapping his way with a stick that sweeps dangerously across the road. These images, full of energy and menace, suggest strongly that the springs of action in this story lie with the pirates.

The details Wyeth has added to Stevenson's narrative at every turn magnify the impressiveness of the pirates. In the first illustration, Bones is posed like a monumental statue on a cliff, seen from below. His stance, his billowing cloak, and his telescope held like a weapon make him at once the archetypal seaman on the lookout and a commanding figure—much more imposing than the sick old pirate of Steven-

son's story. The figure of Blind Pew is never very clearly described by Stevenson, but Wyeth has given him the face of a death's head, with broken teeth. And the fingers of his outstretched hand, which claw at the air in a threatening gesture, are echoed in the thrusting tree branches of the wintry scene and especially in the shadows of those branches which lie across Pew's path. The effect is thoroughly chilling.

The pictures for the second segment of Stevenson's story, "The Sea Cook," are more static, more emblematic. In the first, Jim Hawkins says goodbye "to Mother and the cove" (57). In the next, Jim enjoys a quiet moment in the galley of the Hispaniola with the friendly sea cook, Long John Silver. Taken together, this pair of pictures is designed to emphasize the contrast between the safety of the cove and the dangerous and deceptive world into which Jim is moving.

In his depiction of the first scene Wyeth employs color, composition, and original added detail to give the reader a feeling for the complex emotional tone of the moment. The composition of the picture is quite striking. Dazzling sunlight illuminates the left side of the picture, where a sturdy woman stands weeping, her face buried in her apron. Jim is turned away from her, advancing toward the viewer and into the dark shadows cast by the house, which somewhat obscure his face. He is seen in outline, like Bones and Pew; and, like the blind Pew, he carries a stick which extends before him. The picture presents the moment of choice as Jim leaves home to pursue the pirate treasure, and he is shown pausing "on the sill of shade." There is a certain poignancy in the situation which is not grasped by the Jim Hawkins who, as Stevenson describes him in this moment, thinks only of the captain and the treasure. Stevenson's Jim has no weeping mother to make his leavetaking difficult; indeed, the reader is specifically told that Mrs. Hawkins was in good spirits as her son left, and for Stevenson's Jim it proves surprisingly easy to turn the corner and put "home out of sight" (57). Wyeth's picture, however, picks up the faint undertones of tragic retrospect which appear in the narrative of his own adventures by an older and wiser Jim Hawkins, a Jim who can describe his own boyish day-dreams of adventure this way: "Sometimes the isle was thick with savages, with whom we fought; sometimes full of dangerous animals that hunted us; but in all my fancies nothing occurred to me so strange and tragic as our actual adventures" (53). Stevenson's reminder here of the fallibility of the young focal character lends a certain plausibility to Wyeth's suggestion in his illustration that Jim might not have "seen" his mother's tears.

Wyeth makes the seamen of the "faithful party" (164) square-shouldered, clear-eyed, resolute, and unmarked by a brutal past. They have no broken teeth, sabre scars, sinister tattoos, or appalling deformities. Among the pirates, Pew is blind, Bones scarred, Black Dog has lost two fingers, and, of course, Silver has lost a leg. The very idea of the pirate with one leg haunts Jim's nightmares in the beginning of the story; and yet when he meets Silver the boy is struck by his pleasantness and his normality. Wyeth dramatizes this by taking care, in his picture of Jim and Silver in the galley, to disguise Silver's handicap. As Jim stands (in the same pose as Billy Bones atop the cliff), hands on hips, leaning backward to compensate for the roll of the ship, a thoughtful Long John regards him quietly, head bent, face in shadow, his tell-tale leg concealed from view.

The third part of the story, "My Shore Adventure," features two illustrations. In one, the leaders of the "faithful party" hand out loaded pistols "to all the sure men" (101); in the other, a feral Ben Gunn leaps "with great rapidity behind the trunk of a pine" (111). Wyeth stresses here the ironic twist of fate which awaits the treasure hunters: the weapons of these strong men will guarantee neither their survival nor their triumph—these will depend instead on the sly, childlike castaway. Wyeth's portrait of Ben Gunn is a clever visual allusion to the traditional "resourceful" image of Robinson Crusoe, and readers reminded of it may be encouraged to accept a little more readily the perhaps excessively convenient activities of Stevenson's deus ex machina later in the story.

The section Stevenson calls "The Stockade" has two pictures which clarify the differences between the "faithful party" and the pirates. In the first, the dutiful Captain Smollett defies the pirates, running up the Union Jack on the roof of the blockhouse with his own hands. This scene offers a vivid contrast to the similar scene on the book jacket in which the pirates hoist the Jolly Roger. Wyeth gives Captain Smollett snowy linen, a carefully powdered wig, and a most dignified bearing. All these proclaim him to be an eighteenth-century gentleman, above manual labor. When he climbs to the roof of the rude blockhouse and removes his coat to run up the Union Jack, the significance of the moment is clearly asserted by the details supplied by the artist. Stevenson's hints concerning body language, gesture, clothing, architecture, and iconic symbols like the flag are translated

into visual specifics by Wyeth, who shares with the inexperienced reader his own knowledge of the elaborately coded symbolic systems human beings have contrived to convey information about themselves. In the second picture for this section, in contrast to the world of order and dignity suggested by Smollett's gesture in raising the flag, the savage pirate crew, armed to the teeth, swarm "over the fence like monkeys" (161). Like Stevenson, Wyeth tends to show the reader the moment just before a bloody confrontation—but the pirates look strong and menacing as they move into the foreground, almost seeming to threaten the viewer, and their bestial appearance contrasts effectively with Captain Smollett's elegant rectitude.

To the innocent eye of a reader concerned mainly with action and adventure, Jim Hawkins's great triumph in the story must seem to be the sequence in which he single-handedly steals the Hispaniola from the villains. But a close reading of Stevenson reveals that here, when he seems most free, Jim is caught up in circumstances beyond his control, and this paradoxical situation is well imaged in the pair of pictures Wyeth provides for the next section of the story. When Hawkins relates the next section of the story, "My Sea Adventure," Wyeth shows the reader what Jim sees through the window of the ship's cabin where two of the pirates, Hands and O'Brien, are "locked together in deadly wrestle"; this is followed by a picture of Jim's confrontation with Hands. The first of these pictures in effect shows a murder, and the second depicts the split second before a fatal accident: Hands is about to hurl the dagger which will cause Jim's pistols to discharge and so, in effect, bring about his own death. In the first picture, Wyeth shows Hands and O'Brien struggling for a knife (not mentioned in the text) and the reader is free to conjecture that this is when Hands acquires the weapon which he will throw at Jim in the next picture. In the fight scene, Wyeth adds a discarded jacket, an overturned chair, and a bottle rolling about the floor among scattered cards, as if to indicate what "drink and the devil" have done to the combatants.

In these pictures Wyeth capitalizes on the unsettling effect produced by the roll of the ship. In the scene with Hands and O'Brien, the lines of the wall and floor indicate that the ship is rolling badly, and the effect is even more striking in the next picture, where the steady line of the sea on the horizon and a bit of land visible in the corner of the picture suggest that the ship, which has gone aground on a sandbar, is canted at a forty-five degree angle. The lines of the mast and the rigging lead upward and converge on the figure of Jim, who clings to the mast, pointing two pistols down at Hands, who holds the knife he is about to throw. Jim's face is an important focal point here. It is close to the viewer and only in light shadow; but, inexplicably, it is so badly blurred that the expression cannot be read. The pitch of the ship suggests the uncertainty of the world in which Jim is moving, and Wyeth's blurring of Jim's face is perhaps an attempt to convey visually that what is about to happen will do so without Jim's volition. Like Stevenson, Wyeth wishes to attenuate Jim's responsibility for the killing of Hands, which becomes nothing but a reflex action. Jim, whose firing of the pistols is neither conscious nor deliberate, is well imaged in the featureless automaton of Wyeth's illustration.

Wyeth concludes his set of illustrations with three magnificent pictures for the section Stevenson called "Captain Silver." The first shows what Jim saw through a loophole in the Stockade wall: a semicircle of pirates cutting the Bible so that they can pass Silver the "Black Spot." Wyeth contrasts the Bible-cutting of the superstitious and self-defeating sailors, posed and lit like some kind of satanic ritual, with a picture of Long John swinging along on his crutch, a purposeful figure of demonic energy who easily pulls the helpless Jim along on a rope "like a dancing bear" (244). This illustration serves as an emblem of the real relationship between Jim and Silver. The figure of the boy struggling at a rope's end evokes the image of the doomed, hanged man Wyeth devised for the title page and may remind the reader of how often Wyeth has chosen to show the young Jim echoing in stance and gesture the pirates with whom he will eventually recognize a fearful kinship.

The title-page illustration for *Treasure Island,* as is usual with Wyeth, had suggested the nature of the essential conflict in the story. In it the pirates look furtively about as they bury their loot, projecting fear and guilt in every gesture. One crouches in despair with his head in his hands, while another is in the act of drawing his sword to protect himself against invisible enemies. These figures are painted brilliantly in realistic detail, but about them and above them swirl billowing, dreamy clouds, and in the sky overhead Wyeth has lightly sketched the huge, translucent image of a hanged man. Part of the horror of this figure is its helplessness as it dangles, arms bound, head bowed, above them. The hanged man symbolizes their fate, their future, their deepest fear. Yet, significantly, they do not seem to see him. They are armed to face a more immediate enemy and are blind to what looms above them. This picture strikes the keynote of Wyeth's version of the story, stressing the themes of helplessness and tragic blindness that in Stevenson's narrative are conveyed by the voice of the older Jim as he reflects on the exciting treasure hunt which initiated him into the ways of a corrupt world.

The final picture of a series, like the opening picture, occupies a powerful rhetorical position. If Wyeth had used his title-page illustration to suggest the atmosphere of guilty fear which pervades the book and to hint at the tragic blindness with which its protagonist stumbles through his adventures, here he had to convey the hollowness of Jim's triumph at the end of the story and the boy's dim recognition both that the treasure had been fatally tainted by all the crimes committed for it and that he and Silver have more in common than he would like to admit. In his final illustration, Wyeth shows us the treasure cave at last. He catches the disillusioned tone of Jim's description of the treasure that had been the occasion of so much "blood and sorrow," such "shame and lies and cruelty" (265) by choosing to make the cave not the "large, airy place, with a little spring and a pool of clear water, overhung with ferns" of Stevenson's description (275) but a dark brown cavern with a great curved roof, like the inside of a giant mouth. In this deeply shadowed final picture Wyeth suggests the rueful self-knowledge of the older Jim by showing the blind, unthinking boy who had left on his quest with such bright dreams as a faceless creature hunched over his treasure hoard, letting the glittering coins slide down his fingers into storage bags like some fairy-tale gnome or like a sad allegorical embodiment of greed.

An illustrator's vision, as I have suggested, can have a powerful impact on the way a reader experiences a text, and Wyeth's pictures embody the story in a very different way from, say, the fluent drawings of Louis Rhead or the mordant sketches of Mervyn Peake. Stevenson as author and Wyeth as illustrator seem unusually well-matched. Wyeth's pictures for *Treasure Island* translate the ironic doubleness at the heart of the written narrative into effective visual terms and open up alternative aspects of character and unexpected thematic and structural nuances for the reader's consideration. Perhaps they are especially effective in projecting the darker strain in Stevenson; Wyeth once confided to his mother that "for some reason or other *Anything* that I appreciate keenly and profoundly is always sad to the point of being tragic" (quoted in *An American Vision* 4). But, as many a dazzled reader can attest, they also do full justice to the romance, the glamor, the purely aesthetic appeal the pirate myth held for them both. Stevenson's and Wyeth's characters may do the darkest of deeds, but the pictures presenting them are invariably beautiful.

Works Cited

An American Vision: Three Generations of Wyeth Art: N. C. Wyeth, Andrew Wyeth, James Wyeth. Essays by James H. Duff, Andrew Wyeth, Thomas Hoving, and Lincoln Kirstein. Boston: Little, Brown & Co., 1987.

Scholes, Robert. *Semiotics and Interpretation.* New Haven: Yale University Press, 1982.

Stevenson, Robert Louis. "Bagster's Pilgrim's Progress." In *Familiar Studies of Men and Books: Criticisms,* vol. 5 of *The Works of Robert Louis Stevenson.* South Seas Edition (32 vols.). New York: Charles Scribner's Sons, 1923.

———. *The Black Arrow: A Tale of the Two Roses.* New York: Charles Scribner's Sons, 1916.

———. *David Balfour.* New York: Charles Scribner's Sons, 1941.

———. *Essays.* 1892. Reprinted with an introduction by William Lyon Phelps. The Modern Student's Library. New York: Charles Scribner's Sons, 1918.

———. *Kidnapped.* New York: Charles Scribner's Sons, 1913.

———. *Treasure Island.* New York: Charles Scribner's Sons, 1911.

Wyeth, Betsy James, ed. *The Wyeths: The Letters of N. C. Wyeth, 1901-1945.* Boston: Gambit, 1971.

Lucy Rollin (essay date 1999)

SOURCE: Rollin, Lucy. "Depictions of the Mother Child Dyad in the Work of Mary Cassatt and Jessie Willcox Smith." In *Psychoanalytic Responses to Children's Literature,* edited by Lucy Rollins and Mark I. West, pp. 141-50. Jefferson, N.C.: McFarland and Company, Inc. Publishers, 1999.

[*In the following essay, Rollin draws comparisons between the works of Mary Cassatt and noted Brandywine illustrator Jessie Willcox Smith, arguing that the artists' formative relationships with their families—particularly their mothers—had a direct influence upon their later artistic careers.*]

Mary Cassatt and Jessie Willcox Smith became successful painters by focusing on images of mothers tenderly caring for their children—a subject with roots in depictions of the Madonna and child in medieval art and one which remains perennially popular. Both Pennsylvanians, one generation apart (though they never met), the similarities in their work are striking. Smith's most recent biographer, Edward Nudelman, notes that Cassatt's aquatints hung in Smith's home, and that, "more than from any other living artist, Smith's art drew its impulse and sentiment from that of Cassatt" (31).

There are some intriguing differences between their styles, however. While both use large, flat areas of color in the Japanese or poster-like style so popular with other Impressionist painters, Cassatt's images are individuals, portraits, beautiful but not sentimental. Smith's images are idealized, the children well-mannered and well-dressed, the mothers invariably young and beautiful—in short, a sentimentalized view of mother and child. Certainly much of this romantic strain in Smith is attributable to her choice of career; early on she elected to become an illustrator, stayed in Pennsylvania, and achieved remarkable success in commercial media such as magazine covers, story and book illustrations, and calendar art. She gave the public what it wanted. Cassatt remained in Paris where she participated in the Impressionist movement, receiving awards and holding individual shows but remaining "an artist's artist," not actively seeking public recognition (Roudebush 75).

But these different choices too are attributable to a deeper cause, one that springs from the different circumstances of their family lives—in particular, their relationships with their mothers, and, tangentially, with other women. This essay will explore this aspect of their lives. Of course, psychobiography is a notoriously risky enterprise. Yet it offers a lens through which to contemplate "the nature and limitations of human choice and commitment" (Coltrera, quoted in Zerbe 46). Certainly women's choices and commitments have, as many historical studies suggest, remained limited in similar ways for many years.

Comparing the lives of two women artists from similar backgrounds, with similar training, only a generation apart, who made difficult choices and achieved particular success, yet who responded to their success quite differently, may shed light on those continuing limitations and suggest other, more positive ways of seeing them.

Certainly the tendency in psychological studies of women artists is to find their characteristic rejection of marriage and children pathologic in some way.

Phyllis Greenacre's work on women artists (1960) takes the classic Freudian stance, assuming penis envy, the close connection of women's art with their biological functions, and the generally troubled lives of women who do not choose traditional feminine roles. She does, however, acknowledge a strong bisexual component in all artists that makes for their "extraordinary empathetic capacity," and comments further that the more complex oedipal situation of girls leads them to caution—"the forerunner of tact"—and to careful balance and diplomacy, all of which, she avers, restrict the artistic impulse (591).

John Gedo (1983) agrees; though he acknowledges that cultural oppression may be partly responsible for women artists' problems, he locates that oppression directly and only within the family, especially in the relationship to the father. Studies such as these assume that the art of such women is a flawed substitute for the fulfillment that marriage and children would have brought them.

Others, however, viewing women's lives differently, find the empathic capacity of women a source of strength. Object relations psychology shifts the emphasis from the relationship with the father to that with the mother as the chief shaping factor in human relationships. Carol Gilligan's now classic study offers the web as a model of women's relational development: women perceive themselves in relation to others, rather than separate from them. Chodorow referred to this phenomenon, and to the mother-daughter relationship that is its source, as the "reproduction of mothering."

More recently, the work of several women psychologists at the Stone Center, Wellesley, Massachusetts, offers a new model for women's development that acknowledges the "centrality and continuity of relationships throughout women's lives" (Surrey, title page). In this model, the mother's and daughter's close relationship with each other provides a "matrix of emotional connectedness" that empowers both of them and leads to the development of a "self-in-relation," as opposed to the more culturally normative idea of the autonomous self.

Instead of individuation, these writers offer differentiation, a process through which we distinguish ourselves from others while remaining related to them. From this viewpoint, the empathy and tact that Greenacre sees as special qualities of women artists take on more positive connotations, and provide, not a restriction to their art, but the very impulse for it, especially in artists like Cassatt and Smith who take the most basic of human relationships as their subject.

Several studies of Cassatt have been published, but only one with a psychobiographical approach: "Mother and Child: A Psychobiographical Portrait of Mary Cassatt," by Kathryn Zerbe appeared in *Psychoanalytic Review* 74 (1), spring 1987. No psychobiographical studies of Smith have appeared, to the best of my knowledge, and biographical studies of her have tended to be relatively brief introductions to generally adulatory descriptions of her work. My method here will be to follow the order of Zerbe's discussion of Cassatt, but to focus slightly more on Smith, setting biographical material about Smith alongside Zerbe's comments about Cassatt, with psychoanalytic speculations about Smith generally based on object relations psychology.

THEIR EARLY LIVES

Mary Cassatt was born in Pittsburgh in 1844, the youngest daughter of a prosperous family. Her father was a real estate investor, who preferred horseback riding to artistic endeavors. Her mother, however, admired French culture, spoke fluent French, and provided every opportunity for her children's cultural enrichment by guiding them through museums throughout Europe. Indeed Cassatt's mother remained a dominant influence throughout the artist's life. Her other children, Cassatt's siblings, tended to be frail and sickly, several dying quite young. Zerbe speculates that Cassatt's eventual choice of artistic subject—robust and healthy children—results in part from a wish to restore the lost siblings to life and health while "defensively denying any rivalry or hatred toward them" (48).

Jessie Willcox Smith was born nineteen years later, in 1863, in Philadelphia, also the youngest daughter of the family. Her father was a financier and provided a comfortable life for his wife and children, educating his youngest daughter in private elementary schools. Curiously, almost nothing else is known about Smith's parents, not even their death dates. She was sent away from home at age 17 to live with cousins in Cincinnati, for reasons which have never been discovered, and returned home to Philadelphia in 1884 only after she pleaded dissatisfaction with her position as a kindergarten teacher (she supposedly said she was too tall to stoop down to them comfortably) and expressed her desire to attend art school. While her parents undoubtedly paid for her schooling, Smith seems to have felt the need to become financially independent. Quite soon after completing her education, she took a position with the *Ladies' Home Journal* in 1889. Evidently she lived at home only a short time thereafter. Little is known about her

"Boating Party" (1893), painting by Mary Cassatt. The Granger Collection, New York. Reproduced with permission.

siblings, except for a brother who became an invalid and for whom Smith cared in later years.

Unlike Cassatt, Smith's relationship with her family, and her mother in particular, was distant, marked more by absence than by nurturing or even presence. If Cassatt was restoring her lost siblings by painting them, it is certainly possible that Smith was doing the same, perhaps even more intensely trying to restore the relationship with her mother.

The recurrent theme of mothers caring for children is powerful in her art, and indeed, one of Smith's first paintings in this mode is strikingly intense, even erotic. "Mother," from 1903, depicts a young mother kneeling in front of a large armchair, her back to the viewer, embracing her child, who looks up at her but whose face is partially obscured by the mother. The mother's dress is slipping off her shoulder, and the child's hand caresses the shoulder. The embrace of the mother is replicated in the embrace of the wings of the chair, and the decorative fabric of the chair contrasts with the simplicity of the mother's and child's skin and clothing, all creating an especially concentrated image of physical closeness, heightened by our seeing neither face clearly.

It is instructive to compare this painting with one of Cassatt's: "Breakfast in Bed" (1897) depicts a young mother lying in bed cuddling her child and watching as the child eats. While this painting also has a physicality similar to that of Smith's, we see both the mother's and child's faces here, two highly individual portraits. The child looks away, while the mother's eyes examine the child almost suspiciously in a sidewise glance. The effect of these different gazes mitigates the intense physical closeness of the two, suggesting an attempt to distance them even while they are together—something that must have frequently marked Cassatt's life, since her mother was not only available to her but intensely involved with her life.

Nowhere else in Smith's canon is a depiction of mother and child so intense as her 1903 painting, though she painted the subject many times. It is as if she learned to distance herself from her own desire for closeness with her mother, yet continued to explore that desire in many modes—probably a healthy reaction to what was evidently an emotional situation she could not otherwise control.

THE PAINTERS MATURE

In 1877, after terminating her studies at the Pennsylvania Academy of Arts because it was too stuffy and moving to Paris, Cassatt met Edgar Degas, who admired her work and invited her to join the Impressionist movement. He became her master, yet in her words, she could now work with "absolute independence" (Zerbe 49). As Zerbe puts it, her painting became "even more highly libidinalized" as she entered this "tumultuous but intimate relationship" (49).

While there is no evidence to suggest that Degas and Cassatt had an affair, her biographers have noticed that her finest work, especially on the mother-child theme, was done during the times when her relationship with Degas flourished. Zerbe speculates that she thus sublimated her desire for a child by Degas, achieving a "compromise formation: as an artist she asserts her own creative powers, vis-à-vis her art, while defending against any desires to be a mother" (50). Moreover, Zerbe asserts, this psychological situation was exacerbated by her father's withdrawal from his daughter's artistic life while her mother's intense interest in it continued; Cassatt was thus propelled "toward a highly libidinalized and enmeshed relationship with her mother" (51).

When Degas arrived on the scene, inserting himself between mother and daughter, he acted as the "de-symbiotizing agent" that her father should have been. Nonetheless, Zerbe suggests, since their relationship was uneven, Cassatt remained in a "developmental arrest at the level of the mother-child dyad," her paintings only partially resolving "her unconscious conflicts regarding her mother" (51-52). Zerbe points out that Cassatt painted two fine portraits of her mother, but never completed a major study of her father (52).

Jessie Willcox Smith also attended the Pennsylvania Academy, found it repressive and stuffy, but graduated in 1888. For a time, despite her successes at the *Ladies' Home Journal,* she then found herself in "a

Illustration by Jessie Willcox Smith from The Water-Babies *(1916), by Charles Kingsley.*

sort of limbo," becoming more publicly visible yet not in the mainstream of professional illustration (Nudelman 20). Determined to pursue a lucrative career, however, she enrolled in the Drexel Institute of Arts in 1897 in order to study under the dean of illustrators, Howard Pyle. "He seemed to wipe away all the cobwebs and confusions" for her (quoted in Mitchell 4). She also admired Pyle because of his ability, which he could evidently teach, to reach imaginatively into the story he was illustrating: "you were bound to get the right composition because you lived these things. . . . It was simply that he was always mentally projected into his subject" (Quoted in Nudelman 23).

Smith's illustrations too have been admired because of her ability to project herself into her subject; she seems able to understand the intensity of a child's concentration, especially while at play. But in Smith's work, good manners always prevail, possibly reflecting the self-control she must have learned early. And no painting of her parents or siblings has ever come to light.

Thus Smith, like Cassatt, found a male mentor. Unlike Cassatt, however, there is nothing in Smith's history to suggest any kind of erotic relationship between them; Pyle encouraged all his pupils, and particularly sponsored Smith's working relationship with her friend and colleague Violet Oakley by procuring a book contract for an edition of *Evangeline* for them. In 1898, Smith left Drexel and moved in with two other women artists, Jessie H. Dowd and Elizabeth Shippen Green. For the remainder of Smith's life, she would live harmoniously with other women, each pursuing her own career yet giving each other financial and emotional support.

Zerbe cites Greenacre and Chodorow on the peculiar nature of the mother-daughter relationship, marked as it is by "fusion, narcissistic extension, and denial of separateness" (54). Just as Cassatt remained close to her mother physically and emotionally, expressed in her work by mothers and children in tight embraces, visual boundaries were softened and even erased between the two. Degas' encouragement of Cassatt's drawing—i.e. the depiction of boundaries—is further evidence of his desymbiotizing influence, but it was not strong enough, Zerbe suggests, to continue once his physical presence in her life lessened.

In contrast, Smith's work is, on the whole, very strongly drawn, possibly suggesting the clear boundaries that evidently were established between her and her mother early in life. However, Smith's attention to fabric, especially the fabric of the mother's dress in her paintings, which often seems to dominate and encompass the child as it nestles in the texture and pattern, may be a substitute for that blurring of boundaries which characterizes Cassatt, and which Smith denied so early but consciously or unconsciously longed for.

Their Artistic Development

Cassatt's mother died in 1895; for the next five years, Cassatt turned to portrait painting. Then, after 1900, she painted very little, becoming, instead, an active suffragette. Her work during this time reveals a definite waning of her powers. Zerbe comments that such an abrupt change "reflects pathological mourning and the employment of manic defenses . . . a disruption of her inner life" (56-57). She suffered frequent bouts of depression, and even explored Spiritualism.

Late in life, living only with a housekeeper and chauffeur, her infrequent visitors found her "blind and lonely, unreasonable and vituperative" (Quoted in Roudebush 89), unable to work or to find solace in friends. Zerbe speculates, "Her tragedy seems to have

predominantly centered upon a denial of her own emotional reactions and feelings in search of her mother's love" (57). Since her art "served indispensable adaptive functions" (57), without it she could not act as a whole person. She seemed unable to function without her mother as well.

Smith's later life was quite different. Contracts for work continued steadily, and she seems to have managed them astutely, often making an illustration for a calendar serve as an illustration for a book and thus reaping a double profit from her work. Eventually she became known among her friends and relatives as "the Mint" because of her financial success and her great generosity; one biographer states that at one time she was responsible for the financial support of eleven children—nieces, nephews, and cousins who were without adequate resources (Schnessel 44). Unlike Cassatt, Smith was found by later visitors to be calm, sociable, spiritually at ease, enjoying theater and opera, her gardens, brisk walks, and especially her relationships with her friends Violet Oakley and Elizabeth Shippen Green, with whom she lived.

Another member of their household was Henrietta Cozens, who arrived at the home Smith shared with the others after Smith's invalid brother had died. She took over the household duties, managing the funds and other household affairs—becoming "mother," in short, to the other three women and freeing them from the daily bother of routine matters to concentrate on their art (Schnessel 37). Each July 4, the women honored the occasion with a celebratory dinner and a reading of the Declaration of Independence, "as each woman listened intently. After the reading, the women rose and signed the reprinted document between the names of the founders of our nation" (Schnessel 44).

In 1914, Green married the man to whom she had been engaged for several years. Oakley concentrated her time working on murals in another city, while Smith built a home for herself and Cozens, on a hill just above their first. The routine there was comfortable and pleasant, with Smith as busy as ever, but maintaining her correspondence with her women friends, her portrait painting, and her occasional visits with art students.

This same year, her large edition of Mother Goose rhymes appeared and was immediately successful. One reason for its popularity may be the softer style of the pictures; the dark outlining so typical of Smith's poster style was muted into more tender shapes and textures. If, as Zerbe notes, the intensifying or blurring of boundaries in Cassatt's work reflected her shifting relationship with her mother, this shift in Smith's style may reflect her sense of rediscovered closeness with a mother-like woman who cared for her needs and gave her undemanding companionship.

Another interesting aspect of these Mother Goose pictures is her depiction of all of the characters as young children; Peter Pumpkin-eater is a small boy, with an even smaller girl, out of natural proportion, in the pumpkin-shell. Such illustrations reduce these lusty characters and their odd situations to tender, pretty moments in a child's life. In her calendar art of the same period, she depicted Little Red Riding Hood's wolf as a tiny toy, and the Beast in "Beauty and the Beast" as a sweet-faced, tea-drinking little monkey. These pictures suggest the attitude of a woman who saw life relatively simply and safely, who maintained a measure of childlikeness, yet who had found in herself a measure of security.

It is a question whether she found this security in spite of, or because of, the absence of her biological mother from her life, and the substitution of another female in that position. Her relationship with Cozens suggests that she enjoyed having household duties cared for, yet she also adopted a kind of patriarchal stance in their relationship, assuming the chief financial responsibility for their home. Certainly she continued to mine the image of the mother and child throughout her series of covers for *Good Housekeeping* magazine; she continued these popular covers for nearly 17 years, from 1917 until 1934, and they undoubtedly added to this magazine's popularity across middle-class and upper-class homes.

As her biographer Schnessel has put it, "Monthly images of children at play and of mother love are not continued out of habit. The magazine's management well understood the appeal her works held for millions of readers" (23). But they must have had an appeal for Smith as well, for they are invariably done with tenderness of texture, gracefulness of design, and expertness of technique, despite their obvious commercial requirements. At this time, she was also in demand as a painter of portraits of upper-class Philadelphia children. No doubt she could have made a handsome living doing this work alone. However, she continued to paint mothers and children, depicting a range of imaginative mother-and-child situations that is quite extraordinary for its variety and its naturalness, as well as for its romance and fantasy.

She must have observed mothers and children closely in life to paint such images, yet the variety of images suggests that though Smith's imagination continually

worked this theme, it does not seem to have done so obsessively. And if, like Cassatt's, Smith's art served an adaptive function, she was able, probably because of its commercial success, to continue using it until the end.

Smith died in 1935, upon her return from her first and only trip abroad, leaving her entire estate of original paintings to Henrietta Cozens. In an obituary, the *New York Times* commented, "The children that Miss Smith painted were reflective and a little sedate, and in her art the maternal note predominated. She seemed to be haunted by the vision of two faces, and the face of one was the face of a mother" (Quoted in Schnessel 21). Certainly Smith herself seems to have been "reflective and a little sedate," and Schnessel finds her work, for all its beauty, "in some ways undeniably sad . . . [Mother love] is a dominant theme that speaks volumes about her own needs and desires, and this is why her art is so deeply touching" (21).

Schnessel's comments may represent the male biographer's inability to understand a woman who seemed so obviously happy without male companionship. Smith's life and art, as here described, lend credence to the notion that a self-in-relation, developed under initially unencouraging conditions, may flourish later in visual images as well as in a peaceful, fulfilled life.

Certainly, these two artists, only a generation apart, experienced virtually the same social obstacles to their careers. Both made difficult choices, lived with limitations, and let their art speak for them. One sought a way of life that separated her physically from her home and from other women except her mother; the other, already separated physically from her patriarchal home and family (and possibly rejected by them), enmeshed herself in relationships that nourished her and her painting. They were both "haunted by the vision of two faces"—that of mother and child, but their responses to the needs and desires engendered by this vision were quite different, resulting in two different kinds of art equally valuable and equally worthy of further study.

Works Cited

Chodorow, Nancy. *The Reproduction of Mothering.* Berkeley: University of California Press, 1978.

Gedo, John. *Portraits of the Artist.* New York: Guilford Press, 1982.

Gilligan, Carol. *In a Different Voice.* Cambridge: Harvard University Press, 1982.

Greenacre, Phyllis. "Woman as Artist" (1960). In *Emotional Growth, II.* 575-591. New York: International Universities Press, 1971.

Mitchell, Gene. *The Subject Was Children: The Art of Jessie Willcox Smith.* New York: E. P. Dutton, 1979.

Nudelman, Edward D. *Jessie Willcox Smith: American Illustrator.* Grena, LA: Pelican Publishing Co., 1990.

Roudebush, Jay. *Mary Cassatt.* New York: Crown Publishers, 1979.

Schnessel, S. Michael. *Jessie Willcox Smith.* New York: Thomas Y. Crowell, 1977.

Smith, Jessie Willcox, illus. *Mother Goose* (1914). New York: Derrydale Books, 1986.

Surrey, Janet L. "Self-in-Relation: A Theory of Women's Development." *Work in Progress,* 13. Wellesley, MA.: The Stone Center, 1985.

Zerbe, Kathryn J. "Mother and Child: A Psychobiographical Portrait of Mary Cassatt." *Psychoanalytic Review* 74.1 (Spring 1987): 45-61.

FURTHER READING

Criticism

Adams, Gillian. "Arthur Rackham's *Fairy Book*: A Confrontation with the Marvelous." In *Touchstones: Reflections on the Best in Children's Literature, Volume Three: Picture Books,* edited by Perry Nodelman, pp. 107-21. West Lafayette, Ind.: ChLA Publishers, 1989.

Overview of Arthur Rackham's career that focuses special attention on his interest in the fantastical.

Cech, John. "Remembering Caldecott: *The Three Jovial Huntsmen* and the Art of the Picture Book." *Lion and the Unicorn,* nos. 7-8 (1983-1984): 110-19.

Analysis of *The Three Jovial Huntsmen* that examines how Caldecott's use of wit, action, and a harmonious balance of art and text made him a galvanizing force for change among picture book artists.

Dooley, Patricia. "Kate Greenaway's *A Apple Pie*: An Atmosphere of Sober Joy." In *Touchstones: Reflections on the Best in Children's Literature, Volume Three: Picture Books,* edited by Perry Nodelman, pp. 63-9. West Lafayette, Ind.: ChLA Publishers, 1989.

Reflects on how the stylized details of Greenaway's A Apple Pie demonstrates a deliberate attempt to depict a harmonious universe of indelible nostalgia.

Duvoisin, Roger. "Children's Book Illustration: The Pleasures and the Problems." In *Only Connect: Readings on Children's Literature,* edited by Sheila Egoff, G. T. Stubbs, and L. F. Ashley, pp. 357-74. Toronto, Canada: Oxford University Press, 1969.

Provides a historical overview of the evolution of children's picture books.

Greene, Ellin. "Randolph Caldecott's Picture Books: The Invention of a Genre." In *Touchstones: Reflections on the Best in Children's Literature, Volume Three: Picture Books,* edited by Perry Nodelman, pp. 38-45. West Layette, Ind.: ChLa Publishers, 1989

Offers an appreciation of Caldecott that praises his attempts to interpret common nursery rhymes as an innovation in the evolution of the picture book genre.

Laws, Frederick. "Randolph Caldecott." In *Only Connect: Readings on Children's Literature,* edited by Sheila Egoff, G. T. Stubbs, and L. F. Ashley, pp. 375-83. Toronto, Canada: Oxford University Press, 1969.

Critical examination of Randolph Caldecott's canon and career as an illustrator.

Lundin, Anne. "Kate Greenaway (1846-1901)." In *Victorian Horizons: The Reception of the Picture Books of Walter Crane, Randolph Caldecott, and Kate Greenaway,* pp. 167-223. Lanham, Md.: Scarecrow Press, Inc., 2001.

Offers a critical overview of Greenaway's artistic canon, including individual analyses of her major works.

Meigs, Cornelia, Anne Thaxter Eaton, Elizabeth Nesbit, and Ruth Hill Viguers. "A March of Picture Books." In *A Critical History of Children's Literature,* pp. 399-406. New York, N.Y.: The MacMillan Company, 1953.

Evaluates the works of several lesser-known picture book illustrators of the Golden Age of children's illustration.

Norton, Donna E. "Early Illustrators of Children's Books." In *Through the Eyes of a Child: An Introduction to Children's Literature,* pp. 54-7. Columbus, Ohio: Merrill Publishing Company, 1987.

Explores the early publishing history of children's book illustration, noting the influence of such Victorian masters as Crane, Caldecott, and Greenaway.

Sendak, Maurice. "Randolph Caldecott." In *Caldecott & Co.: Notes on Books and Pictures,* pp. 21-5. New York, N.Y.: Noonday Press, 1988.

Credits Caldecott as being the father of the modern picture book, arguing that Caldecott's illustrated works feature "an ingenious juxtaposition of picture and word, a counterpoint that never happened before."

Smith, James Steel. "To Read, To Look: The Art of Illustrating Children's Books." In *A Critical Approach to Children's Literature,* pp. 305-32. New York, N.Y.: McGraw Hill Book Company, 1967.

Presents a historical chronicle of the role of illustration and illustrators in the development of the children's literature genre.

Chris Van Allsburg
1949-

American illustrator and author of picture books.

The following entry presents an overview of Van Allsburg's career through 2004. For further information on his life and works, see *CLR,* Volumes 5 and 13.

INTRODUCTION

Van Allsburg is one of the most admired children's book author-illustrators of the past twenty-five years. Combining moody, dramatic drawings with unadorned prose, Van Allsburg creates stories in which the line between reality and the imagination is constantly blurred. His characters generally begin in the everyday world, but soon find that ordinary reality transforms into a realm of surreal and fantastic experiences. Van Allsburg's storybooks have been described as haunting, mysterious, and dreamlike, always celebrating the magnificent powers of the human imagination. While playful and lighthearted in many respects, his picture books often hint at a dark underlying mood of melancholy and foreboding. His skills as an illustrator have earned widespread acclaim from critics who praise his technical virtuosity as well as his highly original artistic vision. His Caldecott Award-winning titles include *The Garden of Abdul Gasazi* (1979), *Jumanji* (1981), and *The Polar Express* (1985). In his 1986 Caldecott Medal acceptance speech, Van Allsburg observed that, "Conceiving of something is only part of the creative process. Giving life to the conception is the other half. The struggle to master a medium, whether it's words, notes, paint, or marble, is the heroic part of making art." Van Allsburg's picture books have often been compared to the surrealist paintings of Salvador Dali, the mystery-suspense movies of Alfred Hitchcock, and the storybooks of Dr. Seuss.

BIOGRAPHICAL INFORMATION

Van Allsburg was born in Grand Rapids, Michigan, on June 18, 1949, the second child of Doris Christiansen Van Allsburg and Richard Van Allsburg. His

father worked at a creamery owned by Van Allsburg's paternal grandfather and eventually moved his family to a burgeoning suburb, where the half-built houses and open fields became Van Allsburg's childhood playgrounds. Van Allsburg attended high school in East Grand Rapids and enrolled in the College of Architecture and Design at the University of Michigan in 1967. He majored in sculpture, graduating with a B.A. in 1972, and went on to earn a M.A. from the prestigious Rhode Island School of Design in 1975. That same year, Van Allsburg established a sculpture studio in Providence, Rhode Island, and married Lisa Morrison, with whom he has two children. His sculptures were first shown in New York City at the Alan Stone Gallery, with some of his illustrations later warranting an exhibit at the Whitney Museum of Art in 1978. In 1977 Van Allsburg returned to the Rhode Island School of Design as a drawing instructor. Encouraged by his wife and editors at the Houghton

Mifflin Company, Van Allsburg created his first picture book, *The Garden of Abdul Gasazi,* in 1979. The work quickly became a critical and popular success, and Van Allsburg began publishing nearly a book a year until 1997, after which he took a five-year break before releasing his next original picture book, *Zathura: A Space Adventure* (2002). To date, there have been three major film adaptations of Van Allsburg's picture books—the live-action *Jumanji* (1995) and *Zathura* (2005) and the computer-animated *The Polar Express* (2004).

MAJOR WORKS

Van Allsburg's first picture book, *The Garden of Abdul Gasazi,* follows the adventures of a boy named Alan one afternoon when the dog he is supposed to be taking care of runs away. The dog, named Fritz, enters the mysterious topiary garden of Abdul Gasazi—at the entrance of which is posted a sign that reads, "Absolutely, positively no dogs allowed in this Garden"—and Alan follows him in. Inside the garden walls, Alan encounters the magician Abdul Gasazi, who turns Fritz into a duck. Some of the black-and-white pencil illustrations from *The Garden of Abdul Gasazi* were included in an exhibition of Van Allsburg's works at the Alan Stone Gallery in New York. In his next picture book, *Jumanji,* two suburban children, Judy and Peter, find a mysterious board game called Jumanji—"a young people's jungle adventure designed especially for the bored and restless"—in a park near their house. They take the game home, despite an eerie warning on the box that whoever starts playing the game will not be able to stop until it is completed. The game itself causes a range of wild beasts to invade their home, including lions, monkeys, and a herd of rhinoceroses. After Judy wins the game by reaching "the Golden City" of Jumanji, all of the beasts instantly disappear, leaving no trace of the massive mess they made in the children's home. Van Allsburg's illustrations for *Jumanji* were created with a Conte crayon to evoke photographic-looking images of the incongruous occurrences described in the story. In *Ben's Dream* (1982), Ben falls asleep while studying for a geography test on the great landmarks of the world. His dream takes him on an imaginary tour of such landmarks as the Statue of Liberty, the Eiffel Tower, the Leaning Tower of Pisa, and the Great Wall of China. When he wakes up, Ben learns that his friend Margaret, who appeared in his dream, had also been having the very same dream.

The Wreck of the Zephyr (1983) was Van Allsburg's first children's book with full-color illustrations. In this story, a young boy walking along the beach comes upon an old man, who proceeds to tell him a fantastic "story-within-a-story" about a boy who discovered a flying boat and soared above the town until the boat fell from the sky in a crash landing. By the end, it seems clear that the old man was once the child who found the flying boat. In illustrating *The Wreck of the Zephyr,* Van Allsburg combined thick Rembrandt pastels with fine-pointed pastel pencils to create dramatic effects, striking for both their realism and their evocativeness. Van Allsburg's *The Mysteries of Harris Burdick* (1984) is a unique work of children's literature in which fourteen evocative drawings, combined with enigmatic lines of text, are offered up to stimulate the reader's imagination, challenging them to invent a story around mysterious juxtapositions of image and text. Each two-page spread of *The Mysteries of Harris Burdick* includes a title and a first-line of a story on the left-hand page, with a moody, enigmatic black-and-white charcoal drawing on the facing page. The first of these offers the title "Archie Smith, Boy Wonder" paired with the line, "A tiny voice asked, 'Is this the one?'" In the accompanying illustration, a boy sleeps soundly in bed while points of light fly in through his window. In another, the title "Another Place, Another Time" is followed by "If there was an answer, he'd find it there," with an illustration of four children traveling by train track through a thick fog toward a magnificent castle that looms off in the distance. In *The Polar Express*—possibly Van Allsburg's most recognized picture book to date—an unnamed ten-year-old narrator describes his experiences one Christmas Eve, when a train called the Polar Express mysteriously appears in front of his house. Invited by a friendly conductor to board the train, the boy joins dozens of children passengers in their pajamas. The train takes the youngsters to the North Pole, where Santa Claus's toy-making empire appears as an industrialized city characterized by massive smokestack factories and thousands of elf-workers. In an annual North Pole ritual, the boy is chosen to be the first child of the year to receive a gift from Santa. He is given a sleigh bell from the harness of one of the reindeer, but soon loses it through a hole in his pocket. After returning home on the Polar Express, the boy awakens on Christmas morning to find the bell as a wrapped gift under his tree. In *The Polar Express,* Van Allsburg created wide double-paged spreads of stunning full-color pastel images, emphasizing the grandeur of the train itself, the landscapes it crosses, and the massive urban empire of Santa Claus. As Van Allsburg noted in his 1986 Caldecott Medal acceptance speech, "A good story uses the description of events to reveal some kind of moral or psychological premise. . . . When I started *The Polar Express,* I thought I was writing about a train trip, but the story was actually about faith and the desire to believe in something."

In the picture book *Just a Dream* (1990), Van Allsburg offers an undisguised message about the importance of environmentalism. Walter is a litterbug who shows no respect for the environment and refuses to recycle his trash. In a dream, he is transported to a nightmarish future in which the natural environment has been destroyed by pollution. When he wakes up, he is inspired to plant a tree in an effort to help preserve the majesty of nature. Van Allsburg composed the text of *The Wretched Stone* (1991) to resemble a captain's ship's log, in which the captain records the strange adventures that befell the crew of a ship called the *Rita Anne.* A large, brilliant stone brought aboard the ship from an island causes the sailors to turn into monkeys. The captain eventually restores the monkeys to human form by reading aloud to them, although the sailors retain their preference for eating bananas. In *The Widow's Broom* (1992), a widow living on a farm retrieves the broom of a crash-landed witch, finding that its magical powers can help her with such tasks as feeding the chickens and playing the piano. *The Widow's Broom* is ultimately a parable about persecution, in which a rural community finds themselves feeling threatened by the widow's strange and powerful broom. *Zathura,* subtitled "A Space Adventure," serves as an indirect sequel to Van Allsburg's earlier picture book *Jumanji.* Two brothers, Danny and Walter—neighbors of Peter and Judy, the protagonists from *Jumanji*—discover a board game which they take home to play. This time, instead of being invaded by jungle creatures, the gamesters find themselves in a world of outer-space adventures as their house flies off toward the purple planet of Zathura. Along the way, the brothers encounter such fantastic events as a meteor shower in their living room, a murderous "Zyborg pirate" robot, a black hole, and time travel. In addition to the picture books he has authored and illustrated himself, Van Allsburg has also provided artwork for several young adult novels written by Mark Helprin, including *Swan Lake* (1989), *A City in Winter* (1996), and *The Veil of Snows* (1997).

CRITICAL RECEPTION

As both an author and an illustrator, Van Allsburg has won near-universal praise for his illustrative virtuosity and his unique artistic perspective. Peter F.

Neumeyer has asserted that, "Van Allsburg's books are art works in the shape of books, art works accompanied by mysterious and thought-provoking stories." Examining nine of Van Allsburg's children's books published between 1979 and 1988, Neumeyer has reached several conclusions about the central thematic concerns that run throughout the author's oeuvre, contending that all of Van Allsburg's books express "the celebration of the imagination" and that his "pervasive theme" is "the Reality of the Imagination." A number of reviewers have remarked upon the cinematic qualities of Van Allsburg's stunning use of visual perspective, which resembles the often dramatic camera angles of motion pictures. In her review of *Jumanji,* Pamela D. Pollack has observed that, "[t]he eye-fooling angles, looming shadows and shifting perspectives are worthy of Hitchcock, yet all these 'special effects' are supplied with only a pencil." Van Allsburg's prose style has been characterized as straightforward and unadorned, with scholars noting his minimal use of adjectives or embellished language. While some have admired the brevity of Van Allsburg's narratives for allowing the artwork and the reader's individual imagination to flesh out the story, others have argued that Van Allsburg's plots are weak and merely serve as devices for presenting his illustrations. However, certain critics have asserted that Van Allsburg's illustrations strongly compliment his minimalist prose by depicting a more complex and nuanced story than that conveyed by the text. Joseph Stanton has commented that, "[t]he startling contrast between Van Allsburg's dull, though carefully crafted, prose and his extraordinary images operates as a continuous irony. It is key to the tension between the ordinary and the marvelous that is his central subject."

AWARDS

Van Allsburg has won numerous awards and accolades throughout his career, including Caldecott Medals for *Jumanji* and *The Polar Express.* He was awarded *New York Times* Best Illustrated Children's Books citations for *The Garden of Abdul Gasazi, Jumanji, Ben's Dream, The Wreck of the Zephyr, The Mysteries of Harris Burdick, The Polar Express,* and *The Stranger* (1986). *The Garden of Abdul Gasazi* won a Caldecott Honor Book citation from the American Library Association and the *Boston Globe-Horn Book* Award for illustration. *Jumanji* and *The Wreck of the Zephyr* were given *New York Times* Outstanding Books citations, and *Ben's Dream, The Wreck of the Zephyr,* and *The Mysteries of Harris*

Burdick were included in the American Institute of Graphic Arts Book Show. Additionally, Van Allsburg received a nomination for the Hans Christian Andersen Award in 1985.

PRINCIPAL WORKS

The Garden of Abdul Gasazi (picture book) 1979
Jumanji (picture book) 1981
Ben's Dream (picture book) 1982
The Wreck of the Zephyr (picture book) 1983
The Mysteries of Harris Burdick (picture book) 1984
The Polar Express (picture book) 1985
The Stranger (picture book) 1986
The Z Was Zapped: A Play in Twenty-Six Acts (picture book) 1987
Two Bad Ants (picture book) 1988
Swan Lake [illustrator; by Mark Helprin] (young adult novel) 1989
Just a Dream (picture book) 1990
The Wretched Stone (picture book) 1991
The Widow's Broom (picture book) 1992
The Sweetest Fig (picture book) 1993
Bad Day at Riverbend (picture book) 1995
A City in Winter [illustrator; by Mark Helprin] (young adult novel) 1996
The Veil of Snows [illustrator; by Mark Helprin] (young adult novel) 1997
Zathura: A Space Adventure (picture book) 2002

AUTHOR COMMENTARY

Chris Van Allsburg (essay date July-August 1986)

SOURCE: Van Allsburg, Chris. "Caldecott Medal Acceptance." *Horn Book Magazine* 62, no. 4 (July-August 1986): 420-24.

[*In the following transcript of his 1986 Caldecott Medal acceptance speech, Van Allsburg discusses childhood influences on his creative process, the stylistic inspirations for* The Polar Express, *and his career as an author and illustrator.*]

The first book I remember reading is probably the same book many people my age recall as their first. It was profusely illustrated and recounted the adventures and conflicts of its three protagonists, Dick, Jane, and Spot. Actually, the lives of this trio were not all that interesting. A young reader's reward for struggling through those syllables at the bottom of the page was to discover that Spot got a bath. Not exactly an exciting revelation. Especially since you'd already seen Spot getting his bath in the picture at the top of the page.

The Dick, Jane, and Spot primers have gone to that book shelf in the sky. I have, in some ways, a tender feeling toward them, so I think it's for the best. Their modern incarnation would be too painful to look at. Dick and Jane would have their names changed to Jason and Jennifer. Faithful Spot would be transformed into an Afghan hound, and the syllables at the bottom of the page would reveal that the children were watching MTV.

In third grade my class paid its first visit to the school library as prospective book borrowers. It was on this occasion that we learned about the fascinating Dewey decimal system. None of us really understood this principle of cataloging books, but we were inclined to favor it. Any system named Dewey was all right with us. We looked forward to hearing about the Huey and Louie decimal systems, too.

The book I checked out on my first visit was the biography of Babe Ruth. I started reading it at school and continued reading it at home. I read till dinner and opened the book again after dessert, finally taking it to bed with me. The story of Babe Ruth was an interesting one, but I don't think it was as compelling as that constant reading suggests. There was something else happening: I just simply did not know when to stop or why. Having grown up with television, I was accustomed to watching something until it was finished. I assumed that as long as the book was there I should read it to the end. The idea of setting the book aside uncompleted just didn't occur to me.

This somewhat obsessive approach to reading manifested itself again during the summer after third grade. My neighbor had a collection of every Walt Disney comic book ever published. I took my little wagon to his house and hauled every issue back to my bedroom. For a solid week I did nothing but read about Pluto, Mickey, Donald, and Daisy. It was spooky. By the sixth day they'd become quite real to me and were turning up in my dreams. After I returned the comics, I felt very lonely, as if a group of lively house guests had left suddenly.

As years have passed, my taste in literature has changed. I do, however, still have obsessive reading habits. I pore over every word on the cereal box at breakfast, often more than once. You can ask me anything about Shredded Wheat. I also spend more time in the bathroom than necessary, determined to keep up with my *New Yorker* subscription.

It seems strange now, considering my susceptibility to the power of the printed word, that I'd been reading for more than twenty years before I thought about writing. I had, by that time, staked out visual art as my form of self-expression. But my visual art was and is very narrative. I feel fortunate that I've become involved with books as another opportunity for artistic expression.

Over the years that have passed since my first book was published, a question I've been asked often is, "Where do your ideas come from?" I've given a variety of answers to this question, such as: "I steal them from the neighborhood kids," "I send away for them by mail order," and "They are beamed to me from outer space."

It's not really my intention to be rude or smart-alecky. The fact is, I don't know where my ideas come from. Each story I've written starts out as a vague idea that seems to be going nowhere, then suddenly materializes as a completed concept. It almost seems like a discovery, as if the story was always there. The few elements I start out with are actually clues. If I figure out what they mean, I can discover the story that's waiting.

When I began thinking about what became *The Polar Express,* I had a single image in mind: a young boy sees a train standing still in front of his house one night. The boy and I took a few different trips on that train, but we did not, in a figurative sense, go anywhere. Then I headed north, and I got the feeling that this time I'd picked the right direction, because the train kept rolling all the way to the North Pole. At that point the story seemed literally to present itself. Who lives at the North Pole? Santa. When would the perfect time for a visit be? Christmas Eve. What happens on Christmas Eve at the North Pole? Undoubtedly a ceremony of some kind, a ceremony requiring a child, delivered by a train that would have to be named the Polar Express.

These stray elements are, of course, merely events. A good story uses the description of events to reveal some kind of moral or psychological premise. I am not aware, as I develop a story, what the premise is. When I started *The Polar Express,* I thought I was writing about a train trip, but the story was actually about faith and the desire to believe in something.

It's an intriguing process. I know if I'd set out with the goal of writing about that, I'd still be holding a pencil over a blank sheet of paper.

Fortunately, or perhaps I should say necessarily, that premise is consistent with my own feelings, especially when it comes to accepting fantastic propositions like Santa Claus. Santa is our culture's only mythic figure truly believed in by a large percentage of the population. It's a fact that most of the true believers are under eight years old, and that's a pity. The rationality we all embrace as adults makes believing in the fantastic difficult, if not impossible. Lucky are the children who *know* there is a jolly fat man in a red suit who pilots a flying sleigh. We should envy them. And we should envy the people who are so certain Martians will land in their back yard that they keep a loaded Polaroid camera by the back door. The inclination to believe in the fantastic may strike some as a failure in logic, or gullibility, but it's really a gift. A world that might have Bigfoot and the Loch Ness monster is clearly superior to one that definitely does not.

I don't mean to give the impression that my own sense of what is possible is not shaped by rational, analytical thought. As much as I'd like to meet the tooth fairy on an evening walk, I don't really believe it can happen.

When I was seven or eight, on the night before Easter, my mother accidentally dropped a basket of candy outside my bedroom door. I understood what the sound was and what it meant. I heard my mother, in a loud whisper, trying unsuccessfully to keep the cats from batting jelly beans across the wooden floor. It might have been the case that the Easter Bunny had already become an iffy proposition for me. In any event this was just the moment the maturing skeptic in me was waiting for. I gained the truth, but I paid a heavy price for it. The Easter Bunny died that night.

The application of logical or analytical thought may be the enemy of belief in the fantastic, but it is not, for me, a liability in its illustration. When I conceived of the North Pole in *The Polar Express,* it was logic that insisted it be a vast collection of factories. I don't see this as a whim of mine or even as an act of imagination. How could it look any other way, given the volume of toys produced there every year?

I do not find that illustrating a story has the same quality of discovery as writing it. As I consider a story, I see it quite clearly. Illustrating is simply a

Illustration by Chris Van Allsburg from The Polar Express *(1985). Houghton Mifflin Company, 1985. Copyright © 1985 by Chris Van Allsburg. All rights reserved. Reprinted by permission of Houghton Mifflin Company.*

matter of drawing something I've already experienced in my mind's eye. Because I see the story unfold as if it were on film, the challenge is deciding precisely which moment should be illustrated and from which point of view.

There are disadvantages to seeing the images so clearly. The actual execution can seem redundant. And the finished work is always disappointing because my imagination exceeds the limits of my skills.

A fantasy of mine is to be tempted by the devil with a miraculous machine, a machine that could be hooked up to my brain and instantly produce finished art from the images in my mind. I'm sure it's the devil who'd have such a device, because it would devour the artistic soul, or half of it anyway. Conceiving of something is only part of the creative process. Giving life to the conception is the other half. The struggle to master a medium, whether it's words,

notes, paint, or marble, is the heroic part of making art. Still, if any of you run into the devil and he's got this machine, give him my name. I would, at least, like to get a demonstration.

An award does not change the quality of a book. I'm acutely aware of the deficiencies in all of my work. I sometimes think I'd like to do over everything I've ever done and get it right. But I know that a few years later I'd want to do everything over a third time.

This award carries with it a kind of wisdom for someone like me. It suggests that the success of art is not dependent on its nearness to perfection but its power to communicate. Things can be right without being perfect.

Though this is the second Caldecott Medal I've received, believe me, it is no less meaningful than the first. Being awarded the Caldecott is an experience to which one cannot become jaded. I am certain of this and stand ready to endure any efforts to prove otherwise.

I would like to thank these people at Houghton Mifflin for their support, encouragement, and, occasionally, commiseration: my editor, Walter Lorraine; Peggy Hogan; Sue Sherman; and Donna Baxter.

I would also like to take this opportunity to thank the people here tonight who have committed themselves to getting children and books together. I know that if it weren't for your efforts my readers would be not only small in size but in number, too.

And finally I'd like to thank Mae Benne and the other members of the Caldecott Committee for this great honor. I accept it as both praise and encouragement.

Good night!

Chris Van Allsburg and Heather Vogel Frederick (interview date 14 October 2002)

SOURCE: Van Allsburg, Chris, and Heather Vogel Frederick. "Chris Van Allsburg." *Publishers Weekly* 249, no. 41 (14 October 2002): 27-8.

[*In the following interview, Van Allsburg discusses the publication of* Zathura: A Space Adventure, *how the book functions as an indirect sequel to* Jumanji, *and his plans for future projects.*]

It's been 20 years since Peter and Judy opened a mysterious board game named Jumanji that unleashed chaos inside the covers of the eponymous picture book and a virtual juggernaut of success for the author and illustrator. In addition to being awarded his first Caldecott Medal (he received a second in 1986 for **The Polar Express**), Chris Van Allsburg also snagged a movie deal and the kind of exposure that most authors and illustrators dream of.

This fall, Van Allsburg is making a return trip to the visual landscape he explored in **Jumanji** with a sequel entitled **Zathura** (Houghton Mifflin, Oct.). "Each of the 20 years that has passed since **Jumanji** has brought a lot of mail from kids asking me what happened to Walter and Danny Budwing," says Van Allsburg. "I thought it might be interesting to figure out the answer."

The characters he's referring to are introduced on the last page, running off with the board game and clearly headed for trouble. Deciding what befalls them caused Van Allsburg "a little trepidation," he says. "Sequels often cross territory that's already been explored in the first effort, and sometimes they're dismissed as not particularly creative undertakings. I wondered if it would be possible to tell a story that actually worked on its own."

And so he decided to have the Budwing boys discover another game wedged in the bottom of the Jumanji box, a game that whisks them off to outer space and a wholly different set of adventures.

"The theme here is slightly different as well," Van Allsburg notes. "The boys have a relationship which I think is a little more pronounced than anything we knew about the siblings in **Jumanji.**"

Not surprising, given that the author-illustrator has become a father himself in the intervening years (he has two daughters) and is now fully versed in sibling relationships. "I didn't have to fish around very much for the patterns of behavior for an 11- and a seven-year-old," he admits with a laugh.

In fact, his daughters served "not only as the behavioral but also the figurative models for the book," he says, explaining that he had to "slick their hair back so I could see their ears. They'd get a little edgy—the last picture I drew was one where they're wrestling, and they were really getting into it."

Fatherhood also brought another significant change in Van Allsburg's life: he gave up teaching at Rhode Island School of Design to be at home with his girls. "I found that the time that I spent away from the drawing board in the classroom, time that brought me a fair amount of pleasure and gratification, was now going to be spent with other young people."

Like **Jumanji, Zathura** is also illustrated in black and white, a medium Van Allsburg notes "is becoming stranger and stranger—it's almost vanished from newspapers, and you never see it in broadcast anymore." At the same time, it has become more intriguing to him, and he points to the Coen brothers' recent movie *The Man Who Wasn't There* as an inspiration. "The quality of light and mood and atmosphere in the film was just so compelling to me; it reconfirmed my conviction that black and white really can do it all," he says. "Plus, it reproduces so much better than color."

Creating **Zathura** took Van Allsburg about six or seven months, he estimates, fairly average for one of his books. "I work on a story for two or three weeks, and once I have a pretty good rough draft I start doing sketches. I do a lot of sketches, because for those 15 images I choose to put in a book, in telling that story in my mind there are 10,000 images. The process of trying to pick the ones that will add as much story value as possible to each page is a critical one."

As for what else he has up his sleeve, Van Allsburg says he's juggling several projects, including something that's been in development as a film for a long time. *Zathura,* meanwhile, has been optioned by Sony/Columbia, which also produced *Jumanji.* Whether or not he will be involved in the making of the movie remains to be seen at this point, he says. "With *Jumanji* I was pretty thickly involved, and I assume that, because I know the producers and they might value the contributions I could make, I might be involved in the development of *Zathura.*"

Still, he hastens to add, "an optioned project is just the first baby step. There's a long stairway to climb."

Chris Van Allsburg and Steven Heller (interview date November-December 2004)

SOURCE: Van Allsburg, Chris, and Steven Heller. "Chris Van Allsburg, Creator, *The Polar Express.*" *Print* 58, no. 6 (November-December 2004): 50, 52, 334.

[*In the following interview, Van Allsburg discusses film adaptations of his picture books and the development of* The Polar Express *as a "performance capture" animated film.*]

This winter, director Robert Zemeckis and actor Tom Hanks, collaborators on *Forrest Gump* and *Cast Away,* premiere an entirely different kind of movie. Their film adaptation of the Chris Van Allsburg children's adventure book *The Polar Express* is a cinematic and technological breakthrough. For this curious tale, about a doubtful young boy who takes an extraordinary train ride to the North Pole and finds along the way that a sense of wonder is eternal for "those who believe," the filmmakers bring Van Allsburg's moodily surreal tableau to virtual life through a digital process called "performance capture," a unique combination of live action and animation that allows the actors to play any age demanded by the script. The technology further allows them to appear within an environment that replicates the tone and texture of the original pastel pictures in the book.

This is not the first time one of 55-year-old Van Allsburg's books has been recast on celluloid. *Jumanji* (1995), directed by Joe Johnston, starring Robin Williams and a young Kirsten Dunst, was an action ad-

venture about children who are quite literally consumed by a jungle-themed board game wherein wild animals come to life. Williams, the "hunter," was lost in the game ages before, and this is his chance to escape. Anyone who remembers the book knows that the live action could not reproduce the sublimely eerie black-and-white pencil drawings. But with *The Polar Express,* the texture of the film is true to the artist's vision.

Van Allsburg's books (including his first Caldecott winner, *The Garden of Abdul Gasazi,* as well as *The Wreck of the Zephyr, The Widow's Broom, Two Bad Ants, Ben's Dream,* and others) are perfect storyboards for films. Each tale builds in dramatic force, while expressing pathos for character and situation. It is not surprising that Zemeckis and Hanks have used *The Polar Express* as a quintessential rite-of-passage tale. Christmas-themed books and films are routinely rooted in common stereotypes but, while the basic setting for *The Polar Express* may perpetuate the myth, the idea of self-discovery sets this narrative apart from most other holiday fare.

In this interview, the soft-spoken Van Allsburg discusses the compromises that came from allowing other artists to transform his book—a perfectly honed narrative entity—into their medium and sensibility, and the challenges and successes that emerged.

* * *

[*Heller*]: **The Polar Express** *is your second feature film. When you created this and* **Jumanji,** *did you see them in your mind's eye as movies?*

[Van Allsburg]: Not in the sense that, when making them, I have ambitions or goals to turn them into films. Nor do I strive to produce stories that I think will lend themselves to reinterpretation as films. I do, however, see the stories I create play out in my mind's eye a bit like a film. When I'm writing a story, the words on the page are actually a description of the series of images that I imagine.

Philip Roth has long objected to having his novels adapted to film since they have been distorted in various ways. Did you have similar reservations?

Authors are not obligated to make their work available to filmmakers. Every author knows that the result of a rights sale can be a disappointing film. I had concerns about *Jumanji* and *The Polar Express,* but comforted myself with the notion that, no matter the outcome, the book would stay just as it was: the original representation of my ideas.

This rationale creates a kind of "no lose" proposition: If the film stinks, it will soon be forgotten, leaving the book as the relevant surviving version of the story. On the other hand, if the film replaces the book as the dominant version of the story, it can only do so if the film is extraordinarily successful, as with *The Wizard of Oz.* In a case such as that, the author's version was displaced by the film. However, having contributed to something that truly succeeds as film entertainment, the author was rewarded in other ways.

How do you feel **Jumanji** *worked as a movie? Did it accomplish what you intended in the original form?*

It did not capture the feeling I strove to create in the book. The book's story and pictures were inspired by the idea of cognitive dissonance: the security of home juxtaposed with the peril of jungle adventure. The atmosphere and style of the drawings emphasize this quality, producing a combination of authenticity and fantasy. It becomes dreamlike, resembling Surrealist art. There is something about it, aside from the content, that is unaccountably menacing or disturbing. This quality of the book went unnoticed by the filmmakers, who chose to make something that felt like a fairly conventional action film. It wasn't bad, but it was not what I had hoped for.

In your conversations with director Robert Zemeckis—who also wrote the screenplay for the film—what was it that attracted him and the star, Tom Hanks, to **The Polar Express***?*

I'm not sure. I think that, like many adults, they started reading a book they assumed was about their children, then realized it was really about them, too. It can stir pretty powerful memories. I think they were both interested in exploring the specific psychology of the protagonist, which is kind of profound, but presented in a very simple story.

The Polar Express *is live-ish action that approximates your drawing, and yet is not traditional animation. Zemeckis had to invent an entirely new process. What did this entail?*

Initially, it entailed ideas about reproducing such subtle elements as the slightly "dirty" and soft-edged quality of the pastel art of the book. That wasn't really feasible, but the book's pictures were used as a reference to guide the artists as they produced the digital environments for the film. The characters were created through a motion-capture process that produces a digitized performance derived from the actions of human actors. Those digitized performances are then located within the digital environments and the director has, at that point, a virtual reality through which he can move the camera and manipulate the lighting.

As author of **The Polar Express,** *you have certain creative rights. In this case, however, another artist has invested his vision and technology. Was it easy for you to cede your creative ownership to someone else?*

It's not easy if I have contemplated the challenge of expanding the story and feel that I have come up with an effective solution. At that point, my ideas for turning the book into a film must compete with the filmmakers'. Their ideas may be different, leading to a contest an author never wins. I believe, however, that artists produce their best work when unencumbered by the need to accommodate the demands of others. So even if my ideas go unacknowledged, I am willing to concede that letting the project proceed with a single vision controlling the outcome is, theoretically, a sound way to make art.

Still, you make your art, and then, based on your concept, another makes his art on top of what you've started. I know this is a common and time-worn tradition, but don't you feel the least bit compromised by the process?

No. Film is such a complicated medium and so different from a book that I accept that it will have little similarity to what I've done. My hope is modest: that a book of mine might inspire a talented filmmaker to create a good film that utilizes what is best in the book.

Did the actors bring to life the characters as you imagined them?

The Polar Express is not really as much about individual characters as it is about a quest or journey. There is a protagonist who is torn between believing in an idea, which he cherished, and not believing in it because it defies reason. This character's condition is effectively dramatized. In fact, it is essentially the theme of the film.

Do you ever picture an individual actor when you are creating a children's book? Is there an actual human analog to your imaginary characters?

Characterization in picture books is necessarily somewhat abbreviated. There simply isn't room in the text to develop a detailed character study. A great deal needs to be accomplished in the pictures. I sometimes have a face in mind when I draw—or, at least, a type. That might mean I have a specific model I intend to use or a determination to find a model whose face resembles the face I've imagined. As for behavior or personality, all the characters are probably some version of myself.

How involved were you in the overall production, like casting, art direction, etc.?

I had some involvement in the beginning, talking with writers and attempting to establish a tone for the film. The director's commitment to making the film look as much as possible like "the book come to life" left little for me to do in the way of influencing the look of the film.

Through motion-capture technology, Tom Hanks [is able to play] a number of different characters. Accepting this casting meant placing as much faith in the technology as the actor. About the actor, I was confident.

I know for a fact that you are an extremely meticulous illustrator. While you routinely experiment with media and form, you are a perfectionist and, therefore, like having control. With this film, was there ever a time when you wanted to trade places with the filmmaker?

Film is an incredibly potent medium, and the idea of having all its elements at my disposal is appealing. It is also intimidating, considering the costs involved, and looks, in some cases, to be a very high-stakes undertaking. I'm not sure I'd be comfortable under those conditions or making all the decisions and compromises that are a part of the deal.

Your work has long had a surreal, fantastic quality with a hint of mischief to add drama. **The Polar Express** *is full of mystery and a certain level of sadness. What was your impetus for the book?*

At first, it was just a story about a train that could go anywhere. When I decided the destination would be the North Pole and the departure date would be December 24th, the story turned out to be about the feelings nine-year-olds have, clinging on Christmas Eve to an idea that is under heavy assault from their own maturing rationality.

Does the script reflect the more melancholy moments of the book? Or did you sacrifice any of the moodiness of the book for greater uplift?

The film story is probably less melancholy, but not as a result of a determination to purge it of pathos. The excitement of the ride north becomes a more dominant emotional component of the story. The lessons imparted to the child passengers in the film are, perhaps, explicitly uplifting. However, the dark palette of the book seems to be intact, and there is, from what I have seen, a sort of subtextural moodiness.

Would you be open to directing your own film?

I can imagine doing it, because I feel I understand it. But I've never studied filmmaking and I don't think I could utter anything close to "What I'd really like to do is direct" and keep a straight face. But yes, I confess. Telling a story with the comprehensive, powerful tools of cinema is a very seductive idea.

GENERAL COMMENTARY

Peter F. Neumeyer (essay date 1989)

SOURCE: Neumeyer, Peter F. "How Picture Books Mean: The Case of Chris Van Allsburg." *Children's Literature Association Quarterly* 15, no. 1 (1989): 2-8.

[*In the following essay, Neumeyer examines the text, illustrations, and overall design of Van Allsburg's first nine children's picture books in terms of the author's recurring theme of "imagination," commenting that several of "Van Allsburg's books declare that Imagination is 'real,' that the world in the mind, including the child's world of fantasy, is actual, true, even tangible."*]

Chris Van Allsburg is a distinguished sculptor who obtained his degree in that art from the Rhode Island School of Design. Thus it is not surprising that Chris Van Allsburg's first children's book has on its cover extraordinary and magically three-dimensional topiary sculptures in the shape of rabbit, duck, seal, and elephant. The 1979 publication of *The Garden of Abdul Gasazi* marked the debut of a new star among children's book illustrators. Appropriately, the book won recognition as a "Caldecott Honor" book. In the subsequent seven years, Van Allsburg won the Caldecott Medal itself twice, for *Jumanji* in 1981, and for *The Polar Express* in 1987.

The outstanding illustrator, David Macauley, has written an eloquent testimonial for Van Allsburg. But it does not take an expert to recognize Van Allsburg's distinction. The nine illustrated children's books he has published have won almost unqualified acclaim and have fascinated adults as much as they have the children. They clearly stand out against the humdrum ephemera that clutter children's bookstores seasonally, and that disappear almost as quickly as they are published. Van Allsburg's books are art works in the shape of books, art works accompanied by mysterious and thought-provoking stories. To examine them carefully is to give oneself a lesson in how picture books work.

I'd like to look at all nine of Van Allsburg's books ostensibly for children, exploring what these books mean, and how they achieve that "meaning." We shall have to look at them with extreme care—to look at all aspects of the books, for in the case of a very good picture book—and Van Allsburg's certainly fall into that category—every part of the book works harmoniously with every other part to create a singleness of effect, to create a "meaning." The prose, the illustration, and the physical appearance of all nine of his books are related.

Six of them appear to make virtually identical statements; three make statements that are closely connected. Six of Van Allsburg's books declare that Imagination is "real," that the world in the mind, including the child's world of fantasy, is actual, true, even tangible. That may be a difficult concept for a child, but one of the remarkable aspects of Van Allsburg's work is precisely this desire to translate a metaphysical concept into verbal and pictorial shape so that it may be comprehended—at some level—by a child.

In order to clarify the statement of the six very similar books, we shall first isolate the statement each makes in the narrative itself. Secondly, we shall look at the illustrations—the manner in which what happens or what is meant is depicted visually. Thirdly, we shall note the language of each statement. And finally, we shall look at aspects of book design, as those aspects, too, help to communicate the meaning.

THE STORY

In three of the books, children fall asleep, have extraordinary adventures, and return from whatever world they inhabited during their sleep, only to find, on their return, some incontestable and objective proof that the land they were in during their sleep was truly and objectively there.

In **The Garden of Abdul Gasazi** (1979) young Alan Mitz is dogsitting for Miss Hester; he falls asleep on the couch, putting his hat under his shirt for safekeeping. Alan dreams that Fritz, the dog, runs into the garden of the magician, Abdul Gasazi. Alan chases the dog, whom the magician, however, has transformed into a duck. As Alan carries the dog-duck home, his hat flies off his head and is caught and carried off by the dog-duck. When Miss Hester comes home, Alan wakes and tells his story as the dog sits watching. Alan is hatless. Miss Hester assures Alan that Fritz had been sitting in the front yard, waiting for her. Alan, feeling foolish, tells himself he won't be duped again, and he goes home. When he has departed, Miss Hester calls Fritz, who trots up to her and drops at her feet the hat Alan had put under his shirt when he fell asleep. Here is empirical evidence of the "reality" of the world of Alan's dream. There's no conclusion possible except that Fritz must, indeed, have been the "duck" that, in Alan's dream, flew off with his hat.

In **Ben's Dream** (1982) the reader/viewer takes the role of the objective observer who finds the reality of the dream world corroborated by two independent witnesses who cannot be making up a story, since the reader observes the "reality" himself. Ben and Margaret pedal their bikes home to study their Geography textbooks—presumably the section on famous monuments of the world. As Ben sits home alone, studying, the rain begins, and as it rains harder, Ben is lulled asleep. Soon, the rain becomes a large body of water outside the window. As various great monuments—the leaning tower of Pisa, the Great Wall of China, and others—pass by, we are constantly aware that we are seeing them from Ben's perspective, since, in each picture, we see a bit of Ben's house, and in some we see parts of Ben. At the end, we learn that Margaret had seen exactly the same monuments, that they had been floating, half under water, for her, just as they had for Ben.

Margaret says to Ben that he would never guess whom she saw as she floated by. But he *does know*; it was Ben, himself, whom Margaret had seen. Now, how could Ben know that? Simple. He saw her too, just as they were floating by the Sphinx. But obviously, Ben could be fibbing, couldn't he? But he *wasn't fibbing*; not at all! We can prove it to ourselves merely by turning back to the page with the Sphinx, half submerged. There we see Margaret looking out of her house; and there, too, in the foreground, is Ben's arm stretched out, waving to her. In their respective dreams, Ben truly saw Margaret, and Margaret saw Ben. And the objective evidence of the merging reality of the two dreams is logically indisputable. We need not rely on the two children's stories. We can see it for ourselves in the objective world of the story.

In *The Polar Express* (1985) a nameless first person narrator tells a story of "many years ago." On Christmas Eve, when very young, he falls asleep. Outside, he hears bells ringing. He looks out his window and sees a train in the snow. He hops aboard, is taken through snowy woods to the North Pole, where Santa and his elves are at work. Santa gives the boy a little silver sleigh bell—"the first gift of Christmas." The next morning, the boy's sister finds one last present under the tree, a little box containing a silver bell and a card that says "Found this on the seat of my sleigh. Fix that hole in your pocket. Signed 'Mr. C.'" The boy/narrator shakes the bell, and it makes the most beautiful sound he and his sister ever heard. But the parents seem to hear nothing, saying "Oh, that's too bad," and "Yes, it's broken." On the last page, the narrator tells us that although once most of his friends were able to hear the bell, there came a time when his sister no longer was able to hear it. But now, although the narrator is old, "the bell rings for me as it does for all who truly believe."

Again, as in *The Garden* and in *Ben's Dream,* when we return with the narrator from the dream world, back to our daily world, Van Allsburg presents us with objective evidence from that other world.

In *Jumanji* the parents of Jody and Peter go to the opera, leaving the children home with toys with which they soon become bored. The children run outside and find a long, thin box with the label, "Jungle Adventure Game" under a tree. They take the game home, and as the children roll the dice and move their markers along the board's spaces through the game's "jungle," they find themselves trapped in a world of lions, monkeys, tsetse flies, monsoon rains, and other tropical hazards, all, seemingly, in their own house. Judy wins the game, arrives at the magical city, shouts "Jumanji," and the children run out, put the game back under the tree, and fall asleep on the sofa.

Their parents come home, bringing with them their friends, the Budwings. The parents wake the children; the Budwings (whose own children are now home alone, as Judy and Peter were) make polite chitchat with Judy and Peter, and then the adults go about their affairs. The children return to the puzzle they had been doing when their parents left, but then, as they look out the window, they see the Budwings' sons, Walter and Danny, running from the same tree, carrying the same long thin box with the magical world of Jumanji within it. They, too, presumably, will enter the hazardous jungle world.

That Judy and Peter had fallen asleep at the outset is not stated explicitly, but it is strongly suggested because the book's objective narrator, not implicated in the story, tells us that they were asleep when the parents came home. Presumably the Jumanji adventures happened in the world of dream. That the Budwing children are now seen running off with the same box at very least establishes the reality of the boxed game which Judy and Peter had found at book's outset, quite likely in their dream. The adults see nothing of this world, however; it is as closed to them as was the sound of Santa's bell in *The Polar Express.* The humdrum adult prosaicness is rendered not only by what they don't see, but by what they say, as well as what we (through the children's eyes) *see* of them.

The Wreck of the Zephyr (1983) is also a story of the reality, this time not precisely of the world of sleep and dream, but of the world of the unconscious. The primary narrator, whom we have no reason to doubt, travels along the seashore and there, on cliffs high above the sea, finds the wreck of a small sailboat. An old man, a secondary narrator, tells him the strange tale of how, years ago, a small boy had gone sailing. A sudden gust caught the sail, the boom swung about, and the boy was knocked unconscious onto the deck. When he "opened his eyes," he found the boat and himself cast high adrift on the beach. Strange sailboats were floating through the sky. In the evening, the boy sneaks out aboard the Zephyr, and does, indeed, make her rise out of the water. Using the stars for a guide, the boy sails the Zephyr through the clouds and the sky until he reaches his town, where the boat falls down through the trees between the village and the open sea. And there the Zephyr sits today; and that is the boat the primary narrator happened upon in his stroll.

Having told the story of the Zephyr, the old man walks away. Knowing story conventions, we may well assume the old man was the boy, who—he said—"never amounted to much." And we are left with the listener, the narrator, whom we have no reason to doubt, and who found the stranded boat that is visible proof of the truth of the boy's experiences with the flying Zephyr.

Finally, the remaining book whose subject is unequivocally the reality of the imagination, *The Mysteries of Harris Burdick* (1984), is more a game or puzzle book than a sustained and plotted narrative like the five above. Still, its point is the same: the celebration of the imagination. In the preface, the man who signs himself Chris Van Allsburg tells us that he first saw the fourteen drawings that comprise

most of the book in the home of one Peter Wenders. When Wenders used to work for a publisher, "Van Allsburg" tells us, a man calling himself Harris Burdick came to visit Wenders and told him he had written fourteen stories and drawn many pictures for them. He brought just one drawing for each of the fourteen stories with him, he said, but he agreed to bring the stories on the following day. But Burdick was never seen again; to this day, he is a mystery. And all that remains are Burdick's fourteen drawings, with dozens of stories inspired by the drawings, written by Wenders's children and their friends. This book consists of the fourteen eerily evocative drawings, with imaginative captions and gnomic single-sentences that read as though they are from some work of which we should know the name.

The remaining books do not repeat the identical point of these first six, but certainly their import is, in varying degrees, similar.

In 1987, Van Allsburg published an alphabet book. Although it does seem to have a unifying theme—the mangling, distortion or obscuring of the letters of the alphabet—it does not, strictly speaking, have a plot. And yet the title, as rendered on the title page, reads as follows:

> The Alphabet Theatre
>
> Proudly Presents
>
> The *Z* Was
>
> Zapped
>
> Performed by
>
> The Caslon Players
>
> Written and Directed by
>
> Mr. Chris Van Allsburg

Indeed, the letters of the alphabet are presented as actors on stage, each letter "appearing" on a stage with curtains drawn aside and with curtained backdrop. The letters, then, too, as actors on stage, are part of the world of illusion.

The two books I would not list as explicit statements of the reality of the imagination are **The Stranger** (1986) and **Two Bad Ants** (1988). Clearly, each is *imaginative.* In the first, the "stranger" is Winter personified, who is accidentally hit by a farmer's truck, who comes to stay with the farm family while he recuperates, and who gives intimations that his very breath is chilling, and, at the end, mysteriously departs.

The second, **Two Bad Ants,** recounts the adventures of two ants who foray with their brethren on a hunt for sugar, are left behind in the house of human beings, undergo terrors in the strange world of giants, and, at the end, make it safely back to the tribe.

The point of this recapitulation of plots is to show that six of the nine books tells a story in which, at the end, there is objective evidence that creations of the imagination are real. In the three remaining, there is, at very least, a playful manipulation of the objective world.

In most of the stories, we rely on the impartial narrator, a narrator whom we assume to be reliable. **Ben's Dream** is the most convincing in making the case since we need not rely merely on what the narrator tells us, but we can actually "see" the proof on the page on which Ben and Margaret wave to each other in their dreams. If we can actually see it, then it really *must* be true.

The Illustrations

The message of the majority of these books is that creations of imagination, especially in the fantasy of children, are objectively real. The stories recounted above say as much openly. But my point is to see how *picture books work,* and to note how the message is conveyed not merely in the bare story line, but by the illustrations too, as well as by the prose style, and even by the appearance or layout of the book.

The illusionistic nature of **The Garden of Abdul Gasazi** is announced on the dust jacket which does not present "pictures," essentially one-dimensional representations of "reality," but rather attempts to surpass the normal flatness of a painting or a drawing. As mentioned at the outset, the dust jacket shows *sculptures*—topiary "carvings" representing animals,

presumably in the magician's garden. The artist has employed a sort of *trompe l'oeil* illusionism not unknown to artists of the Renaissance, who would paint madonnas and Christ child in, say, a window frame out of which, or over which, would hang drapery or grapes apparently so that one is tempted to touch them.

The illusory three-dimensionality is achieved by Van Allsburg, trained as a sculptor, by techniques of *chiaroscuro,* dramatic lighting and shading, as well as by the shadows cast by the topiary plantings and by most other objects later in the book. Additionally, Van Allsburg attains the sense of three-dimensionality by frequently changing the viewer's point of view of perspective, thus almost giving the sense that the beholder is walking *around* the pictured objects. The consequence is that the beholder obtains a sense of roundness, of depth and distance, that gives the entire book a semblance of magic realism—a realism more real than real, which becomes, then, of course, *sur*real.

On the dust jacket of this, Van Allsburg's first book, we should note, too, the dog, a Boston Bull, who, appears in one guise or another (sometimes transformed into a horse with blinkers over its eyes) in subsequent volumes—a sort of Van Allsburg signature, perhaps, comparable to the Noah's ark which Kipling puts (as a rebus for his initials—"R. K.") in odd corners of his illustrations for the *Just So Stories.* On another level, the recurrence of the dog strongly denotes that, among all the volumes in which he appears, there is an underlying unity.

The illustrations, done in black and white with carbon pencil, stress architectural constructions, interiors of houses, sumptuous facades led to by imposing stairways. Significantly, Alan's and Fritz's entrance into the magician's garden is through an archway behind which lies a deep tunnel of trees. This archway seems to stress the sense of depth and perspective in the drawing, a sense strongly suggesting the distance that Alan and the dog travel in their voyage into Alan's dream. In fact, the depth and distance is doubly stressed in this particular illustration in that, outside the archway, there are two parodies of "classic" statues which, however, do not face us, as they normally would in a composed illustration, but which have their backs to us and which seem to be lurching in through the archway, just like Alan himself. In short, it is a deep, long trip that Alan and Fritz take.

In **Ben's Dream,** the actual proof of the reality of the dream world lies not so much in the statement by Margaret and Ben that they saw each other during their dreams, but even more convincingly, in the proof readers can provide for themselves merely by looking at the illustration in which Margaret looks out the window at Ben, and Ben's arm is waving to her, as they float by a huge Sphinx.

In *The Garden of Abdul Gasazi,* the scenes' reality is heightened by chiaroscuro and by an insistent perspective. And this *sur-*or super reality is part of the strategy of persuading us that Alan's dream world is actual. In *Ben's Dream,* we also have Van Allsburg's habitual use of architectural perspective to give the illusion of depth, as well as the heavy shading, suggesting a light source within the picture. Actually, though, the shading is not subtly graduated as in the previous books, but frequently superimposed on much more distinct lines than in *Abdul Gasazi*—a technique that's also the hallmark of the 1988 book *Two Bad Ants.* But here we have an additional element as well.

In *The Garden of Abdul Gasazi,* the angle of vision is frequently as though the viewer were almost lying on the ground, facing the pictured scene head-on, but from slightly below the point of interest. In *Ben's Dream,* on the other hand, once Ben has fallen asleep, the angles from which the famous landmarks are seen change at dizzying pace from page to page. We have lost our stability, our spatial locus, in the illustrations, and they take on a sense of hallucinatory rudderlessness in space. For, indeed, Ben, in his dream, is, of course, in another world which is not bound by our logical laws of space and time.

In addition to the shifting angles of vision, Van Allsburg has unsettled our perception by an extraordinary and discordant inconsistency in the individual black lines which he uses to define space and objects. Conventionally, in the earliest and the last pages of the book, which represent time when the children are awake, not dreaming, the shading or hatching is sustained and consistent, each surface or each shadow being established by more or less parallel lines. But once the children are in the dream world with its shifting perspectives and points of view, tossed about, as it were, on the ocean of their dreams, the instability of the view is rendered frequently by a cacophonous discordance, by a clash of the individual lines which denote even a single object. What this says is that even though the world of dream is a real one, it exists in a manner quite different from our mundane and daily one.

Finally, denoting a sort of thematic unity with the first book, the Boston Bull Terrier who was Fritz in *The Garden of Abdul Gasazi* here appears in a framed picture. The continuity from the first book, the hook into Alan Mitz's world, is marked by the dog, but perhaps because in *Ben's World* the dream world is more clearly demarcated, more clearly announced, the real dog from the first volume is now in a framed picture. He is merely an image of that real dog.

The Polar Express is a book in which every detail shows the planning, the premeditation, and the excellence of execution of the finest contemporary children's picture books. The dust jacket shows the Polar Express, with its piercing headlight signalling the emphasis on mysterious lights throughout the book. And again, there is distortion as the unconventionally wide illustrations give the impression of wide angle, or even of a fish-eye lens, once again suggesting the distortion of things we experience in our dreams. Carefully, the illustrations are designed so that no crucial element will fall within the sewn channel between pages.

Most strikingly, the width of the "wide angle lens" may be perceived on the page on which three wolves are set against the double spread, wide apart, making the facing pages seem almost wider than they already are. And then the pages are made wider yet by the length of the train that spreads across the pages, brought clearly to the viewer's eye because its length is punctuated by the lights luminating the compartments of the cars, and glowing like an elongated ellipsis across the facing pages. Set in contrast to this width are the vertical trees of the northern forest through which the train passes, and through which the wolves roam. The presumably tall trees are vertical, but they are cut off abruptly by the page format, thus again underlining the width, the breadth of the vision. And such breadth stresses, accentuates, "narrates" the broad space through which the train travels.

Again, too, signalling the continuity with the previous books (thus, again, blending "meaning" in this one with "meaning" in the others), there is the Boston Bull—not an actual dog, but a hand puppet on the narrator-boy's bedpost. Again, the dog is imaginary rather than real, and this coincides with the topic of the book—the relationship of imagination to "reality"—though, of course, the very point of the book is that imagination *is also* reality.

Another noteworthy statement is made by the portrayal of Santa, himself. Van Allsburg's Santa has none of the cuteness or the roly poly jollity of the conventional Christmas card Santa. Rather, he and his reindeer, as depicted in one of the central spreads of the book, have a monumental, a sort of statuesque grandeur and high-seriousness. Santa and the reindeer seem to look out of carved eye sockets almost like Greek statues, and Santa's arms and body, as well as the necks of the reindeer, have a columnar and unrealistic, abstracted roundness and bulk. In their statuesque immobility, they seem removed from life, and thus they enter the realm, perhaps, of symbol.

Related to this symbolic magnification is a hushed silence that lends elevation and dignity to the story. The "hush," which also is part of the reality, is achieved by the muted colors, by the understated prose, by the static quality of the frame around pictures and text, and by the lack of motion as represented in the reindeer, as much as by the story itself.

The significant point about the strange nature of reality is again stressed (and repeatedly re-emphasized) in illustrations such as the first glimpse we have of the North Pole. Our first glimpse of the Pole is a picture of mist, of snow, and of more of the mysterious lights which flicker throughout the book, as well as a reflection of all these mists, snows, and lights. What the reflection is *in,* we do not know precisely. No lake is mentioned in the text, but it seems that there may, or must, be some body of water in which the boy/narrator sees his whole vision of the North Pole twice—in the shimmering, dream-like blur, and then in the very reflection of that blur again. What is real?

Jumanji, done with Conte dust and Conte pencil, in shades of white, gray, and black, is pyrotechnical in its shifting perspectives. Seen sometimes from above, sometimes from below, always some aspect of the scene looms enormously, frequently bringing the viewer closer to the scene than is comfortable. The viewer would like to be adjusted or eased into a more comfortable perspective in relation to what's there. But that is impossible.

Even the contrast between the imaginativeness of the children and the limitation of adults is made humorous pictorially. Van Allsburg renders the parents as prosaic adults who come home from the opera, bringing their friends, the Budwings, with them. How is the "prosaicness" of the adults shown? Perhaps by means of a little joke: we actually never see the adults' faces—merely their not very imaginative costumes in a curious illustration that shows the parents from knee level to neck. And what we see, presumably of Judy's and Peter's father, is a fountain pen

clip protruding from the white dress shirt pocket. Now, a man who has his fountain pen clipped, accountant-fashion, into his white shirt when he goes to the opera. . . . !

In *The Wreck of the Zephyr,* precursor and companion volume to *The Polar Express,* the subject is the "reality" of what transpires in an unconscious state. Like *The Polar Express,* the book is in full color, suggesting that when Van Allsburg deals with great vistas, he resorts both to color and to the elongated format. The difference between the use of the elongated format in *The Polar Express* and in *The Wreck of the Zephyr* lies in the fact that essentially the vector, the line of force, in the former remains horizontal—representing the long voyage, perhaps—whereas in the latter, the impetus is distinctly diagonal in those illustrations rendering the sailboat(s), thus pictorially giving the impression of a boat tossed dizzyingly on the waves.

The reality of what is imagined here takes the specific form of the *surviving,* living reality of what had happened in the past. The primary narrator, a bearded man of middle age (Van Allsburg?)—stands with his back to us, looking after the "old man with the pipe." It is significant that no character in the entire book is ever shown face on. Thus, the whole book seems to be retrospective, looking into the past, as indeed, the words tell us it is.

Just as in *The Polar Express,* a certain stillness imbues the dream adventures that are narrated in this tale—an air evoked by the muted colors. Just as *The Polar Express* gives a pervading sense of dignified silence, so in this book, at least in the night-time scenes the enveloping dark, calm blue is punctuated only by pin-point lights of stars, and of window lights in houses. Finally, too, the Bull Terrier appears in the book's third illustration.

The Mysteries of Harris Burdick, a sort of puzzle or activity book demanding reader participation, more resembles *Ben's Dream* than it does the others. This resemblance is suggested further by the square, rather than elongated, format which it shares with *Ben's Dream.*

Unlike the major, elongated books, *The Mysteries* does not so much state that the imagination is real, as it *implies* the fact. As in all the other books, the illustrations—which this time are not merely illustrations accompanying a text, but are *said* to *be* artifacts, illustrations—blur the line between the "real" and the "imaginative." Being a type of secondary imaginative renderings of the imaginative, they, too, become doubly confusing by their illusionistic, highly modelled "plasticity"—their sculptural realism existing within a dream framework. The effect is again achieved through the techniques of chiaroscuro and the shifting perspectives from picture to picture, making us feel as if we were walking around in reality.

Because of its oddness, one might think that *The Stranger* is one of Van Allsburg's primary statements of the reality of imagination. But it is not. It is the unsettling (both visually and verbally) story of Winter personified—a distinct personality, occasionally wide-eyed as on the dust jacket, occasionally wooden, as in the picture in which he is dancing with the family. The illustration has the static quality of one frame of a film. The story is eerily supernatural, but the subject of the book is not the relationship of this supernaturalness to reality. The story maintains, simply, that the events did happen. We can make of them what we will.

The Z Was Zapped does not have a sequential narrative. The illusory nature of reality, or the reality of illusion, is stated thematically by the animated letters of the alphabet, which perform their action on a painted stage, as well as by the playful prefatory theatre bill. The whole, though, is more a *jeux d'esprit* than a linear exposition of the "reality problem." Pictorial rather than narrative, it is more in the vein of Escher or of Anno's alphabet than the comparable, exclusively verbal high jinx of the late Jorge Luis Borges which, being narrative, entail a verb, and thus a proposition.

Two Bad Ants seems entirely different from all the earlier books. Heightened, shocking in effect because it is viewed from the ants' perspective, the primary reality of quotidian is never called into question, and dream reality is not at issue. The premise of the book is simply that of Gulliver's voyage to Lilliput. Given the fact that the protagonists are a centimeter in size, the rest follows logically.

LANGUAGE

Books, even picture books, generally are story. Van Allsburg—illustrator though he may be—has conveyed his story not merely in pictures, but also in prose. And if Van Allsburg's pervasive theme is the Reality of the Imagination, then we should look with care at the manner in which the prose text has underscored this theme. That is not difficult to do, and we may save considerable time by focusing primarily on *The Polar Express. (Jumanji, The Garden of Abdul Gasazi,* and most of the other books expressing the same theme, follow the same method.)

The objectively proved statement of *The Polar Express* is that a dream is as "real" as a bell. To convey such a concept has required difficult, abstract language of more than one philosopher. But such is not the case with our illustrated books. Backtrack for a moment to the illustrations. These are plastic, super-real in perspective and modelling, and make definitive statements by dimensions and breadth. Their three-dimensional "thereness" is undermined only slightly in some by the blurring of "texture."

And now consider merely the words accompanying the first vision we and the children have (in *The Polar Express*) of the North Pole. Van Allsburg sets the words in a narrow column, enclosed in hard, no-nonsense black lines that seem doubly to emphasize the message, "there's nothing blurry about childhood imagination; it's hard fact." The text declares,

> The mountains turned into hills, the hills to snow covered plains. We crossed a barren desert of ice—the Great Polar Ice Cap. Lights appeared in the distance. They looked like the lights of a strange ocean liner sailing on a frozen sea. "There," said the conductor, "is the North Pole."

What is startling is the very normality, the mundane simplicity of this writing. Every sentence is simple and declarative. With the exception of slight inversion in the last sentence, they all follow the most basic, straightforward sentence pattern—subject, predicate. There is nothing fancy, elaborate, artful—except the effect achieved by the seeming lack of "artfulness." The prose, we might say, is eminently prosaic (as opposed to poetical). And this prosaic writing is worth noting because, like the bass accompaniment to a melody, it keeps being the "ground," the linguistic background against which the miraculous picture story is set. Quite matter-of-factly, our author tells us in this remarkable picture book: children live/dream their very real miracles. Many adults lose that ability. The "I" of the story—obviously an artist, as this book proves—still lives/dreams his childhood miracles. In other words, that miracles and the dreams of children occupy a real time/space is triply emphasized: by illustration, by the obvious clarity and common sense of the prose text, and by the layout, to be discussed below.

What we have seen in the prose of *The Polar Express* is true for all Van Allsburg's books. Instead of saying that Van Allsburg is an illustrator rather than a writer, it is more accurate to say that in the combination of strikingly stylized illustration with clear, serviceable prose that does not call attention to itself,

Van Allsburg gives unique expression to the ordinariness of the extraordinary—for those who have an open eye and the skill to perceive.

The argument that such a prose style is a conscious achievement, rather than a lack of art, lies in the fact that it is a style Van Allsburg progressed to, rather than one he began with. Just as his first book, *The Garden of Abdul Gasazi,* is marginally more baroque—i.e. its pages of text are surrounded by a foliated frieze margin—so the early prose itself is marginally more discursive than the later, containing more adjectival superlatives, as well as more stage business in the form of dialogue.

Moreover, though certainly Van Allsburg's range of prose style is not demonstrably extensive, we do, also, see what may have been a premeditated distinction in *The Mysteries of Harris Burdick,* the book that stands most apart from the others. In that book, although in most instances Van Allsburg maintains his matter of fact style, he does, on occasion, seem to venture a sort of mock Victorian melodrama:

> He had warned her about the book.
>
> Now it was too late.

or

> His heart was pounding.
>
> He was sure he had seen the doorknob turn.

The above deviations from the totally objective are slight variations from Van Allsburg's norm, and even in this book, in which the task of the illustrations is precisely to picture the bizarre, the very extraordinariness of this bizarre quality is underscored by the undramatic style. Thus the straightforward caption, "She lowered the knife and it grew even brighter" accompanies the startling illustration of a frightened, wide-eyed woman about to cut into a pumpkin that glows like a bright lantern. The woman and all surrounding objects are thrown into dramatic and startling relief.

And even though in *Jumanji,* we might find that the text is marginally more elaborate than in *The Polar Express,* by and large, our generalization remains: the repeated theme of Chris Van Allsburg is the reality of the world of the imagination. He makes his point by treating the amazing as though it were absolutely normal, resorting neither to metaphor, to hyperbole, or to other elevating devices of language.

DESIGN OF THE BOOKS

These nine books are all well produced. That is important because it says that the artist's statement is treated with the significance it deserves. It also invites us to attempt to discover the manner in which the thoughtful book production is designed to support or to demonstrate the theme. We will look at several details of this design or production in order to see how it works.

1. Trim size, covers, and front matter: Speaking somewhat loosely, Van Allsburg's books come in three trim sizes: *Ben's Dream* and *The Mysteries of Harris Burdick*—not precisely the same size, but tending to the square; *The Z Was Zapped* and *Two Bad Ants,* not precisely the same size, but distinctly vertical (taller than they are wide); and the remaining five, distinctly horizontal—much wider than they are tall.

Each trim size includes books that clearly state Van Allsburg's thesis both in words and in pictures, so we can draw no conclusion about content from the size of the books. At most, we might say that the two more-or-less square books are both on the order of puzzle books. Playfully and more obviously than the larger books, they set out the problem or visual puzzle that is to be solved.

The five horizontally elongated books, which are, in my view, the most important ones, have handsome cloth covers. *The Polar Express, The Stranger,* and *The Wreck of the Zephyr* seem almost a series, although there are slight variations. The cloth covers are embossed with gold or with silver lettering or illustration. The endpapers are heavy, textured, and strikingly coordinated or contrasted to the cover cloth, as well as to each other. Then, in contrast to many mindlessly assembled children's books, the Union Catalogue front matter is not squeezed onto the title page. There is ample white space, as well as broad title pages with the text set in clean and attractive type. Entering the books, one has the feeling of entering an attractive and uncluttered house through a spacious hallway in which one may prepare for what is to come.

2. Other matter in support of the theme: Van Allsburg says not only that the creations of Imagination are Reality, but he sets himself the writerly-aesthetic task of demonstrating that the two are not demarcated from each other. The space inside and outside the book: now, there could possibly be two different "realities" and "imaginative areas"—one within the context and universe of the storybook itself; the other outside the book, between the reader and the storybook. Both these possible lines of demarcation are dealt with by Van Allsburg.

First, Van Allsburg, like many artists of the illustrated book, but perhaps more purposefully, denies the line demarcating the world of the reader from that of "mere" book by the simple device of omitting page numbers. The reader inhabits the same psychological space as the pictorial narrative.

The second way in which the relationship of the world within the book and the world without may be demarcated is by margins—both white space around pictures and text, as well as by lines around either.

Two Bad Ants may be the most conventional third person narrative with omniscient narrator of any of Van Allsburg's books. The format declares as much, each illustration taking up the major portion of the page. The text appears in the same place below each picture and keeps the same margin. Additionally, this is the only book which has page numbers. In other words, this book says "I'm a fiction; you, dear reader, are outside—listen to the story teller; he knows all."

The Stranger, though certainly much more mysterious than *Two Bad Ants,* has illustrations on right hand pages, each the same size; each with identical and unbroken border. The text is on the facing left-hand page, surrounded by a double line. The double line puts the text in a frame—apart from the illustrations, apart from the reader. There is no missing the fact that one is reading a book "outside one's self"—and again, there are no page numbers fly-specking the page.

The Z Was Zapped is somewhat more intricate. The letters, as said before, appear on stage as characters in a drama, as announced on the title page. The proscenium juts, and each letter has a backdrop and is framed by a curtain. Beyond that, there is white margin. But not always! In some cases, as in the letters "L," "M," and "P," a *shadow* from the three-dimensional-appearing letter falls onto the white margin which is officially beyond the bounds of the illustration. The fine line between the world of the book and the world of the reader has been violated, and the two worlds meld into each other.

The Polar Express may be the most subtle blending of form and meaning of any of Van Allsburg's books. We have already spoken of the emphasis given the long journey by the horizontally elongated format of the book, as well as by the cutting off of top and bottom of trees and all tall items that are vertical. The illustrations begin close to either the left or the right hand margins and extend past the channel and well into the facing page. Only a two-and-a-half inch col-

umn of white is left down the side of the page for the text. The text, straightforward and matter-of-fact, runs part way down the narrow column. Although the illustration is framed in a black line that directly touches it, that black line is virtually invisible where it abuts the white column, and another (seemingly the same) black line frames the text *within the same margin as the picture.*

Enclosing text and illustration within the same margin erases the line distinguishing the world of the reader from the world of the writer, as well as the world of the sleeping child in the story from that of the waking child. Finally, too, the world of the narrator-adult ostensibly now telling the story (and believing in the imagination) is distinguished from the world of the child in which that same adult existed back then, when he lived and dreamed in the imagination.

General disorientation of the reader: Much has been said already about the manner in which the reader is disoriented by Van Allsburg's illusionistic devices of simulated three-dimensionality and his abrupt changes in perspective. At this point, let me add merely that such distortions and swooping perspectives may actually render up this artist's psychological truth. They may not be merely artistic devices. Van Allsburg, I have been told recently, will not fly in airplanes and prefers not to go above the second floor when he is on tour. If indeed Van Allsburg suffers vertigo, how suitable and psychologically economical to transform what might be a debility into a striking artistic signature!

Jumanji and *The Garden of Abdul Gasazi* are black and white; *The Polar Express* and *The Wreck of the Zephyr* are colored. Each makes the case for the reality of the imagination. Only in the case of the most recent book—the realistic, omniscient, conventional third person narrative of *Two Bad Ants*—is a measure of startling *unfamiliarity* achieved by the use of odd combinations of colors which we would not ordinarily associate with each other. That, in conjunction with the highly exaggerated, eccentric linearity, may well be a device to disassociate us and help us to see the world through the barely imaginable vision of an ant—a device used to dislocate us and to heighten the effect of the simple magnification of all objects, a magnification that, of course, is fully reasonable from the ant's point of view (literally).

SUMMARY

My objective has been to attempt to understand how illustrated books mean. My test sample has been the nine books Chris Van Allsburg has produced in the last decade. All of Van Allsburg's books deal with illusion, but six of them seem to say that the waking world is as real as that of dream.

The artist-author, together with the book designer, can state his message clearly, simply, yet unobtrusively, by the felicitous exercise of his craft. By the way of that craft, perhaps a complicated metaphysical theory is made accessible to children, not discursively, but for immediate apprehension. Chris Van Allsburg, has done this through plot, illustrative devices, prose narrative, and book design.

How, then, does a picture book mean? It means by way of the many unique opportunities it affords a skilled author-artist such as Chris Van Allsburg. It means in a manner of which the viewer/reader is not necessarily aware—so it may mean subliminally, or even subversively. Finally, as do Van Allsburg's books, it may mean greatly—may make significant and complex statements about reality. And, all complexity notwithstanding, because of the unique opportunity its combination of the arts affords, the illustrated picture book may—non-discursively—bring extraordinarily complex or subtle understanding to even very young children.

Note

I owe a great debt to Eleanor Cameron, who went over a version of my manuscript generously, patiently, and with a clear critical eye. Lapses that may remain likely are symptoms of occasional foolish stubbornness on my part.

Works Cited

Anno, Mitsumasa. *Anno's Alphabet.* New York: Thomas Y. Crowell Co., 1975.

Kipling, Rudyard. *Just So Stories.* New York: New American Library, 1974.

Van Allsburg, Chris. *Ben's Dream.* Boston: Houghton Mifflin, 1982.

———. *The Garden of Abdul Gasazi.* Boston: Houghton Mifflin, 1979.

———. *Jumanji.* Boston: Houghton Mifflin, 1980.

———. *The Mysteries of Harris Burdick.* Boston: Houghton Mifflin, 1984.

———. *The Polar Express.* Boston: Houghton Mifflin, 1985.

———. *The Stranger.* Boston: Houghton Mifflin, 1986.

———. *Two Bad Ants.* Boston: Houghton Mifflin, 1988.

———. *The Wreck of the Zephyr.* Boston: Houghton Mifflin, 1983.

———. *The Z Was Zapped.* Boston: Houghton Mifflin, 1987.

Joseph Stanton (essay date 1996)

SOURCE: Stanton, Joseph. "The Dreaming Picture Books of Chris Van Allsburg." *Children's Literature* 24 (1996): 161-79.

[*In the following essay, Stanton argues that Van Allsburg's picture books combine the high-art aesthetics of surrealism with the popular culture aesthetics of the "strangely enough" tale. Stanton states that, "[b]ecause Van Allsburg's surrealism is largely manifested in his images and the strangely-enough fantasy is primarily evident in his narratives, these two aspects of his work are largely complementary and do not conflict."*]

The picture shows us a darkly lovely rendering of a Venetian canal with two tight rows of buildings facing each other across a narrow waterway. A small arched footbridge delicately links the two sides. But in the background towers a gigantic ocean liner crashing its way into the far end of the canal. On a facing page is the title of the image, "Missing in Venice," and a caption: "Even with her mighty engines in reverse, the ocean liner was pulled further and further into the canal." Here indeed is a mystery—and a mystery that remains unsolved, because the single picture with its title and caption are all we have. Chris Van Allsburg's collection ***The Mysteries of Harris Burdick*** is, in fact, a collection of fourteen unsolvable, but intriguingly captioned, mystery pictures. According to the tongue-in-cheek introduction, these images, along with their titles and captions, were left by a man supposedly named Harris Burdick with a children's book editor supposedly named Peter Wenders. Harris Burdick and the manuscripts for which each of the images is just a sample were, of course, never seen again, leaving us with fourteen inscrutable fragments.

In interviews Van Allsburg has resisted attempts to pin down the origins and purposes of his picture-story ideas. He has indicated that he, too, finds his books mysterious and cannot offer simple explanations as to where and how they originate.

A question I've been asked often is, "Where do your ideas come from?" I've given a variety of answers to this question, such as: "I steal them from the neighborhood kids," "I send away for them by mail order," and "They are beamed to me from outer space." It's not really my intention to be rude or smart-alecky. The fact is, I don't know where my ideas come from. Each story I've written starts out as a vague idea that seems to be going nowhere, then suddenly materializes as a completed concept. It almost seems like a discovery, as if the story was always there. The few elements I start out with are actually clues. If I figure out what they mean, I can discover the story that's waiting.

(Ruello 169-70)

In this essay I do not promise to offer definitive solutions to the Harris Burdick mysteries or to any of the other bizarre fancies invented by the mind and art of Chris Van Allsburg. I shall, however, propose a theory concerning the traditions that lie behind his remarkable originality. Van Allsburg's work involves, it seems to me, the yoking together of two kinds of traditions that are almost never discussed together—a popular-culture tradition and an avant-garde, high-modernist tradition.[1] The popular culture tradition I have in mind will be referred to as the *strangely-enough tale*. The high-art, experimental tradition is, of course, *surrealism*. It too often happens that the popular arts are completely boxed off from the high arts—more often as a result of academic specialization than of overt snobbery—but some of the greatest innovations in the arts come from the surprising mixing of the contents of various boxes.

Furthermore, because surrealism is a high art with a proclivity for the low, it is of particular importance to understand the ways surrealism can and does connect with popular culture. Also, one should appreciate that, despite the "pastness" of surrealism as a movement of the early to mid-twentieth century, the transaction between surrealism and popular culture continues and flows in both directions: the surrealistically inclined have always appropriated images from popular culture, and popular culture in such forms as magazine advertisements, department-store display windows, and rock videos have often borrowed surrealist procedures and appropriated well-known images from classic surrealist works. As we turn our attention to the children's picture-book genre, we should also bear in mind that, although surrealism is not ordinarily thought of as being aimed at an audience of children, much was made in Breton's manifestos, and in other primary surrealist documents, of the value of a "childlike" outlook. It is not, therefore, surprising that Van Allsburg, a university-trained fine-arts practitioner working in the popular children's

picture-book form should fuse surrealist and pop-culture motifs. What is remarkable, of course, is the wonderfulness of his results. If we can gain some sense of the cultural sources that underlie his work, we can better appreciate his success, even as we allow his mysteries to remain more or less unsolved.

I begin with a discussion of the several books in which the surrealistic element in Van Allsburg's work can be most clearly seen. I then discuss books that incorporate strangely-enough tales, with attention to how surrealistic and strangely-enough elements coexist in several of Van Allsburg's most distinctive books.

The three books that I discuss as primary examples of the surrealistic tendencies in Van Allsburg's work are *The Mysteries of Harris Burdick, Ben's Dream,* and *The Z Was Zapped.* Because the term *surrealism* has been applied in so many ways, I must make clear that the surrealism I have in mind is not primarily the surrealism of André Breton and his closest associates. I am not thinking of automatic writing, found objects, random assortments, and frottages. The surrealism that embodies the irrational or unrational by relying upon the accidental would seem to have little to do with the meticulously designed and arranged works of Van Allsburg. The surrealism I refer to here is the secondary surrealism that derived sustenance, though not methodology, from the liberations effected by Breton and company. I have in mind Giorgio De Chirico,[2] Yves Tanguy, Salvador Dali, Max Ernst and, most of all, René Magritte. It is, of course, terminologically problematic that these artists did not always fly the surrealist banner. What the works of these artists, as well as the works of Van Allsburg, have in common is that they contain "highly detailed likenesses of objects, straight or distorted, or three-dimensional abstractions, in a fantastic and unexpected juxtaposition, or in a setting of a hallucinatory kind" (Murray and Murray 402). This kind of surrealism constructs its dream images with a highly self-conscious sense of form and style. The content of the images may arise from the tapping of the subconscious, but the rendering of the work of art is realized with conscious finesse. Van Allsburg's surrealism is quite deliberate, as he himself has acknowledged: "If all artists were forced to wear a badge, I'd probably wear the badge of surrealism. I don't mean something as extreme as Salvador Dali's melting clocks, but a gentle surrealism with certain unsettling provocative elements" (Ruello 169).

Passionate attention to selected likenesses and the employment of unexpected juxtapositions are essential to my three examples of Van Allsburg's surrealism. Perhaps the readiest way to recognize his affiliation with a certain kind of surrealism would be to compare the humorous stage-set images of *The Z Was Zapped* to certain stage-set images of René Magritte. Throughout his career Magritte employed the stage curtain and the shallow space of a stage as a compositional devise that gave a theatrical air to his images. The advantages of this performance-evoking strategy include the compositional attractiveness of this mode of display, the basic wittiness of making a static image into a dramatic action, and the effectiveness of this style of presentation as a means of heightening audience attention. Magritte works such as "Homage to Shakespeare" and "Wasted Effort" are particularly amusing in their interplay of landscape and stage-set elements. The metamorphosis of the stage-curtain shape into the fragment of sky that we see in both of these works is typical of the transformative play Magritte develops in much of his work. Things often turn into sky or stone in Magritte's pictures. Or shoes become feet or bottles become carrots. A complete catalog of Magritte's warpings of one thing into another would be a very long list indeed. Similar transformations could be noted in the works of many other modern artists (and even in the works of some artists from earlier eras), but the clarity and fastidiousness of Magritte's likenesses make him the surrealistic forerunner most obviously comparable to Van Allsburg.

In *The Z Was Zapped* many of the letters of the alphabet undergo transformations in keeping with an alliterative phrase utilizing the sound of the letter. Thus, we have "The E was slowly Evaporating" as the caption for an onstage *E* that is fading away at the top as it gives off steam. "The G was starting to Grow" shows rootlike appendages bursting out of the edges of a *G*. Similarly, a *J* is shown to be jittery, an *M* is melting, a *V* is vanishing, and a *W* is warped. Other letters are under attack in a variety of ways. The *B* was bitten, the *C* was cut to ribbons, the *F* was flattened by a gigantic foot, the *K* was kidnapped by gloved hands, the *N* was nailed, the *P* was pecked by a nasty-looking bird, the *Q* was quartered by a knife that hangs in mid-air without the support of a hand, the *U* was uprooted, the *Y* was yanked, and, of course, the *Z* was zapped. The natural elements play a role in beating up on the hapless alphabet: lightning zaps the *Z*, an avalanche falls on the *A*, and water soaks the *S*. In addition to the emphasis on absurd transformations of objects, the use of stage settings, and meticulous attention to appearances, Van Allsburg shares with Magritte a knack for witty presenta-tion of body parts (hands and feet in particular) separated from the rest of the body. (The illustrations for *F* and *K* are of interest in this regard.) It is even possible that Van Allsburg, perhaps unconsciously, derived the idea for this book directly from a work by Magritte. Some of the letters that Magritte did as chapter headings for an edition of Lautreamont's *Les chants de Maldoror* are interestingly similar to Van Allsburg's letters. Particularly pertinent is Magritte's drawing of an *R* with an eagle's clawed foot reaching out on one side and a human hand on the other (Hubert 194-205).

The violence of Van Allsburg's alphabet no doubt comes as a surprise to many readers. The brutal way that many of the letters are destroyed or threatened hardly fits with conventional ideas concerning what is appropriate for small children; although superficially Van Allsburg's transformations may seem more ruthless than Magritte's, there is, however, an element of melodrama to Van Allsburg's staged destructions that makes them, ultimately, less unsettling than Magritte's. Although it seems odd that *The Z Was Zapped,* a book ostensibly to be shared with the youngest of children, is in several respects the least gentle of Van Allsburg's exercises in surrealism, it can be seen that Van Allsburg's "unsettling provocative elements" are held under control by our awareness that the artist-writer is having fun with his series of alphabetic horror shows.

Van Allsburg's *The Z Was Zapped* belongs to a genre of whimsical nonsense alphabets perhaps best represented by Walter Crane's *The Absurd ABC,* with its wonderful jumble of motifs from nursery rhymes and fairy tales, but it is the Magritte-like quality of Van Allsburg's ABCs that makes their absurdity distinctive.

Ben's Dream wears the badge of surrealism through the genuinely dreamlike nature of its narrative. Also suggestive of surrealism is its humorous display of famous monuments and buildings. A specific connection to surrealism can be found in the obvious echo of an image from *Une semaine de bonté,* a surrealist montage picture book by Max Ernst.[3] Ernst's image of the Egyptian Sphinx seen through the window of a railroad car is reinvented by Van Allsburg in the image of the Sphinx seen from the front porch of Ben's floating house—in both images the head of the Sphinx is facing exactly the same way. It would not be surprising to hear that Van Allsburg was directly inspired by the example of Ernst's collage novel (Ernst 137). Beyond this specific reference, making famous buildings look ridiculous is entirely in the spirit of the surrealist project. It should be noted, however, that the punchline of **Ben's Dream,** which indicates that both the boy and the girl had dreamed the same dream, is suggestive of the strangely-enough motif. Also, although **Ben's Dream** can be seen to have derived from surrealism, it is too mild-mannered, too gentle in its dreaming to be fully in tune with the disturbing ferocity of the great surrealist masterpieces.

Surrealist qualities of a more unsettling sort are to be found, however, in *The Mysteries of Harris Burdick.* Van Allsburg's startling intrusion of an ocean liner into a canal that I referred to at the beginning of this essay bears a family resemblance to the startling emergence of a train engine from a fireplace in Magritte's *Time Transfixed.* The playful joining of the ordinary to the extraordinary are specialities of both Magritte and Van Allsburg. Van Allsburg gives us an unexceptional suburban street where we discover one of the houses to be blasting off like a rocketship, whereas Magritte gives us a fish washed up on the shore that just happens to have legs where its tail should be. The Magritte resemblance has been suggested by other commentators on Van Allsburg's books. For instance, John Russell, reviewing **The Wreck of the Zephyr,** noted that "some of the images of flight are worthy of Magritte himself."

The literary aspect of the *Harris Burdick* book also has a rough equivalence in Magritte. Magritte made the naming of his paintings into a game separate from the making of his pictures. Much could be said about how this practice helped Magritte put forth the fiction that his pictures were not self-revelatory. Magritte often solicited his literary friends to make up names for his pictures, thereby ensuring a mysterious disjunction between the picture and its label. In one sense Van Allsburg self-consciously cultivates mystery through the puzzling labels he forces us to connect to the *Harris Burdick* pictures, but the stronger effect of the labels is to demystify the pictures, at least to some extent. Each caption implies a particular kind of story. There would no doubt be much more agreement between stories generated from Van Allsburg's captions than there would be between stories generated from Magritte's often-baffling titles.

The fourteen inscrutable fragments that make up **The Mysteries of Harris Burdick** are deft excursions into the fantastic that demonstrate the potential of the picture-book form for combining literary and pictorial means to produce powerful literary-pictorial ends.

Perhaps not everyone would agree with me that *The Mysteries of Harris Burdick* is the best of Van Allsburg's many excellent picture books, but I think it is the best place to look for an understanding of his profoundly whimsical art. Composed as it is of fragments, *Harris Burdick* shows us the artist-writer at play in his workshop.

In this strange workshop, the subgenre that I am calling the strangely-enough tale plays a prominent part. The term *strangely enough* is taken from the title of a popular book of tales published by C. B. Colby in 1959.[4] What made Colby's collection of strange stories exciting for twelve-year-olds of all ages was the attitude he adopted toward the material and expressed in his title. Colby managed to present his brief retellings of startling tales in a manner that suggested they might be true, despite their strangeness. Colby's journalistic plain style of writing was one of the elements that seemed to attest to the truth of the tales. Paradoxically, if Colby had been a better writer, his tales would have seemed more literary and thereby less real.[5] The point is that Colby managed to make many of us want to believe that, strangely enough, something remarkable had *really* happened.

The only claim I am making here for Colby is that his work is typical of the genre and more enduring in its unpretentious appeal than many similar collections that have appeared over the years. *Strangely Enough* is primarily interesting as the most popular and widely distributed repackaging of contemporary oral tradition in the medium of print. Whether he knew it or not, Colby was a recorder of contemporary folk legends, primarily of the kind that Jan Harold Brunvand describes as "urban legends." Most of Colby's material appeared first in a newspaper column that he wrote for a number of years. His solicitation of tales for his column was his primary means of tale collection. The newspaper context has long been an important element in the spread and development of modern folk legends, because the inclusion of a tale in a publication dedicated to the reporting of fact tends to reinforce any assertion, however slight and whimsical, that the tale is possibly true.[6]

I have no idea whether Van Allsburg was directly influenced by Colby's book or by any of the numerous other books and comic books that have presented similar "strange tales," but it is apparent that several of Van Allsburg's books and all of the tales suggested in the fragments included in **The Mysteries of Harris Burdick** make use of the simple but powerful formula found in folk legends. In such tales there is an ordinary context out of which something extraordinary seems to develop. Journalistic versions of such tales tend to be brief and lacking in the histrionics common in oral presentations. Most such tales take no more than a page and a half to recount. The ordinary situation is explicated in a few paragraphs, then the extraordinary aspect is delivered as a kind of punchline. The understated manner of the telling in a newspaper context adds to the plausibility of the tales. Sometimes the situation seems to be falling short of the extraordinary until a chance remark by one of the characters betrays the almost dismissed extraordinariness.

Recognizing the relatedness of Van Allsburg's tales to the journalistic retelling of strangely-enough tales, as exemplified by Colby's *Strangely Enough* collection, provides a way of understanding the reason for Van Allsburg's peculiar flatness of delivery and brevity of exposition, which are among the most distinctive features of his story-telling style. In both Colby and Van Allsburg a flatness of tone and a terseness of narration reinforce the surface plausibility of the tale and stand in striking contrast to the bizarreness of what is taking place. Of course, a critical difference between Van Allsburg's tales and Colby's are the wonderful pictures that Van Allsburg employs to make us witnesses of the strange happenings. The startling contrast between Van Allsburg's dull, though carefully crafted, prose and his extraordinary images operates as a continuous irony. It is key to the tension between the ordinary and the marvelous that is his central subject.

The Garden of Abdul Gasazi is an excellent example of the strangely-enough plot and narrative strategy. In this tale, a little boy named Alan is asked to take care of his neighbor's dog.[7] While Alan is walking the dog, the disobedient animal breaks away and heads into the mysterious garden of the magician Abdul Gasazi. Gasazi's abhorrence of dogs is posted on a sign that declares: "ABSOLUTELY, POSITIVELY NO DOGS ALLOWED IN THIS GARDEN." When the dismayed boy reaches Gasazi's house in the center of the garden, the dog is nowhere in sight. It turns out that Gasazi has either used his magic to transform the dog into a duck or played a clever joke on Alan. The rediscovery at the end of the book that the dog was in possession of Alan's hat, which had been stolen by the duck, sets up a final remark by the neighbor ("Why you bad dog," she said. "What are you doing with Alan's hat?"), which suggests, in fine, understated, strangely-enough fashion, that the extraordinary explanation is probably the right one.[8]

In *Jumanji,* Van Allsburg turns away somewhat from the popular-culture tradition of Colby and his kind and draws on the more self-consciously literary tradition that derives from the nineteenth-century weird tales of Edgar Allan Poe and Nathaniel Hawthorne, among others. This tradition has continued to enjoy vigorous life in contemporary works of literary fiction and in films. Among the many writers and filmmakers whose stories fit the mold of the strangely-enough tale are Alfred Hitchcock, Roald Dahl, Ray Bradbury, and Stephen King. The question of interconnections between the weird tales of the literary tradition and the weird tales collected by journalists (such as Colby) and scholarly folklorists (such as Jan Harold Brunvand) is a rich topic that has not been adequately addressed. For my purposes here it does not seem possible to cleanly separate the collected from the crafted with regard to influence on Van Allsburg; they are two sides of the same coin. Even the most carefully crafted of literary weird tales are aimed at popular audiences. Although the simplicity and blandness of Van Allsburg's narration of *Jumanji* suggest the collected tale, the twists of *Jumanji*'s little plot and the ironies it sets up recall, in certain respects, the tales of such popular modern storytellers as Dahl and Hitchcock. The grim little twist at the end, where the dangerous jungle game is found by two little boys who are well known for not following directions, is suggestive of one of Hitchcock's wittily gruesome, unhappy endings. But the somewhat more sophisticated feel of this tale does not conceal the strangely-enough mechanism.

Although I shall not discuss here all the varied graphic techniques Van Allsburg employed in his books, it should be observed that he has produced approximately one book a year since the appearance of his first book, *The Garden of Abdul Gasazi,* in 1979. For each of these yearly productions, his artistic procedures have changed. Each book is an experimental working out of design and material problems that Van Allsburg has set for himself. Underlying his structures and his choices of picture-making techniques is a sculptural sense that derives from his training and practice as a sculptor. Judging from remarks in recent interviews, Van Allsburg still seems to regard himself—even today, after all his years of success as a picture-book artist—as primarily a fine-arts sculptor who does picture books as something of a sideline. The scene in *The Garden of Abdul Gasazi* where Alan runs through the gate in the hedge to first enter the garden is one of many striking instances of sculptural form in Van Allsburg's work. In that scene, Alan and the two statues that border the gate seem to be three statuary variations on the theme "running boy." The gateway itself seems palpably sculptural. Even the separate leaves and blades of grass possess a certain amount of what philosopher of art Susanne Langer would call "kinetic volume" (Langer, 90). Each of these figurations seems static yet uncannily capable of operating in the viewer's space as well as in the virtual scene. This picture subtly suggests to the viewer that he or she might walk into it. The sculptural palpableness of some of Van Allsburg's pictures offers powerful reinforcement to the strangely-enough element in his work. We are drawn into the spaces of the garden of Abdul Gasazi not simply because his style is realistic but because his sculptural effects break down the barrier between our space and the space of the picture. Van Allsburg's sculptural effects in *The Garden of Abdul Gasazi* evoke a twilight-zone mood and have, at the same time, affinities with the sculptural dimensions of works by Dali, Magritte, and other surrealist artists. Thus, the strange tale of popular culture and the dream image of surrealistic modernism are fused in a peculiarly powerful way.

The Wreck of the Zephyr is perhaps the work most completely conceived in the strangely-enough manner. Recounters of such legends add credibility to their accounts by using the framing device of casting the narrator in the role of a visitor to a scene of fantastic events; there he or she encounters a person residing in the place who tells the tale that the narrator presumably does no more than record.[9] There is a twist at the end of *The Wreck of the Zephyr* where we are left with the implication that the narrator was the boy protagonist of the tale he has just told. Van Allsburg sets up this turn of events well. Most readers are probably taken somewhat by surprise when the old man's limping walk and anxiousness to go sailing hint that he was once the boy who flew the Zephyr. As usual in the strangely-enough tale, the truth of the story rests on the presumed credibility of the speaker as an eyewitness.

The Wreck of the Zephyr represents a new direction in Van Allsburg's picture-book art, because it is his first venture into color. Later statements about his experiments with color indicate that he was dissatisfied with the technique he employed in this book. His efforts to blend pastels in ways that would create painted effects were apparently the source of some frustration for him. Whatever difficulties this book may have caused him seem to have been worth enduring; *The Wreck of the Zephyr* presents striking images that might not have been achievable in other

ways. For instance, the luminescent greens of the ocean in the picture on the jacket of *The Wreck of the Zephyr* could not have been produced with the separate-strokes-of-color technique Van Allsburg used in *The Stranger.*

I have already cited John Russell's comment on the evident Magritte influence on *The Wreck of the Zephyr.* As with many Magritte images, several of Van Allsburg's pictures for this book present key elements as suspended or frozen within the scene. Thus, Van Allsburg's flying boats have an eerie silence and a seeming motionlessness that is reminiscent of the gigantic apples or rocks Magritte hangs over seascapes in such paintings as *The Beautiful Truths* or *The Castle in the Pyrenees.* Although we could also link the marine dreams of Van Allsburg with the dramatically lighted nineteenth-century luminist scenes of such artists as Fritz Hugh Lane and Martin Johnson Heade, the overall effect of these pictures is Magritte-like.

The best selling of Van Allsburg's picture books, *The Polar Express,* captures a strangely-enough motif that recurs in many forms in American popular culture. Van Allsburg's explanation of how this story came to him provides a fascinating glimpse into his way of imagining but provides little by way of interpretation.

> When I began thinking about what became *The Polar Express,* I had a single image in mind: a young boy sees a train standing still in front of his house one night. The boy and I took a few different trips on that train, but we did not, in a figurative sense, go anywhere. Then I headed north, and I got the feeling that this time I'd picked the right direction, because the train kept rolling all the way to the North Pole. At that point the story seemed literally to present itself. Who lives at the North Pole? Undoubtedly a ceremony of some kind, a ceremony requiring a child, delivered by a train and would have to be named the Polar Express.
>
> (Ruello 170)

An image that might have been one of the *Harris Burdick* fragments was developed into a story that resolves itself into a kind of seasonal legend. Although the polar rite of winter around which the story revolves is a product of Van Allsburg's knack for developing fantasy rather than a conscious manipulation of an archetypal motif, the archetypal motif of this strangely-enough tale is not hard to spot. The argument of this tale is the heart-warming contention that "Yes, Virginia there is a Santa Claus." The movie

Miracle on 34th Street is, of course, relevant here. The popular-culture nature of this tale makes it no less important than it would be if it were tricked out in the trappings of classical myth. The truth-pretense of the reality of Santa is perhaps the most widely distributed of all American strangely-enough motifs. Santa is the "flying saucer" that parents profess to believe in as an important game of ritual affection, gift giving, and seasonal celebration.

We might expect to lose the dangerous edge of surrealism in Van Allsburg's embrace of Jolly Old Saint Nick, but when we consider the intrusion of a massive train into a quiet suburban street, the restrainedly demonic nature of Van Allsburg's North Pole with its bizarrely vast snow-covered urban appearance, and the quietly nightmarish hugeness of the crowd of identically dressed elves turned out to hear Santa's speech—when we consider all the elements of this late-night sojourn—we find the surrealist edge of danger subtly implicit. It might even be said that there is something about the visualization of Santa's speech to his army of elves that is reminiscent of the famous filmed sequences of Hitler addressing his storm troopers. Although Santa is treated as an unambiguously benign being in the context of the book, there is an unsettling quality to the North Pole scene that adds an aesthetically interesting element of disorientation to the miraculous presence of the godlike Santa figure.

An even more mysterious mythos figures in the strangely-enough notion that lies at the center of *The Stranger,* a work that resonates on a number of levels. Visits by gods among mortals are commonplace in mythic traditions. Not identified as a powerful immortal, the god appears on someone's doorstep. Often such tales are moral fables concerning the importance of offering hospitality to strangers. Van Allsburg's tale certainly follows this pattern but adds the twist that the stranger in his book suffers from amnesia owing to a collision with a car whose driver afterward takes him into his home. The stranger's exact identity remains unexplained, but he is suggestive of Jack Frost, a being responsible for changing the season from warm summer to cool autumn and cold winter. Because of the stranger's amnesia, autumn does not come to the place where he has stopped. The farm family he stays with benefits from the prolonged warm weather that produces a bountiful harvest. Eventually the truth dawns on the stranger, and he departs to return to his appointed rounds.

Of course, as with *Polar Express,* we can link the story in *The Stranger* to a variety of popular works that share its basic strangely-enough premise. In a number of recent films a godlike personage intrudes into ordinary lives. Most often these beings are presented as aliens from other worlds, but they are typically given Christ-like qualities of spirituality and innocence, as well as certain amazing powers, that mark them as something above and beyond. The cult classic science fiction novel *Stranger in a Strange Land,* by Robert Heinlein, fits this profile, as do the films *Starman, ET, Man Facing Southeast, Brother from Another Planet, Edward Scissorshands,* and *Wings of Desire.* Cocteau's *Beauty and the Beast* provides a largely surrealistic version of this motif. In fact, a surrealistic undercurrent could be claimed for all of the films mentioned above. As always, questions of influence are difficult, but it seems that Van Allsburg's stranger is descended from the godly visitors of ancient stories and has some kinship with the extraterrestrial visitors of recent urban legends and the many films and books those legends have inspired.[10]

It is in the undercurrent of danger and the irrationality of the premise that we sense the surrealist dream developing within *The Stranger.* The strange creatures that invade the ordinary lives in Ernst's *Une Semaine de bonté* are perhaps gently echoed by the kindly, but indisputably supernatural, presence of the stranger in Van Allsburg's book. The lovely and uncompromisingly ordinary depiction of a somewhat sentimentalized and gorgeously autumnal rural world serves, however, to de-emphasize the surrealistic aspect of this quiet fantasy.[11]

The two dimensions of Chris Van Allsburg's work that I have discussed here—surrealism and strangely-enough fantasy—can be found in all of his books to varying degrees. Because Van Allsburg's surrealism is largely manifested in his images and the strangely-enough fantasy is primarily evident in his narratives, these two aspects of his work are largely complementary and do not conflict. Both surrealism and the popular tradition of the strange tale provide opportunities to show that the extraordinary resides in the ordinary and vice versa. Surrealism and the weird tale constitute two different but related ways that dreams intrude on everyday life, and Van Allsburg has learned lessons from both of these living traditions.

Notes

1. It may seem odd to speak of the tradition established in the name of an avant-garde style of art whose founding practitioners passionately declared themselves to be antitraditional, but it is

undeniable that surrealism established stances and styles that have been continued and developed. By speaking of a tradition we are referring to the continuance of some of the ideas and forms of masters such as Magritte and Ernst in the contemporary works of artist-writers such as Van Allsburg.

2. Giorgio De Chirico could be considered a forerunner rather than a continuer of the surrealist movement. Some of his most surrealistic works predate Breton's founding of the movement. Chirico is one of those who did not like the term *surrealism* and did not consider himself a surrealist.

3. A large subject I cannot adequately address here is the important ways surrealist artists were themselves influenced by nineteenth-century children's picture books. It has been persuasively argued, for instance, that Max Ernst's *Une semaine de bonté* was influenced by Lewis Carroll's Alice books and their Tenniel illustrations (Wilson 364-71).

4. I wish to make clear that my adoption of Colby's title as the label for a genre of popular pseudo-nonfiction should not be taken as an unqualified tribute to the literary quality of his work. Certainly there was nothing particularly original about what he put together. Collections such as Colby's had been published before—notably R. DeWitt Miller's *Impossible: Yet It Happened* (1947). Miller's book purported to be a study of the paranormal, a claim that was to be repeated by scores of authors who contributed to the paranormal publishing industry that mushroomed in the 1970s and still prospers. A recent series of such collections by Robert Ellis Cahill sells well at various "spooky" tourist spots in New England. The roots of all this can be traced back to the nineteenth century. Some of the early experiments in photography involved the use of multiple exposures to insert ghosts and faeries into "true" photographs. Such hoaxes and wishful musings have been rife in the flying-saucer and Loch Ness-monster subgenres as well. The superiority of Colby to De-Witt and many others, however, lies in the conciseness of his tale telling. Colby's *Strangely Enough* has maintained its popularity, I suspect, largely because its brief accounts spare the reader the often-pompous machinery of the typical paranormal author's explanation of his "field of research." Colby's stories, which have had numerous reprintings, are unencumbered folk-

tales and provide the kind of pleasure any good story affords.

5. It could be argued that the more self-conscious storytelling style of Rod Serling, for instance, kept his published short stories from lingering in the mind with the peculiar aura of plausibility that inheres in Colby's tales. Serling did, of course, achieve a wide audience for his fictions, especially once he established his type of tale in the medium of television, but Serling's narratives seem to fill a different sort of niche in the popular imagination than do Colby's. With Serling we always knew that he was taking us into an artificial realm known as the "Twilight Zone," but with Colby the extraordinary events seemed to be things that had happened to genuine, though only sketchily characterized, ordinary people with whom Colby had talked.

6. It should be noted that journalistic accounts, even when they debunk the tales, serve to support the further spread of the legends. Published versions are disseminated informally through oral retellings. Tour-group leaders, for instance, often seize upon such anecdotes to entertain their customers. In Hawaii tour guides have gained wide audiences for their versions of such tales. On walking tours, the on-site nature of the tale telling enhances the strangely-enough effect of a story by adding the tangibility of observable buildings, streets, and landscape elements. Even when the conductors of these tours are academically trained scholars, the tales are seldom described as folk legends. It is much more fun for both teller and listener to subscribe to a strange-but-true approach to the material. Further, local tales are seldom related to larger archetypal motifs. For example, the reported tendency of Madame Pele, the volcano goddess, to hitchhike and then disappear from the car is never linked to the widespread legend of the "vanishing hitchhiker," which has been discussed by Jan Harold Brunvand in several of his books. The desire to consider the strange tale as possibly true tends to routinely overwhelm any attempt to debunk the tale. Brunvand claims, in fact, that debunkings merely serve to further the distribution of the tale (153).

7. The bull terrier that first appeared in *The Garden of Abdul Gasazi* developed into something of a game Van Allsburg plays with his loyal fans. This game involves the reappearance of the bull terrier in book after book; in many of the books the distinctive dog makes his appear-

ance in an obscure corner of only one picture. This odd and amusing practice serves to link Van Allsburg's books to one another. The artist confesses to having enjoyed this find-me exercise. As he has pointed out, the dog is most difficult to find in *The Stranger* (Ruello 169). After *The Z Was Zapped* in 1987, however, this visual joke was dropped from his productions for the next three books; *Two Bad Ants* (1988), *Just a Dream* (1989), and *The Wretched Stone* (1991) are entirely dogless. The dog makes an amusing reappearance, however, in *The Widow's Broom* (1992) and can also be spotted in *The Sweetest Fig* (1993). It should be noted that his use of a repeated motif, which in popular culture would be called a "running gag," could be viewed as yet another resemblance to surrealist practice. Magritte, especially, is famed for the repeated appearances of his chess pieces, harness bells, men in bowler hats, and the like. Van Allsburg's overall opus is a unity that allows a playful weaving in and out of a pointless but interesting signature motif; this same element of play in serious art is a hallmark of much modernist art influenced by surrealism. The inclination toward playfulness is a key element in Van Allsburg's embrace of both popular culture and surrealism.

8. The value of noticing the strangely-enough plot of *The Garden of Abdul Gasazi* is amply testified to by the misinterpretations of plot action that are fallen into by Peter Neumeyer in a recent article on Van Allsburg that appeared in the *Children's Literature Association Quarterly.* Neumeyer insists upon oversimplifying the story by making it into a case of the protagonist-fell-asleep-and-dreamed-an-adventure-and-then-woke-up ploy so common in the least imaginative children's books. It is, however, obviously the case that the boy wakes up and has the encounter with Gasazi in a waking state. After the adventure he returns to the house, missing the telltale hat. For the dream plot to be operative, the boy would have to be shown waking up at the end of the story. The strangely-enough plot provides a way of understanding the bizarreness of the tale without resorting to the unpersuasive leap to the it-was-just-a-dream explanation that Neumeyer felt he needed to give. In general, Neumeyer's article is flawed by his desire to render Van Allsburg's books as if they were coded messages rather than works of art. Be-

cause of Neumeyer's quest for "visual literacy," he fails to do justice to the magic and mystery of Van Allsburg's picture books.

9. This plot bears some resemblance to the plots of the many Japanese noh plays, in which a person from the particular place tells a tale of an earlier time. As in Van Allsburg's story, the teller is eventually discovered to be the character whose woes are being recounted. In noh plays this tale teller is usually a ghost.

10. The list of books and films cited here indicates a continuing theme in popular culture, in which Van Allsburg's *The Stranger* has played a part. Several of the films mentioned postdate Van Allsburg's book and are obviously not considered influences on Van Allsburg. Because the theme of the godlike stranger is so ancient and pervasive, it would be difficult to establish a sequence of influences.

11. The seasonal feeling of *The Stranger* is one of its especially attractive features. I can recall no other picture book more effective at rendering autumn and the harvest time. Van Allsburg's technique of painstakingly laying on tiny unblended lines using pastels provides him with excellent means to realize the bright subtleties of autumn colors. His attention to details—such as individual blades of grass in the foreground, separate dots for leaves in middle-ground trees, strokes suggestive of the grain of wooden floorboards, and attractively plausible stylizations to represent distant elements—results in a book that seems to love the look of its subject. Van Allsburg creates strong sculptural effects in several of the pictures in *The Stranger,* such as the soup-serving scene and the pumpkin-loading scene. For the most part, however, we are not compelled to enter the pictorial space as we are in *The Garden of Abdul Gasazi*. The images of *The Stranger* are separated from the audience by a haze of seasonal romance. The viewer is happy to step back and contemplate the seasonal display.

Works Cited

Breton, André. *Manifestoes of Surrealism.* Ann Arbor: University of Michigan Press, 1969.

Brunvand, Jan Harold. *The Vanishing Hitchhiker: American Urban Legends and Their Meanings.* New York: Norton, 1981. (Other Brunvand books include *The Baby Train, The Choking Doberman, Curses! Broiled Again,* and *The Mexican Pet.*)

Cahill, Robert Ellis. *New England's Things That Go Bump in the Night.* Peabody, Mass.: Chandler-Smith, 1989. (Other Cahill works include *New England's Visitors from Outer Space* and *New England's Witches and Wizards.*)

Colby, C. B. *Strangely Enough!* New York: Sterling, 1959.

Ernst, Max. *Une semaine de bonté.* 1934. Reprint. New York: Dover, 1976.

Heinlein, Robert. *Stranger in a Strange Land.* New York: Putnam, 1961.

Helprin, Mark. *Swan Lake.* Illus. by Chris Van Allsburg. Boston: Houghton Mifflin, 1989.

Hubert, Renée Riese. *Surrealism and the Book.* Berkeley: University of California Press, 1988.

Langer, Susanne K. *Feeling and Form.* New York: Scribner's, 1953.

Lautreamont. *Les chants de Maldoror.* Trans. Alexis Lykiard. New York: Thomas Y. Crowell, 1972.

Miller, R. DeWitt. *Impossible: Yet It Happened!* New York: Ace, 1947.

Murray, Peter, and Linda Murray. *A Dictionary of Art and Artists.* New York: Penguin, 1959.

Neumeyer, Peter. "How Picture Books Mean: The Case of Chris Van Allsburg." *Children's Literature Association Quarterly* 15, no. 1 (1990): 2-8.

Ruello, Catherine. "Chris Van Allsburg Interview." In *Something about the Author,* vol. 53, ed. by Anne Commire. Detroit: Gale Research, 1989. Pp. 160-72.

Russell, John. Review of *The Wreck of the Zephyr,* by Chris Van Allsburg. *New York Times Book Review,* June 5, 1983, 34.

Serling, Rod. *From the Twilight Zone.* Garden City, N.Y.: Doubleday, 1960.

Van Allsburg, Chris. *Ben's Dream.* Boston: Houghton Mifflin, 1982.

———. *The Garden of Abdul Gasazi.* Boston: Houghton Mifflin, 1979.

———. *Jumanji.* Boston: Houghton Mifflin, 1981.

———. *Just a Dream.* Boston: Houghton Mifflin, 1990.

———. *The Mysteries of Harris Burdick.* Boston: Houghton Mifflin, 1984.

———. *The Polar Express.* Boston: Houghton Mifflin, 1985.

———. *The Stranger.* Boston: Houghton Mifflin, 1986.

———. *Two Bad Ants.* Boston: Houghton Mifflin, 1988.

———. *The Widow's Broom.* Boston: Houghton Mifflin, 1992.

———. *The Wreck of the Zephyr.* Boston: Houghton Mifflin, 1983.

———. *The Wretched Stone.* Boston: Houghton Mifflin, 1991.

———. *The Z Was Zapped.* Boston: Houghton Mifflin, 1987.

Wilson, Sarah. "Max Ernst and England." In *Max Ernst: A Retrospective,* ed. Werner Spies. Munich: Prestel-Verlag, 1991. Pp. 363-72.

Other Works of Interest

Cummings, Pat, ed. *Talking with Artists.* New York: Macmillan, 1991. (Van Allsburg is one of the artists interviewed.)

Nodelman, Perry. *Words about Pictures: The Narrative Art of Children's Picture Books.* Athens: University of Georgia Press, 1988.

TITLE COMMENTARY

THE GARDEN OF ABDUL GASAZI (1979)

Paul Heins (review date February 1980)

SOURCE: Heins, Paul. Review of *The Garden of Abdul Gasazi,* by Chris Van Allsburg. *Horn Book Magazine* 56, no. 1 (February 1980): 49-50.

[In *The Garden of Abdul Gasazi,* w]hen Fritz, the naughty dog, ran into the garden of Abdul Gasazi, a retired magician, Alan was terrified, for he knew that dogs were not allowed beyond the vine-covered wall. Fritz eluded Alan, who ultimately came to the magician's imposing house and politely requested the return of the dog. His request was granted, but Fritz, who had been turned into a duck, compounded his original naughtiness by flying away with Alan's cap. The story, which goes on to a tantalizing conclusion, serves essentially as an ambitious libretto for a series of carefully composed, technically expert pictures.

Stippled tones of gray and precisely outlined figures generate three-dimensional sculptured and architectural forms. Monumental human beings as well as stylized structures are bathed in light and shade, and all of the illustrations suggest in effect the pointillism of Seurat. Consequently, boy and dog, magician and duck are singularly static, while the pictures are filled with a mystical kind of immobility. Decidedly not a picture book for young children but a large virtuoso production—mannered and bordering on the occult.

📖 *JUMANJI* (1981)

Publishers Weekly (review date 10 April 1981)

SOURCE: Review of *Jumanji,* by Chris Van Allsburg. *Publishers Weekly* 219, no. 15 (10 April 1981): 70.

Van Allsburg, whose art works are on exhibit in major museums, was honored with numerous awards for his extraordinary first book, *The Garden of Abdul Gasazi.* [*Jumanji*] is his second, a weird story illustrated by fabulously realistic drawings of surreal adventures, pictures that are so infinitely detailed in three dimensions that they appear to move, breathe and make sounds. Judy and Peter find a board game, Jumanji, with instructions that it must be finished or go on forever. The first move brings a lion roaring into the living room. In his terror, Peter still acts quickly, decoying the beast into a room and locking the door. Every ensuing move throws the brother and sister into more dangers as they pit themselves against the odds, a desperate try to win and banish the jungle. The artist holds back the thrilling result until the last word.

Pamela D. Pollack (review date May 1981)

SOURCE: Pollack, Pamela D. Review of *Jumanji,* by Chris Van Allsburg. *School Library Journal* 27, no. 9 (May 1981): 60.

Gr. 1-4—Jumanji is a jungle adventure board game come to life via the magic that, in Van Allsburg's world, is always waiting to leak into the everyday. With successive dice rolls, deepest, darkest Africa invades the neat, solid, formally arranged rooms of the unsuspecting players' house. The players—a blasé brother and sister home alone—are momentarily dumbstruck but not really upset. They steadfastly go on with the game as monkeys, grinning with a wicked gleam, raid the kitchen and hunker around the game board; rhinos charge intently through the living room

(and right into one's line of vision); a Python coils on the mantel, its pattern set off by a leafy slipcover design to give a jungle camouflage effect. As in *The Garden of Abdul Gasazi* (Houghton, 1979), which *Jumanji* out-does in story terms, real and unreal rub shoulders in three-dimensional drawings extraordinary for the multiplicity of gray tones the artist achieves and the startling contrasts with brilliant white. The eye-fooling angles, looming shadows and shifting perspectives are worthy of Hitchcock, yet all these "special effects" are supplied with only a pencil.

Denise M. Wilms (review date 15 May 1981)

SOURCE: Wilms, Denise M. Review of *Jumanji,* by Chris Van Allsburg. *Booklist* 77, no. 18 (15 May 1981): 1258.

Jumanji is the mysterious, magical board game Peter and Judy discover in the park and bring home to relieve their boredom. Playing it unleashes a frightening jungle world in their midst, one that recedes only when the players reach the game's end. Van Allsburg's consummate draftsmanship creates stunning, velvet-flat, black-and-white scenes that are endlessly fascinating. Vistas of a familiar household world gone amok are seen from startling floor or ceiling perspectives that heighten the story's sense of slightly sinister suspense. The tone of the text lightens the sense of danger in a fantasy come true, but this remains a potent vision that lingers on and on.

Kirkus Reviews (review date 15 June 1981)

SOURCE: Review of *Jumanji,* by Chris Van Allsburg. *Kirkus Reviews* 49, no. 12 (15 June 1981): 737.

Without pictures, [*Jumanji*] would be a fairly orthodox horror story for kids: a jungle board game, found in the park with ominous instructions, produces at each square the children land on whatever wild creature ("Lion attacks, move back two spaces") or natural disaster ("Monsoon season begins, lose one turn") is called for—until, beset, the two youngsters are throwing the dice wildly to reach the last square ("Jumanji, a city of golden buildings and towers") and free themselves of the jungle terror. This episode, however, is framed, in a conventional picture-book made, by their departing parents' injunction to "keep the house neat" and the parents' return, with guests, after the game is over and all is calm. A second sly jest provides the obligatory twist at the end: a guest's two children are returning from the park, discarded game in hand. What makes the pictures themselves problematic is: 1) the heavy load of portent present from the start (as in Van Allsburg's earlier *The Garden of Abdul Gasazi*), which robs the book of a contrast between the normal, everyday and the macabre; 2) Van Allsburg's freeze-dry surrealism, which renders the turbulence as a static charade, or tableau; and 3) the paradox that imagined horror is more skin-prickling than horror seen—with a child's mouth agape. Van Allsburg's artistic skill seems largely confined to the devising of special effects—these largely dependent, in turn, on oversize close-ups and dramatic angles. Once their shock-value wears off, these are boring pictures—with no feel in particular (down to the inappropriately babyish toys) for a child's world.

THE MYSTERIES OF HARRIS BURDICK (1984)

Adrienne E. Gavin (essay date 2001)

SOURCE: Gavin, Adrienne E. "Enigma's Variation: The Puzzling Mysteries of Avi, Ellen Raskin, Diana Wynne Jones, and Chris Van Allsburg." In *Mystery in Children's Literature: From the Rational to the Supernatural*, edited by Adrienne E. Gavin, pp. 210-17. New York, N.Y.: Palgrave, 2001.

[*In the following essay, Gavin examines several children's mystery books in terms of their innovative narratives, asserting that Van Allsburg's* The Mysteries of Harris Burdick *functions as a "postmodernist picture book."*]

Formulaic mysteries are appropriate for child readers, it is sometimes claimed, not because formula fiction has its place in anyone's reading fare, but on the grounds that, as they read, children are learning about the mode of mystery writing itself. The young, it is implied, do not require nuanced, complex, or allusive mysteries. Similarly, it is asserted:

> The researcher of children's literature cannot operate in the categories of 'originality, novelty, stylistic experiment' . . . as are applied to modern (that is, 20th century) adult literature. Devices and patterns that may seem to betoken lack of originality, plagiarism, secondarity, in adult literature are a deliberate creative approach in children's books.
>
> (Nikolajeva, *Magic*, 118)

Comments like these, which are surprisingly common, have as their subtext a notion that in some way our expectations of children's literature can be 'lower' than our expectations of adult literature.

While formulaic writing and derivativeness may be a 'deliberate creative approach' in some children's texts (as they are in some adult works), it is surely reductive to suggest that we should not expect stylistic experiment and originality in children's literature. This essay examines fiction by Avi, Ellen Raskin, Diana Wynne Jones, and Chris Van Allsburg in order to show the varieties of innovation and originality that are possible in children's mysteries.

Carol Billman describes three levels of sophistication in mystery writing for children. Child readers, she suggests, progress from the formula of fairy tales to formulaic mysteries like the Nancy Drew series which are 'conventional, rather than idiosyncratic or inventional' (32) and 'encourage what Tzvetan Todorov calls "metareading," a process by which "we note the methods of the . . . narrative instead of falling under its spell"' (33). They then move onto more sophisticated mysteries which are 'rooted in the "real" world' and contain 'equivocal rather than completely stereotyped characters' (39). In a third stage, she argues, children read more complex, less codified mysteries which overlap with other genres such as time travel fantasies or historical fiction. Her suggestion that child readers progress consecutively through these levels of mystery is overly schematic. Her admission, however, that mystery's 'best offerings, for whatever age, urge upon their readers [a] constant balancing of the mysterious and the recognized, of the unsettling unknown and the reassuring known' (37) stresses the enigmatic and puzzling elements of the most innovative mysteries for children.

Every mystery, whether formulaic or innovative, requires a secret which lies at its heart and which, by text's end, is either explained or left mysterious. Every mystery also involves the provocation of puzzling in characters and/or readers who are compelled to ponder over possible solutions to the mysteries presented. What distinguishes creative, innovative, and original mystery writing from the more formulaic and derivative is the presence of enigma. Enigma is defined in *The Collins English Dictionary* as 'a person, thing, or situation that is mysterious, puzzling, or ambiguous'. As 'mysterious' and 'puzzling' are already inherent within mystery, it is 'ambiguous' that is the key word here. Innovative children's mysteries contain ambiguity; within them there is a slippery indeterminacy of meaning and solution; something enigmatic and shifting lies at their core, making it impossible to reach absolute conclusions. They encourage puzzling that extends beyond the bounds of the plot and which connects with deeper mysteries of life and art, involving issues of identity, reality, and fictionality. As Joan Aiken suggests, '[t]hings not understood have a radiance of their own. It is a challenge to go back to them, to puzzle and puzzle' (45). As this essay shows, Avi's *The Man Who Was Poe* (1989), Raskin's *The Westing Game* (1978), Jones's *Archer's Goon* (1984), and Van Allsburg's ***The Mysteries of Harris Burdick*** (1984), each in its own enigmatic variation, reveals the possibilities of innovation and originality in children's mystery fiction.

At first glance Avi's *The Man Who Was Poe* might appear to be a formulaic detective mystery. The mother, aunt, and sister of Edmund, the central child character, have all disappeared in separate and mysterious circumstances; there has been a robbery of California gold from the Providence Bank; a dead woman's body is fished out of the water, and various characters are being trailed by other characters through the dark streets of Providence, Rhode Island in November 1848. A dark and mysterious stranger helps Edmund solve these mysteries, the criminals are revealed, the case seems closed. The case, however, is not closed and enigmatic questions remain to puzzle both the reader and Edmund.

Avi's innovation is to introduce into his historical detective novel that pre-eminent and originary detective created by Edgar Allan Poe, Auguste Dupin. In doing so he goes back to the origins of detective formula, but transforms that formula into something far less certain. Avi's Dupin is not a simple borrowing but a complex fictional construct who operates on occasion with the original Dupin's rational and clear-thinking powers of detection. At the same time, however, he is the alcoholic, death-obsessed Edgar Allan Poe himself. He tells Edmund that he is '"the man who *was* Poe. Now I am Dupin"' (143), but later says '"I'm no longer Auguste Dupin. I am the man who *is* Edgar—Allan—Poe"' (161). Avi's text uses intertextuality, metafictional elements, and circularity to create its enigma. It blurs distinctions between creator and created, fiction and reality, and 'Dupin-Poe' and Edmund.

The greater the knowledge a reader has of Poe's work and life the more intertextual significance that reader can see. By adding an appendix—'Something about Edgar Allan Poe'—and by weaving among the more arcane links some specific and explanatory references to Poe's work, Avi ensures, however, that even child readers who know nothing of Poe see mysterious interlinkings between the novel they are reading, Poe's life, and Poe's fictional creations. It is the metafic-

tional qualities of the novel, however, that create most enigma. The mysterious Dupin-Poe (as I call him here, although in the novel he goes by both names severally) agrees to help the desperate Edgar solve the mystery of his missing family, which he Dupinesquely does. He also, however, Poe-like, uses the situation as material for a story he sketches out soon after meeting Edmund: '*Edmund . . . a boy . . . Missing sister . . . The sea — bringer of death . . . abandonment. Release/death . . . The . . . necessity . . . of death . . . The certainty of death*' (30). Dupin-Poe's insistence on his story and the emphasis that story has on the inevitability of the death of Edmund's family members and especially his sister 'Sis'—whose name is the same as Dupin-Poe's late wife—deeply disturbs and horrifies Edmund who insists that his experience is real and that his sister is still alive and can be saved. The twisting together of 'real' and story puzzles both Dupin-Poe and Edmund. Dupin-Poe thinks to himself 'have I gone beyond the writing of words? Could I be writing this boy's *life*?' (56). Edmund is shocked when Poe refuses to help him find his mother and sister and instead writes his story: '"this *isn't* a story,"' he insists (161). Enraged at Dupin-Poe's saying Sis is dead, he tears up pages of the story and eventually has to battle physically free of Dupin-Poe to save his sister.

'Puzzling questions . . . are not beyond *all* conjecture,' Dupin-Poe thinks to himself when considering whether his characters have come to life (173). Such questions are not beyond conjecture, but they are, the novel reveals, beyond answers. Dupin-Poe leaves Edmund with just such a puzzling question on the final page of the novel when he asks him: '"I ask you: in what fashion will your sister live longer. In her life? Or, in this, *my* story that would have been?"' (198). The novel ends in ambivalence. The undestroyed scrap of his story that Dupin-Poe tosses to Edmund is the first paragraph of Avi's novel, with the name Edgar crossed out and the name Edmund added. This drives the reader circularly back to the start of the novel and also confirms the enigmatic nature of the puzzling questions the novel has raised but not answered about the parallels between Dupin-Poe and Edmund. Dupin-Poe notes that for a mystery '*to be effective [there] must be a puzzle*' (80), and speaks of a '"puzzle which, if we could fully understand it would bring . . . truth"' (118). Yet he also claims: '"[l]ies have their own truth"' (144). Avi's novel raises postmodernist questions about truth and lies, life and fiction, and creates a sense of enigmatic mysteries which must be puzzled over but which cannot be solved.

Ellen Raskin's novel *The Westing Game* innovates mystery in different ways. It is overtly a puzzle mystery, designed as a game not just for readers but for the characters themselves who are desperately seeking the solutions to the clues they hold. The 16 heirs of the mysterious Sam Westing, directed by his will, motivated by thoughts of inheriting his two hundred million dollars, and working in teams of two, are trying to figure out who among them has murdered Westing. Each team has different clues and must come to solutions in its own way. Mystery piles upon mystery: Is any one a twin? Who plays chess? Who is exploding bombs? Was Westing murdered? Is he actually dead?

Raskin, as Peter Hunt states, is 'consistently experimental' in her work (150), and a Raskin mystery, as Constance B. Hieatt points out, 'is not of the common or garden variety. All of them offer more than the simple appeal of what Graham Greene calls "an entertainment"' (128). Her works are 'playful and fundamentally mysterious' in postmodern ways (McGillis 154). Billman classes *The Westing Game* as 'a mystery novel of the second degree of difficulty' (35). She demonstrates that the novel moves beyond formula in its use of an 'omniscient narrator [who] flits quickly from one character's mind to that of another' and in its lack of a central detective character (36). She does not, however, see enigma within the novel:

> Raskin presents what readers know to be the familiar ingredients of mystery fiction—wills, detectives, clues, red herrings, even a potential corpse—and serves them up in a new and truly adventurous guessing game. Her variation is not, however, ultimately so lacking in clues for its unraveling as to stymie readers.
>
> (Billman 37)

Billman claims that Raskin 'gives the necessary information to solve the ever shape-shifting crime' (38). This is partially true in that it does become clear to readers that Sam Westing, still alive, must be operating this extraordinary puzzle, but it is not true to say that readers can solve the mystery. The enigma at the heart of this novel is that its puzzle is so confusingly difficult that none of the players except Turtle Wexler ever completely solve it and most readers are unlikely to either without the novel's explanation. Mystery remains as to how all the intricate clues fit together. In a different way than Avi's, Raskin's novel also drives readers back to the beginning to re-look at clues. It also leaves open the question why Turtle does not ever tell anyone else that she has discovered Westing.

Raskin's mystery is innovative, too, in its acute and witty observation of characters' public facades and the private truths that lie beneath. She enters into the puzzling nature of human relationships. As the shin-kicking of Turtle, the highly decorated but unneeded crutches of Sydelle Pulaski, and the social-climbing and bigoted remarks of Grace Windsor Wexler reveal, the characters seek individual attention. Through their involvement in the Westing Game each finds a new and confident sense of themselves and they all go on to live out successfully the American dream that 'Uncle Sam' Westing has urged upon them.

Like Raskin's novel, Diana Wynne Jones's *Archer's Goon* makes use of humour which underneath contains darker puzzles. Like Avi's novel it makes use of metafictional techniques and of characters who have mysteriously mixed identities. As Maria Nikolajeva claims:

> Diana Wynne Jones is an indisputable innovator, and in her books the hesitation principle is most tangible . . . The play with alternative worlds in [her] books becomes a discussion of existential questions: what is reality? Is there more than one definite truth?
>
> (*Children's,* 74)

Archer's Goon is a complex fantasy whose mystery begins with puzzling questions about who is intimidating Howard's father, the famous writer Quentin Sykes, and then moves on to more perplexing mysteries connected with identity, time, and the self.

The enigma at the heart of the novel is 13-year-old Howard himself. He begins with a stable self-identity and then is encompassed by a mysterious and threatening situation which destroys his sense of himself. His family live in a town which is secretly run by seven supernaturally powerful and giant siblings who have, gangster-like, divided up the town and corruptly 'farm' their patches. When Howard's father refuses to write his regular payment of two thousand new words for an unknown member of the giant family, Howard's own family are beset. A goon arrives and takes up residence in their house, music blares constantly, their road is dug up, their gas, electricity and banking are cut off, they are driven to borrow food, and a gang is ready to attack Howard and his sister, Awful, at any opportunity.

Howard tries to solve the mystery of which of the seven beings—Archer, Dillian, Shine, Torquil, Erskine, Hathaway, and Venturus—is causing these terrible problems for his family. In what Nikolajeva describes as a 'paradigm shift' in fantasy structures (*Magic,* 117) and 'an identity variable which seems almost unique' (*Magic,* 117), Howard discovers that he himself is the 'criminal'. Tracking down Venturus, the last and youngest giant sibling, who lives in the future, Howard discovers that *he* is Venturus. He discovers, too, that his giant siblings have been trapped in the town and prevented from moving beyond it to 'farm' the rest of the world, not by Quentin Sykes's words as they had believed, but by Venturus himself who has muddled with time in order to perfect his spaceship. He learns that, because of this, everyone has lived through two repeated sets of 13 years and might be entering into a third identical loop if he does not act to stop his Venturus self.

In her analysis of some other Jones novels, Margaret Rumbold points to the shifting selves in Jones's work and to her use of 'multiple signifiers to reflect the heterogeneous nature of the subject' (22). She suggests that within Jones's *Hexwood* (1993) 'selfhood remains essentially enigmatic (at times arbitrary) and cannot be nailed down' (25). This is also true of *Archer's Goon* in which Howard-Venturus's self is the central enigma which is never fully solved. Learning that he is Venturus both horrifies and embarrasses Howard. He feels his magical powers coming upon him, but knows, too, that this third time through life: 'he [will] have to bring himself up not to be Venturus' (241).

Howard acts to rid the world of the three older giant siblings and in a wonderfully metafictional scene in which observing characters run from window to typewriter to see the same scene unfold, his father finally writes the requested words which, as they are typed onto the page, force the greedy older siblings into Venturus's spaceship, to be shot far into the universe. In Jones's novel 'good and evil are no longer absolute categories' (Nikolajeva, *Children's,* 74). The Goon, for example, changes from being a knife-throwing threat, to being virtually a part of the Sykes family, to revealing himself as Erskine and imprisoning the family, to emerge at the end a loved family friend. Jones's novel innovates through the extremely complex position in which it places its protagonist as both solver of and source of mystery, and ends with an indeterminate future ahead for Howard-Venturus.

Most puzzling and mysterious of all the texts discussed here is Chris Van Allsburg's postmodernist picture book *The Mysteries of Harris Burdick.* At the time it was published it was, as John Rowe Townsend notes, 'the enigmatic Van Allsburg's most enigmatic book so far' (329). The book contains 14 discrete and apparently unconnected black and white illustrations, each accompanied by a title and a caption. Van Allsburg claims in his introduction (interestingly written from the Providence, Rhode Island setting of Avi's novel) that these drawings had been handed to him by a retired children's publisher, one Peter Wenders. Wenders told him, he recounts, that they had been drawn thirty years earlier by a man named Harris Burdick who had brought them in to Wenders as samples to gauge his publishing interest in 14 different stories. Having left the drawings with Wenders, 'Harris Burdick was never heard from again . . . To this day Harris Burdick remains a complete mystery' ('Introduction', n.p.). Burdick's disappearance, Roderick McGillis suggests, 'serves to remind us of the supposed "death of the author" in postmodern art' (154). It also suggests the missing person or body that supplies the impetus to much detective mystery or the fleeting appearance of a ghostly being in supernatural mystery.

Apart from the claims about their mysterious origins, which raises postmodernist questions about truth and fiction, the drawings are in themselves mysterious. Their blackness and whiteness is shaded and slightly indistinct; edges are blurred, creating images of dreamscape. They hint at magic and are uncanny, strange, and eerie in effect. They depict puzzling or impossible things such as a chair with a nun in it flying through a cathedral, or a bird flying off bird-patterned wallpaper. As McGillis puts it, 'they "unclose" [rather than disclose] their meaning, keeping it always mysterious and relative' (154). They disrupt 'expectations based on [the mystery story] genre' by not providing solutions (McGillis 154).

The book encourages readings of different types of mystery: the magical, the frightening, the natural, and the fantastic, and the captions heighten mystery further. Providing clues to the stories behind the drawings, they serve to mystify through their provocative nature. The title 'Archie Smith, Boy Wonder', for example, is captioned '*A tiny voice asked, "Is he the one?"*' while 'Another Place, Another Time' is captioned '*If there was an answer, he'd find it there.*' Each title and caption raises more questions than it answers.

David Lewis, discussing indeterminacy within postmodernist picture books, suggests that

> when we have too *little* information, we often find that issues within a story which we would normally expect to have resolved are in fact undecid-

able . . . outcomes are left unresolved or relationships remain permanently unclear.

(261)

Van Allsburg's book is a perfect example of such indeterminacy. Each illustration is in itself an enigma, its mystery unsolvable and its readers left puzzling. As the back cover of the book states 'the puzzles, the mysteries, presented by these drawings, are not what we are used to. They are not solved for us . . . The solutions to these mysteries lie . . . in our imagination.'

McGillis suggests that the '"perfect lift-off" in the final illustration . . . suggests a departure from the known to the unknown' (68-9). In its plotlessness and indeterminacy Van Allsburg's book clearly moves into 'the unknown', as far from the 'rational', solved world of early detective mysteries as it is perhaps possible to go. He is not alone in this move towards inexplicable mystery. Meena G. Khorana notes that within the work of the nominees for the 1998 Hans Christian Andersen Illustrator Award a common motif is 'the evocation of a mysterious, haunting atmosphere by combining magical and realistic elements' (3).

Collocates of the word mystery such as 'wrapped', 'shrouded', or 'cloaked' suggest something covered-up and secret. In formulaic mysteries the cloak, shroud, or wrapper is removed, exposing what lies beneath. In innovative mysteries such as those by Avi, Raskin, Jones, and Van Allsburg the wrapper or cloak remains in place. It perhaps lifts slightly on rare glimpsing occasions or is seen through dimly when the light is at strange angles, but what is beneath is never clearly revealed. Each of the texts discussed here creates an enigma that cannot be solved and that stimulates readers' puzzlement beyond the bounds of any outline plot. In creating that enigma, these authors use postmodernist techniques such as intertextuality, indeterminacy, and incomplete solutions and introduce metafictional elements. In this way their variations on mysteries sustain puzzles, insist that some mysteries are inexplicable, and reveal the innovative and non-formulaic possibilities of mystery literature for children.

Works Cited

Aiken, Joan. 'A Thread of Mystery', *Children's Literature in Education*, 2 (1970): 30-47.

Avi. *The Man Who Was Poe* [1989]. New York: Avon Books, 1997.

Billman, Carol. 'The Child Reader as Sleuth', *Children's Literature in Education*, 15 (1) [52] (1984): 30-41.

Hieatt, Constance B. 'The Mystery of *Figgs & Phantoms*', *Children's Literature*, 13 (1985): 128-38.

Hunt, Peter. *An Introduction to Children's Literature.* Oxford: Oxford University Press, 1994.

Jones, Diana Wynne. *Archer's Goon.* London: Methuen, 1984.

Khorana, Meena G. 'To the Reader', *Bookbird*, 36 (3) (1998): 2-4.

Lewis, David. 'The Constructedness of Texts: Picture Books and the Metafictive', in Sheila Egoff, Gordon Stubbs, Ralph Ashley, and Wendy Sutton (eds), *Only Connect: Readings on Children's Literature,* 3rd edn. Toronto: Oxford University Press, 1996, pp. 259-75.

McGillis, Roderick. *The Nimble Reader: Literary Theory and Children's Literature.* New York: Twayne, 1996.

Nikolajeva, Maria. *Children's Literature Comes of Age: Towards a New Aesthetic.* New York and London: Garland, 1996.

————. *The Magic Code: The Use of Magical Patterns in Fantasy for Children.* Stockholm: Almqvist & Wiskell International, 1988.

Raskin, Ellen. *The Westing Game* [1978]. New York: Puffin, 1997.

Rumbold, Margaret. 'Taking the Subject Further', *Papers*, 7 (2) (1997): 16-28.

Townsend, John Rowe. *Written for Children: An Outline of English-Language Children's Literature,* 6th edn. London: Bodley Head, 1995.

Van Allsburg, Chris. *The Mysteries of Harris Burdick.* London: Andersen Press, 1984.

Sheri McDonald and Sally Rasch (review date May 2004)

SOURCE: McDonald, Sheri, and Sally Rasch. Review of *The Mysteries of Harris Burdick,* by Chris Van Allsburg. *Book Links* 13, no. 5 (May 2004): 44.

Gr. 2-6—In this fictional picture book, [*The Mysteries of Harris Burdick,*] readers are told that a man named Harris Burdick wanted to publish books based on his mysterious drawings, but never returned to the publisher's office. The drawings and accompanying captions are open-ended, leaving the reader to ponder each mystery. Besides writing about one of the scenes, students could brainstorm vocabulary that describes the moods and feelings represented by the drawings, as well as discuss how setting and characters develop in narrative writing.

THE POLAR EXPRESS (1985)

Marilyn Carpenter (review date 8 December 1985)

SOURCE: Carpenter, Marilyn. Review of *The Polar Express,* by Chris Van Allsburg. *Los Angeles Times Book Review* (8 December 1985): 4.

The Polar Express, by Chris Van Allsburg is an original fantasy that unfolds as a reminiscence of a boyhood adventure. One Christmas Eve a boy wakes to find a passenger train outside his window. It is the Polar Express, full of children going to the North Pole to see Santa and his elves. The story contains drama and magic that children will love. There is a mythical Santa, a magnificent train, energetic reindeer, and snow-painted landscapes. The boy receives a bell from Santa that only rings for those who believe in him. Its beautiful sound is more precious to the boy than any other gift. This theme of wonder and belief in the magic of Christmas is refreshing in a time when children want more, more, more. Van Allsburg is a master at creating memorable illustrations dramatized with rich, dark colors and illuminated by spots of bright light. He achieves a mysterious, magical tone with his art that echoes and expands the story's wondrous theme.

THE STRANGER (1986)

Patricia Austin (review date April-May 2003)

SOURCE: Austin, Patricia. Review of *The Stranger,* by Chris Van Allsburg. *Book Links* 12, no. 5 (April-May 2003): 34.

Gr. 1-4—When Farmer Bailey accidentally hits a man with his truck [in *The Stranger*], he invites the stranger into the house. The man cannot remember who he is, and the family assumes he's "some kind of hermit." Young readers can be encouraged to mine the text and art for clues that reveal the stranger's identity.

Sheri McDonald and Sally Rasch (review date May 2004)

SOURCE: McDonald, Sheri, and Sally Rasch. Review of *The Stranger,* by Chris Van Allsburg. *Book Links* 13, no. 5 (May 2004): 44.

Gr. 2-6—Farmer Bailey hits a mysterious stranger with his truck and brings him home to recover [in *The Stranger*]. Many unusual events happen while the stranger is on the farm. Readers can try to determine the identity of the stranger by using the character clues offered in the open-ended story line.

THE Z WAS ZAPPED: A PLAY IN TWENTY-SIX ACTS (1987)

Phyllis G. Sidersky (review date February 1988)

SOURCE: Sidersky, Phyllis G. Review of *The Z Was Zapped: A Play in Twenty-Six Acts,* by Chris Van Allsburg. *Childhood Education* 64, no. 3 (February 1988): 174-75.

The letters of the alphabet are depicted as performers appearing on stage in *The Z Was Zapped: A Play in Twenty-Six Acts*]. Each letter deals with a disaster; e.g., "The B was badly bitten." The dark pencil drawings are well suited to the mood, which is somber and mysterious. This is not an alphabet for preschoolers. It would be useful, however in a sketching class or, as in *The Mysteries of Harris Burdick,* a good stimulus for creative writing. *Ages 8-14.*

Patricia Austin (review date April-May 2003)

SOURCE: Austin, Patricia. Review of *The Z Was Zapped: A Play in Twenty-Six Acts,* by Chris Van Allsburg. *Book Links* 12, no. 5 (April-May 2003): 33.

K-Gr. 3—The title page [of *The Z Was Zapped: A Play in Twenty-Six Acts*], which looks like a playbill, announces, "The Alphabet Theatre Proudly Presents The Z Was Zapped, A Play in Twenty-Six Acts," beckoning the child to guess what mishaps the letters have suffered. Such scenes as "The I was nicely iced," "The J was rather jittery," and "The W was oddly warped" go beyond the usual fare of vocabulary in alphabet books.

TWO BAD ANTS (1988)

Elizabeth A. Ford (essay date 1989)

SOURCE: Ford, Elizabeth A. "Resurrection Twins: Visual Implications in *Two Bad Ants.*" *Children's Literature Association Quarterly* 15, no. 1 (1989): 8-10.

[*In the following essay, Ford asserts that the visual implications of the illustrations in Van Allsburg's* Two Bad Ants *send a "mixed message" that contrasts with the written text of the story.*]

Few would deny the visual impact of the illustrations Chris Van Allsburg has created for his books. His most effective works, like the sculptural black and white illustrations for *Jumanji,* Van Allsburg's 1982 Caldecott medal winner, and the dizzying perspectives of his *Polar Express* (1986), make it clear that Van Allsburg is following a path of personal iconography and offering readers much visual magic along the way. In his best works, his illustrations do what good illustrations should do, according to Maurice Sendak; they create a "marriage" between text and picture, not only describing, but also extending what is written.[1] His 1988 offering, *Two Bad Ants,* which has a stylish power of its own, takes the next step on that path, but also gives some troubling hints suggesting where Van Allsburg's vision may be leading him and his readers. In *Two Bad Ants* the illustrations do more than extend the written word. They create a subtext; they tell another story.

The text offers a simple plot in *Two Bad Ants.* The queen of an ant colony tastes sugar and quickly orders her scouts out on a mission to find and bring back more. On this quest, which is successful, two bad ants go AWOL, opting for sugary satiation in a suburban sugarbowl instead of duty. Their gluttony is punished by near extinction as they meet with every disaster a kitchen can produce. They are almost boiled, nearly drowned, partially cooked and finally electrified. They do escape and gratefully return to their own world, apparently happy to conform if conformity means survival.

The quality of the illustrations accompanying this cautionary tale is high. The low-in-tone flat wash backgrounds and masterly line drawings are evidence of Van Allsburg's considerable talents, which he obviously enjoyed applying to this story. He exploits size and perspective—an approach that has become a trademark—to create a most effective ant view of the human world, transforming the familiar, via ant-eye, into the unexpected. This device gets an instant response from small readers. The two five-year-olds I shared the book with were entranced by visual proof that a human mouth could look like a cave to the two ants afloat in a cup of coffee (18-19). The lighting is equally effective. The unearthly glow that partially illuminates the darkness of the ant world contrasts nicely with the harsh brightness of the kitchen. Technique is not the problem here; implication is. More than perspective is being exploited and another kind of illumination infuses these images.

The illustrations suggest a message that is never stated but that is easily divined by any reader. In his review of *Two Bad Ants,* Sanford Schwartz stalks the ambiguity created by the leap between text and page, but never identifies or discusses it. Schwartz's main complaint is that the work seems unfinished, but he does raise a more problematic issue without defining it, first claiming that: "The best thing about *Two Bad Ants* is that it makes you appreciate, perhaps even like, ants. Mr. Van Allsburg's creatures are beautifully shaped. . . . They're like Bugatti roadsters" (63).

Later, however, Schwartz complains that the ants have no personalities, are "little nothings who are brutalized one morning and learn the dreary message 'you should go home again'" (63). I don't think Mr. Schwarz, or any reader and looker, can have it both ways. The tension between ant as likeable object—not living being—and ant as living object of abuse must be resolved. Schwartz's choice of diction, if not his assertions, shows that he knows this. His apt and revealing comparison of Van Allsburg's ants to sports cars glosses his claim that *Two Bad Ants* might make readers "appreciate" ants. Visually, these ants are clearly mechanized things, as cars are things, and although one can like a car, the appreciation of objects is surely different than affection for living beings. Although few can be expected to like ants—as if by common consent they have been placed on some lower rung of animate life—it seems dangerous to encourage the notion that they are things, as it would seem inappropriate to encourage this view of any living creature.

If the text does not, the illustrations for *Two Bad Ants* do encourage a desensitized view of ants (and therefore all insects?). The first evidence of this is in Van Allsburg's use of perspective. At the beginning of the tale, which is told in a straightforward manner, the ants in the illustrations are larger than life, lords of their own world. The first illustration of an enormous scout carrying back a magnified crystal of sugar makes his discovery seem as significant as Prometheus bringing fire to man—Van Allsburg is *not* humorless (4). The next plate offers a majestic view of the queen ant tasting the crystal (5). A close up drawing of her head and parts of her wing and body fill the image area; readers can only guess how large she really is, and her power is nicely implied by her size: she is too big to fit upon the page. Although smaller than she is, her ant scouts are still clearly at home in their surroundings, not dwarfed by them. As long as the ants stay where they belong, they are pictured as beings in control. After they crawl in through the kitchen window, however, they are dramatically reduced by the human context in which they are placed. Of course ants *are* small and must look small in relation to the kitchen appliances, but the visual message carries another layer of meaning.

Because they are smaller, the two bad ant "things" are easily cut down to size by the powerful world of bigger, mechanized things, things that must be operated by a human agent. Van Allsburg chooses to focus on the human inhabiting the kitchen only once; a mouth and the end of a nose appear over the rim of a coffee cup to form the treacherous cave the ants fear. But if humans do not often appear, they are evident by implication. Someone must spoon up the sugar, operate the toaster, turn on the disposal. Close-ups in the kitchen seem to be through the anonymous human's eyes. These are no longer enlarged views of ants in action, but windows through which the ants' ordeal is seen. Van Allsburg's game is to close in on the ants as they are tortured, and this seems particularly manipulative because of the attitude towards their experience that is encouraged.

The illustration before the ants' first negative experience—a swim in hot coffee—shows the beginning of their fall from the sugarbowl into the "boiling brown lake" (shades of *Paradise Lost*?) (17). The text accompanying the two-page illustration showing their immersion in the coffee explains that this is a traumatic experience, not just a swim: "crushing waves fell over the ants. They paddled hard to keep their tiny heads above water" (18). But the five-year-olds to whom I read the book laughed gleefully at the ants' predicament, and their response was very definitely to the illustration: a reader's response to picture more than word. This illustration is designed to be laughed at. The ants look amazed to find themselves in the cup which becomes a large body of water for them, but they do not seem to be affected by the temperature or the motion of the coffee "waves." It is funny to see the ants bobbing in the coffee, feelers erect, apparently undamaged. My small friends equally enjoyed the ants' descent into the hell of the toaster and subsequent pop up. Even though the text explains that the toaster was becoming "unbearably hot," the illustration does not interpret this as a painful experience. The ants seem to be having a great time bouncing on the toast as if it is a trampoline.

The most popular illustration, according to my friends' reaction, is the one showing the ants' spin in the garbage disposal. There the ants are, whirling in a melee of garbage, looking like refugees from the twister sequence in *The Wizard of Oz*. Again, the text gives some weight to their experience, claiming they emerge "bruised and dizzy" from the "whirling storm of shredded food and stinging rain" (27). The illustration, however, demonstrates that they are undamaged figures of fun. One of the ants even appears to be smiling as he whirls upside down in the disposal. The damage the ants sustain as a result of all these traumatizing occurrences is minimal. Their antennae are cutely bent after their final ordeal when they are shot from an electrical socket by the strength of the current, "speed" lines indicating the force of their trajectory. Van Allsburg comments that the ants are "stunned senseless and blown out of holes like bullets from a gun" (29). He also explains that they must rest, but all damage from this episode is put to rights quickly in the illustrations, for the ants are perky, and their antennae are fine in the next plate as they return home (30-31).

My two readers responded to my questions about the story and pictures by explaining to me that the two ants were bad to come in the house and that funny things happened to punish them, but that they went home "without hurts." Clearly they got the visual message that the ants were impervious to all ordeals.

Van Allsburg's illustrations may make children laugh, but some joyless truths are being served up with the smiles: ants are indestructible. You can do anything to them, and they will bounce back unscathed. It is fun to watch them being boiled, minced and electrified because they are just things, "like Bugatti roadsters," too little to matter. How, and to what other living things will these "truths" be applied? The concept of punishment presented by these illustrations is very different than the violence meted out in traditional literature, where the connection between evil and retribution is usually made very clear, and where the truths dealt with are universal.

The violence of these images seems reminiscent of, and perhaps more dangerous than, the violence delivered by a whole cartoon genre of which the "Road Runner" is the most familiar example. The punch line of each of these cartoons has always been the extinction and resurrection of Wiley Coyote. When burnt to a crisp he would regenerate, when hammered flat he would rebound, when dismembered, he would reassemble. These tasteless sages of pain are considered to be unfit for small viewers by enlightened parents and teachers. Here, however, are a new pair even better at resurrection, for they come unabashed and unmarked through terrors that would instantly kill real ants. The violence is the same, and children still get the punchline, but the packaging is very different, even entrancing. This expensively produced book, created by an author who is considered "a popular phenomenon" (Bader 298), is surely acceptable reading and viewing, ranking with other prestigious works for children.

Two Bad Ants seems an uneasy contemporary for the 1988 Newbery medal winning *Joyful Noise* by Paul Fleischman, for Fleischman's collection of poetry celebrates the variety, complexity and beauty of the insect world. Insects smaller than ants speak, giving voice to realities of their existence, and Eric Beddows's illustrations speak with the same joy. Although it is encouraging that the same year's output contains these widely divergent views, I think all of us know which book will be the most popular; Fleischman's and Beddows's work is much greater in concept but quieter in presentation, while Van Allsburg's book has a more obvious appeal.

Van Allsburg's special talent for presenting new perspectives heightens his attraction. The drawings of these indestructible ants, perhaps more than the written narrative of their adventures, will stay with young readers when the book is returned to the shelf because the images *are* a story in themselves, a subtext superimposed upon the text. My analysis of these drawings cannot answer the question, "What should illustration do?", but it can begin formulating an answer by commenting on what Van Allsburg's illustrations are doing.

In ***Two Bad Ants,*** instead of extending the text, offering what Sendak calls a "juxtaposition of picture and word," a "marriage" (Cott ix), the illustrations create a divorce at the most crucial level of meaning; Van Allsburg says one thing and draws another. What he says is that the ants' experience is real. What he draws is a world in which this is not so. No one would want Van Allsburg not to draw whatever he desires, but in a world becoming daily more conscious of the importance of all earth-dwellers—even those as small as two bad ants—he should be aware of the mixed message he is sending.[2]

Notes

1. Maurice Sendak discusses the connection between drawing and text in his dialogue with Jonathan Cott which introduces Cott's edition of *Victorian Color Picture Books* (See Jill May's apt review of this reference work in the Spring 1988 issue of *Children's Literature Association Quarterly,* 39). Sendak is speaking specifically about the darkness in Randolph Caldecott's work when he says, "something hurts. Like a shadow passing over very quickly. And it is this which gives a Caldecott book—however frothy in its rhythms, verse and pictures—an unexpected depth at any given point within the work, and its special value" (xi). His fascination with the "shadow" is surely, however, an apologia for his own work, and certainly offers a perspective on Van Allsburg, in which the element of "shadow" is increasing.

2. Anyone who doubts the strength of the violence beneath the surface of Van Allsburg's work should also look at *The Z Was Zapped* in which the letters of the alphabet are systematically destroyed. This is, of course, less troubling than the violence done to the "living" protagonists in *Two Bad Ants.*

Works Cited

Bader, Barbara. "The Caldecott Spectrum," *Newbery and Caldecott Medal Books, 1975-1985.* Lee Kingman, Editor. Boston: Horn Book, 1985.

Cott, Jonathan. "A Dialogue with Maurice Sendak," *Victorian Color Picture Books.* New York: Chelsea House, 1983.

Fleischman, Paul. *Joyful Noise: Poems for Two Voices.* New York: Harper and Row, 1988.

Schwartz, Sanford. "Felons in the Sugar Bowl," *New York Times Book Review.* November 8, 1988, 63.

Van Allsburg, Chris. *Two Bad Ants.* Boston: Houghton Mifflin, 1988.

———. *The Z Was Zapped.* Boston: Houghton Mifflin, 1987.

📖 *JUST A DREAM* (1990)

Gail Goss (review date June-July 2001)

SOURCE: Goss, Gail. Review of *Just a Dream,* by Chris Van Allsburg. *Book Links* 10, no. 6 (June-July 2001): 44.

Preschool-Gr. 3—Walter doesn't treat the earth with respect [in ***Just a Dream***], choosing to throw trash on the ground and not recycle. Then Walter's bed travels in his dream into an over-crowded and polluted future. The dream inspires him to plant and care for a tree so that he might help prevent such a future.

Lee Bock (review date February 2003)

SOURCE: Bock, Lee. Review of *Just a Dream,* by Chris Van Allsburg. *School Library Journal* 49, no. 2 (February 2003): 97.

Gr. 2-5—Careless about the environment, Walter imagines an earth without trees [in ***Just a Dream***], littered with trash, and the air terribly polluted-is this the world of the future or only a dream? Masterful, full-page illustrations feature luminescent, surreal paintings.

THE WRETCHED STONE (1991)

Ellen Fader (review date January 1992)

SOURCE: Fader, Ellen. Review of *The Wretched Stone,* by Chris Van Allsburg. *Horn Book Magazine* 68, no. 1 (January 1992): 62-4.

The unusual literary device of a ship's log chronicles the astonishing events that occur during the last voyage of the *Rita Anne* [in ***The Wretched Stone***]. All the initial signs are favorable; pleasant weather at the beginning is a good omen, and the captain is impressed by his literate crew. Many enjoy borrowing books from his library, and some are accomplished storytellers. One month into the journey, an uncharted island is explored with an eye to finding water and fresh fruit, but the island is not hospitable. Instead, the captain brings aboard a strange, heavy object; one surface of the rock is flat and glassy and emits a "glowing light that is quite beautiful and pleasing to look at." After a week, the crew's strange, obsessive behavior convinces the captain that the men have contracted a fever from the rock, and he plans to have it thrown overboard. A trip into the hold, where the sailors have barricaded themselves with the stone, reveals a macabre sight: the men have turned into grinning monkeys, and they are unable to understand their captain's words. After a lightning storm disables the stone, the captain discovers that when he reads to the sailors, they recover some of their alertness; in fact, "those who knew how to read recovered most quickly." Even so, the crew will never be

quite the same again: the sailors seem to have developed an "unnatural appetite" for bananas. Although Van Allsburg clearly has a message to convey, he has added to the book an enjoyable and necessary dollop of humor. The story has a quiet, understated, yet suspenseful tone; most of the plot's considerable drama is conveyed in the impressive illustrations. Van Allsburg's choice of palette is reminiscent of that of N. C. Wyeth, and certain double-page spreads recall Wyeth's familiar sweeping skies. The highly saturated tones and the composition of the paintings command attention. The brief text is positioned in white boxes on the near middle of each left-hand page, but because the paintings have such energy and movement, these rectangles never seem distracting—their placement only serves to reinforce the author-illustrator's theme about the power of the printed word.

THE WIDOW'S BROOM (1992)

Joann H. Ericson (review date spring 1993)

SOURCE: Ericson, Joann H. Review of *The Widow's Broom,* by Chris Van Allsburg. *Childhood Education* 69, no. 3 (spring 1993): 173.

The author weaves a tale of mischief and intrigue [in ***The Widow's Broom***], from the portentous opening illustration of dangling legs, tumbling broom and plummeting witch's hat and cape to the closing portrait of Minna Shaw nodding gently and peacefully in her rocking chair. Minna stalwartly defends the magical broom's activities against the rising complaints by her neighbors. The subtle illustrations, artfully executed in black-and-white duo-tone, echo the Van Allsburg tradition. *All Ages.*

Patricia Austin (review date April-May 2003)

SOURCE: Austin, Patricia. Review of *The Widow's Broom,* by Chris Van Allsburg. *Book Links* 12, no. 5 (April-May 2003): 36.

Gr. 2-6—When a widow begins to use a witch's broom that has fallen into her field [in ***The Widow's Broom***], she finds that it has many talents. It can feed the chickens, play the piano, and sweep all by itself. Neighbors who fear what they don't understand want the broom destroyed. The situation in this mysterious tale can be compared with the Salem witch trials and other eras in history.

📖 *A CITY IN WINTER* (1996)

Elizabeth Devereaux and Diane Roback (review date 9 September 1996)

SOURCE: Devereaux, Elizabeth, and Diane Roback. Review of *A City in Winter*, by Mark Helprin, illustrated by Chris Van Allsburg. *Publishers Weekly* 243, no. 37 (9 September 1996): 84.

A none-too-kid-friendly mixture of war story and bureaucratic satire, this tale of a 10-year-old queen's quest to regain her throne [*A City in Winter*] suffers from a proliferation of heavy-handed and portentous philosophical passages. "I began my journey to the city in blindness and confidence," says the queen, "which, if you think of it, is how we must all live, given the nature of our origin and the certainty of our destination." Helprin (*Winter's Tale*; *A Soldier of the Great War*) is at his weakest in his panoramas of an epic war, which are frequently confusing; and strongest in conveying the farcical and magical aspects of the evil Usurper's empire. For example, the enslaved queen is put to work in the yam section of the palace's starch kitchens; she later tours a storage structure of over 600 floors, including a shop for the repair of winter clothing used by podiatrists attached to the rhinoceros-horn carving apprenticeship program. Two-time Caldecott winner Van Allsburg emphasizes the story's dramatic moments rather than its humor. With characteristic poetic stillness and rich depth of color, his paintings cast a warm glow over the icy city. Although the deliberately cryptic narrative style makes for lackluster reading, the book's handsome design with its use of page ornaments and its production on high-quality paper will make it attractive to collectors of finely illustrated works. *Ages 10-up.*

📖 *THE VEIL OF SNOWS* (1997)

Sybil S. Steinberg (review date 29 September 1997)

SOURCE: Steinberg, Sybil S. Review of *The Veil of Snows*, by Mark Helprin, illustrated by Chris Van Allsburg. *Publishers Weekly* 244, no. 40 (29 September 1997): 90.

[*The Veil of Snows,* t]his pseudo-poetic fantasy is the third in Helprin and Caldecott winner Van Allsburg's trilogy that began with *Swan Lake*. It continues the saga of an unnamed queen defending her country against the evil Usurper, but shows only brief glimpses of the savvy humor of *A City in Winter.*

The narrator here is an unnamed former torture victim who has been promoted to knight and chief strategist for the queen. Members of the perfidious Tookesheim family, fawning helpmates to the Usurper in the previous book, have now corrupted the queen's empire. Once the Usurper begins a fresh assault on the kingdom, the rest is war—and tragedy ensues. The queen's logic becomes tangled to the point of being laughable: for example, after insisting her men carry a wounded soldier with them (which understandably slows their escape), she is "astonished" to find the troop travels more slowly than they would have otherwise. A mute, starving child is rescued and extravagantly nurtured by the queen, then never mentioned again. Throughout, profound yet impenetrable bits of wisdom are doled out by the narrator. Referring to the queen's potential separation from her infant son, he intones: "The saddest thing in the world was for a parent to have his child loosed upon the wing. . . ." The lavish volume features a few richly magical paintings that rank among Van Allsburg's best work: red trees being lifted up by pulleys to the top of a castle, cattle catapulted through the air. Only these make the book worthwhile.

Susan Dove Lempke (review date 15 November 1997)

SOURCE: Lempke, Susan Dove. Review of *The Veil of Snows*, by Mark Helprin, illustrated by Chris Van Allsburg. *Booklist* 94, no. 6 (15 November 1997): 560.

Gr. 4-7—At the end of *A City in Winter* (1996), the unnamed queen stands poised to lead the rebellion against the evil usurper. This sequel, [*The Veil of Snows,*] narrated by a singer turned soldier, begins many years later, after the queen has herself been overthrown. The teller describes his meeting with the queen, who, sounding very much like a real-life contemporary right-wing politician, explains that her land is on the verge of destruction thanks to idiotic journalists, schools that entertain but do not teach, "talking boxes that take the place of books," and foolhardy disarmament. Helprin writes lyrical passages on the power of song and creates stunning images, all of which are gorgeously realized by Van Allsburg. Like its predecessor, this handsome book is recommended for "all ages" by the publisher, but Helprin's decidedly nonlinear storytelling and his subtext seem pitched more to adults who like political fables than to children wanting a good fantasy.

Nancy H. Stevens (review date 1998)

SOURCE: Stevens, Nancy H. Review of *The Veil of Snows*, by Mark Helprin, illustrated by Chris Van Allsburg. *Childhood Education* 74, no. 5 (1998): 323.

This book [*The Veil of Snows*] is the third collaboration by Helprin and Van Allsburg, following *Swan Lake* and *A City in Winter.* This compelling, highly descriptive tale of the struggle between good and evil is told in the context of a kingdom fighting against a malevolent Usurper. The author focuses on the power of the human spirit and its ability to overcome adversity. This beautifully written and illustrated book will enthrall readers.

ZATHURA: A SPACE ADVENTURE (2002)

Diane Roback, Jennifer M. Brown, and Jason Britton (review date 24 June 2002)

SOURCE: Roback, Diane, Jennifer M. Brown, and Jason Britton. Review of *Zathura: A Space Adventure,* by Chris Van Allsburg. *Publishers Weekly* 249, no. 25 (24 June 2002): 54.

Twenty years after *Jumanji* (1981), Van Allsburg picks up where he left off, with Danny and Walter Budwing discovering an oblong box in the park [in *Zathura: A Space Adventure*]. Walter dismisses the box as "just some dumb old game," but his curious younger brother takes it home anyway. While Walter watches TV, Danny glances at the game's "jungle adventure" board, then turns his attention to a *second* board with an outer-space theme and "a path of colored squares leading . . . to a purple planet called Zathura." Just then, "with a click, a small green card popped out of the edge. . . . He picked it up and read, 'Meteor showers, take evasive action.'" The boys don't act too surprised when a giant meteor falls into their tastefully appointed living room, but they do get excited when they see only stars and dark sky outside their windows. Several dice-rolls later, they're scrambling to evade a homicidal robot and a scaly "Zyborg pirate" climbing backward through the meteor-hole in the ceiling (its face goes unseen). As the boys play, their sibling rivalry gives way to cooperation, and grouchy Walter comes to appreciate his little brother. Van Allsburg illustrates the surreal events in a grainy charcoal-black that seems to shimmer on a rough, cream-colored ground. His deathly quiet images—double spreads this time—have a frozen stillness that leaves all color and activity to the imagination; with each new threat, the book seems to hold its breath. Van Allsburg reuses some devices, and Zathura, like Jumanji, is a satisfying enigma. The puzzling conclusion, involving a black hole and time travel to an earlier illustration, will have devotees scouring the first book and its sequel for clues. *All ages.*

Wendy Lukehart (review date November 2002)

SOURCE: Lukehart, Wendy. Review of *Zathura: A Space Adventure,* by Chris Van Allsburg. *School Library Journal* 48, no. 11 (November 2002): 139.

K-Gr. 5—For more than 20 years, readers of *Jumanji* (Houghton, 1981) have had to wonder what happened when the Budwing brothers opened the box that Peter and Judy had frantically discarded in the park. The wait is over [in *Zathura: A Space Adventure*], but the wonder continues in this masterfully executed sequel. Walter's physical torture of his younger brother and Danny's annoying behaviors are classic sibling stuff, but savvy readers will recognize that this lack of camaraderie does not bode well here. The simple jungle board does not appeal to Walter, however, so it is not until another game board is uncovered at the bottom of the box that the action begins. This time, the children face the challenges of space, time, and dimension as they read the game cards: "The polarity on your gravity belt is reversed" and "Your gyroscope is malfunctioning." Their journey to the planet Zathura allows Van Allsburg to depict Walter plastered against the living-room ceiling or being swallowed by a black hole. As ringed planets and spaceships swirl past the windows, the boys find their way to teamwork and even affection. Van Allsburg's choice of highly textured paper adds interest and character; the patterned wallpapers are especially effective as homey counterpoints to the surreal story. The creamy background provides warmth and contrast to the black-and-gray sketches, so convincing in conveying depth of field. One can't help but anticipate the encore.

Deborah Stevenson (review date November 2002)

SOURCE: Stevenson, Deborah. Review of *Zathura: A Space Adventure,* by Chris Van Allsburg. *Bulletin of the Center for Children's Books* 56, no. 3 (November 2002): 128.

Well, this certainly has a familiar ring: a couple of bored siblings left to their own devices find a board game, and once they begin playing they find themselves plunged into a world they can only exit through the game itself. This time, [in *Zathura: A Space Adventure,*] however, the siblings are Walter and his little brother, Danny, and the game (chosen in preference to a dull-looking adventure called *Jumanji*) is a space odyssey involving travel from Earth to the planet Zathura. As the kids play, Walter loses his gravity, almost sliding off into outer space, Danny gets too much gravity and turns into a human bowling ball, and a robot determines to destroy them (they're "alien life forms"), but fortunately Walter slips into a black hole that takes him—and Danny—back in time to before they started their dangerous game. This is essentially a rerun of *Jumanji* in a new location, but the space adventures are sci-fi cool, and some audiences will appreciate the additional tension provided by the thorny relationship between the brothers. The shadowy black-and-white tones of Van Allsburg's illustrations recall 1950s science-fiction films, with their noirish shadows and spookily reflective surfaces; the eerily even smoky texture of house and boys alike is sometimes monotonous but intriguingly suggests machine-engineering in its regularity, and the sharp dark outlines are both a vivid contrast and an emphasis of the other-worldly distance of even the everyday proceedings. The schmaltzy ending (Walter transforms into a nice older brother) is disappointing, but youngsters may still get a thrill from this literary blast-off.

Gillian Engberg (review date 15 November 2002)

SOURCE: Engberg, Gillian. Review of *Zathura: A Space Adventure,* by Chris Van Allsburg. *Booklist* 99, no. 6 (15 November 2002): 603.

K-Gr. 3—On the twentieth anniversary of *Jumanji,* Van Allsburg picks up right where his Caldecott Medal book left off, with [*Zathura: A Space Adventure,*] a similarly terrifying adventure set this time in outer space. Danny and Walter Budwing, last seen on the final page of *Jumanji,* find the magical game box in the park. They discover a second game board inside, decorated with space images. Once home, they begin to play, and like *Jumanji*'s Peter and Judy, they are instantly catapulted into the game's parallel universe, which this time involves meteor showers, pirate aliens, violent robots, wild shifts in gravity, and a black hole that finally loops the brothers back to the park, before the chaos began. Despite the new setting, there are few differences between this book and its predecessor; the exquisite surreal black-and-white illustrations once again show neat domesticity

blown apart by magic. And like *Jumanji,* this book creates a delicious tension between the action in the words and the frozen scenes of impending disaster. Here, though, there's another layer: the brothers' rivalry. At the beginning, Walter thinks younger Danny is just an annoying "little fungus"; by the end, Walter is protective and loving: "Me and you, together." *Jumanji* fans and newcomers alike will delight in this continuation of the story, which ends openly, leaving plenty of room for the game to wreak more havoc in the future.

Betty Carter (review date November-December 2002)

SOURCE: Carter, Betty. Review of *Zathura: A Space Adventure,* by Chris Van Allsburg. *Horn Book Magazine* 78, no. 6 (November-December 2002): 741-43.

Van Allsburg's *Jumanji* (rev. 7/81) concludes: "Two boys were running through the park. They were Danny and Walter Budwing, and Danny had a long, thin box under his arm." An unspoken question hangs in the air—will they play the game? Twenty years later, *Zathura* supplies the answer: of course they will. Danny looks inside the *Jumanji* box and finds a second game board hidden below the jungle adventure. This one shows "flying saucers, rockets, and planets in outer space, with a path of colored squares leading from Earth to a purple planet called Zathura and back to Earth." When Danny throws the dice, the two boys, still inside their house, are hurled into the heavens. Each succeeding turn brings a new threat (from a rampaging robot to an attacking space ship) as they frantically continue play, first individually and then as partners, in a desperate attempt to return home. Conceptually tied to *Jumanji, Zathura* is visually different. The luminescent near-photo-realism of the first book is replaced here with coarser textured illustrations appearing as if the gray shading were created with a fine sponge. Stuffed with heavy furniture; bold, patterned wallpaper; and the Budwings' household clutter, the pictures create a claustrophobic intimacy that magnifies the danger. A distinct black line outlines the boys, forming a fragile barrier between the brothers and their environment and creating the illusion that they are cutouts pasted on pages depicting the transmogrification taking place around them. *Zathura* fails as a sequel, for Van Allsburg reworks his original idea rather than expanding it. The book does, however, succeed as a series entry, delivering a familiar plot device within a different setting. It also stands alone, allowing uninitiated readers surprise at both the fact of interaction and the events themselves. Unfortunately, there is no surprise in the book's heavy-handed message promoting sibling harmony. A saccharine dialogue ends this homily as Walter discards the game, perhaps for yet another two characters to find in a succeeding volume. "'Come on,' he said, 'I've got a better idea. Let's go play catch.' Danny smiled. 'You mean together, me and you?' Walter put his arm around his brother. 'Yeah, that's right,' he said. 'Me and you, together.'"

Lynne T. Burke (review date December 2002-January 2003)

SOURCE: Burke, Lynne T. Review of *Zathura: A Space Adventure,* by Chris Van Allsburg. *Reading Today* 20, no. 3 (December 2002-January 2003): 33.

It's baaack! The 1982 Caldecott-Medal winning book *Jumanji* introduced a magic board game that plunged a pair of siblings into a bizarre jungle adventure. On the last page of the book, the discarded game is seen being picked up by the unsuspecting Budwing brothers.

In this story [*Zathura: A Space Adventure*] Danny and Walter Budwing, who have trouble enough just surviving each other, discover another game board jammed into the bottom of the box, and this one is really out of this world. In fact, the moment the dice are rolled they find themselves plagued by aliens, zero gravity, and a host of other space-related phenomena, including a refrigerator-sized meteor that crushes the TV.

Van Allsburg's stunning black-and-white drawings masterfully blur the boundary between fantasy and reality. It is impossible to determine which is more improbable—an attack by a Zorgon pirate ship or two rambunctious brothers who finally figure out how much they need each other.

FURTHER READING

Criticism

Bodmer, George R. "The Illustrated Postmodern." In *The Image of the Child,* edited by Sylvia Patterson Iskander, pp. 76-82. Battle Creek, Mich.: Children's Lit. Assn., 1991.

> Compares Van Allsburg's *The Mysteries of Harris Burdick* with the works of Jon Scieszka and the critical theory of Jack Zipes.

Freeman, Judy. Review of *Zathura: A Space Adventure,* by Chris Van Allsburg. *Instructor* 112, no. 8 (May-June 2003): 52-3.

> Offers a brief assessment of *Zathura: A Space Adventure.*

Van Allsburg, Chris. "Caldecott Medal Acceptance." *Horn Book Magazine* 58, no. 4 (August 1982): 380-83.

> Van Allsburg accepts his Caldecott Medal for *Jumanji* and discusses his development as an author and illustrator.

Van Allsburg, Chris, and Lynne T. Burke. "Author/Illustrator Chris Van Allsburg." *Instructor* 113, no. 5 (January-February 2004): 22.

> Van Allsburg offers advice to young writers and comments on his own creative process as an author and illustrator.

Additional coverage of Van Allsburg's life and career is contained in the following sources published by Thomson Gale: *Children's Literature Review,* Vols. 5, 13; *Contemporary Authors,* Vols. 113, 117; *Contemporary Authors New Revision Series,* Vols. 38, 120; *Dictionary of Literary Biography,* Vol. 61; *Literature Resource Center*; *Major Authors and Illustrators for Children and Young Adults,* Eds. 1, 2; *St. James Guide to Children's Writers,* Vol. 5; and *Something about the Author,* Vols. 37, 53, 105, 156.

How to Use This Index

The main reference

> **Baum, L(yman) Frank**
> 1856-1919 .... **15**

lists all author entries in this and previous volumes of *Children's Literature Review*.

The cross-references

> See also CA 108, 133; DLB 22; JRDA;
> MAICYA; MTCW 1; SATA 18, 100; TCLC 7

list all author entries in the following Gale biographical and literary sources:

AAL = Asian American Literature

AAYA = Authors & Artists for Young Adults

AFAW = African American Writers (Charles Scribner's Sons, an imprint of The Gale Group)

AFW = African Writers (Charles Scribner's Sons, an imprint of The Gale Group)

AITN = Authors in the News

AMW = American Writers (Charles Scribner's Sons, an imprint of The Gale Group)

AMWR = American Writers Retrospective Supplement (Charles Scribner's Sons, an imprint of The Gale Group)

AMWS = American Writers Supplement (Charles Scribner's Sons, an imprint of The Gale Group)

ANW = American Nature Writers (Charles Scribner's Sons, an imprint of The Gale Group)

AW = Ancient Writers (Charles Scribner's Sons, an imprint of The Gale Group)

BEST = Bestsellers (quarterly, citations appear as Year: Issue number)

BLC = Black Literature Criticism

BLCS = Black Literature Criticism Supplement

BPFB = Beacham's Encyclopedia of Popular Fiction: Biography and Resources

BRW = British Writers (Charles Scribner's Sons, an imprint of The Gale Group)

BRWS = British Writers Supplement, (Charles Scribner's Sons, an imprint of The Gale Group)

BW = Black Writers

BYA = Beacham's Guide to Literature for Young Adults

CA = Contemporary Authors

CAAS = Contemporary Authors Autobiography Series

CABS = Contemporary Authors Bibliographical Series

CAD = Contemporary American Dramatists (St. James Press, an imprint of The Gale Group)

CANR = Contemporary Authors New Revision Series

CAP = Contemporary Authors Permanent Series

CBD = Contemporary British Dramatists (St. James Press, an imprint of The Gale Group)

CCA = Contemporary Canadian Authors

CD = Contemporary Dramatists (St. James Press, an imprint of The Gale Group)

CDALB = Concise Dictionary of American Literary Biography

CDALBS = Concise Dictionary of American Literary Biography Supplement

CDBLB = Concise Dictionary of British Literary Biography

CLC = Contemporary Literary Criticism

CMLC = Classical and Medieval Literature Criticism

CMW = St. James Guide to Crime & Mystery Writers (St. James Press, an imprint of The Gale Group)

CN = Contemporary Novelists (St. James Press, an imprint of The Gale Group)

CP = Contemporary Poets (St. James Press, an imprint of The Gale Group)

CPW = Contemporary Popular Writers (St. James Press, an imprint of The Gale Group)

CSW = Contemporary Southern Writers (St. James Press, an imprint of The Gale Group)

CWD = Contemporary Women Dramatists (St. James Press, an imprint of The Gale Group)

CWP = Contemporary Women Poets (St. James Press, an imprint of The Gale Group)

CWRI = St. James Guide to Children's Writers (St. James Press, an imprint of The Gale Group)

CWW = Contemporary World Writers (St. James Press, an imprint of The Gale Group)

DA = DISCovering Authors

DAB = DISCovering Authors: British

DAC = DISCovering Authors: Canadian

DAM = *DISCovering Authors: Modules*
  DRAM: *Dramatists Module;* **MST:** *Most-Studied Authors Module;*
  MULT: *Multicultural Authors Module;* **NOV:** *Novelists Module;*
  POET: *Poets Module;* **POP:** *Popular Fiction and Genre Authors Module*
DA3 = *DISCovering Authors 3.0*
DC = *Drama Criticism*
DFS = *Drama for Students*
DLB = *Dictionary of Literary Biography*
DLBD = *Dictionary of Literary Biography Documentary Series*
DLBY = *Dictionary of Literary Biography Yearbook*
DNFS = *Literature of Developing Nations for Students*
EFS = *Epics for Students*
EXPN = *Exploring Novels*
EXPP = *Exploring Poetry*
EXPS = *Exploring Short Stories*
EW = *European Writers* (Charles Scribner's Sons, an imprint of The Gale Group)
FANT = *St. James Guide to Fantasy Writers* (St. James Press, an imprint of The Gale Group)
FW = *Feminist Writers* (St. James Press, an imprint of The Gale Group)
GFL = *Guide to French Literature,* Beginnings to 1789, 1798 to the Present (St. James Press, an imprint of The Gale Group)
GLL = *Gay and Lesbian Literature* (St. James Press, an imprint of The Gale Group)
HGG = *St. James Guide to Horror, Ghost & Gothic Writers* (St. James Press, an imprint of The Gale Group)
HLC = *Hispanic Literature Criticism*
HLCS = *Hispanic Literature Criticism Supplement*
HW = *Hispanic Writers*
IDFW = *International Dictionary of Films and Filmmakers: Writers and Production Artists* (St. James Press, an imprint of The Gale Group)
IDTP = *International Dictionary of Theatre: Playwrights* (St. James Press, an imprint of The Gale Group)
LAIT = *Literature and Its Times*
LAW = *Latin American Writers* (Charles Scribner's Sons, an imprint of The Gale Group)
JRDA = *Junior DISCovering Authors*
LC = *Literature Criticism from 1400 to 1800*
MAICYA = *Major Authors and Illustrators for Children and Young Adults*
MAICYA = *Major Authors and Illustrators for Children and Young Adults Supplement*
MAWW = *Modern American Women Writers* (Charles Scribner's Sons, an imprint of The Gale Group)
MJW = *Modern Japanese Writers* (Charles Scribner's Sons, an imprint of The Gale Group)
MTCW = *Major 20th-Century Writers*
NCFS = *Nonfiction Classics for Students*
NCLC = *Nineteenth-Century Literature Criticism*
NFS = *Novels for Students*
NNAL = *Native North American Literature*
PAB = *Poets: American and British* (Charles Scribner's Sons, an imprint of The Gale Group)
PC = *Poetry Criticism*
PFS = *Poetry for Students*
RGAL = *Reference Guide to American Literature* (St. James Press, an imprint of The Gale Group)
RGEL = *Reference Guide to English Literature* (St. James Press, an imprint of The Gale Group)
RGSF = *Reference Guide to Short Fiction* (St. James Press, an imprint of The Gale Group)
RGWL = *Reference Guide to World Literature* (St. James Press, an imprint of The Gale Group)
RHW = *Twentieth-Century Romance and Historical Writers* (St. James Press, an imprint of The Gale Group)
SAAS = *Something about the Author Autobiography Series*
SATA = *Something about the Author*
SFW = *St. James Guide to Science Fiction Writers* (St. James Press, an imprint of The Gale Group)
SSC = *Short Story Criticism*
SSFS = *Short Stories for Students*
TCLC = *Twentieth-Century Literary Criticism*
TCWW = *Twentieth-Century Western Writers* (St. James Press, an imprint of The Gale Group)
WLC = *World Literature Criticism, 1500 to the Present*
WLCS = *World Literature Criticism Supplement*
WLIT = *World Literature and Its Times*
WP = *World Poets* (Charles Scribner's Sons, an imprint of The Gale Group)
YABC = *Yesterday's Authors of Books for Children*
YAW = *St. James Guide to Young Adult Writers* (St. James Press, an imprint of The Gale Group)

CLR Cumulative Author Index

LAIT 5; MTCW 2; NFS 3; NNAL; RGAL 4; SATA 75; SATA-Obit 94; TCWW 2; YAW

Dorris, Michael A.
See Dorris, Michael (Anthony)

Dorritt, Susan
See Schlein, Miriam

Dorros, Arthur (M.) 1950- **42**
See also CA 146; CANR 93; MAICYA 2; MAICYAS 1; SAAS 20; SATA 78, 122

Dowdy, Mrs. Regera
See Gorey, Edward (St. John)

Dowdy, Mrs. Regera
See Gorey, Edward (St. John)

Doyle, A. Conan
See Doyle, Sir Arthur Conan

Doyle, Sir Arthur Conan 1859-1930 ...... **106**
See Conan Doyle, Arthur
See also AAYA 14; BRWS 2; CA 104; 122; CANR 131; CDBLB 1890-1914; CMW 4; DA; DA3; DAB; DAC; DAM MST, NOV; DLB 18, 70, 156, 178; EXPS; HGG; LAIT 2; MSW; MTCW 1, 2; RGEL 2; RGSF 2; RHW; SATA 24; SCFW 2; SFW 4; SSC 12; SSFS 2; TEA; TCLC 7; WCH; WLC; WLIT 4; WYA; YAW

Doyle, Conan
See Doyle, Sir Arthur Conan

Doyle, Brian 1935- **22**
See also AAYA 16; CA 135; CANR 55; CCA 1; JRDA; MAICYA 1, 2; SAAS 16; SATA 67, 104; YAW

Doyle, Malachy 1954- **83**
See also CA 191; SATA 120

Dr. A
See Asimov, Isaac; Silverstein, Alvin; Silverstein, Virginia B(arbara Opshelor)

Dr. Seuss **1, 9, 53, 100**
See also Geisel, Theodor Seuss; LeSieg, Theo.; Seuss, Dr.; Stone, Rosetta
See also AAYA 48

Draper, Sharon M(ills) **57**
See also AAYA 28; CA 170; CANR 124; MAICYA 2; SATA 98, 146; SATA-Essay 146; YAW

Drapier, M. B.
See Swift, Jonathan

Drescher, Henrik 1955- **20**
See also CA 135; MAICYA 1, 2; SATA 67, 105

Driving Hawk, Virginia
See Sneve, Virginia Driving Hawk

Drummond, Walter
See Silverberg, Robert

Dryden, Pamela
See St. John, Nicole

D.T., Hughes
See Hughes, Dean

du Bois, William Pene
See Pene du Bois, William (Sherman)

Duder, Tessa 1940- **43**
See also CA 147; CANR 96; MAICYA 2; MAICYAS 1; SAAS 23; SATA 80, 117; YAW

Duke, Kate 1956- **51**
See also CA 188; MAICYA 2; SATA 90, 148

Duncan, Lois 1934- **29**
See also AAYA 4, 34; BYA 6, 8; CA 1-4R; CANR 2, 23, 36, 111; CLC 26; JRDA; MAICYA 1, 2; MAICYAS 1; SAAS 2; SATA 1, 36, 75, 133, 141; SATA-Essay 141; WYA; YAW

Dunne, Marie
See Clark, Ann Nolan

Duvoisin, Roger (Antoine) 1904-1980 ...... **23**
See also CA 13-16R; 101; CANR 11; CWRI 5; DLB 61; MAICYA 1, 2; SATA 2, 30; SATA-Obit 23

Eager, Edward (McMaken) 1911-1964 .... **43**
See also CA 73-76; CANR 87; CWRI 5; DLB 22; FANT; MAICYA 1, 2; SATA 17

Eckert, Horst 1931-
See Janosch
See also CA 37-40R; CANR 38; MAICYA 1, 2; SATA 8, 72

Edgy, Wardore
See Gorey, Edward (St. John)

Edmund, Sean
See Pringle, Laurence P(atrick)

Edwards, Al
See Nourse, Alan E(dward)

Edwards, Julie (Andrews)
See Andrews, Julie

Edwards, Julie
See Andrews, Julie

Ehlert, Lois (Jane) 1934- **28**
See also CA 137; CANR 107; CWRI 5; MAICYA 1, 2; SATA 35, 69, 128

Eliot, Dan
See Silverberg, Robert

Ellen, Jaye
See Nixon, Joan Lowery

Elliott, Don
See Silverberg, Robert

Ellis, Sarah 1952- **42**
See also AAYA 57; CA 123; CANR 50, 84; JRDA; MAICYA 2; MAICYAS 1; SATA 68, 131; YAW

Emberley, Barbara A(nne) 1932- **5**
See also CA 5-8R; CANR 5, 129; MAICYA 1, 2; SATA 8, 70, 146

Emberley, Ed(ward Randolph) 1931- ... **5, 81**
See also CA 5-8R; CANR 5, 36, 82, 129; MAICYA 1, 2; SATA 8, 70, 146

Ende, Michael (Andreas Helmuth) 1929-1995 .... **14**
See also BYA 5; CA 118; 124; 149; CANR 36, 110; CLC 31; DLB 75; MAICYA 1, 2; MAICYAS 1; SATA 61, 130; SATA-Brief 42; SATA-Obit 86

Engdahl, Sylvia Louise 1933- **2**
See also AAYA 36; BYA 4; CA 29-32R; 195; CAAE 195; CANR 14, 85, 95; JRDA; MAICYA 1, 2; SAAS 5; SATA 4; SATA-Essay 122; SFW 4; YAW

Enright, Elizabeth (Wright) 1909-1968 ..... **4**
See also BYA 3; CA 61-64; 25-28R; CANR 83; CWRI 5; DLB 22; MAICYA 1, 2; SATA 9; WCH

Epstein, Beryl (M. Williams) 1910- **26**
See also CA 5-8R; CANR 2, 18, 39; SAAS 17; SATA 1, 31

Epstein, Samuel 1909-2000 .... **26**
See also CA 9-12R; CANR 4, 18, 39; SAAS 17; SATA 1, 31

Estes, Eleanor (Ruth) 1906-1988 .... **2, 70**
See also BYA 1; CA 1-4R; 126; CANR 5, 20, 84; CWRI 5; DLB 22; JRDA; MAICYA 1, 2; SATA 7, 91; SATA-Obit 56

Estoril, Jean
See Allan, Mabel Esther

Ets, Marie Hall 1893-1984 .... **33**
See also CA 1-4R; CANR 4, 83; CWRI 5; DLB 22; MAICYA 1, 2; SATA 2

Ewing, Juliana (Horatia Gatty) 1841-1885 .... **78**
See also DLB 21, 163; SATA 16; WCH

Fairfield, Flora
See Alcott, Louisa May

Falconer, Ian 1959- **90**
See also CA 197; SATA 125

Farjeon, Eleanor 1881-1965 .... **34**
See also CA 11-12; CAP 1; CWRI 5; DLB 160; MAICYA 1, 2; SATA 2; WCH

Farmer, Penelope (Jane) 1939- **8**
See also CA 13-16R; CANR 9, 37, 84; DLB 161; FANT; JRDA; MAICYA 1, 2; SAAS 22; SATA 40, 105; SATA-Brief 39; YAW

Feelings, Muriel (Lavita Grey) 1938- **5**
See also BW 1; CA 93-96; MAICYA 1, 2; SAAS 8; SATA 16

Feelings, Thomas 1933-2003
See Feelings, Tom
See also BW 1; CA 49-52; 222; CANR 25; MAICYA 1, 2; MAICYAS 1; SATA 8; SATA-Obit 148; YAW

Feelings, Tom **5, 58**
See also Feelings, Thomas
See also AAYA 25; SAAS 19; SATA 69

Ferry, Charles 1927- **34**
See also AAYA 29; CA 97-100; CANR 16, 57; SAAS 20; SATA 43, 92

Field, Rachel (Lyman) 1894-1942 .... **21**
See also BYA 5; CA 109; 137; CANR 79; CWRI 5; DLB 9, 22; MAICYA 1, 2; RHW; SATA 15; WCH

Fine, Anne 1947- **25**
See also AAYA 20; CA 105; CANR 38, 83, 105; CWRI 5; JRDA; MAICYA 1, 2; MAICYAS 1; SAAS 15; SATA 29, 72, 111

Fisher, Aileen (Lucia) 1906-2002 .... **49**
See also CA 5-8R; 216; CANR 2, 17, 37, 84; CWRI 5; MAICYA 1; SATA 1, 25, 73; SATA-Obit 143

Fisher, Dorothy (Frances) Canfield 1879-1958 .... **71,**
See also CA 114; 136; CANR 80; CWRI 5; DLB 9, 102, 284; MAICYA 1, 2; TCLC 87; YABC 1

Fisher, Leonard Everett 1924- **18**
See also CA 1-4R; CANR 2, 37, 77, 98; CWRI 5; DLB 61; MAICYA 1; SAAS 1; SATA 4, 34, 73, 120; SATA-Essay 122

Fisher, Suzanne
See Staples, Suzanne Fisher

Fitch, John IV
See Cormier, Robert (Edmund)

Fitzgerald, Captain Hugh
See Baum, L(yman) Frank

Fitzgerald, John D(ennis) 1907(?)-1988 ..... **1**
See also CA 93-96; 126; CANR 84; CWRI 5; MAICYA 1, 2; SATA 20; SATA-Obit 56

Fitzhardinge, Joan Margaret 1912-
See Phipson, Joan
See also CA 13-16R; CANR 6, 23, 36; MAICYA 1, 2; SATA 2, 73; YAW

Fitzhugh, Louise (Perkins) 1928-1974 .. **1, 72**
See also AAYA 18; CA 29-32; 53-56; CANR 34, 84; CAP 2; CWRI 5; DLB 52; JRDA; MAICYA 1, 2; SATA 1, 45; SATA-Obit 24

Flack, Marjorie 1897-1958 .... **28**
See also CA 112; 136; CANR 84; CWRI 5; MAICYA 1, 2; SATA 100; YABC 2

Fleischman, Paul 1952- **20, 66**
See also AAYA 11, 35; BYA 5, 6, 8, 11, 12, 16; CA 113; CANR 37, 84, 105; JRDA; MAICYA 1, 2; MAICYAS 1; SAAS 20; SATA 39, 72, 110; SATA-Brief 32; WYAS 1; YAW

Fleischman, (Albert) Sid(ney) 1920- **1, 15**
See also BYA 4, 11; CA 1-4R; CANR 5, 37, 67, 131; CWRI 5; JRDA; MAICYA 1, 2; SATA 8, 59, 96, 148

Fletcher, Ralph 1953- **104**
See also CA 73; CANR 132; SATA 105, 149

Forbes, Esther 1891-1967 .... **27**
See also AAYA 17; BYA 2; CA 13-14; 25-28R; CAP 1; CLC 12; DLB 22; JRDA; MAICYA 1, 2; RHW; SATA 2, 100; YAW

Literary Criticism Series
Cumulative Topic Index

This index lists all topic entries in Gale's *Children's Literature Review* (CLR), *Classical and Medieval Literature Criticism* (CMLC), *Contemporary Literary Criticism* (CLC), *Drama Criticism* (DC), *Literature Criticism from 1400 to 1800* (LC), *Nineteenth-Century Literature Criticism* (NCLC), *Short Story Criticism* (SSC), and *Twentieth-Century Literary Criticism* (TCLC). The index also lists topic entries in the Gale Critical Companion Collection, which includes the following publications: *The Beat Generation* (BG), and *Harlem Renaissance* (HR).

Topic Index

CLR Cumulative Nationality Index

AMERICAN

CLR-113 Title Index